Reforming Suburbia

The publisher gratefully acknowledges the generous contribution to this book provided by the General Endowment Fund of the University of California Press Associates.

Reforming Suburbia

*The Planned Communities of Irvine,
Columbia, and The Woodlands*

Ann Forsyth

UNIVERSITY OF CALIFORNIA PRESS

Berkeley   Los Angeles   London

The following chapters were previously published in different form and appear here by courtesy of their original publishers and the author: chapters 2 and 7: Ann Forsyth, "Who Built Irvine? Private Planning and the Federal Government," *Urban Studies* 39, 13 (2002): 2507–30; chapter 4: Ann Forsyth, "Ian McHarg's Woodlands: A Second Look," *Planning* (August 10–13, 2003): 10–13; and chapter 6: Ann Forsyth, "Planning Lessons from Three US New Towns of the 1960s and 1970s: Irvine, Columbia, and The Woodlands," *Journal of the American Planning Association* 68, 4 (2002): 387–415.

University of California Press
Berkeley and Los Angeles, California

University of California Press, Ltd.
London, England

Library of Congress Cataloging-in-Publication Data

Forsyth, Ann, 1963–
    Reforming suburbia : the planned communities of Irvine, Columbia, and The Woodlands / Ann Forsyth.
        p.   cm.
    Includes bibliographical references and index.
        ISBN 0-520-24165-7 (cloth : alk. paper).—ISBN 0-520-24166-5 (pbk. : alk. paper)
        1. Planned communities—United States—Case studies.
    2. Irvine (Calif.)   3. Columbia (Md.)   4. Woodlands (Tex.)
    I. Title.
HT169.57.U6F67   2005
307.76'8'0973—dc22   2003028078

Manufactured in the United States of America
14   13   12   11   10   09   08   07   06   05
10   9   8   7   6   5   4   3   2   1

The paper used in this publication meets the minimum requirements of ANSI/NISO Z39.48–1992 (R 1997) *(Permanence of Paper).*♾

CONTENTS

ILLUSTRATIONS

TABLES

ACKNOWLEDGMENTS

I would like to thank Vivian Bailey, Scott Bollens, Jeff Bronow, Maggie Brown, Armando Carbonell, Bob Dannenbrink, Bill Finley, Robert Fishman, Jackie Goggin, Frank Hotchkiss, Len and Ann Ivins, Padraic Kennedy, Joseph Kutchin, Peter Marris, Lanny Morrison, Rick Peiser, Harry Richardson, Joe Rutter, David Sills, Ruth Steiner, Daphne Spain, Robert Tennenbaum, and Ray Watson for commenting on drafts of this book or providing important insights on my draft findings. Katherine Crewe and Guy Stuart read the whole first draft, earning my sincere appreciation. Dolores Hayden, David A. Smith, and Frederick Steiner all gave exceptionally helpful critiques of the next draft. Some of these readers disagree quite strongly with me—seeing me as either an apologist for or an unfair critic of these developments. However, all helped me to develop my positions, and I hope that they see that while I have not written the book that they would have developed from their own experiences, I have tried to be fair to the various sides. Yuki Kato at UC Irvine chose to do her master's thesis on racial segregation, examining the same three developments, and I enjoyed our interactions tremendously.

The James Irvine Foundation and the Lincoln Institute for Land Policy provided grants to support this study. Additional practical and financial assistance came from the Taubman Center for State and Local Government at Harvard University, especially its director, Alan Altshuler; and from Peter Rowe, dean of the Harvard Design School, where I was working at the time that I conducted the study. The Irvine Company also offered me a few thousand dollars in research support, with no strings attached and no reporting requirements, but after some thought, I decided not to use it. They did, however, copy slides and some plans for me. Robert Elliott of the Irvine Company and Robert Heineman of The Woodlands Operating Company compiled density data, and Dennis Dunn of the Rouse Company provided copies of Columbia's land use plans. I received tours of Columbia from Gerald Von-Mayer of the Howard County planning department, and of The Woodlands from Roger Galatas, former president of The Woodlands Corporation; John Powers, parks and recreation director for The Woodlands Community Services Corporation; and Jim O'Connor, home builder. My thanks for all this help.

At Harvard, Sarah Calderon, Ruby Henry, Jerome Chou, Yetunde Olaya, and Ned Thomas did important library work. Robert Gilmore assembled maps that did not make it into this book but helped my analysis. Elissa Malcohn good-naturedly transcribed most of the interviews and was a truly terrific resource. At Minnesota, David Lowe helped with final details.

Although the development companies have thrown out many documents over the years, in the cases of Irvine and Columbia, many of these have found their way into collections at the University of California, Irvine, and the private Columbia Archives (now affiliated with the Columbia Association). Barbara Kellner and Robin Emrich at the Columbia Archives were particularly helpful. There are a number of Title VII–related files in the National Archives that discuss The Woodlands. My thanks also to the staff of the Howard County Historical Society and the Loeb Library at Harvard. A number of individuals and organizations very generously allowed access to their files or correspondence, including Gerald Brock, Bob Dannenbrink, Bill Doebele, Herbert Gans, the City of Houston Planning and Development Department, Johnson Fain Partners, Joseph Kutchin, Land Design Research/HNTB, Len and Ann Ivins, James McAlister Sr., Richard Reese, Ray Watson, and Don Webb. In addition, a number of other people had conversations with me about the work or helped me to locate people and data, including Nicholas Bloom, Scott Bollens, Jeff Bronow, Karen Chapple, Bernard Frieden, Bill Gayk, Jack Jones, Victor Kao, Robert Marans, Bob McGee, Josh Olsen, Rick Peiser, and Roger Ralph.

I presented work in progress at UC Irvine, Macquarie University (Australia), Queens University (Canada), the University of Massachusetts at Amherst, and the University of Minnesota, and at conferences of the Association of Collegiate Schools of Planning (ACSP) and American Planning Association. I also organized a tour of Columbia at the 2002 ACSP conference. My thanks to Maggie Brown, Ray Burby, Fred Jarvis, Barbara Kellner, Padraic Kennedy, Robert Marans, Cy Paumier, Joe Rutter, Mal and Mimi Sherman, and Bob Zehner for their terrific contributions to that tour.

At the University of California Press, my particular thanks to my first editor, Charlene Woodcock, who had great enthusiasm for the project, and to Sheila Levine, who kindly took over her role once Charlene had left the Press.

Thanks also to those whom I interviewed, the majority in formal, in-person interviews, with a number followed up by second interviews or exchanges of correspondence. A handful involved shorter, more informal interviews or exchanges of emails and faxes. My thanks to Larry Agran, Lynne Aldrich, Pearl Atkinson Stewart, Uri Avin, Vivian Bailey, Alistair Baillie, David Barrett, David Baumgartner, Al Bell, Rick Bishop, Liz Bobo, Ron Bourbeau, Marsha Bousquet, Paul Brady, Jerry Brock, Richard Browne, Maggie Brown, Pat Brown, Jeff Bronow, Steve Burkett, John Buzos, Laurie Casey, Rick Cermak, Ed Chance, Antonia Chayse, Jerry Cope, Ken Coulter, Tom Cox, Sam Crozier, Jack Crumpler, Robert Dannenbrink, Kristen Day, Joel Deretchin, Dennis Dunn, Robert Elliott, Ed Ely, Bill Fain, Frank Faridoni, Mary Fegraus, Bill Finley, Monica Florian, Colin Franklin, Paul Frederiksen, Laura Fuji, David Fulp, Marlene Gafrick, Roger Galatas, Herbert Gans, Rev. Donald Gebert, Debbie Gentry, Tom Glenn, Marsha Gorrie, Robert Gorrie, Vernon Gray, Norman Grossman, Larry Haegel, Tom Harris, Peggy Hausman, Robert Heinemann, Lenneal Henderson, Peter Hersh, Don Hilderbrandt, Mina Hilsenrath, Chuck Hinton, David Hitchcock, Frank Hotchkiss, Jodie Hopkins, Paul Ireland, Ann Ivins, Len Ivins, Christopher Jencks, Eric Jessen, Jack Jones, Dan Jung, A. G. Kawamura, Morris Keeton, Steve Kellenberg, Padriac Kennedy, Jerry Kirchgessner, Bill Kogerman, Margie Kraemer, Alan Kreditor, Rick Krieg, Joseph Kutchin, Larry Larson, Adele Levine, Robert Litke, Mary Lorsung, Kathy Lottes, Leo Molinaro, Julie Martineau, James McAlister Sr., Dick McCauley, Bob McGee, Marsha McLaughlin, Cynthia Mitchell, George Mitchell, Jean Moon, Lanny Morrison, Tim Neely, Judy Nieman, Jim O'Connor, Stan Ofterlie, Plato Papas, Cy Paumier, Jack Peltason, Biff Picone, John Powers, Richard Ramella, Richard Reese, Joel Reynolds, Michael Richmond, Leonard Rogers, Norma Rose, John Rutledge, Joseph Rutter, Al Scavo, Steve Schiboula, Carol Schroeder, May Ruth Seidel, Mal Sherman, Rabbi Martin Siegel, David Sills, Sat Tamaribuchi, Robert Tennenbaum, Ken Theisen, Larry Thomas, Bruce Tough, Coulson Tough, Rebecca Truden, Sheri Vander Dussen, Gerald VonMayer, Peter Walker, Wallace Walrod, Jim Wannemaker, Ray Watson, Don Webb, Natalie Woodson, and Bill Woollett.

Much of this book is previously unpublished; however, parts were drawn from my previously published work. My thanks to the publishers of *Urban Studies, Journal of the American Planning Association,* and *Planning* for permission to used revised versions of three articles.

Chapter 1

The New Community Experiment

It was the late 1960s and early 1970s. The planners, designers, and developers were in their twenties and thirties or just a little older. They were trying to reshape the U.S. suburban landscape by creating "new communities" at the Irvine Ranch in Southern California, Columbia in Maryland, and The Woodlands in the suburbs of Houston, Texas. Working intensively with tens or hundreds of millions of private dollars at their disposal, they designed and built new social organizations, physical forms, legal structures, and marketing programs. They left big plans that over several decades have continued to shape new landscapes. Together the development teams of the three new communities profiled in this book tried out and refined many of the techniques that are currently promoted by the smart growth movement, and they did so at a large scale. Where they succeeded, in areas such as community identity and open space preservation, they have provided support for current smart growth proposals. Where they did not, in areas such as housing affordability and transportation choices, they have shown that contemporary smart growth proposals may need to be revised.

This book tells the stories of Irvine, Columbia, and The Woodlands—how they were designed and how they turned out—and tells us what we can learn from them as we plan for the future.

OVERVIEW

The U.S. "new community" movement of the 1960s and 1970s attempted a grand experiment. In response to criticisms of contemporary trends in suburban development, akin to today's criticisms of urban sprawl, developers and the professionals that they employed embarked on the construction of communities that differed in many ways from the prevailing pattern of suburban development. This book examines the results of these efforts in three of these new communities: the Irvine Ranch in Southern California, Columbia in Maryland, and The Woodlands in the suburbs of Houston, Texas (ordered chronologically). These communities represent successes in the eyes of the new community movement. The book examines the ways in which they are successes and whether they constitute a model for today's planners, designers, developers, and civic leaders interested in alternatives to urban sprawl.

In the 1950s and 1960s, early post–World War II suburban expansion was criticized for its ugliness, cultural conformity, social isolation, and environmental problems. From the 1950s through the 1970s, some real estate developers and parts of the planning and design professions responded to these complaints. They proposed master-planned new communities throughout the United States related to the new town programs then active in Europe. Ranging in projected population from ten thousand to five hundred thousand, these communities were planned to be phased, coordinated, socially balanced, environmentally aware, and economically efficient. Their developers wanted to create whole communities rather than simple subdivisions. By avoiding many of the problems of uncoordinated incremental growth— or sprawl—they imagined both improving urban areas and creating a real estate product that would sell.

While about 150 of these new communities were publicized in the 1960s and 1970s, not all the proposed developments were built.[1] In addition, the developments differed in character. Some developments were relatively small—much closer to ten thousand than one hundred thousand in population. Although the ideal of the new community was the comprehensive new town, with employment, retail, cultural facilities, and recreational opportunities, many were more like bedroom suburbs, either in their initial concept or because of scaling back the development after construction had commenced.

This book examines three of the biggest and most comprehensive of the satellite new communities. Irvine, Columbia, and The Woodlands were all initially planned in the 1960s and 1970s but used many techniques currently advocated by the various antisprawl movements, such as smart growth and new urbanism. Still under construction and with relatively few discontinuities in their planning and development, they can now offer the lessons of several decades of continuously implemented cutting-edge suburban design and planning from the private sector. How well have these planned communities avoided the problems of sprawl? Have they created more sustainable or livable places? Are the techniques that they used still viable alternatives, or are they now part of the problem? Can private-sector planning achieve important public purposes?

People are often skeptical about the financial implications of adopting innovative planning techniques. At the cutting edge of urban design and development thinking, the three case study developments have still worked within the constraints of a conservative market and a need for short-term cash flow as well as long-term profits. Demonstrating that innovative planning and financial success are not necessarily mutually exclusive, the three developments have survived over decades and have been built much as planned, although at a slower pace than initially anticipated. To paraphrase one of the early consultants working on the Irvine Ranch, the developments have made a significant market in their regions for things perceived, at least at the time of their initial planning, as risky development products—attached housing, racial mix, and forest understories left in residential lots and business parks. Although they were helped by their locations in very fast-growing regions, they also picked up a large proportion of each region's growth. The planning teams did not solve all the problems attributed to suburban growth, and in an international sense the developments are hardly sustainable in environmental terms, but they pushed the envelope of development practices in the private market in the United States. Some people bought into the whole new community package; some came for the good schools and convenience; but the developments captured a market, and they did this at a large scale.

While having very different emphases, each development has made a significant number of innovations and conforms to what are still considered to be cutting-edge planning and design strategies. For example, the U.S. Environmental Protection Agency and the Smart Growth Network define smart growth as having dimensions of mixed land use, compact building design, a variety of housing types, walkable neighborhoods, distinctive identities and sense of place, open space preservation, connection to existing communities, transportation choice, efficiency, and collaborative planning (U.S. EPA 2001). The new urbanism has similar objectives, although it often packages these aims in nostalgic architectural styles (Leccese and McCormick 2000; see appendix A). The developments demonstrate all of these smart growth principles except connection to existing communities and collaborative planning, and even these have been incorporated to some extent, particularly as the developments have aged. While looking quite different from new urbanist projects in terms of architecture and street design, the new communities fulfill most of the new urbanists' underlying aims, and they do this at a grand scale.

The developments are large and have strong overall visions, and those are important parts of their character. However, they are also are made up of clusters of planning and design techniques and strategies that can be implemented at a smaller scale and are of much wider interest to both the public and the private sectors. These features mean that these developments are not just dinosaurs from another period, of interest only to those able to assemble tens of thousands of acres for a single project. Rather, the urban design and planning strategies that they initially promoted and used are still of relevance today. These strategies include broad concepts for organizing the landscape into socially mixed villages, overlaid with a pattern of movement corridors and activity centers and framed by the natural landscape. They also include the detailed design of residential blocks, mixed-use centers, infrastructure layouts, and parking lots. The lesson of these developments is that many techniques for achieving such aims as protecting open space or creating convenient places to live are still relevant. They can be encouraged at a large scale by governments.

However, even when successfully implemented, not all of these techniques have achieved the outcomes they were intended to produce, particularly in the areas of transportation and housing. These failures still have a great deal to teach the current period. As I show in chapter 6, they are likely to be failures as well of the current generation of suburban smart growth and new urbanist projects. These new developments are likely to repeat the failures of the past unless they learn from them.

In competing in the market, developers had a palette of strategies to choose from to provide an alternative to sprawl. While taking many risks, they ultimately had to select strategies that would sell to tens of thousands of ordinary Americans who could choose to go back to sprawl if it turned out to be significantly cheaper. Compared with the new communities, sprawl generally *has* been less expensive because it externalizes the costs of development so that they do not appear in the sales price but only over time. In the incremental suburban growth of new communities, services are often delayed to be supplied later by government, permanent open space is left for others to provide, and development patterns are constructed to make private transportation the only viable option. For the three case study developments in this kind of market, the quest for financial returns placed a number of constraints on innovation and caused tensions within the development companies about appropriate goals. All of the developments struggled with the issues of affordable housing and transit. The Irvine Ranch's gated areas along the coast show how marketing concerns can undermine the goal of a physically integrated development. While Columbia has been very successful in racial integration, it came up against limits in terms of economic mix. The creeping increase in lawns in the ecologically focused Woodlands shows a compromise between the market-based suburban ideal and design for water quality and habitat protection.

Intertwined with the story of how these developments tried to avoid the problems of sprawl and to survive financially is a second story about the character of private planning and development in terms of comprehensiveness and the relationship to the public sector. Building innovative developments took tremendous effort. Even with the backing of exceptionally rich and powerful individuals and corporations—with huge amounts of money and so-phisticated political connections—it has been difficult to create and imple-ment the entire range of strategies generally considered necessary for com-prehensive development. Each development has also gone through periods when short-term profitability triumphed over long-term urban planning as internal development company goals.

The developments have certainly fallen short of their own and others' ideals, but they represent marketable urban innovation, what it is possible to sell to large numbers of people with other options. Sometimes the new communities have pushed the envelope enough to provide a significant al-ternative to generic suburban development, and at times they have not man-aged it, with many lessons for the current time.

To do much more, outside of some small niche developments such as many of those constructed by new urbanists, would be to go beyond the market, and thus require new kinds of government intervention. I say new kinds of government intervention because government policies, from zoning to road building, have also encouraged sprawl. Governments are also divided into agencies and departments that have distinctive geographies and spe-cializations with little communication among them, making comprehen-siveness particularly difficult. In addition, the governments that these new communities initially dealt with changed over time, not least because of the growth of the new communities themselves. The developers of the new com-munities had a strong interest in developing according to the plans they had marketed to residents. However, no specific government agency was allocated to their new communities. This meant that the developers were thrust into a role of coordinating multiple public agencies and maintaining this coor-dination over decades. The problems encountered in this by these politically savvy and prosperous corporations show the difficulties of doing really com-prehensive urban development in the United States, development of the kind that can provide a real alternative to suburban sprawl. Comprehensiveness and coordination were difficult for these rich landowners; they are likely to be equally difficult for branches of government.

In this private approach, the developments also staked out an unusual place in planning and design. The physical concepts for the projects fell within the tradition of physical land and site planning for suburban devel-opment. In the United States, this form of planning had traditionally been done by members of the architecture and landscape architecture professions in working for private clients. However, the large size of these new commu-nities and their comprehensive aspirations made them more akin to public planning for cities in which the public sector works for the public interest. Key early staff in both the Irvine Ranch and Columbia, although trained as architects, were actually recruited from public-sector planning positions. The private developers sponsored the formation of public utility districts, donated land for public facilities and public parks, and built public spaces. They also created spaces and institutions that were public-private hybrids—using covenants, conditions, and restrictions to supplement zoning and building codes, and putting in place resident and homeowner associations responsible for maintaining open spaces. These features demonstrate unusual combinations of public and private planning styles and development aims and show the internal complexity of both the public and private sectors.

Overall, the private sector is certainly capable of innovation in the area of land use planning, but this is very difficult to sustain over a long period. The internal quest for short-term profits, or at least positive cash flow, and the external difficulties in coordinating with governments and other entities make this a challenging process even when the developer possesses a great deal of expertise and goodwill. The case studies show a high level of sophistication in terms of comprehensive planning. However, they also show the difficulty of implementing these ideas, given that the private sector is competing in a marketplace where sprawl is often cheaper and where there is often no one in the public sector able to take a comprehensive view. The limits to the capacity of private-sector planning to organize the landscape to create an alternative to sprawl are a recurring theme in this study and the subject of the second half of the book.[2]

THE CASES

The earliest of the case study developments, Irvine Ranch, is based on a historic landholding in California's Orange County.[3] It has been developed by the Irvine Company (TIC), a group that has had three ownership regimes during the development period (see table 1). By 2000, after four decades of development, the Irvine Ranch housed around 200,000 people, with 143,072 within the core area of the City of Irvine. Development is planned to continue for around three or four more decades. The new community was first outlined by architect-planner William Pereira in 1960 as a "university-community" of 100,000 people on ten thousand acres, anchored by the University of California campus that had been proposed for a site on the ranch in the late 1950s. The campus was the focus for Pereira's southern sector master plan, covering the coastal thirty thousand acres of the ranch and approved by the county in 1964. By 1970, an in-house team had expanded the plan to propose around half a million people across well over sixty thousand acres of the ninety-three-thousand-acre Irvine Ranch.[4]

The basic concept of the Irvine Ranch breaks the development into three parts. A coastal section was planned as an extension to Newport Beach and as coastal housing. Over the years the extent of this part of the development has been reduced as habitat and coastal access issues have become more important. The central valley between UC Irvine and the Santiago foothills is

TABLE 1   Basic Data on Irvine, Columbia, and The Woodlands

General Features	Irvine, CA (Census Data for City of Irvine Only)	Columbia, MD (Census Data for CDP)[a]	The Woodlands, TX (Census Data for CDP)[a]
Developer	The Irvine Company (TIC)—majority owned by the James Irvine Foundation until 1977; by a consortium including Donald Bren until 1983; and since 1983 by Donald Bren	James Rouse Company affiliates, with early backing from Connecticut General Insurance (now CIGNA)	George Mitchell of Mitchell Energy and Development; sold in late 1990s to Crescent Operating, Inc., and Morgan Stanley
Metro area/state	Orange County, CA	Baltimore, MD (and Washington, D.C.)	Houston, TX
Proposed population in early plans	Over 400,000 (1970 TIC and 1973 City of Irvine plans)	110,000	150,000 (1972 HUD project agreement)
Population (2000 census)	143,072 in city, more in nearby areas, totaling 200,000	88,254 in 2000 census; 88,370[b]	55,649
Households (2000 census)	51,119	34,199	19,881
Approximate current size (acres)	Originally 93,000; 29,376 in City of Irvine; 29,758 in 2000 census	14,272;[c] 17,705 in 2000 CDP	Originally 17,000 acres; by 2000, 27,000; 15,284 in 2000 CDP
Starting date	1959: UCI campus study; 1964: southern sector plan approved (W. Pereira); 1970: overall plan completed	1962: first land bought; 1965: plan approved by Howard County; 1967: first projects completed	1964: first land bought; 1971: HUD approves Pereira-McHarg Plan; 1974: first buildings occupied

SOURCES: City of Irvine 2000, 2002; Irvine Company 1970c, 2001a, 2002d; Rouse Company 1999, 2002, n.d.; TWOC 2000a, 2001; U.S.A. and TWDC 1972; U.S. Census 1990, 2000.

[a] CDP = census designated place.
[b] From Rouse Company 1999.
[c] From Rouse Company, n.d.

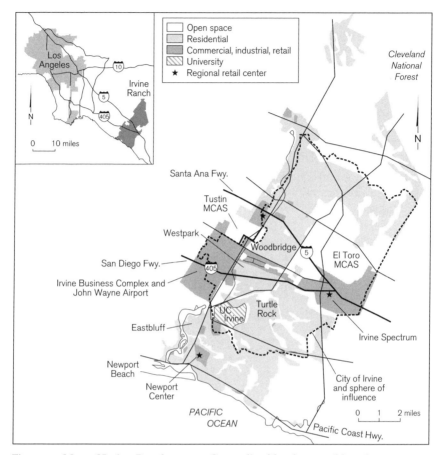

Figure 1. Map of Irvine Ranch, 1990s. Generalized land use and location compiled from several plans. The 1990s were chosen as the period for this map because by that time open space areas were in place. Based on plan drawn by Robert Gilmore.

the core ranch area and is mostly encompassed in the City of Irvine, a municipality containing more than two-thirds of the ranch's population. The northern hills areas will have little development because of many site constraints. A central spine of commercial and industrial development runs down the central valley area—divided into two main sections, the Irvine Business Complex and the Irvine Spectrum (see figure 1). The new community of Irvine covers the entire ranch area and is the focus of this study. However, most residents of the City of Irvine consider it to be the real Irvine. Throughout, I use the term *Irvine* sparingly, specifying instead the Irvine Ranch or the City of Irvine to indicate the particular location.[5]

The early Pereira planning included extensive work analyzing urbane college towns seen as the best models for a university community (e.g., Oxford; Heidelberg; Princeton; Palo Alto; and Cambridge, Massachusetts). While the Pereira modernist urban design lacked most of the richness of these places, the Irvine Ranch's later planners thought much more than has been generally appreciated about neighborhood planning, environmental legibility, open space, and pedestrian networks. The development was seen by its planners as a large "canvas" for suburban design, with notable innovations in attached housing and landscaping of the suburban public realm. Diagrams from the Irvine Ranch's early planning show careful consideration of different village layouts and an interest in the various scales at which "man" relates to the metropolis and region.[6] By the 1970s the development was also actively marketing to new household types, and its later planning has focused more attention on the site scale. Throughout this community's development the Irvine Company has faced a series of environmental controversies and has been the focus of litigation and a target for activism. However, it has made significant changes in response, with over half the ranch now slated for open space and habitat protection.

In 2000, the Irvine Ranch ranked number two among master-planned communities in the United States in terms of home sales, which were 2,377 units (Lesser 2002).[7] It has become a center for the Asian American population of Orange County; the City of Irvine was 32 percent Asian descent and 57 percent non-Hispanic white in 2000 (see appendix B). Its business parks now form one of the largest business districts in California. This was not an accident; like the other case study new communities, the Irvine Company courted industries, particularly in the technology field, and its business parks became "one of the great successes of real estate history" (Interview 0319). In 2000, the *Ladies' Home Journal* named the City of Irvine as the top city in the United States for women on the basis of its low crime rate and other quality-of-life features, although it dropped to fourth place in 2001 and fifth among the new category of small cities in 2002 (Best Cities 2001, 2002).

Columbia, in Maryland between Baltimore and Washington, D.C., is the most well-known of the new communities among planners and designers, engaging numerous experts and generating more research interest than the other developments. The development is organized into a town center and nine villages, each with a mixed-use village center. Its residential component will be largely completed in the early 2000s, with a population near one hundred thousand on about fourteen thousand acres (it is "about" fourteen thousand because the developer bought and sold land over the decades, and so

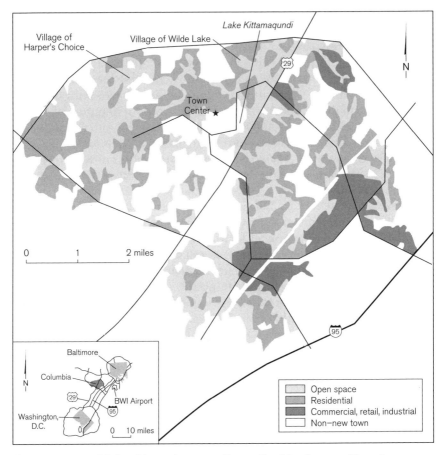

Figure 2. Map of Columbia, early 1970s. Generalized land use and location were compiled from several plans of the period, reflecting the design at the end of the most intensive initial planning phase. Based on plan drawn by Robert Gilmore.

the size has varied from year to year) (see figure 2). Columbia is best known for having made very significant early attempts at economic and racial integration, maintaining a population that has been about one-fifth African American throughout its history. Its increasing Asian-descent population led to a count of 64 percent non-Hispanic whites in 2000. In its early years this integration was a pioneering effort. In 1963, as initial planning was occurring, almost 84 percent of Howard County's "colored" school population still attended "colored-only" schools.[8] Columbia was approved at the county level in 1965, and it was not until the 1966–67 academic year that the final racially segregated school in Howard County was closed (Ephross 1988, 41–

42). The development opened in 1967, the same year that Maryland made interracial marriages legal.

One innovative part of Columbia's planning process was the core team of fourteen outside experts and four people from the Rouse Company who worked through the social planning of the area with the support of other staff and consultants. They met fairly often for about six months from November 1963 to the middle of 1964 (Michael 1996; Tennenbaum 1996b). This sociological focus reflected Rouse's disillusionment with the then-popular architectural and physical approach to planning. He thought it was inhumane, and he wanted urban development to promote human growth and values such as lifelong learning, civic participation, and the mixing of diverse populations (Rouse 1963a).

Rouse, who held deep Christian beliefs, also saw Columbia as a way to help inner urban areas. The new community was seen as providing opportunities for a diverse group of people to leave urban areas that had become obsolete, and also as creating a model for revitalizing the older cities in turn (Rouse 1963a). Columbia was the most self-conscious of the developments about its place in the history of planning and development. A Rouse Company staff member, Wallace Hamilton, was employed with the initial social planning work group, writing a history that was never published.[9] Columbia also made a number of less well-known innovations in environmental planning, village center design, and project management. This social and technical focus contrasted with the Irvine Ranch's physically oriented southern sector plan of the same period.

The Woodlands, north of Houston, opened in 1974 and had a population of over fifty-five thousand in April 2000. Its developer until the late 1990s was oil and gas magnate George Mitchell. In the 1960s he bought several tracts of land and prepared a preliminary master plan for a fairly standard residential and light industrial development. However, he was attracted by new federal programs, Title IV and Title VII, which could provide loan guarantees for new town development. Although opening in 1974 in the midst of the dramatic real estate downturn, The Woodlands was the only one of thirteen projects selected for these federal programs that did not default on its financial obligations (U.S. HUD 1984; Morgan and King 1987) (see figure 3).

Looking for a firm to do the final Title VII proposal in 1970, the year of the Irvine Company general plan, a Houston planner suggested that Mitchell read Ian McHarg's 1969 *Design with Nature.* Tremendously inspired, Mitchell had McHarg work with William Pereira on the master plan for The Woodlands (Morgan and King 1987; Middleton 1997; Sutton and McHarg 1975). This led the development to be designed to protect water systems, allowing aquifer recharge and limiting runoff. The Woodlands combines this emphasis on hydrology with a striking aesthetic that uses largely unmanicured woods to mask and buffer development. The editorial notes by McHarg and

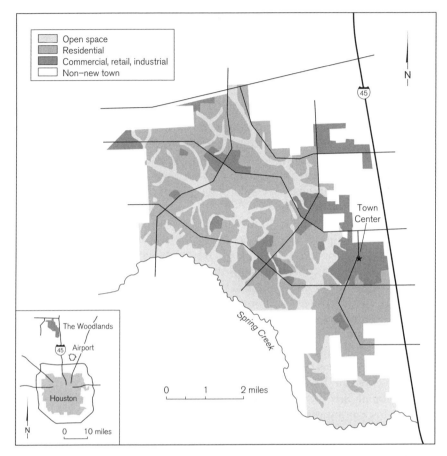

Figure 3. Map of The Woodlands, mid-1970s: generalized land use and location for the development during its Title VII period. Based on plan drawn by Robert Gilmore.

Fritz Steiner in the 1998 collection of McHarg's writings claim, "The Woodlands is one of McHarg's most influential projects. It is the best example of ecologically based new town planning in the United States during the 1970s" (McHarg 1998, 325). In the early 1970s Mitchell also recruited over a dozen professionals who had worked on Columbia, as well as several who had worked on the Irvine Ranch or the UC Irvine campus.

Initially planned for about 150,000 people on approximately fifteen thousand acres, the land area has expanded to over twenty-five thousand acres. The current population target is not clear, although growth has been very rapid in the late 1990s and early 2000s under new owners, with home sales of 1,679 units, or around 4,700 people, in 2000 (Lesser 2002). Like Columbia, it is unincorporated but lies in a county with a particularly low level of services. While it is in the extraterritorial jurisdiction of Houston, it has not yet been annexed. Most typical local government service functions, except schools, water, and police, are supplied by one of the largest private nonprofit governments in the United States. The Woodlands also made some social innovations, particularly the cooperation of religious denominations and the provision of social services through an organization called Interfaith.

Overall, the three new towns have been evaluated as some of the best of their kind.[10] They are particularly comprehensive or complete, with more jobs than households, varied cultural facilities, and extensive recreational areas, in addition to residential and retail development. Out of fifteen planned new communities in their pioneering NSF-funded study, *New Communities USA,* Burby and Weiss (1976, 97) listed Columbia, Reston, and Irvine in that order as having the greatest adherence to the new community concept. In the longer term Reston ended up having a more fragmented planning process because of its significant financial difficulties. The Woodlands was not inhabited at the time of the Burby and Weiss research. However, it had unique success as a Title VII new town and in terms of its ecological planning.

Even with all this sophisticated planning and design activity and the numerous assessments of how they exemplify the new community idea, these developments are not liked by everyone. The Irvine Ranch is often accused of being purely a real estate venture with very monotonous architecture and no social concern. In contrast, Columbia is characterized as far too utopian and having an illegible urban design that has weathered badly. Finally, The Woodlands is portrayed by some as a poor copy of Columbia with a declining commitment to ecology. As I explain below, these are harsh criticisms, often reflecting a partial or outdated view of the developments. That is, they are often inaccurate. However, in some dimensions these criticisms are correct and as such are particularly interesting, because, as the book shows, the developments really fare well when evaluated against current ideas from the smart growth movement about what makes good urban development. Their failed dimensions suggest a need for change or at least refinement in these contemporary ideas.

COMMON FEATURES

The three developments share many characteristics that make it possible to evaluate them as a group. While not perfect, their planning was based on long-term visions and involved cutting-edge professionals with strong urban design ideas. They involve big land areas, excellent locations for attracting a range of activities, and they attracted rich developers, who all aimed to make profits.

Visions

The three case study developments were based on the strong planning and design visions, and in professional circles they are deemed to have realized those visions continuously over a number of decades. The visions were comprehensive and forward looking, although with very different emphases. They responded to a number of social phenomena of the period, including suburbanization, the rise of dual-income families, general mobility, and a quest for community. The developers created a package that emphasized ordered diversity, community interactions, and closeness to nature, using the visions in marketing to attract many residents who bought into and monitored the visions. The visions were at least in part about providing an alternative to sprawl—aesthetically, socially, and ecologically.

To develop and implement these visions required people. The three case study developments shared many of the same professional networks—networks of developers, of big-name planners and designers, and of people interested in urban reform. As well as in-house staff, each of the developments employed a number of important consultant planners, designers, and other experts in major and minor roles. Those working on the case study new communities in planning, landscape, and building design included such important figures as Ian McHarg, William Pereira, Peter Walker, Anne Spirn, and Frank Gehry. Other experts were brought in from time to time as consultants or brain trusts, particularly in Columbia, where such visiting experts included Kevin Lynch, Herbert Gans, Christopher Jencks, and Chester Rapkin. James Rouse (developer of Columbia), George Mitchell (developer of The Woodlands), and key planners and executives from the Irvine Ranch, such as Ray Watson, were all active in public debates about growth. Ray Watson had graduated from Berkeley, starting in the same architecture class as Bill Finley, senior development director for Columbia.[11] George Mitchell attended intensive education programs for new community developers run by Rouse at the Urban Life Center in Columbia. Several professionals worked on more than one of the communities as either consultants or staff. Others had links with key networks interested in urban reform.[12]

These professionals set about quite self-consciously rethinking the character of suburban development and metropolitan form as a whole. Columbia and The Woodlands started with stronger initial visions, but the Irvine Ranch's large size gave it an unparalleled capacity to learn from earlier development and respond to changing circumstances. While the developments varied in their overall atmosphere, members of all the early planning and design groups were part of an extraordinarily exciting process that launched careers. "We never left the office. We worked day and night. . . . It was like planning for D-Day. We had a tremendous sense of wanting to get it done. We were all learning. Most of us were intellectually flexible. We were survivors. We were smart and intelligent and willing to give up our personal lives to make this happen" (Interview 0502). But there was a dark side:

> The personal toll it took on people's lives, the divorces, the erratic behavior. . . . I guess as the result of their reaction to stress. They were doing something so different and so gigantic that it took people out of themselves, and they sometimes acted in ways that weren't normal to them. It was just extraordinary, really, now looking back on it with some maturity. But it was very difficult not to be caught up in it. If you were involved in it, you were involved in it 150 percent. (Interview 0521)

Overall, this was a moment in history when teams of professionals came to believe that they could dream dreams and see them built, that they could reshape metropolitan areas over the coming decades, and that they could provide models for the rest of the country. It was a time of tremendous hope and innovation, and in these three developments many innovations were implemented.

In creating an alternative to sprawl, these developments all experimented with new suburban design frameworks. Aesthetically, what is most striking about all three is the use of landscape to create identity: in the Irvine Ranch, this is formal and modernist, set off by areas of coastal sage scrub; in Columbia, rustic and wooded; and in The Woodlands, a somewhat ungroomed forest. They also experimented with the location and layout of village "centers," the creation of edges to development, and the relationship between road layouts and social groupings. For urban designers focused on center cities, these issues may seem peripheral. However, from a suburban perspective, they have been part of an extremely interesting attempt to remake the suburban landscape.

The practice of planning for large private developments falls to several professions. The initial planning of these developments also coincided with a period of some transition in the field of city planning. Degree programs in city planning had commenced before World War II but were increasing in number. These generally had started with a physical and administrative approach, exemplified by those planners who did general plans, zoning, and development regulation for municipalities. However, during the 1960s the field increasingly embraced both social concerns and analytical techniques from the social sciences, reflecting the profession's ethical commitment to serving the public interest and its technical aspirations. Planners increasingly saw themselves as rational problem solvers who were moving beyond their early commitment to a "set of narrowly architectural goals and to land use and design programs for realizing them" toward a more systematic and politically informed kind of practice (Gans 1968, vii). Many local government planners in the 1960s and 1970s were trained in city planning during this time of change, although some had been architects.

However, the new community planning teams—those who laid out the components of the developments—were dominated by architects and later landscape architects, and detailed infrastructure layouts were the work of engineers. This created a confusing terminology, as different professions used different terms for the work of laying out these cities: the architects saw themselves as doing planning or urban design; the landscape architects, as doing either land or environment planning. All had been trained to focus on the physical world—built or vegetated. Those with training in the social science or administrative approaches to planning and related fields were also on the development teams, sometimes laying out the built elements and open space but often working on coordination, government relations, or special areas such as community facilities and transportation. When the differences among the groups are important, I distinguish among the city planners, architect planners, land planners, and other planning types. Overall, this complex mosaic of skills and approaches caused a number of tensions. However, in terms of the trajectories of the professions, the new communities were located at an intersection of their fields, which allowed innovation.

Size

All three case study developments are very large—with final populations projected to be from one hundred thousand to over four hundred thousand and with land areas from fourteen thousand acres to over ninety thousand, including large amounts of open space and significant employment areas. Their size is related to their comprehensive philosophy. Many facilities depend on a large population, as many key innovations do. A critical mass of jobs also needs to exist in a new town. The smallest of the three, Columbia, was planned for just over one hundred thousand people because the development team considered it hard to be sufficiently comprehensive under that number. The Irvine Ranch was already in place, but the Irvine Company could have made easier profits by selling land for subdivisions. Instead it chose to keep land intact to enable a more comprehensive approach. For comparison, one of the largest of the new urbanist developments, Disney's Celebration, has a current population of about thirty-five hundred and will build out at twelve thousand to fifteen thousand in an area of forty-nine hundred acres plus a forty-seven-hundred-acre greenbelt (Celebration Corporation 2001). This is much smaller and makes comprehensiveness much more difficult.

The large areas and long development timetables of these new communities have made it impossible to avoid difficult development problems. These developments faced the oil crisis and property crash of the 1970s and growing concerns about habitat protection in the 1980s and 1990s. They have also dealt with ongoing changes in household structure, the role of government, and information technologies. As big developments in fast-growing locations, they have had to engage fully with thorny problems such as open space, transit, and affordable housing—problems that smaller developments can leave for others to solve. In their later phases, the developments have had to deal with issues of democratic participation by those who moved in earlier, raising ongoing questions about vision and professional expertise. In time, tens of thousands of residents who had bought into the plans were in place to debate areas of continuity and change. Bigness also made mistakes and failures more visible. However, in the absence of an extremely powerful government coordinating agency, large size was essential for achieving a real alternative to sprawl.

Locations

All three case study developments were located in some of the fastest-growing regions of the 1960s, and they managed to capture and concentrate a significant amount of that growth. As the main monograph on The Woodlands explains: "In the decade 1960–1970 metropolitan Houston added 540,000 new residents, a population growth only exceeded by the Anaheim–Santa Ana, California areas and by Washington, D.C." (Morgan and King 1987, 35).

In Joel Garreau's 1991 book, *Edge City,* Columbia was already classed as an "edge city," a center for jobs and retail, and during the 1990s its high-tech sector expanded further.[13] The Irvine Ranch area contained edge cities at Irvine Spectrum and John Wayne Airport, as well as an emerging edge city at Fashion Island (within Newport Center). The City of Irvine estimated 168,000 jobs in the city alone in 2000 (City of Irvine 2002). In 1991, Garreau classified The Woodlands as an "emerging edge city," and it has since added significant office and research space. Its mixed-use town center is currently under intensive development and includes high-rise buildings and a major retail area.

This employment growth was not an accident; all three developments courted growing industries, and in all three cases these included significant information technology and biotechnology clusters. I actually started this study intending to look at urban development in areas with large high-tech employment concentrations and realized that, in a number of such locations, master-planned communities were an important urban type. However, the three case studies have been exceptionally successful in capturing this employment, and the large numbers of jobs set these communities apart from other development projects that have turned out to be essentially residential and retail ventures. Because all three developers maintain significant ownership of commercial and even industrial areas, the employment concentrations are part of a long-term investment strategy.

Rich Developers Aiming for Profits

These new towns were developed and funded by some of the wealthiest individuals and corporations in the nation. While each development had financial problems, none failed in the sense of having to sell off large parcels or depart dramatically from its initial concept in order to make quick sales. In this, the wealth of the development companies and their backers was crucial. The elite social networks of the developers also helped them gain approvals and get regulations changed.

For all three, profit has been an important aim, although it has not been a matter of short-term profit at all costs. Obviously these were business ventures that would stay in business only if they made money. For Columbia, profitability was also important to Rouse, because a profitable development would be copied by others as a model. The three developments certainly represent large investments. In figuring a ballpark estimate of the housing value alone, if we multiply Columbia's approximately thirty-five thousand housing units in 2000 by a building cost of $100,000 in 2000 dollars, that would represent $3.5 billion in just housing units, *excluding land and infrastructure values*. Similar figures for The Woodlands are $2 billion; the City of Irvine, $5.4 billion; and the remaining third of the ranch, a couple of billion more just for housing units. This does not include the many other components of the new towns, from business parks and shopping centers to civic facilities and open space. These additional elements would increase the housing unit cost several times. If we use census data for 2000, the value of housing in the City of Irvine alone would be approximately $17 billion (assuming rental and ownership units have approximately the same value). While this certainly inflates the overall value in the city, where renters (occupying 40 percent of the housing units) likely live in somewhat less expensive units than the owner-occupied ones, it excludes the other parts of the ranch where land is generally higher priced. Of course, the developers did not construct all of this; for example, most developed the land by subdividing it and providing infrastructure but had others build much of the housing. However, these kinds of figures give a sense of the scale of the overall value of the developments. The Irvine Ranch in particular, with its very expensive land, enormous business parks, and successful shopping centers, has a huge current value. In comparison, the most expensive public works project in U.S. history, the Boston Central Artery Tunnel project, has a cost of $14.6 billion (Altshuler and Luberoff 2003, 76, 116).[14]

However, even with this huge scale, or because it is huge, profitability is difficult for such developments. There certainly are areas where money can be made. Infrastructure can be laid in a coordinated and cost effective manner. The mixtures of uses in new communities can attract larger firms and businesses to these relatively remote suburban locations, allowing profitable commercial and industrial land development as well as increased home sales to workers. Mixed uses can also help development companies ride out downturns in individual real estate sectors. The overall package of amenities typical of new communities is meant to attract a profitable sector of the housing market.

However, because prices of land escalate once development starts, land must be bought up front. The costs of holding the land over decades can be enormous—interest on loans, delayed profits from the investment, and property taxes. Land sold in the final stages, in the almost fully developed new community, can return far more than its cost, but in a decades-long development timetable, it can be a long time before these profits are realized. The initial servicing to attract people to the new towns is also expensive. Smaller developments often make people travel to amenities, and governments eventually supply them on site. New communities pay for amenities before they are needed, adding to their financial problems. While gated areas are highly profitable, in trying to keep to the new town concept, Columbia and The Woodlands have only recently included such sections, and they are still quite limited. In Columbia, it is only a condominium complex in the town center area with an unimposing wrought-iron fence. Even the Irvine Ranch built its first gated village in the City of Irvine only in the late 1990s.

This quest for profitability within the new town concept has set the U.S. new town experience apart from the rest of the world, where governments have sponsored such developments for wider aims, including regional development. Within the United States, this long wait for returns has also distinguished new town developers from most others involved in land development. This issue of private for-profit planning is one I return to below where I sketch out alternative approaches to examining this kind of development.

DIFFERENCES

In comparing these developments, however, we find a number of key differences. The Irvine Ranch is much larger than the other developments, and when the initial development was proposed, the Irvine Company had owned the land since the nineteenth century, using it for agriculture. This gave the developer the initial advantage of not having to purchase land, although, because the development was sold in 1977, for much of its development period the land price has been factored in. In addition, because the Irvine Company owned so much land, it was highly vulnerable to increases in property taxation. Before California's Williamson Act was passed in 1965, land that was in the path of development could be taxed at its development potential, and there was no way to get around this situation. The government's action of raising property taxes and proposing a University of California campus on the property essentially forced development.

The Irvine Ranch's location in Orange County was also important politically. Orange County was a key area for Republicans in the 1950s and early 1960s. Richard Nixon, born in Yorba Linda, Orange County, was vice president during the Eisenhower administration, from 1953 to 1960, when the initial proposals for a University of California campus were being developed. He became president from 1969 to 1974.[15] More truly conservative, Ronald Reagan was governor of California from 1966 to 1974 and then president from 1980 to 1988. In the 1966 gubernatorial election, 72 percent of Orange County votes went to Reagan, leading the state, and a number of the people whom I interviewed in Orange County had pictures of President Reagan in their offices (McGirr 2001, 209). Even today local council hearings in many Orange County municipalities open with the Pledge of Allegiance and a devotional moment. In all but one of the dozen public meetings that I attended in the Cities of Irvine and Santa Ana, this was a moment of prayer or a reflection on a biblical text led by a Christian minister. This socially conservative image was reinforced economically by Southern California's heavy reliance on the defense industry.

In this development context, the Irvine Company managed to thrive. However, the company seems to have stayed out of the most conservative politics. It certainly fought against many environmental regulations but eventually gave in or made compromise deals. Unlike the other developments, the Irvine Ranch area was incorporated quickly as the City of Irvine and through annexations to adjacent municipalities. This meant that the Irvine Company gave up some control as developer, although it has generally followed a pattern of getting development approval from the county, then having its land annexed with approvals in place but facing local government development standards.[16] The development also managed to include a more socially liberal group associated with the university, and by the early 1970s it was using market segmentation to increase sales to both traditional and nontraditional household types. Certainly, the Irvine Company has not been a hotbed of liberalism, but it has had a mixed set of policies reflecting more liberal ideas as well as the social and political conservatism of the county.

Maryland, the location of Columbia, is a border state between the North and the South, and Baltimore in particular was still very conservative in regard to racial issues at the time of Columbia's planning. Columbia's development generally emphasized social issues more than the other two developments, including an engagement with the social changes of the 1960s and a critique of physical planning. In the early days of the development, the Columbia concept of racial and economic integration was stronger and more generally shared than the visions in the other two developments. In inter-

views a number of early development team members—all white—recalled
critical remarks addressed to them by colleagues in Baltimore who were per-
plexed at the open housing policy in Columbia. Rouse and several of his employees were also very articulate in promoting the Columbia concept over a
number of decades.

Those involved in the early stages of Columbia equated the work environment of the Rouse Company and the more general life of the community with Camelot. Its planning was in fact connected with the milieu of social change in the Kennedy and Johnson administrations, and its location
near Washington, D.C., also helped Columbia's national profile. It was relatively easy for James Rouse to go to Washington to testify before various congressional committees. In turn, Washington powerbrokers interested in urban change could visit Columbia, and consultants could work on small parts
of the project.

The Woodlands was placed in the extraterritorial jurisdiction of the City
of Houston, well known as the major city in the United States without zoning. This gave it relative flexibility in land use—both the other two developments had more complex approval processes—and also made it part of
a unique regional market for master-planned communities that impose their
own land use controls within a sea of unregulated suburban subdivisions.
The development to date has built a far larger proportion of its housing as
single-family detached units than the other two developments and in turn
attracted a far larger percentage of nuclear families. The Title VII designation
of The Woodlands gave it some special opportunities as well as a number of
responsibilities, both in terms of planning goals and bureaucratic reporting.

A final set of differences involves the issues of financing, ownership, and
profitability. Initially all three development companies bore the name of their
founders, and had not started off in the new community business but had
a major income-producing arm in another area. For the Irvine Company it
was agriculture; for the Rouse Company, mortgage banking and shopping
center development; and for Mitchell it was oil and gas production. All three
companies still perform most of these functions, even though all have been
sold or, in the case of Rouse, had their founder retire.[17] Additional financing came from insurance and pension funds as well as banks. While different from one another, agriculture, insurance, and oil and gas exploration
are all businesses that require what is known as patient money.

However, the Irvine Company had a different relationship to land development, having owned land that it was essentially forced into developing.
Its founder was also long gone, and there was not even an Irvine at the helm
by the time of the decision to develop in 1959. In contrast, both Columbia
and The Woodlands were the pet projects of the founders of their publicly
traded companies. They also took bigger financial risks, partly because they
had to buy land and partly because they promoted a more unusual initial vi-

sion. However, while personally identified with the development, James Rouse, who had more experience with development, seems to have been less financially exposed than Mitchell. Rouse was not a majority shareholder of the Rouse Company or of the subsidiary that developed Columbia, Howard Research and Development. The Rouse Company did not fully own the majority share of the Columbia development until 1985, when it purchased the approximately 80 percent share owned by CIGNA, formerly Connecticut General Life Insurance (Rouse Company, n.d.; Breckenfeld 1971, 308). The federal government did guarantee a number of loans to The Woodlands through the Title VII program. However, my reading of the financial arrangements is that The Woodlands developer, George Mitchell, owned the majority of his company and had his personal fortune on the line during the early stages to an extent unparalleled in the other developments. While people mentioned that he had very significant separate investments in the tens of millions, he still stood to lose. One of his admirers explained, "He had more courage than any businessman I've ever met in my life. With all of the debt, all of the leverage, all of the everything, he was unfazed. He had ice water veins. He had absolutely no fear" (Interview 0507).

In spite of the different degree of exposure of the company founders, the internal conflicts over the costs of the development were intense in both the Rouse and Mitchell companies.[18] The staff of the major income- and profit-producing arms—mortgage banking, shopping centers, oil and gas—disliked seeing their money frittered away on what they perceived as utopian new towns. They feared financial ruin at the hands of the young teams of idealistic design and planning staff and the slightly ruthless project managers, who between them were creating those innovative yet risky developments. This was a personal fear in these publicly traded companies, in which many employees owned shares: jobs could be lost and stock prices could decline. The staff of the profit-producing arms tried to keep control, and in both cases in the first few years after the developments opened, when debt was at its peak, many changes in personnel occurred, with Rouse and Mitchell having to take more account of the conservative parts of their companies. They were perceived by many as losing control of their companies for a period.

It is harder to know all the details about the Irvine Ranch: it has remained a private company, while the other two companies, both public, have been forced to release more information. In the Irvine Ranch, there were certainly professional and interpersonal disagreements. There was also turbulence in the mid- to late 1970s due to the forced sale of the company following changes in U.S. tax law. However, the development team took fewer early financial risks, and the project seems to have been more continuously profitable. As a private company, it could also make different choices about investments without having to take account of publicly traded share prices.

This is not the whole story, however, in terms of vision and profitability.

Columbia and The Woodlands are now run by employees of public companies essentially working out the initial visions—and since late 2003, the Rouse Company owned not only Columbia but a 52.5 percent interest in The Woodlands. Recent modifications have generally aimed to maintain or even increase profitable development, including higher-density, gated residential areas and various forms of commercial space. In contrast, the Irvine Company is owned entirely by Donald Bren, who seems to have been increasingly interested in an environmental legacy. From the late 1980s onward, he has gradually sold and given land for habitat conservation, with over half the ranch currently slated for open space and habitat areas in time frames ranging from seventy-five years to perpetuity. Certainly he was prodded by vigorous local activism promoting the preservation of open space. Some of this land was also traded for higher-intensity development elsewhere, in a process labeled phased dedication, in which certain amounts of land are dedicated for open space in return for building permits.[19] Open space marketed well can increase the value of other properties. However, the open space areas are still significant in size. This shows both the capacity of private companies to do things that would not be attractive to the shareholders of publicly traded corporations and the different paths that developments can take over time, even while adhering to one basic concept.

The rest of chapter 1 examines where these new towns came from, explains how I studied them, and outlines the argument of the book. In doing this I define a number of terms, such as *new community* and *neighborhood*—terms with a wide range of meanings even among those involved in the urban development professions. Even the term *suburb* is open to some dispute (Harris 1999). Many in the United States use a definition based on political boundaries, in which suburbs are locations within a metropolitan area but outside the central city. Where center cities are large and new, this has obvious limits, because much of the central area will be made up of relatively recently built detached houses that are indistinguishable from the structures in other local government areas labeled suburban. For this book a functional definition is more relevant and useful. This kind of definition proposes that a suburban physical form is one that is dominated by detached houses and automobile-based transportation, no matter what its political jurisdiction, or one that is in a part of the metropolitan area largely built since World War II. The latter form includes earlier settlements engulfed in the outward spread of urbanization. These areas also include a variety of activities and environments beyond detached houses and strip shopping centers. The new communities in this study added to this variety.

THE SUBURBAN CRITIQUE

The three developments all aimed to solve at least some of the problems of incremental and uncoordinated suburban growth, a kind of environment referred to as urban sprawl. While there had been criticisms of suburbia in the pre–World War II period by such writers as Lewis Mumford, it was in the 1950s that such criticisms really took off, fueled in part by the massive building boom that was occurring. For the first half of the twentieth century, housing starts in the United States were generally under about 0.5 million each year. In the second half this suddenly increased to about 1.5 million and remained consistently over 1 million (Hise 1997, 156). Suburbs sprang up across the country, located almost anywhere within commuting distance of urban jobs. Whether the construction was by big developers or small builders, municipalities everywhere were inadequately prepared. Lagging infrastructure, boxy houses, and strip shopping areas became easy targets for social and aesthetic critiques.

The new subdivisions created instant physical environments and social settings in a way that seemed unprecedented to early critics. Urban historians working in the 1960s and 1970s discovered that this situation was not quite so new as it seemed and that high levels of housing mobility had been a fact of life in the United States throughout the twentieth century (Monkkonen 1988, 27–19). Still, the speed of construction in the postwar period meant that in larger developments whole new social groupings were created with unusual speed. As suburbanization continued, spreading outward and filling in areas that had been jumped over in early development, areas of undeveloped land or open space became rarer in the suburban environment. The energy crisis of the early 1970s also briefly alerted people in the United States to another range of environmental problems that particularly affected automobile-dependent areas and detached houses.[20]

A number of popularly successful books criticized suburban areas directly or pointed out emerging social problems or negative trends set there (see reviews in Eichler and Kaplan 1967, 4–10; Popenoe 1977, 2–8; and Gans 1963). Such books include Reisman's *The Lonely Crowd* (1950), Keats's *The Crack in the Picture Window* (1957), Whyte's *The Exploding Metropolis* (1958), Gordon and coauthors' *The Split Level Trap* (1960), Friedan's *The Feminine Mystique* (1963), and Blake's *God's Own Junk Yard* (1964). Columbia's developer, James Rouse, joined this chorus through a number of speeches and papers in the early 1960s. He explained in 1966:

> Our cities grow by sheer chance—by accident, by whim of private developer and public agencies. A farm is sold and begins raising houses instead of potatoes—then another farm. Forests are cut; valleys are filled; streams are buried in storm sewers. Kids overflow the schools; a new school is built. Churches come up out of the basements. Traffic grows, roads are widened, front yards cut back. Service stations, Tasty-Freezes, hamburger stands pockmark the old highway (a good spot for a strip shopping center, and somebody builds it). Traffic is strangled; an expressway is hacked through the landscape and this brings cloverleafs (now there is a spot for a regional shopping

center and somebody builds it, too). Then office buildings, high-rise apartments, and so it goes.

Thus, bits and pieces of a city are splattered across the landscape. By this irrational process, noncommunities are born—formless places without order, beauty or reason, places with no visible respect for people or the land. Thousands of small, separate decisions made with little or no relationship to one another, nor to their composite impact, produce a major decision about the future of our cities and our civilization—a decision we have come to label "suburban sprawl." What nonsense this is! (Rouse 1966b, 2–3)

Of course, many older and well-loved cities have grown in a similar incremental manner, and it is the essence of both the capitalist market and democracy for thousands of small decisions to add up to something bigger.[21] However, forty years later, new urbanists were still making similar criticisms, showing the significant parallels between the perceptions of problems in the 1960s and those in the current period:

> For the past fifty years, we Americans have been building a national landscape that is largely devoid of places worth caring about. Soulless subdivisions, residential "communities" utterly lacking in communal life; strip shopping centers, "big box" chain stores, and artificially festive malls set within barren seas of parking; antiseptic office parks, ghost towns after 6 PM; and mile upon mile of clogged collector roads, the only fabric tying our disassociated lives back together. (Duany et al. 2000, x)

Not all the critics and analysts of the 1950s and 1960s focused on scattered generic suburbs. Some authors began to examine large-scale developments that had received more planning attention, including such "packaged suburbs" as Park Forest, near Chicago, and Levittown, New Jersey (also Clark 1966). This means that the suburban critique also included a critique of some of the more highly planned developments of the period, the precursors of the new communities in this study. The new community planners were trying not only to do better than generic subdivisions but also to improve on more highly planned developments.

Park Forest was a focus for about one-third of Whyte's (1956) journalistic cum sociological study of *The Organization Man*. This development was opened in 1948, with the earliest neighborhoods designed by distinguished landscape architect Elbert Peets (Randall 2000). Whyte's account focused on the effects of large corporations and bureaucracy on American men and argued that the Protestant ethic of individual hard work was being replaced by a social ethic of conformity. Whyte concentrated on the highly mobile class of professionals working for a variety of for-profit, nonprofit, and government organizations. He saw these men as working in a group and *belonging to* the organization rather than *working for* it. In Park Forest, the home of many workers in such organizations, Whyte uncovered very active socializing in this transient young professional population. What would today be seen as a location high in social capital was at the time seen as somewhat shallow with its hectic social life led by the wives of these organization men. Whyte argued that the suburbs were the best place to witness this new social ethic and that they were representative of the future:

> The packaged villages . . . have become the dormitory of the new generation of organization men. They are not typical American communities, but because they provide such a cross section of young organization people we can see in bolder relief than elsewhere the kind of world organization man wants and may in time bring about. Here I will go into the tremendous effect transiency has had on the organization people and how their religious life, their politics and the way they take to their neighbors reveal the new kind of rootedness they are looking for. (Whyte 1956, 10)

Like Park Forest, the three case study developments in this book, because of their locations, attracted many of these kinds of corporate and government workers. All have heavily marketed a hometown image to a mobile population, and in the early years the entire populations of the case study developments were by definition transplants.

While Whyte was critical of organization men, Gans was not so damning in his study of the packaged development of Levittown, New Jersey. Gans's *The Levittowners* (1967) used survey research and participant observation to argue that suburban living did not fundamentally change its inhabitants as had been implied or stated in earlier critiques. However, a significant group of women did suffer from unhappiness after their move, mainly because of isolation—particularly young mothers without a car, working-class women missing family and friends, Jewish women, and women whose husbands were often absent (Gans 1967, 226–27). Interestingly, Gans had been involved with Whyte's earlier study when a graduate student at Chicago, producing a paper on Jewish organizations in Park Forest. Gans also became part of the Columbia social planning work group. At the time of Gans's involvement with Columbia, the book on his Levittown research had not yet been published, but he had produced early accounts (e.g., Gans 1963).

While not examining a planned suburb, Berger's *Working Class Suburb* (1960) also took a more benign view. From interviews with a group of relocated suburban Ford Motor Company production and maintenance workers, Berger found that this working-class group did not change much on moving to a suburban area, and in particular he found little of Whyte's frenetic socializing. While interest in politics increased and friendships changed, the population still voted Democrat and were not driven to join organizations or attend religious services as had been claimed in earlier work. Women's lives changed more than the men's, however; for example, their civic participation increased while men's decreased (Berger 1960, 62).

By the 1960s and 1970s, then, some had begun to question the unrelenting criticism of sprawl. Some even defended suburban areas, which while "highly segregated along marginally differentiated cost lines, [are] not one endless row of homogeneous split-level traps inhabited by a conforming middle class that is hyperorganized and hypersociable" (Hadden and Barton [1973] 1977, 54; also Gans 1963). However, in general, low-density sprawl was attacked repeatedly for its aesthetic problems, lack of a sense of identity, social inequities, economic inefficiency, and environmental damage. As with the debates of the 1990s and the early 2000s, it had relatively few academic and professional defenders, although quite a large market.

THE NEW COMMUNITY PROPOSALS

These debates about the massive postwar development boom provoked discussion from within the professions responsible for urban development, and not just from sociological and cultural analysts. One idea that achieved some support as an alternative was that of the new community. It drew on the traditions of physical planning—strongly linked to architecture and landscape architecture—but also on the new fields of social science and ecology. It seemed to answer the criticisms of sprawl while maintaining most of the benefits of suburban living that had attracted people to the suburbs in the first place.

At its loosest definition, *new community* is a term used mostly in the United States to describe large master-planned areas of at least two thousand or twenty-five hundred acres, although very-high-density new communities could be smaller (Eichler and Kaplan 1967, 23; Ewing 1991, 2). Some have used the term for developments that are largely residential. However, most have distinguished between fairly self-contained new communities and less comprehensive packaged suburbs or master-planned communities. The more self-contained new communities are also called new towns. However, in the United States new towns have been private-sector for-profit developments, whereas new towns elsewhere have been generally developed by public and nonprofit developers.

The more comprehensive definition of *new community* was promoted by the Urban Land Institute (ULI) and other professional groups in the 1970s. For example, a ULI publication reporting on the Irvine Ranch's development laid out the definition of new communities or new towns as large developments that:

- were planned with a mix of land uses,
- created opportunities for neighborhood- and community-level involvement in governance,

- encouraged interaction between different "social, economic, age and racial groups,"
- provided significant employment,
- had a range of housing prices to promote economic mix,
- displayed an overall commitment to aesthetic values, open space preservation, human scale, and personal identity, and
- provided opportunities for both interaction and privacy. (Griffin 1974, 3–4)

In the terms of the Twentieth Century Fund Task Force on governance of new towns, such communities should "offer all the appurtenances and advantages of existing cities without their glaring disadvantages" (Hanson 1971, 4; also Campbell 1976).

In the United States in the 1970s those treating new communities as a form of new town differentiated among at least five types of such developments, and most of the terms are still used. Freestanding new towns were completely independent and generally in rural or remote locations. Satellite new towns were balanced, or had the right mix of uses to be self-contained, but were in the orbit of a larger metropolis and an integral part of a metropolitan area. All the new towns in this study are of this sort. In the late 1960s and early 1970s, large center-city developments were labeled new-towns-in-town; examples include Battery Park City, in New York. Add-on new towns, also called growth centers, were developed as extensions to existing small towns. Finally, some analysts included company new towns as a special form of new community based on one major industry or employer, for example, freestanding mining towns (Hanson 1971, 5; Griffin 1974, 4).

Proponents made many claims for new towns. Alonso ([1970] 1977) summarized these as accommodating urban growth without stressing existing areas, particularly with migrant groups; saving money by providing services at an efficient scale; preserving the countryside and open space; stimulating the economy; providing healthy, socially balanced environments that promote choice; and experimenting with new building and urban forms. To critics such as Alonso these claims seemed to be without basis, and the widespread advocacy of new towns seemed grounded more in factors such as self-interest and romance than evidence of actual improvement of urban life (also Clapp 1971). As Alonso explained:

> Some of the advocacy is probably self-serving, as in the cases of congressmen or federal bureaucrats seeking to maintain diminishing constituencies, self-aggrandizing professional groups, and of business firms in pursuit of new markets. For many, glimmering images of simpler, future Camelots combine the American nostalgia for the small town with the biting reality of our complex urban problems. But mostly the idea of new towns has some magic that fires the imagination, stirring some Promethean Impulse to create a better place and way of life, a calm and healthy community of crystalline completeness.

These romantic associations make it difficult to analyze the new towns strategy as a rational policy. (Alonso 1977, 175)

With all these reasons for new towns, it is not surprising that the idea drew from a number of sources. While there have been new towns built throughout history, the U.S. new community idea of the twentieth century had some very specific precedents. It drew on the turn-of-the-century garden city idea, the modern movement in architecture, and a more direct and indigenous American nostalgia for small towns. It also reflected the increased capacity of the postwar building and development firms to take on larger projects (Eichler and Kaplan 1967, 36). Other sources informed the detailed design within the developments, including emerging work on environmental perception, ecology, market segmentation, urban and community sociology, and innovations in housing and shopping center design. However, garden cities, modernism, small-town nostalgia, and the capacity of builders were important intellectual contexts for the idea of building a new town in the first place. This variety of sources was an important part of their appeal, as people from very different positions and perspectives could at least agree that new towns were an interesting and viable option.

The Garden City Tradition

For many people the garden city tradition is central in the new town movement. It involves a complex cluster of approaches emerging from the United States, Britain, and continental Europe in the late nineteenth and early twentieth centuries. The garden city approach rejected the nineteenth-century industrial city and embraced the emergence of new transportation technologies. Early examples included elite suburbs and company towns designed by landscape architects and planners. In 1898, Ebenezer Howard published a book initially titled *Tomorrow: A Peaceful Path to Real Reform,* which drew on these ideas to create what was to become the classic expression of the garden city idea. Howard's garden cities were compact and self-contained communities of approximately thirty thousand people on one thousand acres surrounded by five thousand acres of rural land inhabited by a further two thousand people. These cities would have a form of common ownership of land and be tied to one another by train lines to create a network of settlements called the social city. This idea was promoted widely in Europe and the British Empire (Hall 1988; Fishman 1987).

The most influential proponents of this approach in the United States were the members of the Regional Planning Association of America (RPAA). This group included Clarence Stein, Henry Wright, Benton MacKaye, and Lewis Mumford and met in the 1920s and early 1930s. They proposed a variation on the social city called the regional city, a series of self-contained new towns of varying size, linked together with limited-access transportation routes or townless highways. By limiting access, these automobile-based transportation routes could function like regional train lines, linking separate cities without causing the strip development that the group disliked. These ideas—the garden city, social city, and regional city—would create distinctive environments unlike the suburban subdivisions by then creeping outward from center cities.

The RPAA developed a small scheme, Sunnyside Gardens, in the 1920s. It created a second, larger development, Radburn, just in time to fail during the Depression. The RPAA's ideas were also the basis of the greenbelt towns of the New Deal era, although like Radburn itself this program was scaled back and only three were built. However, Greenhills, Ohio, and Greenbelt, Maryland, were featured in *The City*, a 1939 movie based on Mumford's *The Culture of Cities*, and thus were much viewed (Knepper 2001, xv–xvii). The RPAA group was not the only bearer of the garden city tradition. Landscape architect John Nolen was a prominent planner of garden city–style developments in the first three decades of the century (Rogers 2001).

However, Radburn was the early demonstration of a number of key ideas taken up in the new community movement. The 640 dwellings that were built became a site of pilgrimage for both the planning profession and new community builders, including those building Irvine, Columbia, and The Woodlands (Radburn 2002). Most important was taming the automobile by relegating it to the outside of a "superblock" and separating pedestrian circulation. Automobiles could penetrate the edges of the superblock only by entering culs-de-sac, onto which the houses backed, allowing vehicular access only at their rear and preserving the core or interior of the superblock for pedestrians walking through open space. Houses fronted onto this open space and a separate system of pedestrian paths that were threaded among the houses. Eventually most new community developers kept the idea of linked open space systems but rejected the reversal of the house orientation, using instead a "modified Radburn" layout.

The Radburn layout was being developed at about the same time as another idea, Perry's neighborhood unit, and was often combined with it. They were both illustrated in the Regional Planning Association's Plan for New York of 1929. Like Radburn, the neighborhood unit was imagined as a superblock layout with major roads along the outside, providing a natural edge to the neighborhood and also providing access to other parts of the metropolis. This idea used arterials both to separate neighborhoods from one another and to link them to the wider metropolitan area. Shops were along the edge, and the elementary school and other civic buildings were in the center. Socially the neighborhood unit was meant to create a villagelike structure of relative social homogeneity, to provide a haven in the diverse and complex urban world (Silver 1985; Perry 1929; also Banerjee and Baer

1984). However, once the idea took off it was taken up by many who promoted a mix of incomes, household types, and so on, *within* the development, and so its physical form was used to house a variety of social arrangements. Perry inferred that closeness would create interactions among people, but even before the first case study new communities were proposed, the idea that propinquity would result in actual friendships had received significant criticism (Mann 1958). While many remember Perry's unit as rigid and suburban, he actually proposed neighborhood units of a variety of densities and land areas, including center-city and suburban examples, although the basic idea was to have a unit based on the catchment of an elementary school. The unit would house six thousand to ten thousand people, depending on the household structure (Perry 1929, 1939).

Generally, the hope of groups such as the RPAA was that these early ideas and prototypes would lead to something much larger, much more like the European new town programs. The three greenbelt cities of the New Deal seemed to show that government in the United States was capable of such work. As Lewis Mumford wrote in the introduction to Stein's *Toward New Towns for America* ([1950] 1957):

> Sunnyside Gardens and Radburn and the Greenbelt towns were but finger exercises, preparing for symphonies that are yet to come: preliminary studies for the new towns that a bolder and more humane generation, less victimized by the false gods of finance, will eventually build. These planners dreamed generously; and their dreams will survive the weaknesses and imperfections of their execution. They achieved an outstanding degree of success, even when the economic tide was running against them, and then the more favorable political currents, represented in America by the New Deal and the more constructive elements in the labor movement, were not yet in motion. Their relative success and increasing influence is a pledge of what may be attained in the future under happier conditions. (Mumford 1957, 17)

Modernism

Modernist architects were also intrigued by the possibility of building new towns. Some developments in the garden city tradition used modernist architecture—for example, Greenbelt, Maryland. Some concepts, such as the superblock, were used by both modernist architects and those influenced by Radburn. However, the modern movement in architecture had its own separate new town tradition with several prominent examples designed in the 1950s, including Chandigarh (initial design began in 1951) and Brasilia (design began in 1957). Both drew on the work of Le Corbusier either directly or indirectly through his students. Such new towns included sculptural modern buildings set in large open spaces. Different land uses such as work, residential, or circulation were allocated to different zones. This reflected debates in the Congrès Internationaux d'Architecture Moderne (or CIAM) and in particular the Athens Charter of 1933 (not published until later) (Frampton 1985, 271).[22]

As with James Rouse in Columbia, many of these architects saw new towns as providing a model for the redevelopment of center cities. As Bauhaus architect Walter Gropius commented in a conference on urbanism in the 1940s: "Carefully planned new towns, more appropriate for showing the way to a greater economy and to better conditions for living, would provide us with the experience necessary to prepare the blueprints for the second and more complicated later step in planning, that is, the rehabilitation of large old cities" (cited in Steiner 1981, 2).

Of the three developments, the early Pereira plans for the university community and the southern sector of the Irvine Ranch are the most clearly modernist in this architectural sense. In the late 1950s and early 1960s, when Pereira was doing this work, the modern movement in architecture was still largely unquestioned as a style among architects. However, by the 1960s, this older tradition of modernism was being replaced by more critical groups such as Team 10 and architect-theorists such as Robert Venturi and Charles Moore (Scott Brown 1967). The other developments, coming later, were certainly modern in a philosophical sense: Columbia relied on social scientific knowledge and systems analysis, and The Woodlands on ecological science. Both used contemporary architects of some caliber, including Frank Gehry in Columbia. All three developments were influenced by 1960s and 1970s modern housing and shopping center styles from California, with clean lines and use of exposed wood. However, their overall design and planning owed more to the garden city tradition and a humanistic approach to building than to high-style, midcentury architectural modernism.

Small-Town Nostalgia

The idea of small towns influenced some of the professional models that these new communities referred to. For example, the New England village was attractive to many in the RPAA, who went on to develop the Radburn model. The 1939 movie *The City,* narrated by Lewis Mumford, presents in approving tones images of Shirley, Massachusetts, the home of RPAA member Benton MacKaye. Perry's neighborhood unit was in a sense re-creating the village in the city.

However, the connection to small towns was also more direct. Of the three developers, James Rouse was the most clearly enamored with the small-town ideal. As I explain in chapter 3, recreating the small-town atmosphere in a metropolis was a key idea for Rouse, who remembered his own childhood in such a place. Rouse had also promoted "clearly defined" neighborhoods at a "human scale" in his earlier urban renewal work (Rouse 1959, 3). The text describing the initial plan for Columbia articulated this clearly: "The villages permit a scale of life reminiscent of the small towns which form such a rich heritage of America. In place of monotonous, sprawling suburbs stretching in endless ranks across much of the country, the villages of Columbia will offer a vitality and a scale of living too often sacrificed today" (CRD 1964c, n.p.).

All the developments have marketed themselves using the same kind of language: The Woodlands in the 1990s called itself America's Hometown. It is, of course, important to distinguish between the marketing of these developments, which has varied over time and has often presented an oversimplified and nostalgic view of community, and the actual ideas of those developing the new communities' physical and social structures. However, the idea of the small town influenced each of the developments' planning, particularly Columbia and The Woodlands.

Community Builders

The new communities were not just the result of ideas about planning and design. Structural changes to the building industry both provoked the new community idea and allowed it to occur. Before World War II, urban homebuilders had been small, averaging 3.5 units each per year. However, the largest 2 percent of builders provided 30 percent of units. Some developers were called community builders in this period, and they focused on building higher-quality suburban areas (Weiss 1987). In the period of 1945 to 1960, the group of the larger builders expanded, with 4 percent of the firms producing 45 percent of the units. Most were what is termed merchant builders—builders that purchased land, made site improvements such as utilities and streets, constructed houses, and also marketed them (Eichler and Kaplan 1967, 20–21). Many of these builders worked on projects that were primarily residential areas. However, among their numbers was a new kind of builder—the "community builder," that is, the builders of new communities. In general the new communities of this period were much larger in scale and more comprehensive than had been possible to build earlier, creating significant differentiation from the merchant builders. As Eichler and Kaplan explained in their 1967 study of new community builders, mainly from California:

> The operating style of a community builder is very different from that of a merchant builder. This stems almost entirely from the different goals each has set for himself. Both seek profits from real estate development. But the merchant builder expects these profits from the rapid turnover of a product which he manufactures and merchandises to the consumers; the community builder's profits will come mainly in the latter stages of a long-range undertaking. (36)

While they were called community builders, these companies generally developed land and built some of the apartments and commercial and industrial buildings. With some exceptions, such as an Irvine Company subsidiary, Irvine Pacific, the community builders stayed out of the home-building business.

With this kind of big-picture, long-term view, the best of the new community developers were actively involved in debates about the future of cities. They hoped to overcome the emerging problems of the suburbs and to create better urban environments through planning and design innovations. For example, Columbia's Rouse saw the private sector as having a special role in urban development in both center-city and suburban areas—mass producing new towns as a solution to sprawl, as the sector had done so successfully with other products.

> We now have no machinery, no process, nor organized capacity in the United States to put to work the knowledge that exists among us about planning for the future growth of our cities. Many of us are involved in building the pieces of a city but for the most part the whole city is nobody's business, neither government's nor industry's. We have assigned a vague responsibility to local government to provide for orderly growth, but we have given it neither the power, the process, nor the financial capacity with which it can fulfil that responsibility. The most advanced planning and zoning concepts in America today are inadequate to preserve our forests and stream valleys and maintain open space. They cannot produce well formed communities with a rich variety of institutions and activities and a wide range of choice in housing: density, type, price, or rent. As a matter of fact, zoning has become almost a guarantee of sprawl rather than a protection against it. Frightened communities, with no alternative processes available, leap to the illusion that low-density residential zoning will preserve a way of life and protect against rising taxes. The one-to-three-acre zoning that results simply extends a thin coat of suburban sprawl over another widening area. Nor have we developed the capacity in the home building industry for producing well-planned, large-scale urban development.
>
> City building has no General Motors, or General Electric—no IBM, no Xerox, no big capital resources to invest in the purchase of large land areas, no big research and development program unfolding new techniques to produce a better environment. There are no large corporations engaged primarily in the end-product production of the American City. City building—the development of houses and apartments, shopping centers and office buildings—is the business of thousands of small corporations, no one of which has within its own resources the capacity to invest millions of dollars in land holdings to be planned and developed over, say, ten to fifteen years. Except for the occasional accident of large landholding remaining in single ownership in the threshold of urban growth, there seems to be no vehicle, public or private, by which planning and development can occur on a scale sufficiently large to provide sensitively for nature or man. (Rouse, quoted in Breckenfeld 1971, 177–78)

This idea of private enterprise creating a solution to urban sprawl is typical of the U.S. new community movement. The U.S. system of government frequently trusts the private sector to carry out important public purposes that are government responsibilities elsewhere, most notably in the heath care system. While new towns in other countries have been quite similar in their urban designs and planning concepts, government powers have provided their underlying coordination and support. This has given them certain advantages in some social and economic dimensions. They have generally been more successful than U.S. developers at providing housing for those with low incomes, although in the 1950s and 1960s, income *mix* was not necessarily much better there because European new towns were often dominated by lower-income groups.

The role of the private sector in new town development was certainly controversial because of the ambiguous place of the development companies in relation to formal government. They were not the kinds of short-term profit-taking speculators that are easily criticized. They had sophisticated plans that were on the cutting edge for their regions and periods and, for the large part, were both more innovative and more implementable than the planning being done by the public sector. In this they had some parallels with Rouse's concept of the potential for creating a Xerox for urban development. As they recounted their roles to me, most members of the planning and design teams described themselves as making heroic efforts to do better than sprawl.

However, to do this kind of planning work, the developers had to maintain power over their property—economically and politically. They had to make sufficient profit to maintain ownership of the land. They had to have enough influence over government staff, elected officials, and even voters to prevent government disruption of the development process. This was a particular issue because these developers often broke the rules or worked within a regulatory context that gave a great deal of discretion to government—changing zoning, increasing densities, defining wetlands. Depending on one's position, the development companies could be seen as manipulating public opinion and doing backroom deals with elites or as educating a conservative marketplace about the benefits of better planning and heroically coordinating disorganized government bodies. Below, I examine the issue of private planning, and in chapter 7 I return to these issues of the power of the community building companies and the relation of this power to public purposes.

FEDERAL NEW COMMUNITY EVENTS AND PROGRAMS

In the end, the federal government did intervene more actively to support new towns, creating a more explicit role for government for a short period in the late 1960s and 1970s. In part this reflected the excitement of influential development, planning, and design professionals who were intrigued by the new community concept. Although the private-sector effort at creating new towns was far more important in terms of scale, the public-sector effort did provide a catalyst or focus for some significant debates and experiments. Of course, this distinction between public and private new towns is misleading. All of the U.S. new communities were private, and all of them took advantage of government programs and policies, but the level of support varied.

Of the three case study developments, the Irvine Ranch and Columbia were not directly funded by the federal government except for grants for specific infrastructure investments and housing projects that were part of generic federal programs. Like other suburban developments, they were also helped by such federal activities as tax advantages for homeownership and federal highway funding, but these gave no particular advantages to new community development over more generic sprawl. In fact, some of the design covenants and maintenance funding mechanisms used by new community builders made it harder for homebuyers to get mortgages backed by the Federal Housing Administration (FHA).

As I explain in chapter 4, there were high hopes for national urban initiatives during the 1960s and early 1970s. The National Committee on Urban Growth Policy recommended building one hundred new towns of one hundred thousand people each and ten new towns of one million (Mields 1973, 186–91). However, in this period the federal government was actively involved in only thirteen new communities. The Woodlands was one of the thirteen. This support was under Title IV of the Housing and Urban Development Act of 1968 and, more important, Title VII of the Housing and Urban Development Act of 1970, which allowed loan deferrals and guarantees for new communities as well as some eligibility for grant funding (U.S. HUD, NCA 1976; U.S. HUD 1984).[23] These acts were administered through the U.S. Department of Housing and Urban Development, which included a special unit that changed its name several times but was eventually called the New Community Development Corporation. Ultimately the recession of the early 1970s, poor locations, developer inexperience, and problems with HUD's management and with program design meant that most of the Title VII new communities experienced significant financial difficulties. Of the Title VII developments, The Woodlands has been constructed closest to its original plans, but the U.S. government has since avoided direct involvement in the new community business (Evans and Rodwin 1979; McGuire 1975; Smookler 1975; U.S. HUD 1984, vi–vii; U.S. HUD, NCA 1976).

STUDYING THE EARLY NEW COMMUNITIES

The newer generation of new communities—both federally supported and more fully private—was intensively examined in the 1960s and 1970s. The

Ford Foundation was particularly active in a very wide variety of urban issues, including sponsoring the 1959 founding of the Harvard-MIT Joint Center for Urban Studies, a group that in the early 1960s did extensive work on
a new town in Venezuela (Peattie 1987). Ford also funded a study of the California new community experience that involved Irvine's Ray Watson as well
as extensive interactions with the developers of Columbia (Eichler and Kaplan 1967; Watson 2002; Finley 2001).

In the 1970s the Urban Land Institute, an organization of development
professionals, created the New Communities Council, and the American Institute of Architects sponsored conferences exchanging experiences about
new towns. Conferences across the country debated issues such as social diversity, the new-town-in-town (or large-scale center-city redevelopment), and
the role of regional planning (e.g., Perloff and Sandberg 1973). The federal government contributed by providing opportunities for professionals
to come together to debate new communities, for example, in a 1977 exchange with the Soviet Union, in which the U.S. delegation was led by the
Irvine Company's Ray Watson (U.S./USSR New Towns Working Group 1981;
Watson 2002). Affluent property developers also took private and corporate
trips to examine the new town experience in Europe.

Early on, much of the writing about new towns was largely descriptive, with
the benefits of new towns taken as a given. As sociologist Sylvia Fava pointed
out, having surveyed the relatively small number of empirical studies of the
sociological character of new towns in the United States:

> Essentially . . . New Towns are seen as a solution to many urban and indeed na-
> tional ills for which critical evidence on specific social questions involved is lack-
> ing or ambiguous. Ideology has taken the place of evidence; matters of belief
> have become accepted as matters of fact.
>
>   Such socially-relevant terms as "participation," "balance," "diversity" and
> "optimum size" have seldom even been defined in the context of New Towns
> discussion. New Towns involve assumptions regarding the nature and desir-
> ability of neighborhood interaction; high-rise and multifamily vs. low-rise and
> single-family homes; the impact of density and community size on the human
> psyche; the importance of propinquity as a catalyst for meaningful contact; the
> merits of community self-sufficiency; the benefits of diversity and balance; the
> manner in which housing choices are made; the virtues of local participation
> and decentralization. (Fava [1973] 1977, 114; also Eichler [1969] 1977)

Fava pointed out that these sociological assumptions about new communities had little grounding in actual evidence. By the late 1970s, however, a
growing number of studies sought to investigate more systematically the
claims of the proponents of new communities. There was something of an
industry of new town studies, with the residents of Columbia being particularly patient as the frequent subjects. However, while some earlier research

projects differentiated new communities on the basis of their level of planning, most did not, generalizing from "new communities" that were basically dormitory suburbs for a narrow income range to the mixed-use, more socially balanced new towns in this study.[24] This made for bolder criticisms or defenses but obscured important differences among these kinds of developments.

The largest research project to examine new communities carefully as a type and compare them with less-planned development was an NSF-funded study based at the University of North Carolina from 1972. It resulted in an overview book, seven specialized monographs, and numerous other papers on issues such as quality of life, schools, economic integration, and recreation (e.g., Burby and Weiss 1976; Burby 1976; Kaiser 1976; Smookler 1976; Zehner 1977a, 1977b). The research team interviewed 5,511 residents, surveyed another 974 youth, and interviewed 577 professionals in fifteen private planned developments, in two more with federal support, and in nineteen less-planned suburban areas.

The University of North Carolina analyses pointed out that new communities are difficult to develop, and more incremental growth is less prone to visible financial failure. However, the researchers found some overall benefits. As Burby and Weiss outlined in the overview volume, new communities of the type they studied have strengths in (1) better land use planning and access to community facilities; (2) reduction of automobile travel; (3) superior recreational facilities; (4) enhanced community livability; and (5) improved living environments for low- and moderate-income households, blacks, and the elderly (Burby and Weiss 1976, 7). However, Weiss and Burby listed many areas where "few overall differences were found includ[ing]: evaluations of housing and neighborhood livability; residents' social perspectives, rates of participation in neighboring, community organizations, and community politics, and satisfaction with various life domains and with life as a whole; the provision of some community services; and the organization and operation of community governance" (Weiss and Burby 1976, xiii; see also Burby and Weiss 1976).

When these evaluations were done, the three case study new communities were relatively undeveloped. For example, when the University of North Carolina group studied them in the early 1970s, the Irvine Ranch's population was well under fifty thousand people, and Columbia's was twenty-four thousand. It was not possible to evaluate The Woodlands because its first residents did not move in until 1974, and the interviews were conducted in 1973.

As interest in new towns increased, sociological studies looked at these developments. However, after the 1970s, when these studies flourished, large-scale new communities received much less attention. The three developments certainly have been mentioned in a variety of works, from Spirn's *Granite Garden* (1984) to Davis's *City of Quartz* (1990) and Garreau's *Edge City*

(1991). However, since the 1970s only a small number of books, dissertations, and collections of memoirs have examined the three developments as their major focus (e.g., Burkhart 1981; Kane 1996; Kutchin 1998a; Morgan and King 1987; Tennenbaum 1996a; see also Kling et al. 1991; Rocca 1996; Nishimaki 2001; and Levinson 2003).

Particularly useful are works that have *compared* two or more of the case study developments in this book. Cervero (1995) analyzed commute trips in nine planned developments from the United States and thirty-four from Europe, including all three case study developments. Landscape architects Girling and Helphand (1994) included all three among the sixteen specific cases highlighted in their illustrated historical survey of designed suburban open space in the United States. Ewing (1991) mentions the three in his ULI-sponsored overview of fifty-eight planned communities in the United States. Bloom (2001b) drew on nineteen interviews and archival materials to give a historical account of the key planning visions and subsequent resident life in Reston, Columbia, and Irvine, focusing on civic activism, community life, economic and racial mix, feminism, and cultural activity. This work is comparatively sparse, given both the early interest in new towns and continuing attention to generic urban growth and the new urbanist movement. However, this more comparative recent work on new communities does provide an important background to this study.

THE SUBURBAN CRITIQUE OF THE LATE TWENTIETH CENTURY

While new communities largely dropped from view by the 1990s, concern with suburban development expanded, fueled by debates about urban sprawl and proposals for new urbanism and smart growth, the latest generation of antisprawl proposals. Interest in urban development comes in cycles, and during the 1990s, as in the 1960s, there was an upswing in such interest, with these issues being the focus of literally thousands of popular and professional articles and dozens of books. One of the purposes of this book is to link these new debates about alternatives to sprawl to the older new community experiments.

New urbanist approaches that consider various scales of development—the block, neighborhood, and region—closely mirror the issues considered in the new communities. Smart growth strategies such as clustering, mixing housing types, preserving open space, and creating a sense of identity were all issues the new community developers dealt with in previous decades. In this context the new debates about urban sprawl—and the proposals by those associated with smart growth and new urbanism—do not seem so new. I return to these debates about suburban design and planning in chapters 5 and 6.

PRIVATE FOR-PROFIT PLANNING AND THE CAPACITY TO INNOVATE

This book is not a study of urban politics. Rather, it tells the stories of three developments, focusing on a number of practical questions about how well these private-sector new communities have provided an alternative to sprawl and which of their planning and design techniques are useful today. However, a study that, like this one, examines the realization of planning and design ideas in a suburban context also raises the issue of power. For those who are primarily interested in the techniques, this section is important for understanding issues of implementation.

Here I define *power* as the capacity to get things done in a way that achieves one's purposes. This raises the questions of who possesses the power, how it is exercised, and for what ends. In new community development, one key question relating to the *who* issue focuses on the intersection of power of six sets of actors: (1) planning, design, and other professionals working on the projects; (2) development companies and their financial backers; (3) governments, of which there are many for even one new town; (4) activists, some of whom are residents; (5) residents; and (6) the wider public, most notably those who live nearby.

Each kind of actor has access to a range of options for achieving his or her purposes—the *how* issue. Actors can: (1) directly invest to create developments, the realm of economic power; (2) regulate actions, sue for such regulation, or vote in regulators, an arena of formal political power; or (3) shape the ideas of what is possible and desirable (Mann 1986).[25] The *what* issue is a complicated one—how fixed or changeable are the ends of various actors?

Explaining the relationships among the dimensions of who, how, and what depends on the purposes one has for the analysis. Various fields or disciplines examining urban development and urban design have been interested in different parts of this picture of power and actors, means and ends. Accordingly they have come up with very different analyses of what the crucial issues are in terms of power roles and relations. Three types of analysis seem helpful in this context: urban political theory explains some of the wider political context of urban development; critical studies of real estate examine the internal workings of development companies; and work on planning innovation emphasizes the networks of professionals that generate and disseminate planning and urban design ideas.

Urban Politics

Altshuler and Luberoff, in a study of similarly large projects constructed by the public sector, outline five differing theories of the urban politics surrounding such projects: elite-reputational, pluralist, public choice, elite-structural, and historical-institutional (Altshuler and Luberoff 2003, 49).[26]

The focus of these theories is on who dominates local politics. While there are real differences among the theories, some of these differences merely reflect variation in data-collection strategies (e.g., a survey that asks who ranks as most powerful in a location versus a historical analysis). Altshuler and Luberoff provide an excellent short review of such theories (49–75). Elite-reputational studies of the 1950s, asking who is powerful, found that "corporate elites dominate local politics" (49). Pluralists from the 1960s, generally focusing on controversial issues from schools to urban renewal, found a wide distribution of power. Public choice theorists argue that rational, self-interested, individual decisions in the public domain generally lead to "collectively irrational outcomes" (49), and they examine these outcomes. Elite-structural theories again find corporate dominance, although such dominance may not be immediately apparent. Historical-institutional analyses are not common but focus on the longevity of institutions that create lag in the system, thereby shaping options in the future and limiting individual political preferences to less-than-perfect execution at any particular time.

Overall, these theories focus on how particular groups dominate governments and on problems with realizing public preferences. Geographically, they have often paid most attention to center cities or, at least, existing cities. In these locations, residents and governments are in place, and private-sector projects are limited in scope, but development is also likely to disrupt the lives of existing residents. This is different from the situation of private new towns, where the private entity has a very long development timetable, the area is very large, few people initially live there, and the voters of the counties or cities where such developments are initially approved are rarely residents of the new town land.

Elite-structural theories that have been particularly popular in urban studies, such as regime theory, often distinguish between a location's use value for its residents and its exchange value for developers, pointing out that these two sets of values are at odds (Logan and Molotch 1987). While this may be obscured by a general consensus that growth is good, it is an important distinction. However, at the beginning of a new town, residents are few and the use of the land is largely for businesses such as agriculture or forestry. The population then changes rapidly, and those residents that move in have at least partly bought into a comprehensive planning vision and want the developers to stick to the concept. Typically, residents eventually wish that fewer people than originally proposed be allowed to share the vision, and they may be quite active in promoting that view; but they have nonetheless bought into a plan.

The situation of democratic participation, municipal fragmentation, and the relation between center city and suburbs is also complex. The Irvine Ranch has been incorporated into several cities, with the City of Irvine the largest, but they are part of Orange County, which is a metropolitan area with multiple centers. Columbia and The Woodlands are unincorporated, linked to Howard County and the City of Houston. The developers of Irvine owned their land for a century and did not choose a suburban location; the developers of the other two rightly or wrongly saw their developments as at least part of a solution for center-city problems.

Elite-structural theories are thus not a perfect fit in explaining large-scale, comprehensive, new community developments, but they can illuminate some of the less visible facets of corporate influence on government. They raise the issue of developers shaping ways of talking about developments so that they are seen as beneficial growth rather than as a strategy for corporate gains. Such theories have quite a lot less to say about the internal workings of development companies and about reasons for the adoption of specific design and planning strategies. If historical-institutional theory were to be more elaborated, it might help to explain how new towns are implemented over decades. In this case the slowness of institutional change in governments can be seen as helping new towns, given their long time frames, although it might also be seen as increasing the complexity of the public sector to which developers need to relate.

Critical Analyses of Real Estate Development

As Susan Fainstein remarks in her book *The City Builders* (1994), with few exceptions, more critical analyses of real estate development do not have a long history, although as the 1990s went on, more appeared (Harvey 1973; Gottdiener et al. 1999). This is particularly the case with analyses of specific developments rather than of the sector as a whole, although in regime theory some authors' examinations of the private sector are of use (Logan and Molotch 1987). While Fainstein's work focuses on center-city redevelopment in London and New York, it makes several key points of relevance to this study. Fainstein considered political and economic factors to be key in explaining real estate decisions, but she found that personality and gender issues were also important in deciding what gets built (Fainstein 1994, 4). This is part of a larger finding that real estate development is not a simple economic process, but rather, "the development industry constructs and perceives opportunity through the beliefs and actions of its leaders operating under conditions of uncertainty" (18). For example, Fainstein noted the tendency to build risky projects because the rewards for professionals within the companies and outside them (e.g., governments, banks) are often not wholly related to the profits from a development. Finally, developers can monopolize a site but not the entire market in a metropolitan area; thus, competition is always there (220).

This view highlights the complicated character of real estate decision making, particularly the role of interpretation in the difficult judgments about demand at a future time. It is no surprise then that different parts of the new community development companies building Columbia, Irvine, and The Woodlands had different perceptions about those future markets and about how far planning and design innovations could be pushed before fatally losing sales. Within the companies, this created many tensions of a kind highlighted by detailed analyses such as Fainstein's but less obvious in broader studies. Logan and Molotch make a similar point about the role of ideas and interpretations in real estate: "People dreaming, planning, and organizing themselves to make money from property are the agents through which accumulation does its work at the level of the urban place" (1987, 12). However, Logan and Molotch focus more attention on land speculators, who make money largely because of the actions of others (for example, a government locating a school near their property), although they may attempt to influence that context (29–31). They have rather less to say about land developers who actually plan developments, lay infrastructure, and subdivide land and thus create at least some of the added value of the land through their own actions.

Planning Innovation

It is in the area of development innovation that planning historians who deal extensively with urban design or the earlier civic design have a useful contribution to make because of their interest in how ideas and techniques are diffused and implemented. As Ward explains in his lengthy history of twentieth-century city planning in the advanced capitalist world, there are three main types of explanations of planning innovation and the diffusion of planning ideas: structural explanations; key individuals; and reformist or technical milieus (Ward 2002, 7–8). The first is broadly the elite-structural theory outlined by Altshuler and Luberoff, although Ward uses this category as a general shorthand for explanations that focus on the political and economic context of innovation. Such theories highlight how the political and economic context narrows the range of options and techniques that are even considered as viable. In contrast, the key individual approach focuses on the work of important figures. More common in architecture and landscape architecture, it is still used as a framework for explanation in planning. It asks whether specific people "can be seen as autonomous actors, literally making a difference by their actions" (Ward 2002, 8).

A third approach, between the two, focuses on the milieus or professional networks that produce innovations. Ward explains that this approach "acknowledges both structural context and key individuals but cedes explanatory primacy to the milieus within which new ideas and practices were formed, debated, refined and publicized. In other words, the research focus is the reformist, technical and, to some extent, institutional networks within which new ideas are fashioned into relevant practices" (2002, 8). These networks shape the kind of options that are considered by generating ideas and then framing analyses in terms of these ideas. Work in planning theory has pointed to the power that planners have as debate framers, agenda setters, attention shapers, and storytellers (Schon and Rein 1994; Faludi and van der Valk 1994; Forester 1989; Healey 1996; Forsyth 1999; Marris 1987; Peattie 1987).[27] Innovative milieus work in part by generating arguments about better urban development, which then frame debates about options.

Obviously this kind of explanation provides a reasonable middle ground for examining the way innovative ideas are disseminated, although the structural or contextual component is not elaborated in great detail. Here both the work on urban growth politics and the real estate industry provide needed depth. But theories about the diffusion of ideas are extremely important in a study such as this one, because they can help to explain why particular planning ideas and strategies are adopted.

A Working Synthesis

Together, the three areas of theory paint a picture in which ideas are important. In this picture, development companies have great influence on their locations. Their economic power is generally apparent, but they also exert power in less obvious ways. Some of this hidden influence is exerted via political connections. However, it is also demonstrated by companies shaping common sense about what is possible in urban development. To do this, each development in this study has employed many experts, who have created different public definitions of key development issues. However, such companies are not monoliths but rather are complex organizations with different arms with internally competing goals and competing interpretations of the future market for their products. In particular, the architects, landscape architects, and planners on the development teams have related to wider professional expectations. They have worked at a scale in which the other, alternative employment has often been public work, and many models that they have drawn on have been government led. They have been attuned to public-sector expectations. In contrast, other parts of the companies have more clearly cared about profitability, in a way that is more easily explained by theories focusing on political and economic dimensions. This highlights the hybrid character of such large-scale developments, and the complexity of the edge between public and private sectors. That urban development has occurred can be usefully explained using political or economic analyses; however, the form it has taken, the question of how, requires an analysis of the role of ideas (Forsyth 1999).

METHODS

I chose to examine three new communities rather than do a large survey of many such developments because I wanted to understand in-depth issues of whether and how they had avoided the problems of sprawl. To do this I had to understand how sprawl was perceived at the time they were started, which involved examining original documents as well as doing interviews. To evaluate how they turned out—in terms of their original intentions and current conceptions of sprawl—I used a number of indicators from various periods of the developments, including census data, existing surveys, interviews, mapping, observations of the physical sites and social events at the locations, newspaper accounts, and evaluations by other researchers.

The details of my research methods are presented in appendix C, but overall I used a number of strategies. I conducted formal interviews with 140 people involved with the developments: professionals, developers, civic activists, and government representatives. These people worked on the developments, lived in them, and protested them.[28] They included over a dozen people who worked on more than one of the new communities. Interviewees had a variety of views on the developments and were chosen for their historical knowledge and in order to showcase a range of opinions. To avoid bias, I included those both currently and formerly involved with the projects and people with both central and peripheral roles (Miles and Huberman 1994, 263). I talked more informally with approximately a dozen other people.

Interviews dealt with the developments' histories, strengths, weaknesses, futures, residents, and the roles of government and technology. They also led me to unpublished work—dissertations, theses, conference papers, and studies conducted but never written up. An additional twenty-six relevant oral history interviews were available across the three sites, although they pertained to eighteen of the same people I interviewed.[29] I kept a mailing list of interviewees, updating them about the research and offering them a chance to comment on the draft of this book. Thirty-five people requested copies to review, and fifteen actually commented. Several of those who offered to review the draft had worked on more than one development.[30] Readers from each development included residents, current and former employees of the developers, elected officials, and activists. Reflecting the different governance of the three new communities, readers included the current and former staff of local governments in the Irvine Ranch and Columbia and the current and former staff of the master resident associations in Columbia and The Woodlands.

When quoting from interviews, I do not give the speakers' names; I do, however, generally indicate their roles.[31] I promised anonymity to interviewees and have provided it by documenting their quotations with assigned interview numbers. In the case of joint interviews that involved people of close association, I protect their anonymity by omitting interview numbers and citing only as "Anonymous interview." In other instances, interviewees knew important parts of the stories of the development and were the only source for this knowledge, as some events had not been documented explicitly. Indeed, some of these interviewees requested to be cited as the source. As one planning team member explained to me: "Because of the way we worked . . . being in the middle of things, [we] didn't document anything. We weren't really asked to write reports. That wasn't the style of land developers, write everything down so we can tell everybody what you did. They didn't want anybody to know what you did" (Interview 0428). With the exception of the quotations that present very simple facts, I have checked them all with interviewees and gained their permission to be quoted. Interviewees were very helpful, even though some of them were recounting things that had happened three or four decades earlier.

I also mapped growth patterns,[32] attended public meetings, compiled and analyzed economic and demographic data, examined existing surveys of residents, and photographed the areas. I traced the histories of the developments, locating hundreds of original plans, reports, maps, slides, speeches, and local newsletter, magazine, and newspaper articles, many in private collections only. The Irvine Ranch was the most controversial of the projects, leaving a significant public record. Many of its early planning documents were placed in one of three collections at the University of California, Irvine, library. Columbia was less controversial but had a local independent archive in which many documents had been placed. The Woodlands had no such central archive, but Joseph Kutchin (1998a) had completed a very useful oral history project on Mitchell Gas and Energy Company, many Title VII files had been placed in the National Archives in Maryland, and several former employees generously shared personal collections of documents. I built up a picture of the developments, working between the various forms of evidence in a kind of dialogue. I used the qualitative research program N4 to manage the interview transcripts, and I spent as much time analyzing census data, reading reports, poring over maps, and developing complete timelines. The evaluation of outcomes required more work with indicators such as densities, affordable housing counts, and demographic data.

These big developments had some specific research challenges. Large-scale communities are, in general, shifting targets: land is bought and sold, planning areas expand and contract, development companies reorganize and are renamed. The private master plans themselves are evolving documents, although from time to time, when presented to governments or funders or corporate boards, they are fixed for the moment of presentation. Some development aims and planning assumptions also change over time. Therefore, many numbers reported in this book are approximate or true only for particular periods. The early years of the developments were also periods of high staff turnover and frequent reorganization. Organizations that had presidents and vice presidents sprouted senior vice presidents in between them. Planning was sometimes its own unit and sometimes part of a land development or real estate unit. Sometimes these reorganizations mattered for the outcome of the developments, although often they were important only at the time. To deal with this, I have generally used generic terms for departments, companies, and positions.

CONTROVERSY AND AUTHORSHIP IN NEW COMMUNITIES

In making this argument, I confront a set of expectations within both the academic and the professional communities, and I am very aware that some of my evaluations run counter to others' impressions of the developments. Both *critics* and *defenders* have expressed different views, many strongly held. Overall, my position will seem far too positive to the critics and far too negative to the defenders.

Of the critics, some have compared the developments with their own ideal environments, from gritty center-city neighborhoods and nineteenth-century planned suburbs to quaint small towns. In general, the case study developments fall well short of perfection in this comparison. Others have assessed the developments from their professional position, looking upon them as a distraction from the most crucial urban dilemmas, which are happening in center cities. Many of these critics have not distinguished between the new towns and master-planned bedroom suburbs, seeing both as exclusionary. And still others have been more critical of the overall profit-making aims of the developments and the economic and political strategies used to make those profits.

The case of the Irvine Ranch is particularly striking in terms of such evaluations. I have never before studied a development company that so many people dislike so intensely. The reasons vary: dislike of the development's aesthetic character, disagreement with Irvine Company policies, belief that the best aspects of the ranch's overall design are the result of community activism rather than Irvine Company planning, and criticism of its specific profit-making strategy and use of elite political connections. Indirectly these critics helped me, as the planners at the Irvine Company had been so heavily denounced in the past that they were less fearful of being studied than other development professionals might have been. In contrast, charismatic James Rouse still cast a huge glow over Columbia, and opinions there were more mixed. Given the success of the racial integration in the new town and the less well-founded perception that its economic mix has also succeeded, many professionals wanted to forgive its weaknesses. However, even defenders of the town often mentioned that it is architecturally uninteresting. People had less settled opinions about The Woodlands, but there was a general perception in the landscape architecture community that it is an outstanding example of the work of their field and that any flaws are in implementation, not in the initial design. As I explain in chapter 4, the reality is somewhat more complex. However, many people from outside Texas could not imagine anything positive happening in Houston, and people from Houston were often stunned that anything interesting could happen so far from the center of the metropolitan area.

A final group of critics were internal critics—people who lived in or worked on the developments and wanted to make them better. These people complained about many lacks: affordable housing, interracial socializing, environmental protection, road capacity, transit systems, interesting architecture, democratic participation, and fiscal accountability in the community associations. Ultimately, however, these critics had decided to continue living or working in the area.

I have tried throughout to represent and respect these different critical viewpoints. Many are absolutely correct. However, some rely on comparisons with particular ideals that are not held by all, have been correct at particular stages of the developments and not others, or focus on one aspect of the development when others are also relevant. To say this is to take a stance, because for many critics *any* positive evaluation of these developments indicates that I have sold out to their rich development companies, aging designers, or the developments' middle-class inhabitants. However, in the long term the critics, who are often from the academic community where I work or from the mainstream of new urbanism, have far more power over my future than development companies or middle-class residents in distant locations. As an academic, it would have been far simpler to criticize the developments than to provide the mixed assessment that I give here.

On the side of the defenders, some people who were involved in the developments have felt that their work has been unjustly ignored by the mainstream of planning and design, which has been suspicious of suburbs or caught up in later trends, such as new urbanism. These development professionals have endured what they have perceived as uninformed attacks by proponents of new urbanism, who particularly criticized the loop and cul-de-sac road layouts of the new towns. Planners and designers working on these projects all expressed frustration that such attacks on their work lack thorough analysis. Those who had worked on Columbia were particularly disturbed by such criticism. Having been the most lauded of the new towns of the 1960s, the fall from favor was more noticeable than in the other two developments, which had been more heavily criticized from the start.

For their part, residents who chose to live in these developments found them to be good places to live and worried that the high profile of the developments made them a target for unrealistic criticisms. At the beginning of my research, Columbia had recently been the focus of a number of sensational newspaper articles on racial and economic divisions, and people were particularly sensitive about such critiques (Epstein 2000).

Again, like the critics, I have tried to represent these different viewpoints. I think it is true that the planners and designers of these developments have received too little recent attention, and much attention has been either superficial or unnecessarily negative. Over the years, residents have certainly been put in the situation of having to defend their residential choices in a way they might not have to if they were to live in developments that have lower profiles or are less clearly defined. As I spent time exploring the developments' various centers, villages, and neighborhoods by car and on foot, I came to appreciate their many strengths. My opinion is that they are certainly better than generic sprawl in numerous dimensions, but how much better and in which dimensions are a key focus for this book.

In addition, this book is about controversial projects with literally hundreds of important contributors. In the new communities, as in other large projects, professional authorship has often been unclear because of internal disputes, extensive use of consultants, and limited documentation of early phases due to a desire to protect corporate secrets. The complexity of this situation underlies the variation I found among the people I talked with who had been involved in different phases or parts of the projects and had very different perspectives on who had done the most important work. In all the developments, tracing the roles of the people who left the biggest paper trails and stayed in place the longest was easiest, of course, but their roles were not necessarily the most important. People in governments claimed that they had made major, positive changes to the plans; those from the development companies saw things quite differently. As an early participant in one of the projects said quite bluntly: "You're going to find out there was a lot of fictionalizing based on people who were bit players, and then there's the truth. The people that came on later on . . . [in] these projects don't have a clue as to how they happened" (Interview 0502).

The period in which people worked on each development was also important. Initial broad concept development and subsequent detailed planning of the first villages were often done by different groups, but both tasks required innovative work and intense activity. The kinds of people who were attracted to and could do this work were very different from those who would take on a role as caretakers of the plan, shepherding it through long decades of implementation.

However, in each development a significant amount of design and planning work was conducted after the overall master plan had been developed, during the period that could be seen as "caretaking." For example, in Columbia, open space and attached housing increased over the years. Many of the urban designers and land planners working on this later design saw themselves as essentially redoing the master plan, making significant changes. Although they worked within the overall frameworks and concepts of the three developments, they also moved around many land uses, circulation systems, and environmental features. But did they in fact redo the plans? This is a difficult question to answer, because the concepts were relatively stable, but they were also refined and modified in significant ways.

In addition to differences among those involved with different phases of the new town, within each development those with specific forms of training saw particular kinds of activities as key to realizing the development. This led them to value some roles and dismiss others. Planners, including architect planners and environmental planners working at a development-wide scale, saw themselves as providing the core vision. Landscape architects, architects, and engineers working at a village scale saw themselves as translating vague concepts into actual urban structures with road and park systems and doing the site planning of buildings. Architects saw some key public buildings, commercial centers, and housing units as providing a crucial sense of identity, becoming landmarks that stood out in an otherwise uninteresting environment. Landscape architects, however, generally shaped more of the landscape, and generally the landscape is the realm in which the developments have the most distinctive identities. On the Irvine Ranch, where all buildings were required to be designed by architects (though they often worked for home-builders), this role was slightly different, as both architects and landscape architects created the overall landscape, although significant buildings also created landmarks. Some engineers saw their infrastructure designs as crucial—the work that really completed the development. These were not just self-serving assessments about authorship but sincere judgments about the relative importance of different scales and types of planning and design work. For some the concept was key, and for others the details of implementation were. These assessments also reflected some of the insulation between staff and consultants and between people working on different parts of the development and in different phases.

I do name names when it seems relevant to the story—for example, to show that there were multiple people involved in a design phase, not just a star designer. However, many important contributors have gone unnamed, such as those who worked in planning and design and especially those who worked in important related areas, such as engineering, marketing, and environmental science.

These issues of controversy and authorship are recurring themes in the book but also have implications for the issue of audience. Put bluntly, for a number of events and contributions to these developments, there are multiple irreconcilable versions of what happened and who the key players were. In general these multiple versions of events do not have implications for an overall assessment of the projects or for the substantive message of the book.

However, the relative accuracy of different versions of events has great personal importance to many of those who generously gave their time to be interviewed. Where I am aware of such differences in recollection or perspective, I have, again, tried either to find a factual middle ground or to present multiple views of events explicitly. However, I am sure that I am not aware of all such differences. Overall this shows the complexity and relative high stakes of the developments.

Finally, a book such as this has different disciplinary audiences. As they read drafts, designers wanted more detail about the intellectual histories of the developments; political scientists thought such discussions should be relegated to an appendix in favor of highlighting analyses of power; and development professionals hoped for details about implementation and project management. This book is centrally about planning and urban design issues, but I hope it will be of some interest to others interested in learning from past attempts to provide an alternative to sprawl.

ORGANIZATION OF THE BOOK

The book begins by examining how the development concepts were devised and implemented. Three chapters tell the stories of each development in turn and outline many of their key outcomes.

Next are the more analytical chapters. Chapters 5 and 6 examine how the developments have attempted to create new kinds of social and physical environments and explore whether the developments have done better than generic suburban development. These urban design strategies to provide an alternative to sprawl have dealt with both the internal structure of each new community and its relation to the wider metropolitan region. The final chapter investigates the special role of private-sector planning in terms of how the private development industry intersects with public goals.

The chapters show that these developments fare very well in terms of current thinking in the smart growth movement about issues such as density, pedestrian paths and access, income and ethnic mix, regionalism, neighborhood identity and layout, avoidance of strip commercial development, and open space design. The development teams have grappled with issues of organizing the metropolitan landscape, and the approaches that they have taken still seem quite contemporary. However, their problems with affordable housing and the dominance of automobiles in the developments show limits to some popular strategies for promoting both housing affordability through mixing housing types and alternatives to the car through small increases in density and the provision of pedestrian path networks.

Overall, these three developments have been successful, but that success has had limits. Are smaller local governments or less powerful county or regional planning bodies likely to do better, given the uncertainties of the electoral system and their limited control over private property or other parts of government at any level? Could even the federal government take on such a role, given the contradictory purposes and procedures of its various departments and agencies? The complexity of new community development raises questions about the implementation of similar planning approaches, including smart growth, particularly in situations with less-cooperative, coordinated, patient, and wealthy developers.

Chapter 2

The Irvine Ranch

The Irvine Ranch in Southern California is the largest privately master-planned new community or satellite new town ever built in the United States.[1] Thirty-five miles south of the Los Angeles Civic Center, the ranch was planned in stages, starting with an early college town plan of 1959–60, then moving to a wider coastal development in 1964 and finally to a plan for the majority of the ranch in 1970. Each stage owed much to the tradition of the architect-planner—with a strong emphasis on physical layout, design elements, infrastructure, and formal governance. The Irvine Ranch was also the most continuously profitable of the three case study developments. Its formal design approach and quest for profits combined to polarize opinion about it to a degree unparalleled in the other developments.

This chapter examines the Irvine Ranch's planning, showing how this interest in design related to larger planning concepts. These concepts include the idea of the metropolitan field (although Irvine's planners did not use that term), work on environmental perception and legibility, market segmentation, design for the car, and, eventually, a new suburban aesthetic. This new design for the suburban landscape was demonstrated in the Irvine Ranch's residential areas and in its shopping centers and business parks, which have been economically successful as well as physically distinctive. Key challenges for the development have included housing affordability and environmental issues.

Even a very stable development such as the Irvine Ranch goes through phases or stages as it reaches new levels of development and faces new challenges. The Irvine Ranch's planning and design can be broken into four major phases (see also table 2).

TABLE 2   Irvine Ranch Timeline

Date	General Events	Villages/ Facilities Opening
1860s–1870s	James Irvine I buys ranch with partners, whom he then buys out	
1937	James Irvine Foundation formed	
World War II	Military bases constructed on Irvine Ranch	
1956	Interstate Highway Act	
1957	UC Irvine site-selection study initiated	
1959	Presidency of Irvine Foundation and Company passes to nonfamily members; UC Irvine site selected; initial planning of ranch	
1964	Southern sector plan agreed to by Orange County	Eastbluff
1965	UC Irvine opens U.S. Department of Housing and Urban Development created Williamson Act in California allows land to be taxed at agricultural rates if withdrawn from development for a period of years	University Park
1967	Leasehold policy first changed	Turtle Rock
1969	Taxation Act—affects nonprofits owning for-profit companies	Rancho San Joaquin
1970	Irvine General Plan accepted by county	Walnut, Northwood, and El Camino Real villages
1971	City of Irvine incorporated in central part of the ranch	Irvine Industrial Complex (IIC)
1972		Deerfield
1973	Endangered Species Act	
1975		Woodbridge
1977	Irvine Ranch sold to consortium	
1982		University Town Center
1983	Donald Bren buys out most others— becomes sole owner in 1996	
1984		IIC becomes Irvine Business Complex; Irvine Spectrum; Westpark "launched"

TABLE 2   *(continued)*

Date	General Events	Villages/ Facilities Opening
1988	Memorandum of Understanding over open space and development signed between City of Irvine and Irvine Company	Tustin Market Place
1990s	Habitat protection negotiated over decade	
1998		Oak Creek
1999		Northpark
2002	Open space on ranch reaches 50,000 acres	

SOURCES: Cameron 1979; Griffin 1974; Irvine Company 2002d, n.d.

Phase 1: Modernist master planning, 1959 to 1966: This was the period when the Irvine Company decided to get into the development business and hired the firm of William Pereira and Associates (WPA) to do the initial university community study and the southern sector plan. The Pereira firm did these tasks while also working on the master plan for UC Irvine. The plans for the ranch were all broad in concept, with the detailed designs of Irvine Company properties done both in-house and by other consultant planners.

Phase 2: Metropolitan field, 1966 to 1977: The Irvine Company presidencies of Bill Mason (1966 to 1973) and Ray Watson (1973 to 1977) were distinctive. During this period the Irvine Company built up a great deal of its own planning expertise, using it to expand planning to the whole ranch and develop the first villages. Mason had been an engineer with the Irvine Company since 1959 and vice president of land development since 1965. On his early death, he was replaced by Watson, who was trained as an architect and had been with the Irvine Company as a planner since 1960. Unlike presidents trained in business and brought from the outside, Mason and Watson provided continuity and a commitment to physical planning. In this period, the first major parts of the 1960 and 1964 plans had either recently opened or were opening, including the university (1965) and Newport Center (1967). The general plan for the central sector of the Irvine Ranch was created in 1970, and the major signature Village of Woodbridge opened in 1975. The company planners drew conceptually from work on environmental perception and the organization of multicentered cities, and this work either guided or rationalized Irvine Company planning. The Irvine Company jointly sponsored an urban design study with the city, produced in 1977, and with the 1973 City of Irvine general plan document it symbolized a coming of age of the public sector.

Phase 3: City building, 1977 to late 1980s: The sale of the company to a consortium in 1977 led to the departure of much of the Irvine Company's upper management and the scaling back and dispersal of planning and urban design functions. Donald Bren, a member of the consortium, bought out most of his partners in 1983 and still owns the Irvine Company privately. During the 1980s the company did not expend major efforts on overall urban or land planning, although detailed design was an emphasis. Bren's tastes for Mediterranean architecture and lavish plantings featuring palms were a very visible part of this change.[2] However, the City of Irvine was coming into its own, conducting numerous planning studies and actively negotiating with the Irvine Company over development issues.

Phase 4: Irvine as landscape, late 1980s onward: While development progressed, in this period environmental activism started to have a large effect on the development, eventually leading to the removal of over half the ranch from development. This period shows a commitment to the physical public realm in the redefinition of open space design, counterbalanced by the increasing number of gated subdivisions, particularly near the coast. Although certainly not starting with the same social vision as Columbia, it did achieve a certain amount of social mix, and by 2000, of the three developments, the City of Irvine was the least white, with about one-third of its population of Asian descent.

BACKGROUND TO THE DEVELOPMENT:
THE IRVINE FAMILY

Up to the 1960s the Irvine Ranch, the largest landholding in Orange County, was a huge and highly profitable agricultural enterprise. The owners of the Irvine Ranch were used to managing land and holding it through bad times, and they did not expect quick or constant profits. Such patient money is very important in large-scale urban development. In many countries, patient capital is supplied by government.

The Irvine Ranch is composed of wholes and parts of three Spanish and Mexican land grants. At its maximum size, it was around 115,000 acres—over a fifth of the area of current Orange County and eight times the land area of Manhattan. By the late 1950s the ranch still had 93,000 acres intact and formed a continuous swath from the Pacific Ocean to the Santiago Hills beside what is now the Cleveland National Forest, and from Laguna Beach to Newport Beach (with the latter initially built on sediment deposited in the tidal area on the edge of the Irvine Ranch) (Cameron 1979, 4).

California became a part of the United States in 1850. While many landowners managed to maintain their Spanish and Mexican land grants, proving title to the new U.S. government was expensive, and high interest rates and droughts in the 1860s forced landowners to sell. James Irvine I, a San Francisco merchant who had made his money during the gold rush, worked with partners to assemble the Irvine Ranch in the 1860s. He bought out his partners in the 1870s. On Irvine's death in the 1890s, his son, James Irvine II, inherited the entire ranch and incorporated it in West Virginia as the Irvine Company (Cameron 1979, 1–5; Cleland 1962).[3]

Histories of the ranch tend to focus on the family dynamics of the Irvines—a rich and powerful family with some mysterious deaths (Irvine Smith 1971, 7–9). The agricultural innovations of the ranch have also received some attention. The ranch became one of the world's largest Valencia orange orchards and was also known for such products as walnuts, avocados, and lima beans (Cameron 1979, 5; Cleland 1962). For the purposes of this book, however, two elements of this early history are most important—provisions for keeping the land intact and the tradition of long-term investment.

In 1937 James Irvine II transferred 51 to 54 percent—accounts disagree—of the ranch to a nonprofit foundation as a means of both stopping Irvine heirs from splitting up the ranch and avoiding estate taxes. Previously the ranch had had been held by the family (Cleland 1962, 144–46; Kane 1996, 218; Irvine Smith 1971). The provisions of the trust included the following recommendations for the most stable investment for the foundation:

> This land holding is preserved and sustained at its present state of development, with such improvements, if any, as may be justified in the future. Portions of the land adjacent to and near the Pacific Coast and Newport Bay might from time to time be advantageously disposed of in various small parcels or units, and hill and unimproved property in larger units; but the great central valley acreage, together with such lands as are essential to the maintenance of the water supply thereto, should in the judgement of the Trustor, be held and operated as a unit. (quoted in Cleland 1962, 145–46)

This policy was a success for several decades—even after James Irvine II died at age 80 in 1947. Up to 1967 the Irvine Company developed its coastal residential areas as leaseholds rather than selling land outright, as a way of both maintaining the acreage intact and avoiding paying tax on land sales (Griffin 1974, 10; Kane 1996; Brower 1994, 9). Some areas were sold, however, mainly in the central valley, and these "window" areas became a problem for planning later on. The proceeds were used to pay for significant agricultural infrastructure investments, mostly water supplies, without having to take on significant debt (Cameron 1979, 6–7).

During World War II, the U.S. government requisitioned land in the central section of the Irvine Ranch: 2,318 acres (eventually 4,738) for the El Toro Marine Corps Air Station (MCAS) along the southern side and 1,600 acres in Tustin to the north for a naval blimp base, later converted to a Marine Corps helicopter base (Planning Center 1996, 1–9). This acreage was in addition to land developed into the Orange County Airport (now the John Wayne Airport), created in the 1920s along the northern edge of the ranch and made public in the late 1930s (Cleland 1962, 132–33; City of Irvine 2003). The large size of the Irvine Ranch made it attractive for such military and aviation uses, just as in the 1980s and 1990s its size made it attractive to those wanting to create large-scale habitat preserves. The military bases helped structure the Irvine Company's design of the Irvine Ranch, leading to the placement of industrial and business sites under the flight paths, as military bases are even noisier than civilian facilities. Both military bases closed in the 1990s. Tustin is being developed for a variety of uses. After much controversy it was decided in 2002 that El Toro will be redeveloped as the 2,700-acre Great Park and mixed-use areas rather than reused as a civilian airport (City of Irvine 1999, 2003; ETERPA 1998; Pasco et al. 2002; Planning Center 1996).

The Irvine Company was not totally in support of these wartime land takings. As former ranch manager William Hellis explained in an oral history interview:

> The acquisitions of the military on the Irvine Ranch were certainly not desirable, but they had the right of eminent domain and we were dealing with an overall military situation which we couldn't combat. . . . The lighter than air [Tustin] base was placed over on Red Hill Avenue, which was very much against our desires. We offered them a site in the mesa country in the area, a little to the south near the old ranch house at a very much reduced price. The land which they took had high agricultural value and had most of the sources of irrigation water and wells which we had developed on this property. Failure in getting them to move the base entirely was to do with the captain who seemed to have the authority to do as he damned pleased without much regard to economics. (Hellis 1992, 43)

In fact, the Irvine Company was briefly successful in getting the base shifted half a mile to the southeast, with foundations poured, but then the captain had the site moved back to the original and current location. He did this even though the construction was much more costly than in the location proposed by the Irvine Company (Hellis 1992, 44). The El Toro base location cut off a planned water gravity feed, but the Irvine Company was able to preserve the right to complete its irrigation system. It also retained many rights to water on the Tustin base, all crucial to its operations, as Colorado River water was not yet available (Hellis 1992, 45). This story shows the grand scale at which the Irvine Company was used to working.

The presidency of both the company and the foundation stayed in the family until 1959. At that time Myford, the last male Irvine in the immediate family, died of a bullet in the head and two in the stomach, ruled a suicide. Joan Irvine, a grandchild of James Irvine II and owner of 22 percent of the stock, had become an Irvine Company board member in 1957 but had a difficult relationship with most of the other members.[4] By her own account she frequently took legal action against the Irvine Company, five of whose seven board members were appointed by the foundation (Irvine Smith 1971). In 1959, the company's presidency passed to Arthur McFadden, who was also a trustee of the Irvine Foundation.[5] Company president McFadden was owner of some former Irvine agricultural land in the central valley, active in a number of local agricultural associations, and member of a family with long associations with Newport Beach (Hellis 1992, 32–33; Cleland 1962, 146–47).[6]

It was during the McFadden presidency that the Irvine Ranch was opened up to both aerospace and electronics plants and to the University of California (Brower 1994, 13; Cleland 1962). However, McFadden's appointment was always seen as temporary, and in 1960 he was succeeded by Charles Thomas, a former head of Trans World Airlines (TWA) and before that secretary of the navy from 1954 to 1957 in the Republican Eisenhower administration (Cleland 1962). These appointments started a long succession of non-Irvine presidents, and eventually changes in U.S. tax policy forced the sale of the company by the foundation in 1977. While the history of the presidency of the company has captivated a number of authors, most important to this argument was its relative stability into the late 1950s (Cleland 1962; Brower 1994).

At over ninety thousand acres, the ranch had never been a family farm; the Irvines had not even moved to live on the ranch until 1906, after the San Francisco earthquake and fire, and the foundation has always been based in San Francisco. The agriculture was at an industrial scale; the crops and livestock were chosen for their likely returns; and at various stages, grazing, crops, and orchards were the dominant uses. In the 1860s there were around forty thousand lambs born each year on the ranch; by 1960 there were 325,000 orange trees and no sheep (Cleland 1962, 142–43). The company estimated that its agricultural water system was the "largest private water system ever built in the United States and, possibly, ever built in the world," and it involved creating a water district to deal with downstream water rights (Cameron 1979, 6–7). This led to a continuing tradition of planning, coordination, and public-private interactions that provided a model for the later new community proposal. It was an enterprise that had to take care of the land over a long period of time and be content to wait for its investments to give returns.

This situation remained until the 1969 U.S. Taxation Act made the nonprofit ownership of a for-profit company difficult, requiring very large distributions of dividends to charity each year. This led to the sale of the ranch in 1977. After a highly publicized bidding war with Mobil Oil Corporation as a major bidder, it was sold to a consortium that included Joan Irvine, and then was bought out six years later by one of the consortium's members, Donald Bren. The changes were not completely independent of the Irvine Ranch, as Joan Irvine had found out about the 1969 tax act and lobbied heavily for it in order "to wrest control of the Company from what she considered to be the slow-moving Foundation" (Cameron 1979, 25; Brower 1994, 37; Irvine Smith 1971). While the sale of the company seems a dramatic change, and considerable controversy and drama occurred at the time, Bren has continued to hold the development as a private company. The basic structure of the ranch's master plan has not changed, although Bren's preferences for Mediterranean architecture and palm trees have reshaped some of the detailed design, and open space has expanded considerably.

PHASE 1: MODERNIST MASTER PLANNING, 1959 TO 1966, AND PHASE 2: METROPOLITAN FIELD, 1966 TO 1977

The First Steps:
Development Pressures and Early Planning

In 1940 Orange County had a population of one hundred thirty thousand, clustered along the northern edge near Los Angeles County, in seaside settlements, and in a number of largely agricultural towns spread among its orchards and fields. With no natural barriers separating Orange County from Los Angeles County, in the postwar period urbanization crept southward from L.A., extending the Los Angeles grid. The urbanized land area increased from 40 square miles in 1950 to 261 square miles in 1970 with the rapid development of the area north of the Irvine Ranch (Griffin 1974, 6–7). As the author of an early ULI account of the ranch's planning explained:

> Not surprisingly, the mushrooming expansion of Los Angeles exhibited many of the less desirable features of urban sprawl, proliferation of government jurisdictions, widespread strip commercial development and mile after mile of unimaginative tract subdivisions. The fragmented pattern of land ownership prevailing in northern Orange County must be viewed as a contributing factor to this situation since each property owner sought to maximize the value of his own property without necessarily giving sufficient consideration to the requirements of the area as a whole. (Griffin 1974, 7)

The 1950s were a time of some development on the ranch, with a number of subdivisions created around Newport Beach and additional land leased for research and development facilities by the Aeroneutronic division of the Ford Motor Company, a defense contractor, and the Collins Radio Company, later part of Rockwell International, in the late 1950s (Cleland 1962, 150). The Irvine Company did not place restrictions on the development, so land was only partly developed, if at all, and then resold and subleased to different tenants for quite different uses (Brower 1994, 14). This continued the tradition of small land sales, or land leasings, to raise capital for agricultural production, but also showed some of the problems of insufficient control.

Meanwhile, the freeway system was also gradually moving down into Orange County. Even before the interstate system was designated in 1956, other national and state highways were being developed, with a version of Interstate 5 appearing in the 1939 Expressway-Transit plan for Los Angeles County and running through the ranch (see Taylor 2000, 200). The Irvine Company, of course, already owned its land, and so it did not deliberately seek out land near interstates, as most other new community developers did, but rather the California State Highway Commission placed the roads through the company's landholding. Initially, these had some negative effects. As had happened with the two military bases, the Irvine Company made efforts to revise routing so that its agricultural production would not be disrupted too much. For this reason as well as concern about additional barriers crossing its land, the company negotiated with the highway commission about the alignment of the Santa Ana Freeway (Interstate 5), which, as a concession to the company, was eventually placed along an existing highway rather than realigned "further south through Tustin" (Hellis 1992, 39). Similarly, the San Diego Freeway (Interstate 405) alignment though the Irvine Ranch to its junction with the I-5 was negotiated, although it did "destroy some fine agricultural land in the foothills" (Hellis 1992, 39). In regard to both freeways, the Irvine Company stood up for its interests in retaining access across them so that it could keep up agricultural production. However, the Irvine Company also offered to give a higher alignment for the Pacific Coast Highway, free of charge because the realignment would make coastal development more feasible, but this was rejected by the district engineers and highway commission (Hellis 1992, 40–42).

In 1957 the firm of Pereira & Luckman was asked by the University of California to locate two sites for new Southern California campuses. The firm selected twenty-one sites, narrowed them to five, and chose one on the Irvine Ranch as the best site in its subregion, taking into account likely urban patterns by the end of the century. Statewide, the other campuses proposed at this time were the Santa Cruz and San Diego sites. By the time of the actual selection, the Pereira & Luckman firm had split in two, and Luckman prepared the final University of California report (Charles Luckman Associates 1959). However, Pereira did the subsequent feasibility and planning work for both the University of California and the Irvine Company.[7]

The Irvine Ranch certainly would have developed eventually. Development had already started to skip over it to the southern part of the county.

Farther south in the county, the fifty-two-thousand-acre Mission Viejo development was planned between 1963 and 1966 and developed by then-competitor Donald Bren, showing the extent of demand even farther from the core Los Angeles area. County property taxes were increasing substantially, and it was not until 1965 that the state passed the Williamson Act to allow reduced taxes for land in agriculture. By the time of the 1965 act, the Irvine Company's decision to develop had already been made, although the company did take advantage of the tax breaks in subsequent years. However, in spite of these other factors pushing development, the University of California campus proposal and the need for an associated college town were undeniably important catalysts, and they shaped the character of the Irvine Ranch's development.

While the UC Irvine site selection structured the initial development, this did include some input from the Irvine Company, as the freeway location had. At the time of the proposals, in 1959, the president of the Irvine Company, McFadden, was also a member of the UC Board of Regents, although he was reputedly also opposed to the land donation (Kane 1996, 221). The company board was slow to make a decision but finally reluctantly recommended the university plan to its shareholders. Joan Irvine was, however, a strong supporter of the plan, as she had a great deal to gain financially from development, and she garnered much publicity for her position (Schiesl 1991, 58; Kane 1996, 222). Part of the reason for the company's reluctance was the wording of the foundation's mandate, which did not allow them to give donations to entities supported by taxpayer dollars. They eventually concluded that the donation was a good business decision rather than a work of charity (Kane 1996, 222).

Following tentative agreement by the Irvine Company, economic feasibility of a college town of around one hundred thousand people on ten thousand acres, which they called the "university community," was established by October 1959 (William L. Pereira and Associates 1959, 1960). This spurred the planning of this early version of the Irvine Ranch new community well before the other two case study developments. The core idea was for a development largely in the southern part of the ranch, near but not right on the coast. The university was at the geographical center of the college town. The development was to have fifty-three hundred acres in residential use and the rest in commercial, university, research, transportation, and greenbelts. To the north the proposed development extended just over the San Diego Freeway, and to the west it was bounded by the proposed MacArthur Freeway. Along the western side were placed research and development facilities and medium-density housing; the eastern side was primarily residential (William L. Pereira and Associates 1959, 1960). This was laid out fairly diagrammatically. The university, however, was planned in much more detail, organized in a star shape, with six quadrangles radiating from a circular central park area.[8] The gateway quadrangle, containing such facilities as the main library, was placed adjacent to the town center area and linked to it by a pedestrian bridge. The town center was to serve the university and wider community with a town square, offices, shops, civic buildings, an inn, a farmers market, and housing. Ultimately, only some of these activities were placed in the center (William L. Pereira and Associates 1963, n.p.).

The Irvine Company soon came to see the necessity for master planning a larger area of the ranch beyond the 10,000-acre university community. They hired William Pereira and Associates again to assess what should be done. WPA recommended starting development in the southern sector, including almost all the ranch area to the coastal side of the San Diego Freeway between Newport Beach and Laguna Beach, as well as in an area across the freeway close to the Orange County Airport. The Pereira firm worked on planning the southern sector while it was also doing the campus master plan, preparing a general plan document in 1963 (Wilbur Smith and Associates 1961; William L. Pereira and Associates 1963, 1964a, 1964b, 1970). The Irvine Company also reorganized itself internally to create a planning "collaborative comprising an integrated research, design, and management team of planners, architects, landscape architects, engineers, economists, and market analysts within the company, and a number of outside consultants" (Kreditor and Kraemer 1968, I-7). The company drew concepts from the 1963 Pereira document and submitted the Southern Sector Master Plan to Orange County in 1964, gaining approval for this plan of 34,089 acres (Kreditor and Kraemer 1968, I-7, 8; William L. Pereira and Associates 1964a, 1964b).[9] The vast majority of the land was to be residential—24,444 acres, or 71 percent. Major centers were proposed at the university and Newport Center. Coastal development was largely low density, with some higher-density clusters described as Mediterranean-style hill villages (William L. Pereira and Associates 1964a; Griffin 1974, 24).

What is left of the 1964 southern sector plan are two documents from the presentation to Orange County: one of twenty typescript pages with an attached map, and the other of seventeen pages of roughly laid-out charts and maps (William L. Pereira and Associates 1964a, 1964b). In 1966, Ray Watson, then head of the Irvine Company land development, hired two young academics, Kenneth Kraemer and Alan Kreditor, to work through the Irvine Company files and produce a larger document synthesizing the planning work up to that date that involved refinements to the southern sector plan. They had to do this at the Irvine Company offices, as it was not practicable to take a great volume of materials away (Kreditor 2000). Their thick unillustrated internal report is quite different in feel from the plans presented by the Irvine Company to the county. However, in content the document reflected the same set of ideas (Kreditor and Kraemer 1968).

This southern sector plan was developed just a little earlier than the general Columbia plan, and the core area that had been the original university community was about the same size as Columbia. However, it was quite different in focus, reflecting the presence of the university and Pereira's interest in physical design rather than the social issues that were dominant in Columbia. Pereira was in some ways an odd choice, although the Irvine Company made much of this flamboyant architect-planner in its advertising. Pereira had primarily done building design and master planning for corporate campuses until the firm received commissions, such as the Irvine Ranch, in the 1960s, although the Pereira & Luckman firm did do public work, such as the site location study for the University of California. This was a period when a number of similar firms were expanding into planning work because of a strong demand for planning from both the public and the private sectors (Eichler and Kaplan 1967, 40). It is always hard to judge intentions, but for many architects such work was a means of obtaining large building commissions, and Pereira certainly used the Irvine Ranch work in that way, designing several buildings at the mixed-use Newport Center and at UC Irvine. However, as will be seen in subsequent chapters, such physical master planning also demonstrates the blurring of the boundaries between public- and private-sector work in this period. Professional opportunities came from both public and private sectors, and the planning and urban design approaches were rather similar.

In 1970 the last major plan was presented to the county, covering circulation and land use issues for most of the ranch (Irvine Company 1970c). Titled the *Irvine General Plan,* it was prepared internally by the Irvine Company under Ray Watson, as senior vice president for land development, and Richard Reese, as head of planning, although they obviously worked with a team from a number of fields. A close reading of the plan and interviews with planners involved in the period indicate that Pereira's work was incorporated into the area south of the San Diego/I-405 Freeway (Interview 0326). Slides of diagrams in the successor office to Pereira (Johnson Fain Partners) indicate that he was involved with concepts for some other parts of the ranch; however, a tremendous amount of additional work was done internally by the Irvine Company in the late 1960s.[10]

The 1970 general plan envisaged 430,000 people on fifty-three thousand acres in the City of Irvine, although the plan excluded parts of the ranch that had been included in the southern sector plan, so that the total planned area was over sixty-six thousand acres and the total population was also higher (Irvine Company 1970c; Griffin 1974).[11] The plan divided the ranch into three sectors (see figures 4 and 5). The southern sector was already largely planned. The central sector was in the main agricultural valley area, at that time filled with orchards and field crops. With a band of the southern sector, including the university and its environs, the central sector became the basis for the City of Irvine. A spine of commercial and industrial development runs down this central valley area, which was eventually divided into two main sections: the Irvine Business Complex and the Irvine Spectrum. Finally, the hilly northern sector, containing grazing land and some orchard areas, backed onto the Cleveland National Forest. This area was never seen as having much development potential and was not included in the plan. While today the development on the ranch seems fairly continuous, it can be seen as comprising several different components. The core new town of the City of Irvine takes up the largest part of the ranch, with other parts falling in several other cities. While there have, of course, been a number of changes to the 1970 plan, the basic locations of housing, employment, and transportation remain much the same.

The version of the 1970 plan presented to Orange County dealt with land use and circulation issues only. It was a large document, eleven inches by seventeen, with forty-six unnumbered pages. On most pages a map of the central and southern sectors of the ranch took up two-thirds of the area, with a narrow band of explanatory text on the right side, frequently only a paragraph or two in length. Few specific numbers or details were in the text. Firmly focused on physical needs, it examined a wide variety of land uses, including residential, industrial, commercial, school and college, recreational, open space, and public uses. Its circulation system involved a detailed road hierarchy, but the text mentioned streetscape design and the future option to introduce transit along the "environmental" corridors. Environmental corridors were mixed-use areas that formed a U shape through the central valley and around the northern part of the central sector, although the northern sections were dropped in the late 1970s (Cameron 1979, 29). *Environmental corridors* is a confusing term, so I generally refer to them as activity corridors.

Interviewees remember the circumstances of the planning process quite differently, but archival evidence shows that the submission of the plan provoked a flurry of responses from county government, requesting more information. People from the county and some from the Irvine Company remember the company coming up with a largely completed plan, revolving around land use and circulation, and presenting it to the county (Interviews 0110, 0325, 0221). Other Irvine Company planners remember a closer working relationship with those county planners. However, in this view, when senior vice president for land development Ray Watson decided to make a very high-profile presentation of the plan, it provoked negative political pressure from opponents of the Irvine Company and its plan, so that the county then required a more complete submission (Interview 0326). The county had also recently developed guidelines for assessing large developments, responding to proposals in 1967 and 1968 to develop some of the "window" areas on the ranch—the parcels that had been sold earlier to fund infrastructure (Kane 1996, 238). While the plan had been some time in the making, draw-

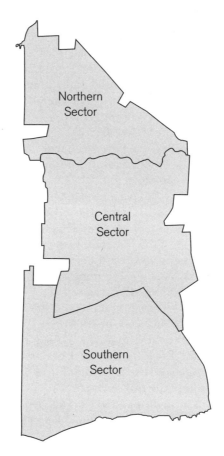

Figure 4. Map of Irvine Ranch key planning sectors, based on 1970 Irvine Company general plan document.

ing on the work of a variety of people and incorporating the existing southern sector plan, this high-profile presentation of a "new" plan in the context of these new guidelines was provocative and controversial. As I explain below, the plan was fairly quickly supplemented with other studies and with the planning process of the new City of Irvine (after 1971), but at the time the 1970 document seemed a fairly brief presentation of a major initiative.

The county responded to the submission by indicating that it wanted consideration of a wider range of issues including "conservation, recreation, air transportation, public investments, community design, safety, human, economic and environmental quality" (Mason 1971, capitalization removed). Even in the areas dealt with by the plan, the county planning staff had

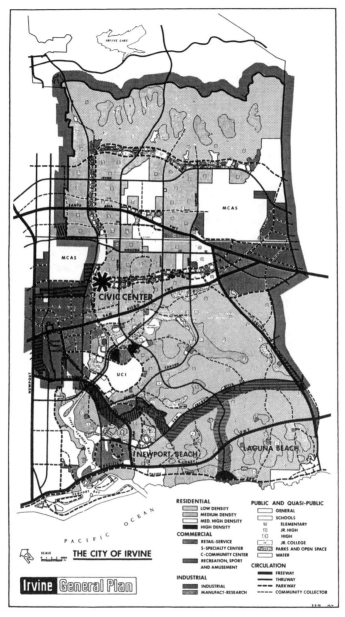

RESIDENTIAL
- LOW DENSITY
- MEDIUM DENSITY
- MED. HIGH DENSITY
- HIGH DENSITY

COMMERCIAL
- RETAIL-SERVICE
- S-SPECIALTY CENTER
- C-COMMUNITY CENTER
- RECREATION, SPORT AND AMUSEMENT

INDUSTRIAL
- INDUSTRIAL
- MANUFACT-RESEARCH

PUBLIC AND QUASI-PUBLIC
- GENERAL
- SCHOOLS
- [E] ELEMENTARY
- [J] JR. HIGH
- [H] HIGH
- [JC] JR. COLLEGE
- PARKS AND OPEN SPACE
- WATER

CIRCULATION
- FREEWAY
- THRUWAY
- PARKWAY
- COMMUNITY COLLECTOR

THE CITY OF IRVINE

Irvine General Plan

Figure 5. Irvine general plan map, 1970. This was the last major plan before the City of Irvine was formed, and it laid out the general concept for the majority of the developable area of the Irvine Ranch. Source: The Irvine Company. Reprinted with permission from The Irvine Company.

concerns about loss of agricultural land, the detailed designs of villages, a lack of specific plans for affordable housing or mass transit, traffic projections, and flood control (Orange County Planning Department 1970a, 1970b; Toner 1970). At the end of 1970, with the stipulation that these issues should be incorporated into the county general plan, the Orange County Planning Commission agreed to the new Irvine Company plan (see also Barton-Aschman Associates 1971).

The change of focus also provoked a response from the UC Board of Regents, some of whom objected to this departure from earlier plans, as the focus in the 1970 plan was much less on the university than in the early 1960s plans (Simon 1970). Admitting students from 1965, UC Irvine was starting just as student unrest over the Vietnam War was taking hold on university campuses, and student culture drew away from mainstream middle-class norms. Although the initial university community proposal had been centered on the campus, by the late 1960s universities were less attractive as a central focus for a new community. Irvine Company marketing that had emphasized the university in the early 1960s changed to wider quality-of-life issues in the early 1970s (Kane 1996, 235). In 1967 the Irvine Company placed its offices in Newport Center rather than close to the university. The 1970 general plan indicated the location of the City of Irvine civic center between the I-5 and 405 freeways rather than adjacent to the university, as had been originally indicated in both 1960 and 1964. Eventually the City of Irvine moved the civic center even farther to the north, onto a separate parcel on the edge of a residential area. However, the reaction of the university to the 1970 plan was not all negative. Analyses by the staff of UC Irvine indicated that an enlarged City of Irvine would have a number of advantages, particularly a stronger tax base for a higher level of services. The Board of Regents approved the alteration (Kane 1996, 236).

Incorporation and the City of Irvine General Plan

While these planning ideas were being developed, buildings were going up and people and businesses were moving in. In 1971 the City of Irvine was incorporated, partly to head off annexations from neighboring areas and partly because a new county board of supervisors was less sympathetic to the Irvine Company (Kane 1996, 235). Incorporation had always been envisaged, but its exact timing was not proposed in advance; instead, it occurred in response to these circumstances.[12] Only the middle two-thirds of the ranch is in the City of Irvine; six other municipalities contain parts of the ranch. Of these, Newport Beach has been more affected than other municipalities, as it gained intensive development at Newport Center along with some larger coastal residential areas. However, only the City of Irvine was conceptualized as a complete new community. This has created some confusion over the years, as the City of Irvine is the centerpiece of the development, but the developed area of the ranch is much larger.

New communities have been heavily criticized for setting up private homeowner or resident associations as shadow governments, and as I explain in chapters 6 and 7, the Irvine Ranch certainly has many such groups that maintain common open space and enforce covenants, conditions, and restrictions (CC&Rs). Columbia and The Woodlands also have such groups, with the difference that at the village scale they include both owners and renters. In addition, all these developments have formal governance such as county governments, school districts, and utility districts, which have elected representatives and provide services. However, of the three, only the Irvine Ranch adds a layer of multipurpose municipal government. Many new community developers avoid incorporation because it injects additional uncertainty into the development process and gives voters the power to derail the long-range plan. However, this loss of control by the development company can benefit the provision of services and provide outlets for democratic participation. I return to this issue of the relationship of private developers to public life in chapter 7.

In terms of planning, the Irvine Company's overall proposal had been approved by the county and was the framework for the subsequent development on lands that were in the county's jurisdiction. This meant that the core ideas have remained, although with some refinements, as I explain later in the chapter. However, once the incorporation occurred, the residents had a strong role in shaping the City of Irvine, and the master plan of the entire ranch became even more complex, a composite of the Irvine Company's ideas and the plans of the City of Irvine and the surrounding municipalities.

When the City of Irvine incorporated, it was required to prepare a general plan quite quickly, and it had to conform to the California law that required sections or elements on land use, circulation, housing, conservation and open space, transportation noise, seismic safety, scenic highways, waste management, and fire and geologic hazards safety (Wilsey and Ham [1973] 1974, I-1). The city added elements on population/economics, public facilities, urban design, implementation, and, in later years, parks and recreation (1980), energy (1984), and growth management (1993) (Kane 1996, 254). The firm of Wilsey and Ham was chosen to complete the new city's general plan. It had done the plan for the new community of Foster City in the Bay Area as well as a number of municipal general plans (Eichler and Kaplan 1967, 39–40). The consultants completed a plan in 1973, and it was amended and refined in 1974. Befitting a new city, this planning process, with numerous committees, was much more participatory than the early Irvine Company planning. In fact, the city first worked with consultants Haworth and Anderson and 162 volunteers to prepare an interim policy plan, adopted in 1972, and then had even more participation for the general plan of 1973 (Kane 1996, 245). As a city staff member from the period explained:

> We came up with a list of about ten major areas of interest. Things like agriculture, the economy, public safety, the schools—a whole bunch of things. We didn't have any staff, didn't have any money either, so the council asked for volunteers to serve on committees. . . . They always met with no staff. They did the analysis. They identified the issues, and they made recommendations. And all the stuff came back to the city council, and we handed that to the planning firm we'd hired to do our first general plan and said, "Here's the basis for the policy plan." (Interview 0408)

The first city plan presented quite varied alternatives for road and transit systems (e.g., grid, loop, linear, and tree structures), for open space, and for villages. It came up with three land use options. All three had an overall land use and transportation structure similar to that of the Irvine Company plans, but they varied in intensity of development, including options with much lower populations. A follow-up study on fiscal impacts found cost savings with higher-density development (Marshall Kaplan Gans and Kahn 1976, s-17). Eventually a fourth option was chosen in 1977 (City of Irvine 1980, I-3). The population was lower than in the 1970 Irvine Company plan, but the overall arrangement of land uses and transportation reflected the earlier proposals of the company.

The land use plan was also coordinated with the 1977 *Urban Design Implementation Plan,* jointly sponsored by the city and the Irvine Company (Dannenbrink 2002). The plan was developed by the firm of Wallace, McHarg, Roberts and Todd (WMRT 1977). While this was the same firm that had worked on environmental planning in The Woodlands in the early 1970s, this connection between the two plans was not as close as may at first appear. WMRT was a large firm with a number of specialties and offices, and the 1977 City of Irvine plan was an urban design rather than an environmental planning document, like that for The Woodlands. However, the 1977 plan helped the city and developer come to an agreement about basic urban design principles (Dannenbrink 2002).

The Overall Planning Concept in "the Place Where Urban Sprawl Ends"

This staged planning process—college town, southern sector, general plan, then planning by the City of Irvine and other cities—unlike that of the other two developments, makes it quite difficult to say when the new community of Irvine opened or began. Some minor development occurred before this planning process, and sections of development opened continuously. Important milestones included the opening of the University of California campus in 1965, the incorporation of the City of Irvine in 1971, and Woodbridge, the first major village started after the 1970 Irvine Company plan was made and opened in 1975. Although a development does not need to have a specific opening day, the staggered openings did make the Irvine Ranch seem more like several developments than like a single new town.[13]

Partly because of these numerous steps, the early planning for the Irvine Ranch is often said to lack vision. This is both true and false. Compared with Columbia and The Woodlands, where teams of young planners and designers worked under the thrall of charismatic leadership and cutting-edge ideas in social sciences and ecology, the Irvine Ranch's initial planning under Pereira seems to have come from the mainstream of modernist design by the architect-planner. Pereira certainly espoused ideas about making Irvine into a great university city, an urbane place with a dense fabric. However, his modernist urban design and architecture bore little resemblance to his espoused models such as Oxford and Heidelberg. It is also not clear from either the plans or Pereira's built work whether he had the tools to come closer to these models. He talked about high-density mixed-use areas, unpretentious shops, and pedestrians, but his actual architecture on the UC Irvine campus consists of big concrete boxes covered in three-dimensional cast concrete panels, floating in a sea of open space.

Even the 1970 plan, drawing on a wider range of sources and going far beyond Pereira, is very broad brush in its overall character and does not have the obvious urban design, social, or ecological visions that the other two developments have articulated. On the Irvine Ranch, more than in the other developments, vision became most tangible in its detailed design. This design has always involved strong landscape forms, a restricted planting palette, and an architecture that has appealed to a broad market rather than being high style. Because the ranch was so big and development was to reach over so many decades, it was obvious from the start that designs would need to evolve and that different concepts would come into prominence at different periods. The Irvine Company has had a process for gaining feedback from residents, allowing planners, designers, and developers to learn from earlier projects. Interviews with now-prominent professionals working on the Irvine Ranch in the 1970s indicated that this approach gave them tremendous flexibility to try new ideas within the overall urban structure and the practice of using landscape as a dominant element.

Looking beyond the broad master plans to the wider set of specialized planning documents and built work, we see a more specific and detailed vision emerge. Four areas are particularly striking: the idea of the metropolitan field (although it was not called that); environmental perception, particularly the concept of legibility; market segmentation; and planning for the car. In addition, by the 1990s, the City of Irvine and the Irvine Company had grappled with the issue of jobs-housing balance, clearly contributed to a new suburban aesthetic, and reoriented their approaches to habitat and open space. I turn to those issues at the end of the chapter.

Metropolitan Field.   In areas like Southern California, and increasingly everywhere in the United States, a new kind of metropolitan area had very obviously come into existence during the early part of the twentieth century. This was an urban, or metropolitan, field with multiple centers. As I explained in chapter 1, the ideas of the social or regional city of Ebenezer Howard and the Regional Planning Association of America had focused on the concept of a multicentered city set in a landscape of agriculture and open space. In contrast, in what I call the metropolitan field, city centers were dotted in a largely urbanized landscape. I use the term *metropolitan field* to distinguish it from other related terms, such as the RPAA's *regional city* (described in chapter 1). However, it was not the term used at the time; then, there was no consistent term.

Columbia and The Woodlands were certainly not protected from being engulfed in such metropolitan landscapes, but their overall self-contained planning was much more reminiscent of the garden city and RPAA philosophies. The Irvine Ranch was different, embracing an alternative vision. As one of the early planners explained:

> I do believe in the thing called the regional city [his term for the metropolitan field]. And as a consequence, that is the reason that I have less excitement about the [new urbanist] Celebrations of the world, which I think are nice little enclaves unto themselves, but basically we live in a regional city. We travel that way, we live that way. And each subcommunity . . . whether it's Irvine, Newport Beach, whatever it is, has something within it that contributes to that regional city, whether it is a performing arts center, a park, an industrial area, [so] that when you add it all up we have these nodes of activity, in Kevin Lynch's language, all over. And I do believe that the very thing that bothers people, maybe, who are not familiar with this area, Orange County, is, it seems like there is no central something. And I don't think there's a natural central anything anymore; [the region] is too large for one big central place. Those are bygone days that have long passed. And in fact, therefore, we have the University of California Irvine, which is an important part of the county, not just to the City of Irvine. We have [the Irvine] Spectrum, which is an important part of this region. We have the performing arts center over here. We have Newport Center. We have the ocean. We have lakes. We have Disneyland [outside Irvine]. (Interview 0406)

The metropolitan field in this sense is not unstructured, but it has a structure that permits multiple paths and activities. Advertised as "the place where urban sprawl ends," the Irvine Ranch was marketed as an organized, convenient, clean, and open environment, one of "tomorrow's cities" (Irvine

Company 1970b, 20). There were certainly tensions over the vision, with the Irvine Company's designers generally having a higher-density, more mixed-use, and more urbanized vision than many of the residents of the City of Irvine had or even, at times, the company's own marketing department. However, the overall urban design strategy organized the metropolitan field, without returning to earlier, more centralized urban forms, and came to have an appeal to many. As a civic leader from the City of Irvine explained: "When I first came here, I missed the city not having a core, because I grew up and you went downtown. But downtown, I think, is an idea whose time has come and gone. We have many cores now" (Interview 0324).[14]

Environmental Perception and Legibility. The three case study developments, including the Irvine Ranch, are all based on the concept of a "village" structure. This divides the developments into named areas that provide houses, shops, schools, and recreational areas. The new community as a whole is made up of a mosaic of such villages along with townwide or even regional employment areas, commercial and mixed-use districts, open spaces, and civic facilities. Obviously the idea of breaking down the development into units had some history, most notably in the neighborhood unit concept of the 1920s. The Irvine Company planners were quite aware of this history.

However, they departed from it. Under Ray Watson, who headed planning until 1966, then land development, and then the company from 1973 to 1977, and Richard Reese, the head of planning, urban designers were inspired by the then-recent work of Kevin Lynch (Dannenbrink 1976, 2002). Lynch's work was attractive to the design teams because he provided a way of structuring the metropolitan field, creating a sense of place within clearly defined districts.

In his 1960 book, *Image of the City,* Lynch proposed that mental images of the city may vary among individuals and groups but that it is possible to detect a public or a shared image (Lynch 1960, 7, 46). Drawing on his studies of the spatial perceptions of middle-class professionals in the center city areas of Los Angeles, Boston, and Jersey City, Lynch suggested that some environments are more legible, or "imageable," to the general public than others (9–10). By this he meant that their parts "can be recognized and can be organized into a coherent pattern" (3). Lynch acknowledged that over time people can find their way around even the most confusing and monotonous landscapes, but a well-structured environment can be more quickly legible and also allow for new experiences over time. To analyze environmental legibility, he came up with a vocabulary of city elements. These included *paths,* "the channels along which the observer . . . moves"; *edges,* "linear elements not used or considered as paths"; *districts,* "medium-to-large sections of the city . . . which the observer mentally enters 'inside of,' and which are recognizable as having some common identifying character"; *nodes,* or strategic spots that one can enter into, which are junctions or concentrations of activities and may be the core of a district; and *landmarks,* which are reference points, like a node, but are not entered by the observer (Lynch 1960, 47–48).

Lynch's basic point was that an environment with more of these elements is a better environment. For example, a city where people identify many of these elements has more options for wayfinding, more components of the city that can be invested with meaning, more options for collective memories, and so on. The "highly imageable" city will seem "well formed, distinct, remarkable" and will be valued by both insiders and outsiders (Lynch 1960, 10). Exemplary areas include parts of San Francisco, Boston, and Manhattan.

Lynch's work focused on existing environments that had been imbued with significance by residents. In the Irvine Ranch, the planning teams had to create a landscape using physical elements that they assumed, or hoped, would be perceived as important parts of a legible city. This has been a common use of the Lynchian vocabulary, with designers assuming that they can create meaningful landmarks and districts. The appendices in Lynch's book, however, show that many of the elements remarked on by the lay professionals in his research were not visible during his field observations because they were cultural elements such as ethnic neighborhoods. Conversely, some elements that he perceived in the field were invisible to the middle-class professionals who were less sensitive to architectural character. Lynch also later modified his framework (Lynch 1981).[15] However, in a new community, Lynch's early work provided useful guidance for planners and designers trying to create distinctive spaces.

This work was new and influential at the time of the Irvine Ranch's main planning in the 1960s and 1970s, particularly as Lynch conveyed his ideas to a generation of graduates at MIT and as the slim book was increasingly read in professional circles.[16] Lynch's work influenced the early development of the ranch's Eastbluff Village, opened in 1964 (Watson 1999). The 1970–71 *General Plan Program Urban Design Element* by the Irvine Company clearly cited Lynch's work. The report recommended *The Image of the City* and proposed a "new urban form that eliminates urban sprawl and creates an imageable environment" where "the differentiated parts will be integrated into a visual whole that is coherent, meaningful, memorable, and highly pleasurable" (Irvine Company 1970–71, 3; 1972a). The 1972 statement of development objectives for the university town center called the site a key node and proposed it have "at least one key vertical landmark" (Irvine Company 1972b, 9). Diagrams and sketch plans from Woodbridge, the first major village planned after the 1970 Irvine Company general plan, were clearly labeled using terminology from Lynch's work, including *edges* and *paths* (see also Lynch 1960, 46–49; Watson 1999; Dannenbrink 2002) (see figure 6).

Intra·Village grid pedestrian circulation system on neighborhood paseos connecting lake and activity corridor.

Each Village Quadrant comprised of neighborhood units spatially identified and structured around neighborhood nodes and focal points at intersecting paseos

Village edge buffer

Existing eucalyptus hedgerows integrated into system of paseos.

Inter-Village trail system

Village quadrant spatially formed by village environmental components (activity and lake corridors and village edge)

Inter-Village trail system (pedestrian, bicycle and equestrian)

VILLAGE NEIGHBORHOOD

Figure 6. Concept diagram for Woodbridge, with landscape architecture by SWA, early 1970s. Source: The Irvine Company. Reprinted with permission from The Irvine Company.

The 1977 urban design plan sponsored by the Irvine Company and the City of Irvine used interview techniques reminiscent of Lynch in investigating the public image of the city, and it also used some Lynchian terms (WMRT 1977). As two senior planners from Irvine Company explained:

> Kevin Lynch's book influenced me a lot, and . . . the studies he did where he interviewed people in Boston: where do you live? Draw me the edge, and draw me where it is, and draw me where the center is. . . . Bartholomew's book on planning [drawing on Perry's neighborhood unit idea], where it says a neighborhood has an elementary school, must have *x* number of people, and all that

kind of stuff, we threw away and abided by Kevin Lynch's ideas. . . . We didn't do it every time, but we tried to create or pick the strongest edges we can have. . . . We were more interested in creating identifiable places. (Interview 0406)

I always memorized Kevin Lynch and all this urban design stuff. That was a great mentor for me. That to me was like getting the stone tablets on top of the mountain: "Oh my God, you can really organize urban space." (Interview 0326)

By 2002 the Irvine Company articulated these ideas in a set of "community planning principles based on the development and implementation of more than a dozen villages during the past 40 years" (Irvine Company 2002b):

So What Makes a Good Community Plan?

Identity. Open space, parks, trails, recreation facilities and distinctive entries should assist in creating a special sense of community character. Many times, this character is created by natural landforms. This sense of character sets the community apart from neighboring villages.

Distinct edges. Each community's edge should help create strong identity, and should only be interrupted a minimal number of times for traffic to enter and exit. This reinforces the community's identity, and helps improve traffic flow both inside and outside the community.

Neighborhoods. Larger villages are organized into neighborhoods with small parks as their focus.

Village center. Each community should have a unifying feature that serves as the heart of the community. Sometimes it is a pedestrian-oriented park, shopping center, school or daycare center.

Streets. Streets are designed as public, landscaped spaces, for both pedestrians and autos.

Home design. A wide variety of home designs and neighborhood site plans should contribute to the character and quality of the village.

Landscaping. Landscape in a community provides an overall fabric and texture that ties the community together as a cohesive place. The landscape and open space design should be responsive to the uniqueness of the site conditions and opportunities.

A careful balance. The blending of development and open space should be balanced and thoughtful. (Irvine Company 2002b)[17]

Obviously, in this document, district identity, edges, and landmarks are strong values, as are the concepts of balance and variety, which I return to in chapter 5.

Rather than becoming social units, villages designed from a Lynchian perspective became identifiable districts within the wider metropolis. That the areas have been criticized by some as aesthetically monotonous shows the difficulty of operationalizing Lynch's approach, because creating a strong unifying identity necessarily reduces variety. My own evaluation is that the distinctive character of villages does promote wayfinding, as Lynch proposed. In addition, because the villages were not defined by such social institutions as schools or supermarket catchments, the planners were allowed more experimentation with the size of villages. In the Irvine Ranch they have varied from under four thousand people to over twenty-six thousand.

This Lynchian approach does not mean that the villages in the Irvine development have been devoid of social meaning, that they have been merely visually coherent units. In fact Lynch's work was based on empirical research on the meaning and sense of the city. One internal Irvine Company memo, setting out planning principles for the central sector, clearly laid out this interest: the centrality of social relations in physical planning, the importance of basing work on "empirical research related to social intercourse," and the need for "rational, comprehensive planning" to attend to a variety of physical scales at which social relationships occur, from the block to the region (Ashley 1969, 2, 3).

A group of master's students at UC Irvine explored these issues in the late 1990s in a cluster of papers sponsored by Ray Watson of the Irvine Company but supervised by faculty. They surveyed 720 households in the Irvine Ranch and received 243 responses from three villages—Turtle Rock (an early village), Woodbridge, and Westpark (a recent, higher-density, predominantly renter village). Although this was a small sample, the students supplemented it with other information. Using a measure developed by Nasar and Julian (1995), they discovered that the villages had relatively high and similar senses of community (Van Zandt 1999, 17; Macey 1999, 57–68; Purpura 1999; also Wallace 1999; Jackson and Smith 1999; Kelley 1999). While certainly some bias was present, the high satisfaction of residents of the City of Irvine, responding to more random surveys reported in chapter 6, supports these findings. As I discuss in chapters 3 and 5, designers of other new communities often had extremely high expectations that were not fulfilled. However, on the Irvine Ranch the expectations about the social function of the villages were low, or realistic, and so they have all likely been attained.

Lynch's work was not only about districts. At the ranch scale the 1970 plan also created a number of centers or nodes that were related to the region rather than to particular villages or even the ranch. Newport Center has been developed for mixed use, including housing that surrounds a large mall called Fashion Island. A regional shopping center was planned at the junction of the Interstate 5 and 405 freeways, and eventually it was built as an entertainment and shopping center surrounded by the Irvine Spectrum business park. The university has also become a center, as have the beaches. This shows the link between the idea of the metropolitan field and the work of Lynch.

Lynch's identifiable districts were not the only area in which planning for the Irvine Ranch referred to work on perception. Irvine's designers also used work on perception to create both its signage and signage regulations, an important component of the Irvine Ranch development's response to the aesthetic problems of sprawl. The 1975 Irvine Company sign manual started with a thirteen-page summary of research on human perception and visual communication, color, and legibility of lettering (Irvine Company 1975). It espoused a minimalist view of signage, proposing a small number of small signs with a limited design palette and arguing that through good design a clear message could be articulated without the visual clutter often associated with urban sprawl.

Social Mix through Market Segmentation.   Planning for the Irvine Ranch was firmly focused on the physical. However, social and physical issues were also linked. As I explained in chapter 1, in the 1950s a growing number of commentators, professionals, and developers came to see that suburban development had not taken enough account of social change or social diversity. By providing large areas of similar housing units, such development promoted social homogeneity, acting in a manner seen as regressive because of its effect on the potential for human growth and learning in those suburban locations. The development in Columbia was greatly influenced by these debates and actively promoted the mixture of ethnic and economic groups.

However, new community developers had more self-interested reasons to want to counter this trend toward homogeneity and to market to a variety of household types. Each of the developments was trying to capture fairly large percentages of the buyers and renters in its region, and to do this the marketing teams could not afford to ignore large groups of consumers. In order to attract firms to industrial and business parks, new community developers, such as the Irvine Company, also had to show that they could provide sufficient housing for a range of workers. To manage this, each development had to aim for as wide a range of people as possible. While the Irvine Ranch's early development had been in the expensive coastal areas, the 1970 plan opened up a wider range of locations. That is not to say that the Irvine Ranch has ever been a mecca for people seeking low-cost housing, and, as I describe later, affordable housing has been an issue of some tension, particularly in the City of Irvine. In terms of racial issues, Irvine was never legally segregated, but neither did it make many active attempts to market to nonwhites (Dientsfrey 1971). However, from the 1970s onward the Irvine Ranch did need to provide a range of housing price levels and styles in order to obtain a larger share of the market.

Even in the 1960s, the Irvine Company experimented with housing unit designs. By 1980, 48 percent of houses in the City of Irvine were attached, compared with 61 percent in 1990, but still a large number for Orange County in the 1970s. These attached units were perceived as risky in mar-

Figure 7. Diagram of Woodbridge showing diverse housing types, reflecting the sophisticated market segmentation used in that village, 1970s. Source: The Irvine Company. Reprinted with permission from The Irvine Company.

keting terms. This was the period when residents had moved to the suburbs to get away from apartments, but the Irvine Company planners wanted to provide attached houses for design reasons, to save green space. By the time of the Woodbridge development, planned in the early 1970s, the Irvine Company was also experimenting with very elaborate market segmentation,

to appeal to different household types (Agid 1972) (see figure 7). As one
of the planning team members explained in reference to Woodbridge:

> The fine-grain mix—that was more of a marketing kind of a thing. . . . In [the
> earlier development of] Turtle Rock we left some land. We built single-family
> first and bypassed a higher-density residential site and a commercial site. And
> when the people moved in, they immediately went to the city council and said
> rezone that back to housing; we don't want those things. So the fine-grain
> mix concept came out of the necessity to develop, build, and market all den-
> sities and all uses simultaneously. We found out absolutely in Woodbridge that
> you could put a low-income house on the lot next door to a single family de-
> tached tract, and nobody thought a thing about it when they bought their
> home, because those were just people like them. It didn't scare them at all,
> and it didn't hurt the marketing at all. So that's how that fine-grain mix came
> out. And that was also the origin, at least for us, of this concept . . . put a prod-
> uct in, in every market segment, from the lowest income to the highest in-
> come. Try to have everything you bring online at one time, in every enclave
> of land. (Interview 0326)

Thus the Irvine Company achieved mix for reasons of design and sales.
It did not promote a strong vision of social equity as Columbia was doing in
the same period. While the 1960 land use plan for the college town had been
introduced as aiming to "provide an economically balanced community," this
meant a mixed economy, not a mixed-income population (William L. Pereira and Associates 1960, 3). As I explain below, market-rate affordability
is a problem that has never been resolved in Irvine. However, while it has
been attacked for its high costs and lack of social concern throughout its history, as I explain in chapters 5 and 6 it compares favorably with the other
two case study developments in terms of government-sponsored affordable
housing and ethnic mix. Thus through design, marketing, and local political action, the Irvine Ranch development has achieved much the same results as the ostensibly more visionary developments, particularly in the City
of Irvine, where government has been active at times in promoting affordable housing.

Design for the Car.   Starting in the 1920s, planners and designers began
to think seriously about the way that cars could change the city. Architect
Le Corbusier placed towers in a park with freeways; Frank Lloyd Wright
imagined a very low-density urbanism of one-acre lots. The neighborhood
unit and related planning at Radburn tried to tame the car by placing main
roads around the unit to provide a boundary or edge, dividing the area
from the rest of the city. However, these roads were also the means of linking units together into a larger metropolis. In Radburn this idea was operationalized using a superblock, with culs-de-sac and loop roads bringing

cars into but not through the unit. Pedestrians were thus able to wander through the center without being bothered by cars. This kind of superblock planning was also used in modernist urban designs such as public housing projects.

Planners for the Irvine Company drew freely and loosely on these earlier ideas. Irvine's various planners used the freeways as a framework for development. They created identifiable residential and industrial districts surrounded by a loose grid of landscaped arterials leading to concentrated and convenient shopping areas. Irvine Company planners are still proud of their lack of strip shopping development. The interiors of villages contain numerous traffic-calming features with fairly extensive pedestrian path systems. Not all these design elements came directly from the Irvine Company planners and consultants. For example, the berms and elegantly screened walls that line the arterials along village edges do reflect Irvine Company design philosophies but also take their character from City of Irvine requirements for noise attenuation (Dannenbrink 2002). However, the necessity of planning for the car was a strong imperative in the Irvine Ranch. As one early landscape architecture consultant explained:

> [Irvine] was also the best effort so far to really accommodate the car. You know Radburn included it but it was [just] a way of getting to work. But Southern Californians live in their cars. I know I would try to get rid of them, and Ray [Watson] would make me put them back. And I do think that it really was the best effort in the country to design with the automobile. . . .
>
> But it is probably the best of the places designed for the car. And what was also incredible was that they kept track of how ideas worked out, and there was a correction process. I didn't see that work being done in Columbia. (Interview 0401)

While automobiles were to be the dominant mode of transportation on the Irvine Ranch, early plans do mention buses, and the structure was put in place for other modes of transportation (Kreditor and Kraemer 1968, IV-32). The early City of Irvine general plan was even more futuristic, proposing 80 to 150 foot transit rights-of-way for such technologies as monorails (Wilsey and Ham [1973] 1974, sec. 6, 17–18). As an Irvine Company planner active in the 1970s explained:

> Woodbridge is the prototype village for the entire central basin. There was to be a donut of those kinds of villages with employment in the center of each one. And by aligning all of the commercial centers and employment centers in each village, you then created a condition under which a public transportation system would be viable, the goal of which would be to have one-car families. Not zero-car families, but one-car families, so that people could work without having to have separate cars. (Interview 0306)

While the transit rights-of-way were eventually dropped by the city, the mixed-use activity corridors of the early Irvine Company plans are the corridors where regional light rail has been proposed (Orange County Transportation Authority 2002). However, objections from nearby residents may reroute the rail from the more residential parts of the corridor, again showing the challenges to providing popular alternatives to the car in locations such as Irvine.

Woodbridge

Woodbridge, with a land area of 1,786 acres and a population of twenty-six thousand, was the first village completely developed according to the 1970 Irvine Company plan and the City of Irvine general plan. One of the main activity corridors in the larger ranch plan went through the center. Woodbridge shows the underlying village concept, the idea of mix, and the influence of Kevin Lynch. In some ways it is just a bigger and more complicated version the early smaller developments, featuring small lots and linked open space. However, those who worked on it saw it as a very special project—with more small parks and much more housing mix than could be achieved in a smaller development. It was also wildly successful from a sales standpoint. As one of the planning team members explained:

> The timing was perfect because we were just coming out of the recession. It opened up on Father's Day, and we had—I think there were six thousand applications for 350 homes. We had the big lottery. We had to arrange this whole thing for people to come out for two weeks, where they could put a card in for selected houses. It was an amazing process. Talk about perfect timing. We were spending all this time and money and energy at the time when the market was dead, people were going out of business. And so, by the time that the plan came out and we were actually implementing it, it was the perfect time because everything was on the upsurge. (Interview 0110)

It was also the end of an era, in that it was opened in 1975, just before the sale of the company and the scaling back of centralized land planning functions. The new owners were much more oriented toward development than planning and design. So Woodbridge, meant to be a prototype for future developments, became more a product of its times. However, a number of features were replicated in later developments, particularly as the development was used to illustrate sections of the WMRT urban design plan of 1977.

The rest of the story of the Irvine Ranch revolves around several controversies, including the sale of the company, affordable housing, and habitat protection. It also had a number of successes, although not everyone agrees they were successes, particularly its experimentation with the visual character of suburbia and the growth of its research parks.

PHASE 3: CITY BUILDING, 1977 TO LATE 1980s,
AND PHASE 4: IRVINE AS LANDSCAPE, LATE 1980s ONWARD:
AESTHETICS, ENVIRONMENT, AND DAILY LIFE

Sale of the Company and Rise of the City

As was previously explained, in 1977 the Irvine Company was sold after something of a bidding war. It was bought for $337 million by a consortium of several people, including Joan Irvine, Alfred Taubman, and Donald Bren. In 1983 Bren bought out almost all the other shares. Taubman used his proceeds to buy Sotheby's; Joan Irvine sued for more money and won, although not the sum she had originally wanted and not until 1990 (Flagg 1990).

Interviews indicated that many in the senior management had sided with the competing Mobil Oil bid in 1977 and left soon after the new owners took over.[18] The new owners also proceeded to disperse the central planning and urban design group, so others not in the senior ranks left as well. The sale of the company also had a number of implications for coordination among the physical components of the Irvine Ranch. As I have explained, much of the vision of the Irvine Ranch was really shown in the details of suburban design, and these details were beyond those required by the city. With a planning and design staff dispersed to different parts of the organization, some observers felt that the coordinating function had been lost. As one urban designer explained: "Everything broke down when the company was taken over, because they didn't believe in all that kind of design control. And so everybody had their separate parking lots with spiked fences between them, and the landscaping wasn't coordinated, the signing wasn't coordinated" (Interview 0326). However, others remembered it as a period in which the urban design received continued attention, although some compromises were made for marketing reasons and because the City of Irvine did not want to have to maintain large open spaces.

Planners who had been employed in the City of Irvine during the 1970s and 1980s remembered it as an exciting period, with the expansion of the industrial area around the airport and its transformation from the Irvine Industrial Complex to the Irvine Business Complex. It was also the time of the construction of a number of large new villages, such as the fairly high-density Westpark (Interviews 0309, 0312). There was a sense, for these planners, that the city contributed some of the energy and innovation that had previously existed largely within the private sector:

> I also think—this maybe sounds a little self-serving, but I think that in the first half of the 1980s decade there were a lot of people who were fairly young and creative, who came together in all the jurisdictions on the public side and private side, which I don't think exists anymore. You start looking at the creativity that existed in the City of Irvine, and in the County of Orange, and in the Irvine Company, as well as many of the other cities around here that were very

active and creative and dynamic, and I think a lot of the things that happened at that time were generally good things. (Interview 0309)

While this professional energy was oriented toward growth for the early part of the 1980s, by the late 1980s no-growth and slow-growth ideas came to dominate the council, leading to a large turnover in senior staff. However, in a sense this was just a new direction of energy from growth to the protection of open space. In fact, the Irvine Company continued to develop its land, at first making deals to allow more density elsewhere in return for open space protection and later just protecting such space.

Newer phases of development have certainly required a great deal of negotiation among residents, government, and the developer. The process of getting approvals for major sections was quite elaborate by the 1990s, with zoning approval alone taking three years for Planning Area 27 in that decade. However, there has been an underlying agreement that the developer can keep building. As with the other two developments, the developer has also had a very strong role in framing options for regulations about land use. As a City of Irvine planner explained:

> The zoning is prepared by the property owner, the Irvine Company, and they submit it to the city for review. In some communities the city takes the lead on that. . . . There have been some criticisms that the Irvine Company doesn't plan anymore. I myself don't think that's true. I think that their planning staff is very talented and that they really do pay attention. They spend a lot of time traveling and looking at what works here and what doesn't. And then when they come back, they'll say we put this in the plan; we saw this in such and such a place, and we thought it really worked, and here's why. And they're also receptive to ideas that we have. . . . So, it's interesting in that they take the lead on developing the zoning. But we do have a role in reviewing it and working with them to decide what's the feel of the community going to be? What kind of a place is this going to be? How does it add to what's already in the community? (Interview 0403)

In terms of local politics, in the early years the Irvine Company did not contribute to local elections, something that interviewees commented may have given added power to other landholders who did make such contributions, particularly those holding window areas (Sills 2002). Over the years, however, the Irvine Company has put money into fighting ballot measures at the local, county, and state levels and made other high-level campaign contributions, including contributions against the California Coastal Act in the early 1970s and for roads projects in the 1980s and 1990s (Pincetl 1999, 201). These interactions among city, county, and company set the stage for a number of key controversies over housing and jobs, design, and the environment.

Housing and Jobs

Irvine has for a long time been an expensive development in an expensive region. For its critics, this is the end of the story. However, as is generally the case, a close reading shows a more complicated picture both in the private market (in its market segmentation) and in government sponsorship of affordable housing. This became a very controversial issue in the 1970s and 1980s, as the business parks expanded and housing for workers did not keep up.

In the United States, private-sector homeownership is supported by the government in a number of ways. For higher-income earners the most important of these are income tax deductions of mortgage interest and the lack of capital gains taxes on homes.[19] Veterans Administration loans have also been important in the Irvine Ranch area, renowned for its connections to the defense industry. At the lower end of the market is Federal Housing Administration (FHA) support of mortgages that has allowed low down payments (Carliner 1998, 302).

For many years property on the Irvine Ranch did not take advantage of FHA loans because of its policy to lease rather than sell land. This matter was complicated for a number of reasons. For one thing, the Irvine Company and Foundation were used to holding the land as a whole. Also, in the 1950s the Irvine Company had had unfortunate experiences selling land for industrial development and seeing that development fall short of high standards. Also, some other new towns had been developed on long-term leases, most notably the Australian national capital of Canberra. And finally, because the land had been held for so long, its sale also involved a very large tax bill.

Irvine's problems with the FHA were not unique. Columbia faced a similar situation over its methods for maintaining open space, which, as I explain in chapter 3, involved legal arrangements that were also against FHA rules. Columbia responded by gaining special FHA approval on an experimental basis for its practices. The Irvine Company did not do this for its leasehold policy. To the Irvine Company's defense, however, this kind of FHA approval was not easy to obtain and was not extended even to the federally supported Title VII new community of Park Forest South, which wanted to use a Columbia-style lien system (Burby 1976, 38, 44).

The leasehold policy was first changed for a parcel in east Tustin in 1967. The Irvine Company under Ray Watson wanted to develop the land for a moderate-priced housing market and to gain access to FHA financing. Watson presented the Irvine Company board with a study showing that "the projected market advantage of fee over leasehold more than made up for the tax consequences of selling our low basis land" (Watson 2002). This new

TABLE 3 Federal Funds to Orange County and the City of Irvine

	Orange County			City of Irvine		
	FY 1987 (in 1996 dollars)	FY 1996	Change (%)	FY 1987 (in 1996 dollars)	FY 1996	Change (%)
Direct Federal Expenditures or Obligations						
1. Total direct expenditures or obligations	10,263,660,391	9,686,990,473	−6	340,458,095	348,194,659	2
Department of Defense	5,200,189,565	2,539,043,701	−51	226,221,333	233,305,644	3
All other agencies	5,063,470,826	7,147,946,772	41	114,236,762	114,889,015	1
2. Total grant awards	594,645,105	1,245,319,385	109	55,083,804	76,778,343	39
3. Total salaries and wages	898,509,565	924,263,078	3	—	—	—
Department of Defense	466,041,436	356,919,939	−23	—	—	—
4. Total direct payments for individuals	3,721,260,840	5,256,472,555	41	396,391	16,786,328	4,135
Retirement and disability	2,615,237,983	3,166,974,775	21	—	—	—
All other	1,106,022,856	2,089,497,780	89	396,391	16,786,328	4,135
5. Total procurement contract awards	5,024,797,521	2,241,843,783	−55	284,977,901	254,591,000	−11
Department of Defense	4,450,941,989	1,910,490,000	−57	225,841,160	228,941,000	1
6. Other federal expenditures or obligations	24,447,360	19,091,672	−22	0	38,988	New
Other Federal Assistance						
7. Direct loans	15,998,269	7,471,118	−53		150,512	New
8. Guaranteed loans and insurance	3,956,494,638	8,090,590,431	104	3,806,760	22,931,421	502
Total (excluding loans and insurance)	39,429,225,438	36,584,853,913	−7	1,247,611,837	1,290,311,305	3
Total per capita	18,197	14,386	−21	14,107	10,271	−27
Defense direct + procurement per capita	4,454	1,750	−61	5,112	3,680	−28
Defense direct + procurement % total	24%	12%		36%	36%	
Total including loans and insurance	43,401,718,345	44,682,915,462	3	1,251,418,597	1,313,393,238	5
Guaranteed loans per capita	1,826	3,181	74	43	183	324
United States resident population (people)	2,166,801	2,543,168	17	88,437	125,624	42

SOURCE: Oregon State University Libraries 2002.

policy was extended to other new sales in 1968, giving buyers the option of buying or leasing, and eventually was extended to existing leases. Part of the transition to really committing to urban development and the eventual elimination of most agriculture involved the decision to sell residential land.

While several interviewees mentioned their own Veterans Administration housing loans, interviews with representatives of the Irvine Company and data from the recent Consolidated Federal Funds Reports (available from 1983 for incorporated areas) indicate that the FHA has had a relatively small direct role in the City of Irvine (Andrew Parker 1997). As table 3 illustrates, by 1987 the City of Irvine had a very low level of new loan guarantees and insurance per capita at only $43 (1996 dollars) compared with $1,826 for the county. Although it had increased by 1996, it was still only $183. While these figures include a number of federal programs, such as student loans, they obviously indicate low levels of such support for Irvine.[20] Much more important in Irvine was defense spending, as I explain below (Forsyth 2002b).

In providing housing aimed specifically at low-income earners, the Irvine Ranch has had a mixed history. The early developments in the 1960s were mainly at the higher end of the market, both because they were developed near Newport Beach to take advantage of existing services, and because the Irvine Company needed cash to pay for its large up-front infrastructure costs. Residents of the Irvine Ranch have generally resisted subsidized housing construction. For example, a study of Orange County politics, based on in-depth interviews conducted in 1970 and 1972 with twenty-three residents of an Irvine Company development, found the population to be supportive of ecological issues but against public housing (Lamb 1974). The City of Irvine conducted surveys in the 1970s that came up with very similar findings (Kane 1996, 248). Smookler, one of the North Carolina researchers, describes repeated opposition to higher-density and lower-cost units by both city and county, reinforced by Irvine Company advertising emphasizing a "high-income, homogeneous community" (Smookler 1976, 81–82). In the late 1970s the City of Irvine and the Irvine Company were sued to create more affordable housing—725 units for low-income groups, using Section 8 funding—but this move to increase production was not sustained (Settlement Agreement 1977; Banzhaf 1980).

However, the situation has had some positive aspects, and from time to time the city council and others took the initiative to promote development of such units. Larry Agran, mayor of Irvine over several terms, has been a particular proponent. In 2000, the Irvine Company claimed that the City of Irvine had 3,233 units of subsidized affordable housing, or about 6 percent of its housing stock, although HUD data indicate that as of 1998 only around 700 of these units were federally subsidized (Irvine Company 2000b; U.S. HUD 1998). Many of the units come from such sources as local city-sponsored linkage programs, requiring set asides of affordable housing for people at 50, 80, or 120 percent of county median income. These units are not physically obvious—they have attractive designs—and they do not have a centralized waiting list, making them harder to count (Schiesl 1991). Without this important city initiative, the situation would be far worse.

As was explained earlier, the developers have also made some attempts to appeal to different market segments. In early 2000, new homes started at $144,000, and the Irvine Company was working on more inexpensive market-rate rentals, with costs held down by increasing densities (Irvine Company 2000c). Because of the high median household income in the city—$85,624 in 2000 compared with $64,611 in the county—many of these smaller units are affordable to those earning below median incomes. However, according to the 2000 census, 45 percent of renters and 31 percent of homeowners paid more than 30 percent of their income in housing costs in the City of Irvine. This compared unfavorably with 33 percent of renters and 19 percent of owners in Columbia. However, it was about the same as its immediate context in Orange County, where 42 percent of renters and 32 percent of owners had housing costs of 30 percent or more of their income (see table 10 in appendix B). Overall, Irvine's is a complicated patchwork of a response to affordable housing, both helped and hindered by local activism.

While not directly about affordability, the number of gated areas in the Irvine Ranch is the largest of the three case study developments. Most of these gated developments are near the coast. However, the Village of Northpark in the City of Irvine, opened in the new century, is gated against vehicular access, although internally it has a grid layout inspired by new urbanist debates, and pedestrians can enter through open gates. As I explain in relation to the other two developments, this trend toward gating vehicular access is a powerful one in marketing terms but disruptive to the overall concept of a new community in which the parts are meant to be balanced and interconnected.

The Irvine Company has certainly wanted to maximize profits, and expensive housing has been one way to do this. Many existing residents of the ranch have wanted to restrict additional development, particularly in the lower price brackets. However, a major reason for the affordability problems on the ranch has been the large demand for housing due to the Irvine Ranch's emergence as an employment center (Gass 1976).

The earliest plans were vague about employment, and internal Irvine Company analyses projected fewer jobs than households. For the southern sector, Kreditor and Kraemer (1968, III-12) calculated that under existing proposals there would be 0.5 jobs per household related to the industrial parks. They did not calculate jobs related to commercial areas or the university. A year later an internal memorandum to the Irvine Company's planning staff estimated almost 200,000 jobs and 670,000 residents would be on the ranch by 2000 (Ashley 1969). In contrast, by the late 1990s the City of Irvine had more than 3 jobs per household.

This job growth was partly due to the capacity of the region to capture significant federal expenditures in the defense area (see table 3). Southern California and Orange County in particular have been beneficiaries of military investment, much influenced by congressional lobbying, reflecting regional caucuses (Markusen 1989; Scott 1993).[21] Malecki (1982) analyzed federal research and development spending for two time periods—the early to mid-1960s and the mid- to late 1970s. He found that the Los Angeles standard consolidated statistical area (a consolidated metropolitan area including, at its southern edge, Santa Ana–Anaheim or Orange County) received the highest amount of both defense and total federal R&D expenditures in the country. For both time periods the figures were more than twice those for the second-ranked metropolitan areas (Malecki 1982, 25, 29; also Scott 1993). The Irvine Ranch was able to capture more than its share of this development, offering well-designed research parks easily accessible to the Orange County Airport. Table 3 shows that federal expenditures have been declining in per capita terms, and the City of Irvine has had lower per capita federal expenditures than the county. However, defense expenditures were larger in the City of Irvine than in the county in the late 1980s and mid-1990s, both in per capita and in percentage terms.[22] By the late 1990s the City of Irvine was being touted as one of the new "nerdistans," or high-tech centers (Kotkin 1999). The Irvine Ranch's economy has been broad, with a range of high-technology and manufacturing firms in the area, as well as large shopping areas, but defense was an important base.

The New Suburban Aesthetic

The Irvine Ranch's physical character has provoked strong reactions. Part of this has been to do with the size of the development. The Irvine Ranch presented the planning teams with a large canvas for design, a term people actually used when talking about it during interviews. To explain its large size, the Irvine Company prepared a number of graphics overlaying an outline of the ranch on New York City, Boston, San Francisco, and Washington, D.C. (see figure 8). These kinds of comparisons are frequently used in large developments to help all those involved to understand the scale (Forsyth 1999). Advertising for Columbia in 1967 showed an aerial photo of Manhattan with the headline "Columbia's bigger!" (Rouse Company 1967). However, the Irvine Ranch was so large—eight times the land area of Manhattan—that it was particularly striking.

As I explained earlier, Irvine Company planners and designers aimed to

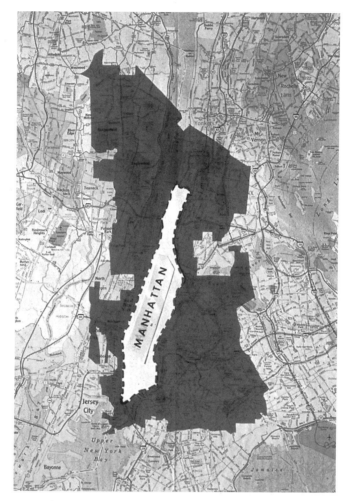

Figure 8. Outline of Irvine Ranch superimposed over New York City. In order to show scale, the Irvine Company created a number of images of Irvine superimposed over major cities. The image is likely from the 1960s. Source: The Irvine Company. Reprinted with permission from The Irvine Company.

deal with this enormous size by creating a sense of place in each village, but this strategy led to a certain uniformity that can be interpreted as monotony. In the older parts of the development, beige tones predominate, and many local stories circulate about "Irvine beige." Aesthetic covenants also are stringently enforced, adding to a sense of uniformity. This issue of covenants is an important one in all three developments and one I explore in more depth in chapter 5.

However, from its earliest days the Irvine Company experimented with architecture and landscape. The early decision to eliminate strip developments and the city berm requirement led to plantings lining most arterials. Villages have always had carefully selected planting palettes that have been well maintained through the work of the Irvine Company and owner associations. In the early 1970s, the City of Irvine conducted two park master planning processes: an overall "interim" plan by Haworth and Anderson in 1973, and a community parks master plan by Ribera and Sue in 1974 (Kelly 1999, 8). The Irvine Company, for its part, worked with Sasaki, Walker and Associates (SWA), who were involved with a number of Irvine Company design projects in the 1960s and 1970s, to create a 1973 outdoor recreation plan for Woodbridge Village that helped shape the 1974 city document. In 1988 a new community park master plan was created by EDAW (Kelly 1999, 8; Dannenbrink 2002). This indicates that a large amount of design expertise, involving several well-known firms, has been incorporated into park planning by both the Irvine Company and the City of Irvine. The same can be said of urban design (e.g., WMRT 1977).

In the late 1980s and the 1990s, the Irvine Company also recentralized some of its planning and design capacities. Higher-density residential developments of this period often used some kind of Mediterranean palette, replacing the "California contemporary" forms of the 1970s. The architects of these developments recently received positive attention for their innovations in suburban housing design (e.g., Conroy 2001). Donald Bren's interest in detailed design has affected this recent development. As one of the Irvine Company staff members explained, because of Bren's concern with formal issues, "we do our tilt-up [industrial] buildings based on Palladian ordering" (Interview 0303). In addition, as the business parks have been redeveloped and expanded, the earlier landscape dominated by one-story tilt-up concrete buildings has been gradually replaced with more varied architecture and a lush modern landscape (see figures 9 to 16). Of course, the landscape has always been important on the Irvine Ranch, but the standards in the 1990s were particularly lavish.

Three regional shopping centers are also distinctive. Open-air Fashion Island in Newport Center was redeveloped from its original Pereira architecture to a more low-key Mediterranean theme in the 1980s. Architecture was by popular shopping center designer Jon Jerde, and landscape architecture by SWA. Its parking lots, an important part of the view from the surrounding hotels and offices, were extensively relandscaped.

The Market Place in Irvine and Tustin is the location of big-box retailers housed in striking, richly colored stucco prisms. The parking lot's planting is oasislike and is punctuated by white columns, pink triangular walls, and

Figure 9. Housing in Woodbridge. Attached units are common in this village, planned in the 1970s. Source: The Irvine Company. Reprinted with permission from The Irvine Company.

Figure 10. Park West Apartments, designed by Frank Gehry. Photographer: Ann Forsyth.

Figure 11. Housing in Westpark. In this high-density village, landscape design is important. Photographer: Ann Forsyth.

Figure 12. Housing in Northwood. Although developer Donald Bren's taste for Mediterranean architecture is evident in recent developments, this area, pictured in the 1990s, shows that builders have supplied a variety of styles. Photographer: Ann Forsyth.

Figure 13. Early Irvine Company aerial photo of business complex, circa 1970s. This early landscape of one-story tilt-up buildings has been replaced with a much higher-density, more mixed-use, and highly landscaped environment, demonstrating the important role of redevelopment even in a new community. Source: The Irvine Company. Reprinted with permission from The Irvine Company.

Figure 14. Landscape in Irvine Spectrum business area. The most recent business areas have been thoughtfully landscaped from the start. Photographer: Ann Forsyth.

Figure 15. Halloween at the University Town Center shopping area, Irvine. Photographer: Ann Forsyth.

Figure 16. Tustin Market Place parking lot. Photographer: Ann Forsyth.

rock-covered berms. The landscape design was by POD and Kirby and Company, and the architecture by the firms of Mexican architect Ricardo Legorreta and LPA, making this area at the cutting edge of big-box shopping center design (Rocca 1996, 97) (see figure 16). POD had earlier designed the landscaping for Park West Apartments, opened in 1970, with "California contemporary" architecture by Frank Gehry (Irvine Company 1970b, 26).

The newest of these major shopping developments, Irvine Spectrum Center, is located at the intersection of the I-5 and I-405 freeways, where an eight-anchor shopping mall was once proposed (Schaaf 1977, 62). This entertainment-oriented center is designed around a looped pedestrian pathway that passes through spaces replicated from historical environments from the Mediterranean area. Its parking lot, viewed obliquely from above, looks like an orchard. Starting without department stores, it now has a Robinsons-May, and Nordstrom and Target stores are planned.

The design approach of the Irvine Company, while not at all fitting in with current elite architectural norms and debates, has attracted some critical attention, most notably a long 1996 essay in the Italian periodical *Lotus*. As the author, Rocca, argues:

> In Orange County, on the southern edge of the conurbation of Los Angeles, the orange groves have been replaced by the largest theme park in the world. The earthly paradise where a providential big brother, the Irvine Company, is indefatigably planning and building spaces for working and living in the best of all possible worlds (and countries). A new and marvelous setting where the beauty of the natural landscape forms a backdrop to subtly impressive office complexes, an international airport, residential communities in the garden-city style, an important university, and gigantic shopping centers. All this on an extraordinary scale: in a list of national economic capacities the county (with a gross domestic product of 60 billion dollars in 1989) would come in the top thirty countries of the world, ahead of Argentina, Austria, or Denmark. (Rocca 1996, 56)

The *New York Times* architecture critic, while commenting that the Irvine Ranch's high densities were "almost subversive" in a suburban context, argued that its buildings were "less architecture than . . . quick, efficient packaging of a comfortable level of middle class taste done as neatly with buildings as Sears or J. C. Penney has ever been able to do it with clothes" (Goldberger 1988).

This approach to creating a suburban environment is at odds with contemporary high-style design ideas and has provoked reflection within the Irvine Company about the appropriate form for suburbia. As an Irvine Company employee remarked:

> I look at the [Irvine Spectrum] entertainment center, and I say, is it right to go to the Alhambra and look at those spaces, the proportions and everything,

and basically poach that form, the style, and bring it to a bean field in Irvine? Is that right? And then I say to myself, well, it's possible that it's wrong. But then I say, would the form or the character that [architects] Morphosis would develop there, with exposed metal and glass and stuff, [be] any better, or is that just another sort of expression that doesn't have any meaning? . . . What do you draw on? It's all landscape. It's hills and bean fields and freeways. . . . So what is the right move? The only thing I can think of is that Don [Bren] and all of us are huge believers in trying to make places where people can enjoy themselves and have a full range of experiences and hang out, because we're all really influenced by European models and great spaces in cities. So, we look for models to clue us in on the scale, spatial design, and architectural design to make those places feel good and great to go to. It's just a little weird because there's no context. It is a stage set. So I haven't come to grips with whether I think it's bad or good. (Interview 0303)

This contrasts with recent design on the UC Irvine campus, which in the 1980s and 1990s employed a number of star architects, such as James Stirling, Frank Gehry, and the firm of Venturi Rauch and Scott Brown, to do major buildings. Of course, the campus had started off with a modernist site design featuring a number of similar-looking Pereira buildings organized in dispersed quadrangles with a huge central park, leaving a great deal of empty space. The new signature buildings have improved the campus greatly, in terms of both their design and making it more pedestrian-friendly (Rocca 1996; Parman 1990).

The author of the *Lotus* essay on the Irvine Ranch explicitly contrasted the high style for these recent buildings on the UC Irvine campus with the "innocuous and traditionalistic" residential landscape, which was characterized as "deeply conservative[;] the residential architecture leaves no room for any independent experimentation " (Rocca 1996, 51). Some popular local opinion mirrors these concerns:

It's a nice place, but I wouldn't want to live there. . . . I once heard a father tell his son, "We live in the Village of Woodbridge," and I had to refrain from yelling, "It's not a village; it's a bunch of houses thrown together." There's no character. I'm sorry, it's antiseptic. The fact that there are no gas stations indicates it's not built for people. It's built for a whole different class of people who don't want problems, who aren't willing to face the real world, I think. And I don't like it. I think it is soulless. (Interview 0308)

However, alternative views exist, with many residents appreciating the orderliness without being overly disturbed by the architecture. In the words of two civic leaders:

I like the newness. . . . I like the fact that it's middle-class and clean and convenient and you can park your car. . . . Today the things you need to have a good life are here. I can get the *Wall Street Journal* and the *New York Times* delivered to my front door, and the *Los Angeles Times*—good papers. There are more good restaurants than I can get to. The performing arts center in the university [means] the cultural life is enriched. Los Angeles is close enough. San Francisco is an hour away. I like the fact that there's a place to park when I go shopping. . . . And with age, the neighborhoods will get differentiated. The trees will take care of the architects. Architects make mistakes; the trees cover them up sooner or later. . . . I'm a happy camper here at Irvine. (Interview 0324)

I remember going to a number of planning meetings during the 1980s outside the city, and people would ridicule Irvine, that it's so homogeneous. And I would point out that we have a diversity of population and businesses and the like. And then I began to be a little less defensive about it: you know, people like the fact that at the end of their work day there is something that is orderly, reliable, dependable. It is not chaotic. It's safe. Their kids are safe. These are not things that we should take for granted. These are things that are community values and are to be cherished and supported. And yeah, it's a little less exciting than living in a neighborhood where you don't know what the heck's going on and you don't want your kids out after dark. (Interview 0219)

In turn, professionals were often quite positive, even about the architecture. Talking about the Irvine Company, a local planner explained:

They want to maintain that variety of streetscape. It's a very thoughtful process. On corner lots, they're requiring builders to come up with a different prototype, so that you don't have a blank side but you have a special design that takes advantage of that corner situation . . . and they really make a statement. So they [have] paid attention to a lot of details that at the city level we might have been able to do but probably wouldn't have. (Interview 0403)

In my interviews, I was struck by the careful attention given to all aspects of physical design in Irvine. At their best, the various generations of Irvine Company urban designers and consultants had a focus on creating a new kind of urban environment in a suburban location and frequently pushed for higher densities and more mixed use than local governments, the public, or marketing teams would accept. This issue of a new form for suburbia has been a contentious one in all three developments and is one I return to in chapter 5.

Environment and Habitat

The story of the Irvine Ranch is at least in part the story of a transformation in perceptions of the land—from an economic view held by the agriculturalists at the Irvine Company, one based on long-term returns, to one more focused on protection of the land itself both for human enjoyment and because of its more intrinsic features. As was explained earlier, the initial Irvine

Company plans envisaged development of the coastal areas, mostly at very low densities, although with a string of higher-density centers. Of the over 34,000 acres of the southern sector plan as it had evolved by 1968, only 2,338 acres were planned for open space—the rest of the land was to be developed (Kreditor and Kraemer 1968, II-2). This open space was described as "reserves for greenbelts, pedestrian ways, golf courses, and other provisions for active and passive recreation" (Kreditor and Kraemer 1968, II-5). The part of the ranch's green area that was considered most important to retain was the land in agriculture in the central valley (Kreditor and Kraemer 1968, II-7). Land that was later seen as habitat and an important legacy was at the time regarded as scrubland and as hillsides amenable for development because of location and views.

However, the 1960s and 1970s were a time of change in California as people came to appreciate the coastal areas in new ways. A growing environmental interest had both selfish and more altruistic motivations—some people were concerned about preserving nature for itself or for future generations, and others about maintaining the surroundings that they had paid a great deal to purchase. They came up against developers who wanted to make money from the land. These conflicting motivations complicated environmental politics.

In the early 1970s the Irvine Company backed down over a plan to develop the upper part of Newport Bay (Schiesl 1991, 68–69; Brower 1994). The Irvine Company had intended to develop a marina, partly through a land swap with the county, but by the 1970s popular opinion was against such developments, and a new county board of supervisors voted down the deal.

After the creation of the California Coastline Commission through a ballot initiative in 1972, the Irvine Company revised its plan for developing land along the coast as well, going through an elaborate multiparty planning process. Eventually it reduced its planned development significantly to 2,600 residential units and 2,150 resort accommodations clustered within a 9,473-acre planning area (Watson 1973; Griffin 1974; Moore 1976; Forma 1998, I-7; Irvine Company 1987). For its part, the Irvine Company had paid fifty thousand dollars toward defeating the coastal ballot initiative, but this was less than two *days'* worth of its property taxes paid to Orange County alone at that time (Watson 1973, 5, 7). Ray Watson, president of the Irvine Company, outlined the company's new approach in a 1973 speech to the Institute of Real Estate Appraisers. His speech indicates the overall company policy of working to keep a seat at the table, responding pragmatically to changing circumstances.

> Where we can, the Irvine Company is becoming an actual working part of public and quasi-public agencies. We have, for instance, joined with others in our industry and the Planning and Conservation League to conduct a *joint* study

leading to possible recommendations on a state land use plan. At one time, developers called conservation groups their enemies. We are now sitting down with our adversaries in the hopes of working together for the better results that all of us want.

Let me assure you that we are not naïve enough to believe that we will always be in total agreement with these groups. . . .

But we realize that if the developer is too rigid, he becomes less effective. . . .

The changing role of the private developer is to understand that society has changed and continues to change, to accept this change as reality, and to become a vital segment of this changing scene so that the inevitable change is guided for the best interests of all the people. (Watson 1973, 6–7)

The 1973 general plan for the City of Irvine had extensive sections on environmental issues, in contrast with their virtual absence from earlier Irvine Company plans (Wilsey and Ham 1974). In the 1980 general plan, open space (18 percent) and agriculture (11 percent) were projected to take up a large proportion of the 44,000 acres in the city and its sphere of influence (City of Irvine 1980, fig. 1-D).[23] In 1988, City of Irvine residents voted for the city to develop a memorandum of understanding with the Irvine Company to transfer development away from areas they wanted preserved for such open space and increase density in other areas (Kane 1996, 260; Pincetl 1999; Memorandum of understanding 1988). Some interviewees expressed concern about this increased density; however, if well designed, it could have the environmentally positive outcomes of raising densities enough to support walking for transportation.

The most large-scale open space issue on the Irvine Ranch has been habitat protection. Starting in the late 1980s, activists made a number of attempts to save Irvine Ranch land with habitat values. In October 1990, the Laguna Beach City Council agreed to buy 2,150 acres of land for seventy-eight million dollars in order to create a greenbelt and protect land from development (Martinez 1990; Brand 1991). In 1991, the Natural Resources Defense Council and an ornithologist proposed listing the California gnatcatcher as a federal endangered species—this bird has a habitat on Irvine Ranch lands. By 1992, the Irvine Company had agreed to protect over 16,000 acres in a county open space preserve and had arranged for the Nature Conservancy to manage it (Irvine Company and Nature Conservancy 1992). In 1993, Secretary of the Interior Bruce Babbitt listed the bird as merely "threatened." At the same time the federal Department of the Interior promulgated a "special rule" to allow negotiations over habitat protection under the fledgling Californian NCCP—the Natural Communities Conservation Program, promoted by then California governor and later Irvine Company board member Pete Wilson (Jasny 1997, chapter 1).

The NCCP process aimed to protect overall habitat and avoid species-by-species and project-by-project negotiations. In 1996, the agreement for a

35,000-acre wildlife reserve was signed, with protection of Irvine Company lands lasting seventy-five years. This included 18,000 acres from the Irvine Company, although as several interviewees pointed out, most of the Irvine Company's land had already been promised to the county or state under earlier negotiations (Jasny 1997, chapter 3). In late 2001, this habitat area was expanded. In the end, the Irvine Company claims that approximately 44,000 acres of the Irvine Ranch will be protected as habitat, with the most recent 11,000 acres protected in perpetuity. An additional 6,000 acres of ranch lands are parks and open space (see figures 17 and 18). During 2001 and 2002, Bren also created a thirty-million-dollar endowment for expenses (Irvine Company 2001b, 2002a). Although preserved for habitat, many areas need restoration, and this is paid for by mitigation fees from landowners. Public funds pay for other items, such as park security. Obviously the private owner of a company is able to make these kinds of donations with an eye to his legacy. It has also not hurt Bren financially. In 2002, with an estimated net worth of four billion dollars, he was ranked the eighty-seventh richest person in the world and by 2003 had risen to the seventy-eighth (Forbes 2002, 2003).

While few people whom I interviewed thought this solution for habitat protection was perfect, most thought it provided at least a good model. As one environmental activist explained in an interview before the last of the donations:

> That is an example of actually piecing together large chunks of habitat and creating a reserve. Now, there may be reasons why that reserve isn't perfect. One of them is that the toll road runs right through the middle of it. Another is that it's time-limited in terms of its duration, and there are probably pieces of habitat that should have been included in it that are not. Also, it's probably not as biologically based as some people would tell you it is. But having said all that, there is a large chunk of land that's been set aside by agreement of developers, environmentalists, and government authorities. And that's a very difficult thing to accomplish in Southern California, where we're used to doing things on a parcel-by-parcel basis. (Interview 0215)

As an another environmentalist explained, reflecting on the process: "I can never say anything bad-bad about the Irvine Company. When you compare it to Philip Morris and the Mission Viejo Company, they're angels, absolute angels" (Interview 0305). In many ways the most recent experience with habitat protection is just a continuation of Irvine Company policy to cut its losses and collaborate when fighting highly organized opposition could be counterproductive.

However, almost everyone working for the Irvine Company complained about the recent implementation of federal wetlands regulations—feeling that these regulations were overenforced in Southern California and that

Figure 17. Inland habitat protection area. Photographer: Ann Forsyth.

Figure 18. Coastal Crystal Cove State Park, with Irvine Company development behind it. Photographer: Ann Forsyth.

they undermined local-level agreements about open space. They also felt that their efforts in other environmental areas such as water reclamation—they have a very extensive water recycling system—and habitat protection were not appreciated. As one planning professional complained:

> And some person [at EPA] just got their Ph.D . . . , and they're basically in control of your land. You play ball or you don't get your permit. So, that has really gotten worse over the last year or two, and it will continue to get worse if you talk to them. . . . As you're aware, the company set aside seventeen [thousand or] twenty thousand acres of land. But for wetlands, we get no recognition of that. . . . The wetlands people don't care that we preserved may be much more valuable wetlands than what we're impacting. (Interview 0228)

In contrast, environmental bureaucrats involved with wetland and watershed issues complained that the Irvine Company was attached to highly engineered drainage solutions to minimize the size of drainage channels and maximize developable land, in accordance with outdated planning ideas based on the premise that wetlands are swamps that should be drained and filled. One noted: "They are really the worst developer I've ever worked with" (Interview 0402). It seemed to many that the Irvine Company sent out bulldozers to scrape off vegetation to ensure that developable land could not be interpreted as wetlands.

With all these controversies, it is not surprising that over the years a number of Irvine Company employees have been involved with governmental relations—although their titles have often included "corporate" or "community" affairs. It is also not surprising that its staff and board members have had strong associations with politics. One of the senior public relations employees at the time of my interviews had worked as press secretary for George Bush Sr. when he was vice president. As of 1999, the company's board of directors included Pete Wilson, Republican governor of California in the mid-1990s. An early president of Irvine Company had been secretary of the navy in a Republican administration, and Bren has been a prominent contributor to the Republican National Committee (Timmins 1993). These links to political elites have fueled criticisms of the Irvine Company from both academics and political opponents.

Living in Irvine

By 1980, the City of Irvine's population was 62,134; by 1990, 110,330; and by 2000, 143,072. The ranch's population was far larger, closer to 200,000. The City of Irvine estimated 168,000 jobs in the city alone in 2000 (City of Irvine 2002).[24] As was stated earlier, this was much more employment per household than was envisaged in the earliest plans. While 78 percent of the

City of Irvine's population was white in 1990, by 2000 those who were white had dropped to 64 percent (compared with 63 percent in California). In the same period those classed as Asian by the census had increased from 18 to 32 percent of the population (compared with a statewide increase from 10 to 12 percent in the same time span).[25] In 1990, 22 percent of the population of the City of Irvine had been born in other countries, with half of those arriving in the previous decade. These were the same proportions as in California as a whole and more than the U.S. figures of 8 and 3 percent, respectively. In early years, reports about racial intolerance occurred, but this seems to have changed over the years. The Irvine Ranch has become an economically and socially diverse area (see table 10 in appendix B).

In this area, where quality of life has drawn many to settle, the most controversial planning issue of the 1990s was the reuse of the El Toro Marine Corps base after it was slated for closure. Although the nearby Tustin base was also closed, its reuse plan for various forms of development went smoothly (Planning Center 1996). In contrast, the proposal for El Toro led to four voter initiatives and very divisive arguments. Those in the north of the county and Newport Beach argued for El Toro's conversion to an international airport to promote economic development and to replace the present John Wayne Airport, which produces aircraft noise in Newport Beach. Those in the south of the county and the City of Irvine argued against the airport because it would increase noise and traffic and decrease quality of life in their area, and eventually their position won.[26] However, in terms of the planning of the ranch, the Irvine Company had already taken account of aircraft noise in the vicinity of El Toro, and even with the airport option, the noise would be less intrusive than under military uses, which are extremely noisy. Both the airport and the alternative plans would increase development in the area—either attracted by the airport or by the vacant land of the former the marine base (ETERPA 1998; Cotton/Beland/Associates and others 1999). The Irvine Ranch—as opposed to the City of Irvine—suffered from aircraft noise and received development under both scenarios. While many in the area saw this as a crucially important debate—and it was—in the larger context, either option would bring development to the new community of the Irvine Ranch. From this viewpoint, it is not so surprising that the Irvine Company did not take a strong stance on the issue.

Although popular rankings have many drawbacks, in 2000 the *Ladies' Home Journal* named the City of Irvine as the top city in the United States for women on the basis of its low crime rate and other quality-of-life features. Although its ranking dropped in subsequent years, it stayed relatively high, as was outlined in the first chapter (Best Cities 2001, 2002). Like the other developments, it was planned assuming a population of highly educated housewives, whom the development teams feared would be bored.

However, the mixed-use designs have been convenient and flexible enough to support change in women's roles.

Overall, the Irvine Ranch has provided a range of environments that have remained popular while fulfilling many of their original antisprawl goals. These were primarily physical planning goals: ordering the landscape, preserving some open spaces, and creating dense activity corridors. The new town of Columbia took a quite different approach, and I turn to it in the next chapter.

Chapter 3

Columbia

In the 1950s, James (Jim) Rouse pioneered the speculative air-conditioned shopping mall. In the 1970s and 1980s, Rouse developed the first festival marketplaces. Both of these innovations in shopping center development were highly popular and very profitable and because of this were replicated enough to reshape urban areas across the United States. Malls created a new community focus for suburban areas. Festival marketplaces like the Rouse Company's Faneuil Hall Marketplace in Boston, Baltimore's Inner Harbor, and South Street Seaport in New York became models for center-city retail. In the civic arena, Rouse was also a key player in national debates about urban issues in the 1950s, one of the people credited with inventing the term *urban renewal*. In the 1980s, Rouse created the Enterprise Foundation to foster work on housing and community development in low-income areas (Gillette 1999).

Columbia was Rouse's project of the 1960s and 1970s, coming after his work on urban renewal and malls and before his festival marketplaces and the Enterprise Foundation.[1] It was meant to do good, creating a "garden for people" as an antidote to out-of-scale cities and suburban sprawl. However, touted early on as "the next America," it was not meant to be merely one of Rouse's civic activities. Rather, Columbia was supposed to be profitable enough that less visionary developers would want to copy the concept, changing the character of suburban development more generally. Rouse employed many experts on the development and used it as a basis for a formal education program about new towns that was run through a subsidiary established in 1968, the American City Corporation.[2] Rouse publicized its principles widely, and in the 1960s and 1970s Columbia's planning attracted more attention than the other two case study developments did. It was frequently mentioned in popular books and articles, research studies, and government inquiries. In spite of this, it was not as profitable as Rouse had hoped, and it was not replicated.

Like Irvine, Columbia went through several phases. When people talked to me about Columbia, the phase of their involvement mattered more than in the other developments (see table 4). The first two periods, in a ten-year window from the early 1960s to the early 1970s, were so intense, innovative, and inspirational that those working on the project often experienced fundamental changes in their lives. Certainly, there was something of this atmosphere in The Woodlands, but as many of the professionals there had come from Columbia, they were experiencing it for a second time. In addition, residents in Columbia in the early years were uniquely caught up in the atmosphere of innovation in a way that was not paralleled in the other case study new communities.

Phase 1: Early Camelot, 1962 to 1967: This is the period when the land was bought for Columbia, the basic concept developed, and the project officially opened. It was a time of secret land deals, skillful work at gaining approvals, innovative planning, and a hothouse atmosphere at the Rouse Company.

Phase 2: High Camelot, 1967 to the early 1970s: In the early years of Columbia the Rouse Company was still innovating and expanding its planning and design staff. Rouse made a number of high-stakes decisions, including taking on huge debt to attract a large General Electric facility. This period came to an end with the departure of many key personnel to The Woodlands and other developments and the property crash of the early 1970s, which affected the Rouse Company deeply and led to dramatic downsizing. Until the downturn, the development was selling well and gaining extraordinary publicity.

Phase 3: Community building, early 1970s until Rouse's retirement in 1979: In the middle and late 1970s, the Rouse Company struggled back from the recession, and Columbia became large enough to demonstrate some of the community-building features that Rouse and his development team had devised. At this time the unincorporated Columbia started to have a significant influence on county politics.

Phase 4: Consolidation, 1980 onward: In 1985 the Rouse Company bought out its long-term lender, Connecticut General, to own Columbia. The company continued Columbia's plan much as it had been first approved, although with some modifications responding to market demands, development opportunities, and resident opposition to development. The Rouse Company planning staff decreased in size over the years, and by the 2000s it was minimal. At the same time the Columbia Association—which develops and maintains parks and open spaces and provides other community services— matured, having become wholly controlled by the residents in 1982.

TABLE 4 Columbia Timeline

Date	General Events	Villages/Facilities Opening
1914	James Rouse born	
1956	Rouse Company goes public	
1958	Harundale enclosed shopping mall	
1961	Rouse starts investigating the possibility of developing a new town in Maryland	
1963	October 29: Rouse reveals that he has been assembling land for Columbia	
1963–64	Work group meets; initial planning done	
1964	November 11: plan presented to county commissioners	
1965	Columbia plan approved by county in July	
	Columbia refinanced by Connecticut General, Chase Manhattan, and Teachers Insurance and Annuity Association	
1966	Construction begins on Columbia	
1967	Columbia's first homes on sale, July	Wilde Lake
1968	American City Corporation started	
1969	Interfaith Housing Corporation breaks ground on 300 units of section 221d3 FHA housing	Oakland Mills Village Center
1971		Long Reach, Mall in Columbia, Harper's Choice Village Center
Early 1970s	Economic downturn affects Columbia	
1974		Long Reach Village Center, Owen Brown Village Center
1979	Rouse retires	
1982	Columbia Association—full resident control	
1985	Rouse Company buys back Columbia from Connecticut General/CIGNA	
1986		King's Contrivance Village Center
1989		Dorsey's Search Village Center
1992		Hickory Ridge Village Center
1998		River Hill Village Center

SOURCES: Breckenfeld 1971; Tennenbaum 1996a; Rouse Company 2002, n.d.
NOTE: For some villages I could find the date of the village opening and for others only the date of the village center opening. For Long Reach, I show both.

BACKGROUND TO THE DEVELOPMENT:
JAMES ROUSE AS A PERSON

Rouse's biography is important because of Columbia's strong identification with the developer.[3] Certainly many people worked on the project and influenced its character, but they were attracted to Rouse as a person and to his ideas about development. Even though he owned only a small part of the Rouse Company and its various subsidiaries, he was a strong moral force, particularly during the 1960s. He was charismatic and had a capacity to make many people feel as if he represented their own aspirations, even if those aspirations were quite diverse.

Rouse was born in 1914 and grew up near Easton, Maryland, in the Eastern Shore area of the Chesapeake Bay. In the 1920s Easton's population was approximately forty-five hundred, and it grew only slowly in subsequent decades. Rouse's father was a broker of canned foods, and James and his brother, Willard, who later joined James in the Rouse Company, generally had a comfortable childhood. It was a somewhat special place—both an agricultural and fishing area and a retirement location for the affluent. Politically it was conservative. The Rouse's own home was large, with a two-acre garden, and the young Rouses made pocket money selling vegetables (Breckenfeld 1971, 201–2). These details are important because Rouse was trying to evoke some of this small-town feeling in Columbia.

In 1934, Rouse started work in the Baltimore office of the Federal Housing Administration but then left for the private sector, working under Guy Hollyday, who later became FHA commissioner in the Eisenhower administration. He earned his law degree in 1937. In 1939 he started his own mortgage banking business in Baltimore (Breckenfeld 1971, 202–3; Gillette 1999).

Rouse became involved with civic activities after the war, initially at a local level in several Baltimore organizations. When Hollyday became FHA commissioner, these activities expanded to the national level. He was named chairman of the Subcommittee on Rehabilitation, Redevelopment, and Conservation of the President's Advisory Committee on Government Housing Policies and Programs, a group that had input into the urban renewal section of the 1954 Housing Act. He helped found the Greater Baltimore Committee, a business group that promoted urban renewal and provided the energy behind the multimillion-dollar Charles Center urban renewal program in downtown Baltimore. In 1961 he was chair of the subcommittee that drafted successful legislation to create a metropolitan planning agency for Baltimore. Nationally in 1954 he helped found ACTION, Inc., the American Council to Improve Our Neighborhoods, a business group that lobbied for urban renewal and included the publishers of *Time* and the *Washington Post* (Gelfand 1975, 280). In the early 1950s he was even Maryland president of the United World Federalists, a group proposing a single world government. These were all valuable civic activities, showing Rouse's concern with public issues, but with the exception of the Charles Center this activity did not produce much built work (Anderson 1964; Breckenfeld 1971, 205–9; Gillette 1999).

Rouse had, however, been successful in business as a mortgage banker. In the late 1940s he also started to develop shopping centers. In 1958 he opened Harundale Mall near Baltimore, only the second mall in the United States to be enclosed and air-conditioned. Southdale, in Minneapolis, had opened a few months earlier but was not as influential as Rouse's development because it was developed by a large department store chain that could afford to lose money on its building. Harundale showed that enclosed malls could be built speculatively and be profitable as well as prestigious (Breckenfeld 1971, 213). Rouse continued to develop shopping malls, increasingly seeing them as a new form of community center for suburban areas (Rouse 1963b). In 1957, Rouse founded the Community Research and Development Corporation (CRD), with 30 percent of its stock owned by the Rouse Company. Until starting on Columbia, the organization built shopping malls and a sixty-eight-acre mixed-use development called Cross Keys, which became the location of the Rouse Company offices for a period (Eichler and Kaplan 1967, 56–57; Gillette 1999). In 1967, the year Columbia opened, three-quarters of the Rouse Company's revenues came from real estate, primarily shopping centers, and only one-quarter from mortgage banking (Breckenfeld 1971, 218).

By the 1960s, after his professional and civic activities in the area of urban development and redevelopment, Rouse had become very disillusioned with the then-prevalent architectural and physical approach of planning. He thought it was inhumane, and he wanted urban development to promote human growth and values, such as lifelong learning, participation, and the mixing of diverse populations. Rouse thought that the scale of U.S. cities in the 1960s was too large and that it promoted "loneliness, irresponsibility, and superficial values" (Rouse 1963a). He was also disappointed with the outward spread of urban areas in a sprawling pattern of development and made a number of speeches and presentations on the issue. However, James Rouse saw the need not just to critique the conditions of the day but also to create an alternative to both unplanned suburban development and inner-city housing. Such a development could both provide opportunities for many different kinds of people to leave the urban areas that had become obsolete and also create a model for in turn revitalizing the older cities.

Behind the scenes Libby Rouse, Jim Rouse's wife for more than three decades up to the 1970s, has also written about her dissatisfaction with the isolation and inefficiency of her own suburban life of the 1950s and early 1960s (L. Rouse 1977). This made her particularly interested in the design of environments to be more supportive of families and cultural development. Libby and James Rouse discussed urban issues on their first date—Libby had just read a work of Mumford's on the city (L. Rouse 1977; Breckenfeld 1971, 196).

By what seems to have been the early 1960s, Libby Rouse was able to critique her personal version of the feminine mystique and imagine alternatives, as she recounted in a talk given in 1977:

> In asking what would Jesus want for the family, I'd muse upon such notions as: Would He want it lonely, bored, driving everywhere? No, He would want families close to one another, more like early tribes or clans. He would want them to be in small communities, so they could be more loving, sharing warmth and friendships, and support of one another. He would want each individual to grow to his fullest. . . . It was out of all this searching for answers, "What would Jesus want for families" that the design of small residential communities (now cul-de-sacs in Columbia) came to be dreamed of in my head. (L. Rouse 1977, 5–6)

The Christian language may make this sound conservative, and her approach is very oriented toward the family, but in fact Libby Rouse's position was not so easy to categorize.[4]

Like Libby Rouse, James Rouse was also a very committed Christian. While he did not talk about his faith in quite the manner of Libby Rouse above, he did, for instance, host the series of Lenten Lunches at the Rouse Company, to talk about life, work, and faith. In 1970 this series was held in Columbia for the first time and featured the five young male "ministers" currently in Columbia and one woman, Mary Cosby (Rouse 1970). Initially Presbyterian, the Rouses were members of a very small congregation, the Church of the Savior, based in Washington, D.C. This group was founded in 1947 by Gordon Cosby (husband of Mary Cosby), formerly a Baptist, and emphasized service as a core value. After Columbia was built, a branch of this group was established in Columbia, the Kittamaqundi Community (Kittamaqundi Community 2002). This was such a strong part of Rouse's life that a number of employees went along to services to understand what made Rouse tick. Rouse certainly seemed to have a special vision, and people were intensely attracted to it and tried to understand it. Eventually contacts with the Church of the Savior offshoot, Jubilee Housing, inspired James and his second wife, Patti, to found the Enterprise Foundation (P. Rouse 2001). It was this set of ideas that also started Rouse on the path toward developing Columbia.

PHASE 1: EARLY CAMELOT, 1962 TO 1967

The First Steps:
Land Purchase, Planning, and Approvals

In 1961 Rouse started looking for land to develop as a new town, surveying land in Howard and Charles counties in Maryland via helicopter. This was a much different process from Irvine, where the land was already held by the Irvine Company. While a large tract of land was available in Charles County, Howard County seemed to have more potential, as it lay in the development paths of both Baltimore and Washington, D.C. One of the board members of Community Research and Development was from Howard County and was active in advocating the location.

Howard County was at that time still rural. Ellicott City, its county seat, had a population of eight hundred, and the overall population of the county in 1960 was about thirty-six thousand. However, growth was accelerating in the 1950s, and some large research and development plants had been built close to where Columbia was to be eventually located (Eichler and Kaplan 1967, 57; Breckenfeld 1971, 224–27). An interstate, I-95, was under construction. Close to the Columbia site although outside Howard County were a number of federal facilities, including the National Security Agency, Fort Meade, and the Social Security Administration.

In May 1962, Rouse started to acquire land in Howard County. He made some initial estimates of costs for a twelve-thousand-acre development: eighteen million dollars for the land, forty-two million dollars for the entire project stretched out over twelve years, and a pretax profit of sixty-seven million dollars (CRD 1962; Breckenfeld 1971, 226–28, 232).

He found financing from Connecticut General Life Insurance Company, which had already financed seven Rouse projects over a two-decade period. The Village of Wilde Lake in Columbia is named after Frazier Wilde, the chairman of Connecticut General. Connecticut General supplied an $18 million loan, later increased to $23.5 million.[5] The loan went to a newly created Howard Research and Development Corporation (HRD), jointly owned by Rouse's Community Research and Development and Connecticut General, which split the profits, although the stock held by CRD was "pledged" to Connecticut General (Eichler and Kaplan 1967, 59; Yankee discipline 1969/1970). The initial deal was a complicated one, but essentially the Rouse organization had a contract for fifteen years to run HRD, while Connecticut General supplied most of the money and controlled the majority of the board, three of the five directors. There was an agreement that if the Rouse Company could not come up with a plan that Connecticut General liked, then Connecticut General had several options for buying out the Rouse Company, all involving the Rouse Company's losing money that it had paid for planning and other start-up costs. Connecticut General also put a cap on the purchase price of land. This was the largest single investment that Connecticut General had made. They held it for two decades but pulled out before Columbia started earning significant profits (Rouse Company 1970, 24; Breckenfeld 1971, 229, 230, 305–6). This shows some of the financial complexity of such large projects.

The Rouse team figured out a zone of about twenty-five thousand acres within which they would purchase land; this involved about six hundred landowners, none with more than one thousand acres (Breckenfeld 1971, 231; Eichler and Kaplan 1967, 60–61; Moxley 1996; Jones 2000). John M. (Jack) Jones, then a young lawyer from Rouse's Baltimore law firm of Piper Marbury, coordinated the land purchases, negotiating sales in widely different locations, initially using six different realtors within the overall purchase zone, trying to keep prices from escalating. Purchases proceeded slowly in 1962 but speeded up significantly in early 1963 after Connecticut General agreed to the loan. In order to disguise the source of the funding, money was funneled in multiple transactions through bank accounts held by six dummy corporations and even through a personal check account held by Jack Jones. All files about the transactions were kept in an unmarked locked office with only three keys (Breckenfeld 1971, 232–34, 236). This kind of intrigue captivated a number of those writing about the development, just as some of the Irvine family fights did for that project.

Eventually—after nine months—Rouse, or more specifically HRD, assembled 15,500 acres from 164 holdings for almost $23 million. This was by no means a contiguous development; there were numerous window or outparcel areas, including existing subdivisions and farms. The Rouse Company has bought some of them over the years; for example, it has purchased commercial areas along Route 29, a highway between Washington and Columbia that goes through the center of Columbia, demolishing buildings to create a parkway. However, Columbia still resembles a Swiss cheese with many non-Columbia holdings within the general Columbia area (Breckenfeld 1971, 242, 262).

Planning and the Work Group

A number of versions of Columbia's planning and development aims were circulated, but they generally included four main elements: (1) creating a complete city with enough jobs for its residents and big enough to support urban amenities such as a college, concert halls, bookstores, and automobile dealers; (2) respecting the land; (3) creating an environment where people could grow; and (4) making a profit (Hamilton 1964h; Hoppenfeld 1967; Breckenfeld 1971, 180–83; J. Rouse 1977; Master builder 1966). Other accounts added such aims as not creating a tax burden on Howard County, setting high standards for design, promoting housing choice, and fostering community interaction (CRD 1964b, 3; CRD 1964c; Hoppenfeld 1963a). While Rouse was undoubtedly sincere in his ideas about creating a place where people could grow, and that vision was the central motivation for many of those who joined the development team, the quest for profits was also undeniable. As Breckenfeld explains in one of the more promotional accounts of Columbia: "In pursuit of his promethean objective, Rouse combines the zeal of a missionary, the vision of a prophet, and the icy cal-culation of a cost accountant." He goes on to say, "The surest way to make the American city what it ought to be is to demonstrate that it is enormously profitable to do it a better way" (Breckenfeld 1971, 169, 172). While some people recalled Rouse as not being concerned enough with the costs of de-velopment,[6] it is also important to note that Columbia became well known in planning and development circles for two different contributions. These were the "Columbia concept" of racial and economic integration and the "Columbia model" or the "economic model," a form of real estate pro forma that projected costs, revenues, and profits for the development on the basis of different land use alternatives.

Planner William (Bill) Finley joined Rouse in late 1962 as project direc-tor for Columbia (CRD 1964c). He had been chief author of Washington's famous 1961 "Plan for the Year 2000" and staff director of the National Capital Planning Commission (NCPC). He in turn hired Morton (Mort) Hoppenfeld, who had been chief urban designer at the NCPC and had worked under Edmund Bacon in Philadelphia, to become director of ur-ban design at Columbia (Hoppenfeld 1961). Both had Berkeley planning degrees, but Finley had started in architecture with Ray Watson of Irvine. Finley played a key role bridging between those involved with design, project management, and financial issues. Robert Tennenbaum also worked at the NCPC briefly and came on board in the planning team as an architect planner (Anderson 1964; Hamilton 1964i; Tennenbaum 1996b, 33; Fin-ley 1996).

Perhaps the most well-publicized innovation in Columbia's early planning process was having a core team of fourteen outside experts and four people from the Rouse Company work through the social planning of the area with the support of other staff and consultants. This team of social experts, a "so-cial planning work group," was to provide social input to the physical plan-ning staff (Hoppenfeld 1963b, 1967, 1971; Michael 1996). They came on board about a year after Finley had started work and just after the develop-ment had been announced to the public. At that stage the land was largely bought, and preliminary site and marketing information was available. Rouse had of course already articulated a position on urban development in a series of talks and papers that he had given in the previous years. The most notable of these was a talk on metropolitan growth given at UC Berke-ley in September 1963 (Rouse 1963a; Hamilton 1964i).

The work group was selected from a number of sources. Some were people that the lead consultant, Donald Michael, knew through his contacts at the Institute for Policy Studies in Washington, D.C. Others seem to have been associated with the Space Cadets, a network of people interested in issues of urbanization, coordinated by work group member Leonard Duhl at the Na-tional Institutes of Mental Health in the 1950s and 1960s (Duhl 1963, 1999).

Only a couple of the group members came from outside the Washington, Baltimore, and Philadelphia areas. This quote from Bill Finley, in a journalistic account, gives the public face of the decision: "'Our first thought,' says Finley, 'was to bring in the senior citizens of the behavioral sciences in America. However, we soon found that we could read pretty much what they had to say. We were anxious for the planning of this town to come from unfrozen minds. So we assembled a rather distinguished group of relatively unknown names in a wide variety of fields'" (quoted in Breckenfeld 1971, 251). The work group included the following people.

1. Donald Michael, the chair of the group and a social psychologist, was then at the Institute for Policy Studies and later at the University of Michigan. A prolific author, he was interested in the systems approach that examined interconnections among issues and phenomena and also worked on various topics to do with social and technological change.
2. Henry Bain was a Washington political consultant who had already worked for Rouse in examining how acceptable Columbia would be in Howard County.
3. Antonia Handler Chayes, the expert on family life and women and the only woman in the work group, had been the technical secretary to the Committee on Education for the President's Commission on the Status of Women. She went on to become a top government administrator— both assistant secretary and undersecretary for the Air Force. During the early 1960s she was part of a Washington power couple—married to Abram Chayes, then a legal adviser in the U.S. Department of State in the Kennedy administration and later a Harvard law professor. She became active in conflict resolution; I had to fit in my 2001 interview around her work trips to the Balkans.
4. Robert Crawford was commissioner of recreation for Philadelphia.
5. Leonard Duhl, from the National Institute of Mental Health, was coordinator of the Space Cadets network and later a professor at Berkeley. He went on to develop the idea of Healthy Cities, which was eventually adopted by the World Health Organization (Duhl 1999).
6. Nelson Foote was a sociologist and manager of the consumer and public relations research program at General Electric and later a professor of sociology at Hunter College.
7. Herbert Gans, a sociologist, had finished both his first book, *The Urban Villagers* (1962), and his fieldwork for *The Levittowners* (1967). He moved from the University of Pennsylvania to Columbia University in the middle of 1964.
8. Robert Gladstone ran an economics and market research firm in Washington.
9. Christopher Jencks, then education editor of the *New Republic* and at

the Institute for Policy Studies, later became a professor at Harvard's Kennedy School of Government.

10. Paul Lemkau taught public health and psychiatry at Johns Hopkins.
11. Chester Rapkin taught planning at the University of Pennsylvania and was the author of a large number of books and reports on land taxation and racial issues in planning. Rapkin was the person who invented the term *SoHo* for south of Houston in Manhattan.
12. Wayne Thompson was city manager of Oakland, California.
13. Alan Voorhees had founded his own transportation planning firm in 1961. It grew to be one of the largest in the world, and he also became the dean of engineering at the University of Illinois at Chicago.
14. Stephen Withey taught psychology at the University of Michigan and was a specialist in communication.[7]

The work group first met in November 1963, only two weeks after Rouse had announced the development. They met every two to four weeks for about six months to the middle of 1964, during a period of intense physical planning. This was also the period of a sophisticated publicity campaign to get Howard County to agree to the needed rezoning (Michael 1996; Tennenbaum 1996b). The work group members produced working papers on various issues, and by July 1964 Donald Michael had integrated them into a thick internal draft report document, "Recommendations for the Social Planning of Columbia: Physical Facilities and Social Organization. Abstracted and extended from the deliberations of the CRD Social Planning Work Group" (Michael 1964). Also, numerous internal memoranda were exchanged among staff in the Rouse Company, including the ones written by staff member Wallace Hamilton as part of a projected history of the project.[8] A few work group members also did more intensive ongoing consulting with Rouse.

Many people writing about Columbia have done what I have just done, outlining the composition and activities of the work group as a matter of some interest (e.g., Breckenfeld 1971; Hoppenfeld 1967; CRD 1964e). However, a number of different opinions exist about the importance of the work group. It was well publicized and is a major part of all accounts of the development. Rouse saw of group of its type as something to be replicated in other developments and promoted it as an idea. However, it should be emphasized that the work group met only for a few days every two weeks for a few months.[9] It was made clear to them at the time that *"precise or vague as your recommendations are, the final decision necessarily will be ours, the developer's, as to whether or not to use them and to what extent"* (Hoppenfeld 1963b, 5, emphasis in original). When I interviewed some of the members almost four decades later, after extremely successful lives in varied fields, they groped to remember details about the sessions apart from a wonderful atmosphere of debate that ended up with much disagreement and relatively meager amounts of specific guidance. Documents prepared for and about the work group and from the files of Herbert Gans and the Columbia Archives certainly show an exciting capacity to question assumptions about urban development.

One interpretation is that the work group was most important in educating Rouse and some of his very early staff, rather than in creating a specific social plan. This education involved a fairly wide-ranging discussion from a group of people who were either well read or had significant practical experience. As Herbert Gans recounted, Rouse "didn't say much. We didn't know what he wanted. It really went all over the place. . . . I don't think we were inhibited by Jim in any way" (Gans 2001). Ideas from these discussions certainly made their way into the planning. For instance, out of the work group's activity came specific ideas about how to foster education and learning as a central focus for the development. The work group also articulated some ideas such as smaller secondary schools, clustering of commercial and civic facilities, a minibus system that was run for a number of years by the Columbia Association, and providing comprehensive health care in what became an early HMO. As I explain below and in chapter 5, the work group also gave fairly specific advice on how to achieve racial and economic mix. The group's idea for a "kings representative," or ombudsperson, to mediate between residents and developer, can be seen in the village associations (Michael 1964). Some ideas were not taken up, including the possibility of a separate school district for Columbia. Overall, the ideas of the work group did have some effect on the form of the villages, neighborhoods, and institutions developed in Columbia (Hoppenfeld 1971). However, as a whole the physical plans still look remarkably like a cross between the neighborhood units that the planning staff knew about from their professional world and the small town that Rouse wanted to evoke.

Apart from their role in educating the Rouse team, perhaps the work group's major role was in being a touchstone for both marketing and subsequent planning. Rouse Company employees who were not centrally involved with early planning talked to me about "work group principles" that were really early planning ideas culled from a variety of sources. Len Ivins, the twelfth person to be hired on the Columbia team, described learning about the work group only through "osmosis" (Ivins 2002). Rouse and other early planners certainly held up the broad ideas of the work group as a source of principles to guide innovative development, even when these were sometimes quite expensive principles to implement. The group was also used in marketing to help attract people to the development who were interested in social issues and who kept such debates alive in a maturing Columbia.

A compelling description of the contribution of the team came in an anecdote from Irvine's Ray Watson, who in his later work on the board of the Disney Corporation brought Jim Rouse to a workshop. "I said to Jim: 'I know of all those consultants you brought in to solve all these problems, all the meetings that happened. What did you get out of that?' And he gave a great answer: 'Rays of light'" (Watson 1999). While this sounds like Rouse's reflection after many years, the idea of rays or shafts of light was used at the time of the work group, as in this quote from a letter from Rouse to Herbert Gans, who had complained about the work group meeting for such a short period: "As to the future, we regard the work group as such an intimate part of our planning process and such a rich source of knowledge and inspiration for our work in Columbia, that we know we will be seeking your 'shafts of light' periodically as the development process moves forward—and we will do our best to keep you fully informed about our progress" (Rouse 1964).

Major Planning Concepts in "the Next America"

Whether or not the work group changed Rouse's mind, they interacted with him over a number of issues. Particularly important were racial and economic mix, the village concept, and the role of education. The Rouse team also developed ideas from examining other new towns, and these also fed into the overall planning concept. Marketed as "the Next America," Columbia was presented as having solutions to many pressing issues.

Racial and Economic Mix.   One of the ideas that particularly interested Rouse was the concept of socially balanced, or socially mixed, communities. This is the idea of planning locations so that they contain a diversity of important social characteristics, including class or income group, age, family structure, tenure, ethnicity, or race. Proponents of social mix have attributed to it a wide variety of aims, many of which are contradictory. These include improving city functioning, aesthetics, and neighborhood stability; raising "standards of the lower classes"; providing equality of opportunity and cultural cross-fertilization; promoting "social harmony by reducing social and racial tensions," and "promoting social conflict in order to foster individual and social maturity" (Sarkissian 1976, 231, 232; Gans 1961a). Social mix has been an important part of a number of experimental communities.

In the United States, suburbanization has involved many of those with some wealth leaving the center cities. This has created what are perceived to be homogeneously poor cities and homogeneously better-off suburbs. Recent scholarship has shown that suburban areas have never been quite as homogeneous as this image indicates, but it is undeniable that there have been many subdivisions with quite uniform price levels (Harris 1999). During the 1960s and early 1970s, commentators such as Richard Sennett argued that this wealth and mobility "opened up an avenue by which men can easily conceive of their social relatedness in terms of their similarity rather than their need for each other" (Sennett 1970, 49). James Rouse made counteracting this trend toward homogeneity and promoting economic and racial forms of social mix a centerpiece of the Columbia project. It was the core of the "Columbia concept."

Once it was decided to promote mix, one of the key issues that Columbia's planning had to deal with was the scale of mix: how finely should each social characteristic be mixed? On one hand was a desire to give each group similar locational opportunities, and on the other was a desire for people to get to know their neighbors, which required that they have some important dimensions in common. In the absence of any conclusive empirical evidence about the best scale of mix, the practice has been to balance tendencies to "ghettoization" with the problems of "dividing and conquering." In Columbia, Gans proposed that racial mix was to be at a fine grain, at the house level, but economic mix was to be a bit more lumpy, at the block level. This reflected his earlier published work that found that some homogeneity of interests and values was needed for friendly neighboring and cast doubt on residential mix as the best method for improving the lot of low-income populations (Gans 1961a, 1961b). Presumably similar incomes would mean similar educational levels, which would make common interests and values more likely. This approach was then transferred to The Woodlands, which adopted approximately the same system.

In practice, social mix is hard to maintain. People move to avoid conflict or to find the best location (which also happens to be the best location for others who share their social characteristics). Prices in popular areas escalate, excluding the bottom of the market. However, Columbia did build in mechanisms for maintaining some forms of mix, such as the variety of housing sizes and types within villages. These are strategies still promoted by groups such as the new urbanists.[10]

Village Concept.   The Rouse team overlaid the idea of mix with the concept of the village. While one of the aims of Columbia was that it be big enough as a whole to provide a comprehensive range of services, Rouse and his planners thought that the entire development was too big to be the basic unit of daily life. Obviously this was not a unique dilemma, but the Columbia solution uniquely reflected Rouse's personal intuitions about good social environments. Recalling the work group process, one of the early Columbia planners explained:

> It was an interesting process. But the bottom line is, Jim [Rouse] knew what he wanted. He wanted the town to be made up of villages, much like the village he grew up in, on the eastern shore. We felt that was a charming idea and a nice way of organizing the town in phases for construction. . . . We're planners, so we had to organize it somehow, and that was a convenient way to do it.
>
> He wanted the small-town feel, people to know each other, people going to the supermarket and recognizing each other, knowing the person that bagged the groceries and meeting your rabbi or minister at the supermarket. . . .

That was the ideal, and that was a very romantic kind of image, which actually happened, particularly in the village centers. It still happens, probably more so than in other suburban areas, or anywhere else. So that worked out very well, this interaction of people that before one only met on a professional, formal level. Suddenly you're sitting next to them in the barber shop or standing in line at the bank. But how to make that happen? . . . He didn't know how to do it. That was the purpose of the work group. The big question was, how big should the cul-de-sacs be? How many families could reasonably form a sub-community? Is a cul-de-sac of 50 houses too big? Probably. The discussions led to an ideal of eight, eight to ten, something like that. The next question is . . . who should live there? Should it be people with homogeneous kinds of lifestyles and incomes, or should we just open it up? We focused more on homogeneous, because it would anyway be defined by home prices. If everyone can afford an x-price house in the cul-de-sac, they're going to be reasonably compatible. (Tennenbaum 2000)

The number of villages has fluctuated over time. A 1964 document presenting Columbia to the county listed ten villages; it was reduced to seven by the early 1970s and then increased again (CRD 1964c; Village Center 1966). The Village of Dorsey's Search was added adjacent to Columbia but outside the new town zoning area. In the most recent version of the Columbia Association's organization, there are nine primarily residential villages, and the mixed-use town center forms the tenth village.

Education.   In a garden for growing people, education plays an important role (Hamilton 1964g). This role is not confined to schools but pertains much more broadly to personal development.

The various units (neighborhoods, villages) were organized around schools, designed so that children of all ages could walk to school. High schools and middle schools were in the village centers. Village size was set at approximately thirty-five hundred families. At the time this number equaled about twelve thousand people and was selected because it was close to the population needed to support both a high school and a reasonable supermarket as well as a variety of specialty stores such as a barber, restaurant, drugstore, and hardware store (Hamilton 1964i). As one of the early Columbia planners explained: "One of the great moments was when we realized that the catchment for a supermarket back in the sixties was about 15,000, 20,000 people, and that was the same for a high school. That was a great moment. We pinned it up on the wall. It wasn't so much true of the middle school. So, there's no purity" (Tennenbaum 2000).

Many innovations were proposed for Columbia. Some concepts, such as "open" schools, were independent of the physical plan, although the design of the school buildings was affected. Other policy proposals, such as having smaller schools than was typical of the period, were intimately linked with the overall design of the development. As part of the Howard County School District, the Columbia team needed to negotiate these changes with the county, making the overall approach more regional. However, the issue of education was larger than fitting schools into villages and neighborhoods; it involved a far broader concept of a community of learning, with adult education playing a key part. A number of the work group papers dealt with issues of continuing education and lifelong learning (Chayes 1964; Jencks 1964; Ephross 1988). I return to this issue later in the chapter.

Ideas from Existing New Towns.   Of course, Rouse and his development team also drew on other ideas taken from the tradition of new town development, particularly European examples. Rouse's professional life and civic activities had given him a number of ideas about the development process that he was able to draw on. He was also obviously deeply concerned about issues of ethics and values. In addition, Rouse, like almost all the new town developers, made the trek to Europe and looked at major examples of older urban environments and more recent new towns. Rouse took such a trip in the middle of 1963 with Mort Hoppenfeld and Libby Rouse (Hamilton 1964i, 2). On that trip Hoppenfeld was intrigued by Copenhagen's Tivoli Gardens, a smaller version of which was for some time planned to be built in downtown Columbia. Neither Jim Rouse nor Hoppenfeld liked the aesthetics of the British new towns; but Hoppenfeld found the Swedish Vallingby and Farsta near Stockholm to be more attractive, integrated with their forested surroundings (Breckenfeld 1971, 256–57).

Mort Hoppenfeld was also inspired by Finland's small new town, Tapiola, close to Helsinki (Tennenbaum 2000). Started in 1952, it was one of the very few private new towns in Europe, although it was developed on a nonprofit basis, supported by welfare agencies and a trade union. Tapiola was planned for seventeen thousand people on 670 acres (twenty-six people per acre). As such, it was quite small—comparable to many of the villages within the three case study developments. Its architecture was modern, but its design was based on neighborhoods where mothers could walk to shopping; roads were separated from bicycle and pedestrian paths; and the whole atmosphere was wooded (Breckenfeld 1971, 94–96). Some of this concept found its way to Columbia.

Overall Physical Concept

Armed with these aims and ideas, Rouse's planners faced a development area of streams, forests, open agricultural lands, and significant window areas. Given their image of the small town, this led to a plan that was conceptually a series of distinct villages, composed of neighborhoods and separated by landforms, vegetation, and parcels of land owned by others. The ideas about social planning were partly integrated with this physical structure, although the same physical form could have supported a number of social arrangements.

Villages, like small towns, would each provide a range of housing options for people from various walks of life. Higher-density housing would be clustered closer to the village centers, partly because it was believed that people in such units would have a lower level of car ownership. This drew on ideas from the social planning work group as well as the garden city tradition and the neighborhood unit. One of the planners explained: "We went up to Radburn, and I had Radburn pinned up on the wall. We were familiar with the Perry neighborhood concept from school, so we knew all about the neighborhood unit" (Tennenbaum 2000).

The village centers were innovative and departed from the classic neighborhood unit in combining commercial areas with recreational facilities such as swimming pools, civic facilities such as community rooms and interfaith centers, and middle and high schools (see figures 19–22). Some facilities—such as an indoor swimming pool or an art center, which could not be supported by a single village—were nevertheless distributed to different village centers, which were then seen as having a particular flavor or specialty. Such centers were close to a new urbanist main street in program, although pulled into a loose cluster arrangement. In early publicity, the image was that of a town square (CRD 1964b, 7; Rouse Company 1966, 17).

As built, the village centers are more spread out, taking the form of a campus rather than a town square. A significant mix of uses still exists, although in many village centers this mix is not at all obvious because the buildings are at some distance from one another, separated by open space and parking and entered from different streets or along different driveways.

The early village centers often included a courtyard area, a much reduced version of the town square, around which were arranged shops and some community rooms. The central shopping areas in later villages have become more linear, closer to mainstream shopping center design. Renovations of centers have also tended to reconfigure courtyard centers into something more linear.[11] Some commentators see this as a real departure from the initial concept (Levinson 2003). In my opinion, outdoor seating, whether it is in a courtyard or along the face of the building, is a fairly minor aspect of the basic structure of a shopping center surrounded by parking. Overall, however, the village centers do have an innovative mix of uses. In many, the civic facilities, such as village association meeting rooms, are well integrated into the core shopping area. I consider the centers to be one of the successes of the Columbia plan. In comparison, in the Irvine Ranch and The Woodlands, offices are often located in with the village centers but without the range of civic space.

Villages were not the only planning unit; each was made up of a small number of *neighborhoods* (Michael 1964, C-1). For planners this is confusing terminology, as these neighborhoods were much smaller than the classic neighborhood unit, itself more comparable to the village. Each neighborhood was to be centered on an elementary school and contain a convenience store, envisaged as locally owned and with a strong social role. However, the structure of Columbia had a specific character, with each early neighborhood diagrammed as a loop road with culs-de-sac branching off that road and multiple neighborhoods clustered around a larger loop road encircling the village center. This village layout resembles a four-, five-, or six-leafed clover, with each neighborhood being a leaf attached to the village center at the core (see figure 21). It is a logical layout when diagrammed, although not so obvious once laid across a landscape. It is quite different conceptually from Irvine's districts.

Not all the neighborhood schools have survived the maturing of the development. Fewer yet of the neighborhood stores that were envisaged as centers of neighborhood life have survived, although many of the buildings have been converted to other uses, such as child care centers.

In addition to the residential villages and neighborhoods, the whole town of Columbia was to have a center. The town center was planned to have a college, hospital, office buildings, community center, high-density apartments, restaurants, theaters, inns, a music pavilion, a lake, and a regional shopping center serving a population from far beyond Columbia (Breckenfeld 1971, 259). Eventually all these things were built. It was originally called a downtown, as the Rouse team saw themselves as creating a new city. Early marketing included images of what appear to be urban universities and center-city plazas. However, "town center" became more marketable in suburbia (Rouse Company 1966). It has two centerpieces: a mall and a lakefront. Like the village centers, the functions of Columbia's town center are spread out, and one does not comprehend them all at once.

The Mall in Columbia, opened in 1971, is an enclosed shopping center and was the largest the Rouse Company had built to that date. Like Fashion Island in Irvine, its early opening was made possible by the surrounding population beyond the new town. Even in the early 1970s, 250,000 people lived within ten miles of Columbia, and 800,000 within 15 miles (Breckenfeld 1971, 301). Although the mall is enclosed, the architects Cope Linder and Wolmsley used a space-frame roofing structure with extensive high-level glazing to create an open-air atmosphere indoors. The Rouse Company had made a significant reputation on indoor malls, so it is unsurprising that the company built one in Columbia. Early diagrams of the town center show the mall oriented on an axis perpendicular to the lake, forming a T-intersection with it. This indicates a stronger connection between the two than has been allowed by the eventual mall axis and location. The mall now runs parallel to the lake and is divided from it by parking garages, a road, and the offices of such

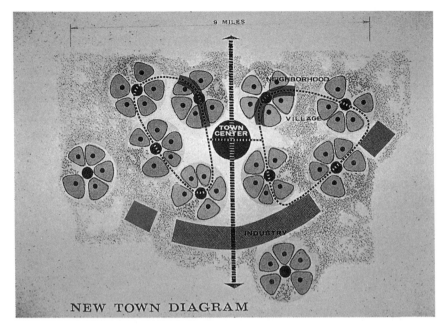

Figure 19. New town, village, and neighborhood concept, Columbia, mid-1960s. Creator: The Rouse Company. Source: Columbia Archives. Reprinted with permission from the Columbia Archives.

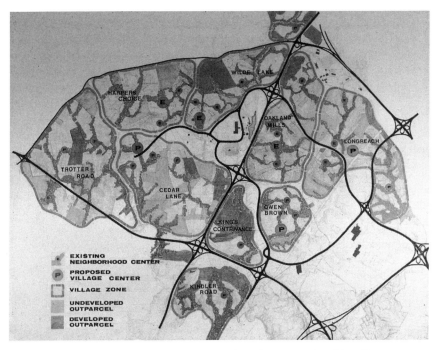

Figure 20. Villages in the landscape, Columbia, circa 1970. Working diagram. Reproduced with permission from Cy Paumier.

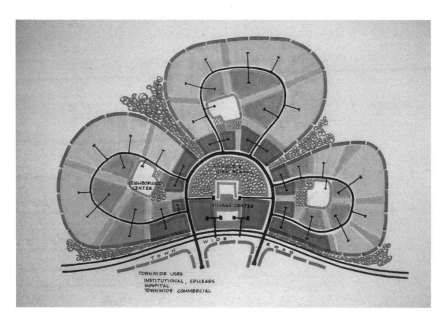

Figure 21. Village concept diagram, Columbia, circa 1970. Reproduced with permission from Cy Paumier.

Figure 22. Wilde Lake Village Center, 1971. Creator: The Rouse Company. Source: Columbia Archives. Reprinted with permission from the Columbia Archives.

organizations as the Rouse Company and the Columbia Association (Plan approved for Village of Wilde Lake 1966, 2).[12] Kevin Lynch, visiting the Rouse Company, also worked with some of the young designers at the company to create a more main-street style alternative, but it was not adopted (Hilderbrandt 2001).

Envisaged for some time as a small-scale Tivoli Gardens, the area around Lake Kittamaqundi is much more low-key and has many fewer visitors than the mall but does provide an attractive open-air gathering space in the town center. While the movie theaters in the area have struggled over the years and were torn down in the early 2000s, the lakefront boasts a number of restaurants, a hotel, and very usable public park space. It is the site of a well-attended summer arts festival and is currently undergoing redevelopment with added offices and high rise condominiums.

The multidisciplinary design firm of Cope Linder and Wolmsley, which had designed the mall, was also responsible for the landscape along the lakefront (Landscape design 1966, 4). This work on both commercial and public or civic space by the same firm is reminiscent of Pereira's involvement in planning and building design for both the Fashion Island/Newport Center area and University of California Irvine. Gehry, Walsh, and O'Malley designed the lakeside exhibit center, the Rouse Company offices, an outdoor concert facility, and the town center fire station. While Columbia never emphasized building design, it nevertheless employed or attracted a number of professionals who became known for high-quality design (Ryder 1976).

The town center, village centers, and neighborhood centers have received a great deal of attention and obviously provide an alternative to the almost random arrangement of shopping, schools, and civic buildings in much suburban sprawl. However, it is interesting to note that in early planning documents these centers were planned to contain a total of 345 acres in commercial (retail) and office uses. However, HRD also proposed an additional 360 acres of commercial and office space in "scattered strategic locations." This additional acreage did not include the allocation of 60 acres for such uses as drive-in banks, auto supply stores, service stations, apparel stores, and drive-in restaurants; 200 acres for a private golf course; and 1,575 acres of industrial land (HRD 1965a, 42–43). This means that the big-box centers developed recently on the edge of Columbia are not quite such a departure from the plan as many would like to think and that the early plans contained quite a large amount of land allocated to opportunistic commercial development.

This physical concept of villages, centers, and "scattered" development had to be fitted into the physical constraints of the site. Plans were circulated in a series of colored folders and were then known as the "green book" or the "red book," depending on the color of the folder. The earliest proposal in the "green book" of 1962 had envisaged five hundred acres of parks and thirty-four hundred acres of low-density greenbelt surrounding the development, a fairly large percentage of open space for the period (CRD 1962; Hamilton 1964i). The early team members were mostly architects with a sincere interest in the landscape that made up for limited training. They worked hard at laying out the development across an underlying rural landscape that was a patchwork of pretty farms, rolling hills, and streams. Early diagrams of the development—before the village structure had been teased out—show green areas along the valleys connecting to the wider network of waterways (Tennenbaum 1996a).[13]

Interestingly, Columbia was being designed at about the same time as Wallace-McHarg's famous 1964 *Plan for the Valleys*. This plan was for a forty-five-thousand-acre section of Baltimore County to the northwest of the city, expected to grow by 110,000 people over forty years (described in McHarg 1969, 79–93). Anticipating McHarg's ecological planning that was a key aspect of The Woodlands, it proposed managing growth to respect natural processes and scenic beauty while achieving profits similar to those of uncontrolled subdivision. It was sponsored by a nonprofit planning council representing about five thousand landowners in the area. McHarg had taught at the University of Pennsylvania since 1954, and Columbia's Bill Finley was a visiting professor during that time. Hoppenfeld had worked at the Philadelphia Planning Commission (Finley 2001; McHarg 1996).[14] McHarg's partner, Wallace, then executive director of the Greater Baltimore Committee, had worked in downtown Baltimore on the Charles Center project, which Rouse was associated with (McHarg 1996, 176). However, with all these connections, McHarg's firm was never involved with Columbia. I asked one of the early planners why McHarg had not been used, and he responded, "We thought he was difficult to work with" (Finley 2001).

Of course, many of the early ecological planning and analysis techniques promoted by McHarg were not totally unique. The use of map overlays for analysis, described in more detail in the next chapter, was not invented by McHarg but had been written about earlier by landscape architects such as Jacqueline Tyrwhitt, who from 1955 to 1968 taught urban design at Harvard (Tyrwhitt 1950). Tennenbaum had studied land use ecology with Paul Sears at Yale and invited Sears to Columbia to advise on lake sites (Tennenbaum 2002).[15] Sears was a prolific author who had written such articles as "Importance of Ecology in Training Engineers" (1947). Other planners and designers had similar backgrounds. It is easy to look back and say that Columbia's early planning looks "McHargian"—and several interviewees used that term—but Columbia demonstrates how such ideas actually existed outside the work of McHarg.

In the late 1960s and early 1970s, after the overall concept was in place but in a period when still much work remained to do on the development, Rouse hired a large number of landscape architects. As expertise in landscape increased, plans were refined to make the naturalistic open space and road design fit the actual form of the land. Some initial decisions could not be changed—for example, placing the town center in what landscape architects saw as one of the better areas of forest—but the refinement was significant in these years.

In Columbia, the villages are divided by this open space network rather than by roads, as in the Irvine Ranch or the classic neighborhood unit idea. Even within villages, smaller areas are divided by wooded paths, stream beds, and parks in a pattern that one of my interviewees described as the open space "mortar" in the "stone wall" of development (Interview 0110). This took advantage of the strengths of the rural landscape but has made the shape of each neighborhood and village difficult to perceive from the ground, because the edges are literally buried in trees, and the landscape character is fairly similar across the entire development. In addition, while quite a bit of architectural variety exists within villages, they are relatively similar to one another. This creates a homogeneity across the residential part of the development, which has the advantage of making Columbia recognizable as a unit but also makes it harder to tell where one is within it. A local Columbia design professional described a conversation with one of Columbia's planners that exemplifies this tension:

> He said that he had recently gone up in a helicopter, and he had flown over Columbia, and he said it was so exciting to see the plan drawings that he had done come alive. And all of a sudden it was obvious what was the driving core of Columbia—what gave it what he thought was its legibility was the open space system. My comment was, "Great, most people don't read it from the air. Most people read it from the car or sidewalk as they walk, and it is illegible.". . . You cannot read the structure of this place from the road, and I think that's the biggest failing. (Interview 0124)

Even in its early days Columbia was criticized for its physical design—its overall plan and its architecture. Many just commented that it was less architecturally distinctive than Reston. Christopher Alexander's 1966 classic article "The City Is Not a Tree" used Columbia as an example of a treelike road structure, which he labeled as artificial and unsuccessful. He contrasted it with the more complex semi-lattice or network structures of natural cities that are based on a transportation grid (Alexander [1966] 1972, 407, 408, 401). However, these criticisms mainly reflect unresolvable differences in approach between Columbia's planners and urban designers on one side and their detractors on the other. The Columbia approach was deliberately more populist, meant to appeal to a broad market, and this meant less high-style architecture and more culs-de-sac than some outsiders expected. It aimed for a middle ground, avoiding the lowest common denominator, rather than being placed at the cutting edge of architectural aesthetics (Architectural

Committee 1970). As I explain in chapter 5, the plan also conceived of the development as a set of environments focused on the life of the resident—the residential cluster, neighborhood, village, and town. It rejected the kind of network Alexander described in favor of this more cellular organization. With this concept of focusing on the human, Columbia's urban designers also imagined that they were making a legible environment (Hoppenfeld 1967, 407).

The first village, Wilde Lake, certainly had a great deal of design attention paid to it, and it became home to most of the early planning and marketing team as well as James Rouse. Many of these people were concentrated in one neighborhood, Bryant Woods, one of the earliest neighborhoods and still very desirable given its closeness to both Wilde Lake and the town center. The physical and architectural structure of the villages is, however, only part of the Columbia village concept, which also includes the social structure of the village resident associations and other civic groups. Later in the chapter I return to this issue of the social reality of the village concept when I discuss social planning in practice.

Approvals and Construction

While this planning was going ahead, Rouse was dealing with the politics of getting the development approved and construction started. The context was the early 1960s in Maryland. The people of Howard County were concerned about the suburban sprawl that was beginning to encroach on their county. Normally Democratic, the county had elected three Republicans as county commissioners who had campaigned for low-density development ("Columbia has already changed the county" 1966). The county had resisted water and sewer extensions and zoning for lots smaller than half an acre. In the context of Maryland and particularly Baltimore at the time, the implications of such an antigrowth approach were not only economic but also racial (Maryland Commission on Interracial Problems and Relations 1955). Howard County voted for pro-segregation George Wallace in the 1964 Democratic presidential primary and for Republican Barry Goldwater in the 1964 presidential election (Breckenfeld 1971, 263). When a court had overruled the commissioners' rejection of a high-rise apartment building, the commissioners had in turn eliminated all high-rise apartments from the county zoning. Part of the political base for this opposition to growth came from comparatively recent in-movers who had come to Howard County searching for a semirural exurban environment (Breckenfeld 1971, 238–39, 262).

During 1963, it had become obvious that someone was buying large amounts of land in this rural county between Baltimore and Washington, D.C. While many rumors circulated about the development, no one really knew who was doing it or what it was until October 29, 1963, when Jim Rouse announced it to the county commissioners at one of their public meetings. He also said that he would have a plan to present to them the next year (Moxley 1996; Breckenfeld 1971, 245).

When the development was announced, the most controversial aspect was its very existence. After that came the issue of race. Describing one of the earliest public meetings, an early development team member explained: "The second thing, and this was right out of the audience, 'Are you going to allow Negroes?' Jim [Rouse] said, 'There's no way you can build a new town without it being entirely open. We will have no restrictions of any kind.' Of course, a lot of people went wild at that one" (Interview 0103). The *Baltimore Sun* made sure that the open housing aspect of the development had a high profile. It still regularly reports on the state of Columbia's race relations, often in fairly sensational terms.

However, the residents of Howard County had a year between finding out about the idea of the development and the presentation of the plan. Rouse and other high-level officers talked to Howard County groups with a basic message that growth was inevitable in the county, and the new town could concentrate development in one orderly location. In hundreds of presentations, Rouse promised that Columbia would isolate its tax burden within its own borders, so that residents of the largely rural area would not need to subsidize the increased level of services in Columbia, particularly for parks and recreation. The project was also discussed more widely, with articles appearing in such locations as *Harper's* (Hamilton 1964j; Anderson 1964).

The plan was presented to the county on November 11, 1964, asking for a special planned community district like the later idea of planned unit development, allowing flexibility to the developer about the location of uses and infrastructure (HRD 1965b, 12; Hamilton 1964k; Breckenfeld 1971, 263–66). Legal counsel for the county advised that the ordinance contained a number of flaws, and in early 1965 the county commissioners stated their dislike of the idea of a California-style special tax district. The tax district would have solved Rouse's problem of creating a tax wall around the development and was attractive because of the capacity to issue tax-free bonds, making infrastructure construction less expensive. The commissioners were also opposed to row house and cluster developments, housing types that were a core element of the Columbia plan. For numerous reasons they feared the kind of row houses prevalent in Baltimore. This had the interesting consequence of casting Rouse as the underdog, and Howard County voters began to express support; various opinion polls showed between 67 and 85 percent in support of the plan (Breckenfeld 1971, 267–70; Rouse 1969; also Sidney Hollander Associates 1965).

Eventually Rouse's legal team, led by Jack Jones, created the Columbia Association (CA), with a levy placed as a lien on taxable property, relating the amount paid to the valuation—up to a maximum of seventy-five cents per one hundred dollars in value. Getting FHA and Veterans Administration approval for the Columbia Association to have first lien on Columbia properties had its own difficulties; VA approval required an act of Congress (Jones 2000).

The zoning issue was resolved when Howard County created a new town zone available for anyone with at least twenty-five hundred contiguous acres. That meant a new kind of zone was created specially for Columbia, but it was also an option for others involved with large-scale developments (HRD 1965b, 12; Breckenfeld 1971, 271). This set overall densities, broad categories of land use such as employment centers and attached housing, and created performance standards. It was quite innovative, allowing flexibility within broad overall parameters. Public support for the new town also enabled Rouse to make a distinction between townhouses (small groups of attached units) and row houses in long lines. As Jack Jones explained in an interview, such zoning changes were in the interest of the local government:

> The so-called Euclidean zoning, which is what you normally talk about, is based upon certain assumptions, which are that you know what's going to be done in each place and that you're smart enough to be omniscient and make fine distinctions between [land use categories] M1, M2, M3.[16] So I sat down with an accountant to check my mathematics. I figured out that if we did twenty-two square miles by traditional zoning, which means you had to lay out each lot and post each lot with zoning notices and have hearings, go through the citizen committee, go through the committee of all the regulatory agencies, police department, fire department, then have a hearing, and then have a final hearing, there would be about 120,000 public hearings. And so, I went before the county council, and . . . that horrified them. Then I came up with a concept called new town zoning, which was based upon three propositions. Number one is that as long as we designated an employment center . . . —and that meant anything that employs people, whether it's a hospital, factory, office building—what difference does it make as long as we met performance standards? . . . But they stuck on making the distinction between [detached] housing and apartments and townhouses. That was a sore issue. But other than that, we were just going to have housing, employment, and open space. (Jones 2000)

By mid-July 1965 the plans were approved with no significant opposition. Most commentators at the time saw it as a great victory that a racially and economically integrated development had been approved by a rural Republican county in Maryland in the mid-1960s. The more cynical saw it as a pragmatic county trying to isolate its growth, but on balance it was remarkable. Another of the professionals working on the early stages of the project explained:

> How Columbia was approved is an absolute miracle. . . . On the day that Jim Rouse walked into the courthouse where the county commissioners met, he basically said, "We want to build an open city which will be an open town in

the middle of your beautiful farm land. And it will be an urban environment. And we have no zoning. And we understand that unless you people sitting up there vote in favor of this, which you have run on a platform against, we cannot and will not build Columbia. And so I understand that you are against it. But if you will give us an opportunity to persuade you that it is a better alternative than being gobbled up by urban sprawl coming up Route 29, then I think there is an opportunity at least to have a fair dialogue." And that's basically what happened. . . . [And Rouse] was as charismatic and as persuasive as anybody in public life I've ever heard when he was a young man. He would create a stunned silence among a sophisticated or nonsophisticated crowd by his eloquence and his grounding in the relationship between physical development, if you will, and human values. And he had a holistic and systems view of the world that very few public figures had at the time. (Interview 0104)

Construction did not start immediately, even though with a twenty-three-million-dollar loan, every day's delay cost five thousand dollars in interest alone (Breckenfeld 1971, 187). Some of the delay was due to normal constraints—engineering and utilities could not be started before the rezoning was achieved. In addition, engineering turned out to be complicated, because the Columbia team tried to innovate—curving roads to save trees, reducing radii in culs-de-sac. Subdivision plats showing streets and lots needed to be approved by the county before the land could be sold. HRD agreed to pay large submission fees to increase the capacity of Howard County to process such approvals. The county planners seemed excited about the opportunity—an excitement not always shared by the county commissioners. The planning director, Tom Harris, had graduated in city planning from the University of Pennsylvania in 1959, studying there at the time of such academics as McHarg and Gans and also doing a studio with Bill Finley (Harris 1996, 2000). Such connections meant that the county staff were knowledgeable about issues and trends, but it still took some time to build capacity in terms of the development approval process.[17]

Adding to these delays was the desire for Rouse Company architect-planners to keep working on refining the project (PADCO ca. 1966; Breckenfeld 1971). Construction finally began three months behind schedule, in June 1966 (Breckenfeld 1971, 273–76). The first homes went on sale in July 1967.

Finances and General Electric

At Irvine, finances were not much discussed in public. Because Rouse ran a publicly traded company and needed to raise the money for the development from the outside, the finances were always more public. Rouse also wanted people to know about at least some of his financial picture because he expected Columbia to be profitable and hoped the profitability would lead others to replicate the planned new town idea. Profit was important in Rouse's thinking because, without it, large institutional investors could not be attracted. In 1962, Rouse had imagined a cost of forty-two million dollars and a pretax profit of sixty-seven million (Hamilton 1964d, 1).

By the middle of 1964, work group member Robert Gladstone figured out that the profit might be as low as four million dollars, given the heavy initial infrastructure costs. This was a low return on such a large investment. This led some rethinking of the project. Commercial and industrial land was increased, open space reduced, and the overall residential density increased from 2.1 to 2.3 units per acre (Hamilton 1964d, 3). The cost of the one-year process of gaining approval from Howard County and the additional year to finalize initial planning was also quite significant.

In December 1965, Rouse refinanced Columbia, putting together loans to repay Connecticut General's initial loan and the Rouse-owned Community Research and Development's own investment in planning and other services. A document put together in 1965, seeking funding, projected a before-tax profit over a fifteen-year development period of over one hundred million dollars (HRD 1965a, 30). The fifty-million-dollar loan that Rouse put together at that time came from Connecticut General (twenty-five million), Chase Manhattan Bank (ten million), and the Teachers Insurance and Annuity Association (TIAA) (fifteen million) (Master builder 1966).[18] Rouse explained the significance of the deal:

> Three great financial institutions agreed that the values created by land assembly, planning and zoning on a large scale exceeded costs by such a margin that they can lend the prospective full cost of land and development and be adequately protected by excess value above the cost of the land. Their decision was therefore very important for the future of city building and for opening up big financial institutions to financing city building. (Rouse quoted in Breckenfeld 1971, 307)

For a new community developer, money is necessary not only to buy land and to put in infrastructure but also to provide enough frills so that the development is perceived as a viable one and develops sales momentum. These frills are costly. In 1967, when Columbia opened, they had only to look to the south to Reston to see the potential for financial failure, and the Reston development team actually shared some of their experiences with the Columbia staff (Ivins 2001). Rouse had a very optimistic development scenario— thirty thousand units sold over fifteen years, although for the first few years the sales were projected to be below the average of two thousand per year (HRD 1965a, 24–25). This kind of volume was higher than anyone had achieved in the Baltimore-Washington corridor. At the time, around fifty thousand units per year were being built in the Baltimore and Washington areas, and twenty thousand of these units were in the corridor between the two (Breckenfeld 1971, 190–91).

Dramatic growth made the high projections seem plausible. Many developments, including the other two case study projects, made high projections during the 1960s and early 1970s. The idea of social mix—providing rental and for-sale units at a variety of market levels and without regard to race—can also be seen as an attempt to increase market share by appealing to a wide variety of potential homebuyers and renters. In the early years Columbia's sales did surpass projections, with land sales for ninety-one hundred homes and apartments by the end of 1970 (Breckenfeld 1971, 193). However, in 1969, Rouse took on even more debt trying to attract a General Electric manufacturing campus to the area, described below.

Here, it is important to understand the culture of the Rouse Company. The people at Howard Research and Development, particularly the designers and project managers, were working in an atmosphere like the dot.com period of the late 1990s, with young professionals working at the cutting edge, rethinking the metropolis, and building their visions. They were expensive visions. It was also the late '60s and early '70s, a time of social experimentation that influenced both the content of the urban vision and the personal lives of the development teams. This was in some contrast with other parts of the Rouse Company that were dealing with mortgage banking and developing suburban shopping centers. To many in these parts of the company, some in the Columbia team seemed wild and profligate in both their personal and their professional lives, with the potential to impose enormous debts on the company. This potential was exacerbated by the large increase in staff hired in the years just before and after opening, at a time when issues such as salary policies and the organizational structure had not been refined (Interview 0520). This caused a great deal of tension into the early 1970s, affecting the development, as also occurred in The Woodlands.

In this high-stakes financial context, the planning team under Finley used new programming techniques, such as PERT (program evaluation and review technique), to keep the project on schedule, and the Columbia economic model, to keep it on budget (Spear 1971). While it took a number of years to finally get the economic model coordinated with the land development plan, this was an enormous step forward in the development industry, which had been relatively unsophisticated about such matters. Columbia's program management techniques became the subject of some scholarly attention (e.g., Apgar 1971a, 1971b). This process was pushing the limits of technology at the time. Calculations for the model were the realm of nerdish staff with mechanical calculators, who would laboriously project profits, losses, and the effects of changing costs, designs, and phasing. To call it a "model" makes it sound quite scientific, and I was surprised at first when people told me about its components—a basic spreadsheet.

As a member of the Rouse project management team in the late 1960s and early 1970s explained:

> I think the thing that's really, really interesting about Columbia . . . is [that] it created a development process, a way of thinking about land planning, the creation of community, taking it through the process of economic forecasting, budgeting, financial feasibility and market research, that heretofore had been basically absent in the real estate industry. A lot of real estate projects were basically conceived on the back of envelopes. And it wasn't very process-oriented. What Columbia did is brought together a number of inputs: public policy, the natural qualities of the land, [and] a very thorough site analysis, even before any planning was done. (Interview 0201)

Even with this more sophisticated management approach, construction did not go smoothly. The economic model was based on a number of assumptions about costs, and as construction came near it was apparent that these had been unrealistically based on nonunion labor. According to Len Ivins, who worked on project management, the two Maryland firms with the capability of doing such a large project both gave extremely high prices. He explained in an interview in 2001: "I don't know whether they had a deal, but their prices were outrageous. It basically would have sunk the project. We could not afford—When we took those costs and translated them to the economic model and the cost of development, we could not have done the project" (Ivins 2001). The response was to bring in nonunion contractors from Rhode Island to start construction. This nonunion aspect of Columbia is not frequently mentioned in accounts of the work as a liberal utopia.

Everyone was aware of costs, so the Columbia team set about trying to increase sales; a particularly big push occurred in 1970 (Ivins 2001; Sherman 2000).[19] Some policies, such as putting custom homes in each cul-de-sac and mixing builders in neighborhoods, were thrown out in order to make sales. One of the first times this happened was when the Levitt Company offered to pay cash for over three hundred lots in the Running Brook neighborhood of Wilde Lake at a time when cash was short in Columbia. The condition of the sale cut architectural approval of the house plans. Other cash flow problems are evident in the fairly high concentration of townhouses and apartments around the Oakland Mills Village Center. People working on the development in the period remembered extraordinary efforts made to make sales.[20]

The development process—let alone the social process of building the community—still had a number of challenges in this period, although the hard economic times of the 1970s had not yet hit. Columbia was to be a satellite community linked to the metropolitan areas of Baltimore and Washington. However, within its boundaries enough jobs had to be available for its population, even if many people went elsewhere to work and others living elsewhere came into Columbia for jobs. This was not just a utopian ideal; it would help sell more housing in Columbia, as at least some workers would shift to be near their jobs.

Creating those jobs was not an easy feat, so in the late 1960s, when General Electric expressed interest in creating an appliance park to employ twelve thousand workers on the eastern edge of Columbia, Rouse jumped at the opportunity. Rouse felt General Electric could put Columbia on the map. He encouraged the company, even though many of his high-level staff were concerned about the cost because he did not own all the land that it was interested in.[21] Eventually, Rouse had to buy an additional 2,139 acres of land for $19 million and add a four-mile rail spur to attract this large employer (Williams 1969; Breckenfeld 1971, 303–8). With this holding, Rouse reached 17,868 acres, and General Electric paid $3.8 million for 1,100 of them. At the 1969 stockholder meeting, Rouse defended the purchase as ultimately adding to profitability. In the late 1960s, the Rouse Company revised Columbia's profit figures upward, with the GE project aiding this (Weiss 1973, 43–44). A 1969 *Fortune* magazine article quoted Rouse as saying, "Over the entire fifteen years of construction . . . , we certainly are going to be able to show a cumulative profit in excess of 20 percent compounded annually" (Businessman in the news 1969, 40).

Connecticut General provided the loan for the new land purchase, and additional loans in 1970 brought debt above $100 million (Breckenfeld 1971, 308). Of course, big developments need big loans, but these were extremely large. The mortgage banking and retail side of the Rouse Company could find much to fear in these commitments. Their fears were exacerbated by other large Rouse Company planning studies conducted during this period for a proposed new town on Staten Island and a metropolitan planning process in Hartford. Land sales fell to $6.3 million in the 1974 fiscal year, down from $22.6 million the year before. At that time HRD had a negative net worth on its formal balance sheets, although appreciation of land values probably placed it in the black (Kennedy 1974).

In fact, General Electric never fully occupied the site, instead changing its strategy to use smaller sites and also moving offshore. Although the Rouse Company bought the land back and the area eventually became a very successful high-tech center, with much growth in the 1990s, this took a long time. Obviously three sorts of businesspeople—land developer, manufacturer, and lender—were tussling here, all trying to keep control over their futures and to maximize profits.

Overall, it is difficult to figure out the profits and losses from the development of Columbia. This is partly because many early transactions involved swaps between wholly owned subsidiaries, and depreciation allowances on buildings reduced pretax profits substantially, acting as if the buildings were declining in value when in fact the equity in these buildings was substantial and increasing. However, Connecticut General certainly lost in 1985 when it sold its 80 percent share to the Rouse Company, at about the time that the development was finally beginning to show profits.

PHASE 2: HIGH CAMELOT, 1967 TO EARLY 1970s,
PHASE 3: COMMUNITY BUILDING, EARLY 1970s TO 1979,
AND PHASE 4: CONSOLIDATION, 1980 ONWARD

Social Planning in Practice

In the period between Columbia's opening and the recession of the early 1970s, there was a lot of hype about Columbia. Articles appeared in *Life, Business Week,* and the *Saturday Review,* part of a general interest in urban issues in the period (Maryland's "new town" 1968; Von Eckhardt 1971). Most articles seemed assured of Columbia's future success and enamored with Rouse as a person. It is also hard to overstate the excitement that many of the earliest residents had, with a significant number moving "from all over the country because of [Rouse's] ideals. They didn't come here for their jobs. People left their jobs. . . . And people gave up careers and came here and relocated, to be a part of this" (Interview 0109). As two early residents recounted to me in interviews:

> What intrigued me was the idea, if you started from scratch, could you do a better job? Could you not repeat and relive the same problems over and over again? That was key for me, moving here. I wanted to be part of something that was new and fresh, had ideals, and to see if it could happen. (Interview 0129)

> Most of us felt that we were in a very important drama, that this was something that had, if not worldwide, certainly a national stage. We had visitors, and there were people who were doing TV shows and people who were doing articles about Columbia and so on. It makes you feel different. (Interview 0131)

The Rouse Company, as previously mentioned, was also continuing to expand in the late 1960s, with many young professionals, also intrigued by the project, coming to work for Rouse. The atmosphere became less of a hothouse but was still innovative. They found a congenial work environment generally open to new ideas, making Columbia a garden for professionals to grow in as much as a garden for the residents. As two of these professionals explained:

> It was really interesting in the Rouse Company that it was your deeds that really made a difference. In a big corporation, what you did was what really mattered most. It wasn't a question of what was your title; it was your spirit of

cooperation. . . . But the best part of it was the Rouse U. part, the Rouse University. We met all these people, and when we all left we had this incredible network. And it's still [in place] to this day. (Interview 0428)

I said to Jim Rouse, "You know, we don't have a very good environment for people with disabilities." So we held a three-day conference, and we had forty people there in wheelchairs. . . . It was very eye-opening. The people who came in the wheelchairs were just so pleased. They said, "We have never been invited to a conference. We have never been on the panels." But I think those kinds of things were possible in Columbia, where I wouldn't have thought of doing it . . . in any other city that I worked in or was a consultant. It would never have occurred to me [elsewhere, but it did in Columbia] because the atmosphere, the vision, generated much more freedom of thought. Even if you couldn't do anything about it, you could think it. You could dare to think it. (Interview 0131)

This atmosphere within the Rouse Company lasted until the early 1970s, when the company was reorganized several times, and many of the key early staff left to work for The Woodlands and elsewhere (Rouse Company 1971). While some key people, such as Michael Spear, research director and later president of the Rouse Company, were still employed, work on Columbia was increasingly involved with maintaining the plan. This is a typical process in new community development—the initial hothouse atmosphere does not need to continue for the life of the project. In the case of Columbia, however, this transition was a difficult one. As a more recent Rouse Company employee explained:

[The Rouse Company] went through that very painful period, and I would say that . . . 1973 to '74 here was like our parents going through the Depression. Once you go through that and see as many employees cast aside almost overnight and all that that entailed, and then grow up through the next twenty years past that, or thirty years past that, you learn some lessons. And you learn that land needs three meals every day, whether you're developing it or not. That whatever you thought it was going to take, it's probably going to take longer. That optimism is a wonderful thing, but reality is different. You learn all these lessons. (Interview 0116)

While this development story was unfolding, people were moving into Columbia, and at least in the early years a number were doing so because of its social innovations. Some of these had to do with social equity, but others were in the area of developing institutions or organizations in Columbia, with the Rouse team taking a very entrepreneurial approach to attracting cultural, health, and educational organizations (Brooks 1971, 279). Many Rouse Company employees lived in Columbia almost from its opening and experienced these social innovations in both their professional and their personal lives. One explained to me:

We were pioneering. We were in Camelot. But all the people were in Camelot. We all knew each other. We were like a wonderful, friendly place. We were experimenting with everything. Jim [Rouse] would throw a ball up in the air: could we have the Corcoran Gallery of Art? Okay, it didn't work out. He started a ballet company. . . . And there would be Jim walking around with David Rockefeller, trying to get money from Rockefeller, and some big designer designing the sets and costumes. . . . So all these things were floating all over the place. . . . Everything was in the experimental stage. You had housing, architect[-designed] housing, that was far beyond and better than anything being offered anyplace. There was an experiment in religious centers, that we would not sell any land for churches or synagogues. The place was socially planned, purposely. . . . (Interview 0210)

This experience was studied a great deal in the 1970s to see why people had moved to Columbia and what they thought of it. The Rouse Company, of course, had its own market research, and the residents of Columbia conducted some of their own studies, but professors and thesis students also flocked to Columbia. Studies ranged from ethnic relations to the changes in bird populations (Geis 1974).[22] Not all of them published work; I found many unpublished studies, theses, commentaries, and critiques and heard of more.[23] Columbia residents seem to have dealt with the fairly frequent interviews and surveys with admirable tolerance.

One of the first studies, by Lansing, Marans, and Zehner (1970) from the University of Michigan, interviewed a random sample of 216 residents of Columbia in late 1969 (with a 92.3 percent response rate).[24] The town's concept or plan was cited by 51 percent of Columbia residents as something that attracted them to the development, with nearness of work a distant second, at 22 percent (people could mention more than one thing). However, when explaining the reasons for their overall evaluation of the community, 47 percent of Columbia's respondents mentioned the accessibility of job, stores, and the downtowns of Baltimore and Washington, D.C. The physical plan was mentioned second, at 22 percent. Of the ten developments examined in the study, "nice and friendly neighbors" had the lowest proportion of mentions by Columbians—only 8 percent (Lansing et al. 1970, 29–49). Subsequent studies have generally found many strengths and some tensions in Columbia.

Columbia Concept.   Columbia had a number of aims that involved self-containment, nature, human growth, and profits. It innovated in the process of planning, physical layout, project management, governance, and education. It was convenient to two large cities and had many of the planned features that generally attract people to new communities. However, the one thing that it is most remembered for is its social mix and its "open" housing policy. Columbia has in fact maintained a population that has been about one-fifth African American throughout its history, although it rose a little to 23 percent by 2000 (in a population that was 64 percent non-Hispanic white). The first child born to Columbia residents was symbolic of its philosophy—a child born to an interracial couple (Clark 1971).

The path to racial integration was not always smooth. The eight full-page and one double-page advertisements for Columbia in 1967, the year it opened, were collected into a brochure by the Rouse Company. These advertisements used over thirty photographs of Columbia but did not contain any people who were obviously not white. However, at the time, the company was very vocal about its open housing policy, the exhibit center displays reportedly included racially mixed groups in most images, the marketing department soon moved to a more integrated image both in advertisements and staffing, and the Rouse Company monitored its market closely (e.g., Sidney Hollander Associates 1970a; HRD 1972; Sherman 1996). In its early period, the Rouse Company, famously, threw out a builder found to be discriminating in sales (Kennedy 1981). As was previously mentioned, this whole approach was seen as brave in Baltimore's racially segregated housing market. One African American interviewee recounted how, before moving to Columbia, her family had moved to a suburb of Baltimore only to have the white population move out. In such a metropolitan area there were many white Christian families who were used to living only with others like themselves and a real estate culture that made people fearful of change. There was a real potential for the Columbia concept to fail and for people who moved there in search of an integrated environment to end up in a segregated one. Working before the 1968 Fair Housing Act, the Columbia sales team could legally track the race of every buyer, which they did to stop large concentrations of one group. They feared that such concentrations could undermine attempts at integration in a period in which a great deal of nervousness about open housing still existed (Sherman 1996). In addition, the Rouse Company sent testers to check the marketing of houses in Columbia, making sure that marketers would refuse to give assurances about the racial character of an area except to say that housing was to be open to all. In the words of a member of the development team in the 1960s: "You have to remember that we had a situation here where we were selling homes in a county where people had run to get out of the city. There was no open housing legislation. They were coming out to Howard County primarily on half-acre, acre, and two-acre lots, to run away from urban sprawl. But even more so to run away from blacks and Jews" (Interview 0210).

However, the open housing policy was not merely visionary but also had some marketing benefits, in that a pent-up demand for integrated suburban environments also obviously existed among African Americans and Jews. Further, many liberals were attracted to suburban living either because of ideas about closeness to nature, or because they genuinely saw it as better for family life, or because it allowed the growing number of dual-earner couples to commute to jobs in both Baltimore and Washington, D.C. In this context, Columbia gave all these populations an alternative to the homogeneous suburban sprawl that had been criticized by so many cultural commentators. Rouse lost sales to the racially biased, but they were already well taken care of in the existing areas. Instead Rouse's early sales team tapped into new markets. Partly for this reason, Columbia is the most Democratic of the three case study developments.[25]

A very comprehensive study of racial and economic integration was conducted by Lynne Burkhart in the early 1970s and published in 1981. Burkhart lived with her family in Columbia for four years in the early 1970s, and for eighteen months she collected data in the new town through participant observation on race and class, or in her terms the "relationship between cultural symbols and politics in Columbia" (Burkhart 1981, 11). As a social scientist, she was trained to question and critique, but she nevertheless became caught up in the ideals of Columbia.

> I felt a strong attachment to the community, the source of which seemed mysterious given my general lack of involvement in active community life. I now think this was a reaction to being part, however peripheral, of a goal-oriented, purposive community. Especially in the early days, the most important goal was a better life for many different kinds of people, particularly for blacks and for those with lower incomes. Indeed, James Rouse, the mortgage banker and developer of Columbia, was considered courageous to plan this kind of racial and class mixing in the mid-1960s, and it is not surprising that I was caught up in the community feeling that was forged around it.
>
> It seemed that living in a "truly integrated" community was important to most people's sense of belonging. Residents talked publicly and privately about the good feeling between blacks and whites in public places. Several years later I still feel that the combination of mutual respect, assertiveness, and friendliness that characterizes casual contacts between blacks and whites in Columbia is unusual enough that it ought never to be minimized as a powerful political and social phenomenon. This racial openness is at once Columbia's most notable success, a catalyst for community spirit, a potential for an important social change in the lives of both black and white residents, and an area where failure would be devastating—to the developer, to property owners, and perhaps most important, to believers in the traditional model of integration, of whom there are still many. (Burkhart 1981, xiv)

In this early period a number of ethnographic, participant-observation, and interview-based studies, however, found that Columbia did better at racial integration than at economic mix, with very fine-grained residential mixing of racial groups. However, some exceptions to this situation occurred among some teenagers, for instance, self-segregating along racial lines in the 1970s (Ben-Zadok 1980, 278; Karsk 1977, 120; Sandberg 1978; Burkhart 1981).

In interviews, early residents, both African American and white, looked back nostalgically at the relative openness of the early years when most of these studies were conducted, a period when social institutions were just forming and there was a sense of both opportunity and togetherness. While the formal community association was still developer dominated, volunteering in other groups was easy. One long-time resident remarked, "This is much more difficult these days if you're not well educated and well-to-do" (Interview 0106). Others talked about the early period when few people lived in Columbia, and those people had high ideals and a common purpose, a unique situation for a suburban area in the 1960s. "It was marvelously successful, I think, in bringing people of different races together. And that was an experience that I would say 75 percent of the people that moved to Columbia at that time had not had" (Interview 0129). However, there was a sense of the different risks for different members of the community even in the early years. As two interviewees explained:

> *A:* Because we were part of an experiment—at least we thought we were—a lot of people kind of joked about the fact that it was scary to leave the reservation.
>
> *B:* Right, they used that term all the time.
>
> *A:* They used that term all the time, to go out of Columbia.
>
> *B:* To go over the line—and there was a great deal of hostility.
>
> *A:* If we were black, it would have been for real.
>
> *B:* Because this was not a friendly . . . area. (Anonymous interview)

My conversations, interviews, and observations of meetings also indicated a widely held perception of a change in the commitment to the Columbia concept. This was confirmed by a 2002 survey that asked opinions of eight hundred randomly selected residents, part of a planning process for the Columbia Association. With a margin of error of plus or minus 3.5 percent, it found long-term residents thought it was important that a certain fading of consciousness about Columbia's "uniqueness as an open, caring community that encourages diversity, community participation and protection of the environment" had occurred. Residents of twenty or more years were much more likely than those of ten or fewer to see this as a problem (62 percent versus 38 percent), as were African Americans versus whites (71 percent versus 41 percent) (Mason-Dixon Polling and Research 2002; also L. Parker 1997). A survey of another eight hundred people the following year, focusing on specific action items for the Columbia Association, found that 82 percent of blacks but only 44 percent of whites thought it was a priority to "distribute educational materials to help Columbia residents understand the original vision of Columbia" (Mason-Dixon Polling and Research 2003).

In general, people I interviewed have a perception of separate African

American and white social worlds in Columbia. This is a difficult issue related to the aims of social mix—is it about fostering intense interaction, or about giving people of all backgrounds or races access to the same environmental and locational opportunities? As I discuss in chapter 5, the issue of whether people of any social group or background actually socialize with those they live near has elicited much debate. While the planners certainly wanted interaction, study after study, including some of those cited by people in the work group, show that people do not form intense bonds with their neighbors just because of proximity. Rather, they have such ties with family and with those with common interests. They may engage in casual neighboring with people close by, and they may even become friends if those neighbors have common interests; however, proximity as such does not lead to friendship.[26] In this reading, the residential dispersion and high levels of diversity in Columbia are enough to give relatively equal access to services and facilities, particularly if this is combined with positive public interactions. However, a lack of close friendship based on proximity is a disappointment to others.

In terms of the residential distribution of racial groups, however, the Columbia concept seems to have continued to work. Analysis of the 2000 census by UC Irvine sociologist Yuki Kato indicates that all three case study developments are substantially less racially segregated than their surrounding metropolitan regions. The lack of segregation holds true for all six racial pairings among the census racial categories of whites, those of Asian descent, and African Americans (Kato 2002). Such fine-grained integration was planned in Columbia and may be the result of housing variety in Irvine. Columbia's integration is the most notable, however, because it is highly diverse, and the extensive African American–white integration is a significant break with the patterns of segregation in the region (Kato 2002). Income figures had not been released at the time of Kato's study, so her analysis was solely of racial groups.

Economic integration has not been as successful as racial integration. Columbia originally announced an intention of providing housing for low-income people, with a figure of 10 percent of households often quoted but not appearing in major planning documents (e.g., Smookler 1976, 66). Instead, early documents talk about the development of housing for people of "low income (but not poverty-stricken) and very well-to-do families" (Michael 1964, c-1). To provide housing for the lowest-income groups, a number of programs were used in Columbia, including Section 235, which reduced mortgage interest for moderate-income families (started in 1968); Section 236, which reduced loan interest for low-income rental developments (started in 1968); and Section 221D-3, which was a rent subsidy for low-income earners (started 1961) (Smookler 1976, 68). Some of these programs were designed to run for a specific period, after which units would be returned to the private market. Rouse was also supportive of the Interfaith Housing task force, established in 1966. By 1970, it had constructed three hundred units on five sites (Smookler 1976, 67). However, the discipline of the economic model necessitated, even before the Nixon administration cut a number of such federal subsidies in the 1970s, that Columbia cut back on providing such housing because it needed to make more money from the land.

It is interesting that by 1998 Columbia did no better than the other two developments in attracting such housing, as all three have about the same amount of government-sponsored or -supported affordable housing, at about 5 to 6 percent. In Columbia, this included just under fifteen hundred, or 4.4 percent, federally subsidized units, including Section 8 vouchers (U.S. HUD 1998). In 1990, Columbia also had a lower poverty rate than the other two developments, at 3 percent, meaning that it housed a smaller proportion of very-low-income people. By 2000, its rate was a little higher than that of The Woodlands (see appendix B).

Throughout its development, Columbia did tap into Federal Housing Administration (FHA) support for homeownership targeted at moderate-income earners, allowing loans with very low down payments insured by the federal government. As was explained in earlier chapters, in the 1960s and 1970s it was a useful source of funding for the lower end of the private market in suburban areas. Columbia managed to gain access to this funding earlier in its development than either the Irvine Ranch or The Woodlands.

Up to 1962 the FHA was associated with guidelines for evaluating property values that emphasized socially homogeneous suburban locations, reflecting the values of the private real estate industry to which the FHA was strongly linked.[27] FHA policies changed in the 1960s, and by 1996, 46 percent of FHA loans went to center cities compared with 37 percent of conforming conventional loans (General Accounting Office 1999, 11). As was explained in the chapter on Irvine, even after the lifting of the restrictions on lending to socially diverse areas, FHA support was not automatic for new communities, because the FHA balked at some innovations. In Columbia it had difficulties with the liens placed on property to secure the fees for the Columbia Association. After some lobbying at the assistant secretary level in HUD, Columbia was granted a special exemption. As was explained before, getting approval for loans from the Veterans Administration was even more difficult but was managed with an act of Congress.

Race and income have intersected in complex ways in Columbia. Many of the early African American residents of Columbia were affluent. Early marketing and survey studies found that African American households had higher average incomes than whites, and later studies found widely distributed incomes in the African American population (Karsk 1977, 17; Ford 1975, 133; Smookler 1976; Schuman and Sclar, n.d.). According to the census, in 1980, 42 percent of the employed black population were in managerial and professional specialty occupations, compared with 53 percent for whites, and the respective poverty rates were 6.0 percent and 2.4 percent. The significant middle- and upper-middle-class African American population in Columbia is a striking contrast with the other two case study developments, which have far fewer African Americans of any income level. However, on average the 2000 census reported that in Columbia people who were "white alone" in 2000 earned $37,066 per capita, and those who were black or African American alone earned $25,810. The poverty rate for whites was 3 percent, and 5 percent of households earned two hundred thousand dollars or more per year; for the black or African American population, the poverty rate was 11 percent, and 2 percent of households earned two hundred thousand dollars or more.

Somewhat as a by-product of the attempt to integrate racially and economically and to retain open space, considerable housing variety exists in Columbia (see figures 23–26). Like Irvine, in 1990, it had only 39 percent single-family detached houses, and in 2000, 42 percent. However, in Columbia there had been ideas of doing much more. While the developers brought the idea of patio or zero-lot line homes from California, there were also suggestions for building units over garages and forms of co-housing that never materialized (Sherman 1996, 2000).

More recently, some of Columbia's market-rate housing has also become run-down, suffering from absentee landlords. This has opened up opportunities for lower-cost market-rate housing. However, the presence of a very small number of poorly maintained and even abandoned units has also prompted the Columbia Association to increase covenant enforcement, with rolling inspections every five years rather than a complaint-based system.

By the 1990s and 2000s, it seemed from my interviews and observations that this economic mix was more visible and discussed in Columbia than it should have been, given the fairly low numbers of poor and low-income people. In interviews and newspaper reports, more affluent people complained about the noise and disruption caused by people living in subsidized units or using Section 8 vouchers. As in Irvine, representatives of the developers complained to me about resident resistance to lower-cost housing options. This may be an issue of perception alone; however, this heightened level of complaint may also be partly based on the character of the housing mix.

Columbia has more federally funded housing for families than the other two case study developments. In contrast, The Woodlands emphasized subsidized housing for seniors, who are perceived as quiet and law abiding, and the Irvine Ranch has a set of local programs that are less visible physically. While subsidized housing developments exist around the village centers in

Figure 23. Residential area, 1980s. Creator: The Rouse Company. Source: Columbia Archives. Reprinted with permission from the Columbia Archives.

Figure 24. Attached housing near Wilde Lake. Photographer: Ann Forsyth.

Figure 25. Apartments over shops in Harper's Choice Village Center. Photographer: Ann Forsyth.

Figure 26. Townhouses in newer business park area. Housing is increasingly being inserted into business areas in all three developments. Photographer: Ann Forsyth.

Columbia, renters using Section 8 vouchers are also spread throughout the older areas of Columbia, even in some of the fancier middle-class townhouse and apartment areas. This gives lower-income households visibility both in middle-class neighborhoods and in rental complexes. In the late 1990s, with only 36 percent of Howard County's population, Columbia had over two-thirds of its assisted units (Bloom 2001b, 173; U.S. HUD 1998).

Overall, the Columbia concept does have a tense side. Interviews, observations, and archival sources indicate that people have been accusing one another of racism since Columbia started. There are some problems apart from social distance and complaints about subsidized housing, not all coming from Columbia but affecting it. This has been particularly evident in the Howard County schools. In interviews and in periodic newspaper accounts, many parents seem to have been very satisfied about the good friendships that have formed between children across racial lines. However, maintaining this has required vigilance. The following anecdote of an incident in the 1990s gives a flavor of the work that has had to be done, although the controversy was resolved.

> The Howard County school system puts out a calendar every year, and in this particular calendar they had a picture of a group of children posing for a photograph. It had all the white kids in front, and the black kids were seemingly jostling for position, their faces in between the shoulders of the white kids. Our view of that was that, okay, now this represents [the] Howard County school system, children eager to learn. But the image that you project here is that education for white kids is an expectation; it's an entitlement. But the black kid has to struggle just to get his face in the picture that represents children eager for education. This is what it said. (Interview 0101).

The issue of different social worlds referred to above may also have some public ramifications, including exclusion from boards and committees based on social networks.

The *Baltimore Sun* has kept an eye out for hints of racial problems in the development and during 2000 ran a series of exposés claiming failure of the Columbia concept. However, on balance this assessment seems overdrawn. In Columbia people have had an exceptional commitment to making a better place in terms of the goals of integration, and this commitment has led to come striking successes. In the words of a planner who worked on the later stages of Columbia:

> The paper likes to play up [integration and racial issues] as a big negative, but there are a lot of places in the country where that wouldn't even come up, wouldn't even be a topic of discussion. People are grappling with it. They're concerned about it. I think there are people of good faith on both sides. So the fact that they can have that free dialogue, I think, says a lot about the success of Columbia. (Interview 0110) (See figure 27.)

Figure 27. Crowd at Columbia birthday celebrations, Lake Kittamaqundi. Photographer: Ann Forsyth.

Overall, Columbia managed to counter the perceived trend toward homogeneous suburbs, particularly in racial terms. Its large stock of attached housing was also available for the nonnuclear households that were growing in number in the 1960s and 1970s. The difficulty of providing housing for low-income people with new construction in the private market is, in hindsight, not so surprising, although disappointing to many, given Columbia's ideals.

Governance.   Columbia is unincorporated, although if a city, it would be one of the largest in Maryland. Most of Columbia's municipal services are provided by Howard County, and since the early 1970s Columbia has regularly elected representatives to the county council. The structure of county government was changed in 1968, from three commissioners to five county council members and a county executive. Currently two council members primarily represent the Columbia area. In Maryland, school districts are also organized at the county level. After some early resentment about Columbia from some elected representatives and residents, relationships have been fairly smooth, particularly once it became apparent that Columbia's fiscal impact on the county had been positive since it opened (Columbia Commission 1971; *Howard County and Columbia* 1971).

As I explained in chapter 2, new communities are often criticized for their private governments and exclusive character. While the Irvine Ranch has homeowner associations with roles limited to common-area maintenance and covenant enforcement, Columbia has a slightly different model that still demonstrates a relatively limited role for the quasi-governmental Columbia Association. Part of the original concept of Columbia was to have a higher level of recreational facilities than the other taxpayers of Howard County would be willing to pay for. This included pathways, parks, swimming pools, lakes, tennis courts and golf course, horse-riding facilities, arts and cultural events, and for some time a minibus and child care (Breckenfeld 1971, 290; Hamilton 1964e).

However, these services needed to be paid for, and a special taxation district was not politically feasible, so the Columbia Association, initially the Columbia Parks and Recreation Association, was created. In its simplest terms, the Columbia Association runs like a government, obtaining loans to provide capital improvements in the open space and recreation areas and paying them back through a mixture of property levies and added user fees for some facilities, such as the swimming pools. This is similar to the situation in municipalities, where governments get loans, put in infrastructure, maintain it, and pay back the loans using property taxes and admission fees. It has not always been a smooth process in Columbia, and dramatic budget cuts occurred during the recession of the early 1970s (Appletree 1978, 3).

The property levies have been confusing for some residents who have felt that the developer has avoided its responsibilities and imposed a cost burden on them. Facilities were also generally put in earlier than a municipality might have chosen to do, and that did impose additional costs in the early days but also provided high levels of services. While many residents have wanted to pay down CA's debt, this opinion has not been universally shared, and in 2003 it still owed over seventy-eight million dollars (Columbia Association 2003, 6; Kennedy 1998). Obviously the open space development had to be paid for somehow—either up front through higher purchase prices for property or over time through the levy. This has not always been clear to residents, however, and many have seen it as a way for the development company to avoid its responsibility to pay for infrastructure. In addition the fees to use facilities such as the pools have seemed to some in Columbia to run counter to its original principles of economic integration.

It has also been confusing for other residents of Howard County, who, seeing the services in Columbia, have demanded higher levels of service without paying the fees. As one employee of Howard County explained:

> There's pretty good understanding, I think, from Columbia residents that they don't run the school system, they don't collect trash, they don't provide police; they don't do a lot of these other things. There's some downside from the

> Columbia citizens' perspective: "I'm paying a separate tax for these services
> that I'm supposed to be getting here, but then I pay my county taxes to pro-
> vide the same services that the county parks do for the Columbia parks." And
> there's constant pressure from people outside of Columbia, saying, "Well, the
> people in Columbia all have pools, but we don't have pools." "Well, you don't
> pay the [assessment] taxes they pay, either." . . . If they use Columbia as the
> benchmark . . . the seventy-five cents per one hundred [dollars Columbia As-
> sociation property levy] is a difference; that's a significant amount of taxes.
> (Interview 0217)

While people from outside Columbia can use the open facilities, such as
parks, free of charge and can pay to use the other facilities, such as the pools,
the fees for non-Columbians are substantially higher, currently double those
of the lien payers.

The Columbia Association has a professional staff, a president who is the
CEO, and a council or board of directors with representatives of each village, elected by residents. Along with the separate village associations, the
Columbia Association seems to have been an important forum for public
debate about issues to do with the Columbia concept, although other important civic organizations have existed. As Burkhart explained, reflecting
on her observations in the 1970s, "There remains a heavy emphasis on the
idea of equal access for all residents to the resources of the community. This
powerful ethic, combined with . . . a quasi-governmental structure modeled
on participatory democracy, results in a continual public debate about issues surrounding [Columbia's] heterogeneity" (Burkhart 1981, 12). Burkhart commented that while middle-class white homeowners tended to be
the ones who ran for public office, the commitment to equality and integration gave others leverage to make demands of groups such as the Columbia Association (Burkhart 1981, 29–30). I observed something similar
years later, for example, while attending a meeting at which middle-class-
looking, gray-haired, white residents argued vociferously with the Columbia
Council for free access for low-income youth to swimming pools.

While the relatively powerless village association boards have been elected
from the start, the Columbia Association Board of Directors started off being dominated by the developer. When there were few residents, the developer feared disruption of the open space planning if early residents were to
take over the board and vote to stop investment in open space or other development (Sunderland 1971). A system was put in place to gradually replace
developer representatives with people elected by the residents in proportions
related to the number of housing units in Columbia. When development
proceeded less quickly than had initially been planned—the early plan was
for a buildout by 1980—this turnover was speeded up and occurred in 1982,
after the original time proposed for it but before the housing unit total had
been achieved (Kennedy 1998). The elected Columbia council now acts as

the Columbia Association Board of Directors (Columbia Association 2002). Residents, both owners and renters, can vote, but each household is allowed only one vote in most villages. Surveys report low voter involvement however, and activists mentioned having more difficulty getting those on the east side of Columbia—mostly the villages developed during the middle stage— involved (Mason-Dixon Opinion Research 1991).[28] Interestingly, most of the academic studies of Columbia's governance occurred in the period before the transition was made to full resident control (e.g., Appletree 1978).

Periodically, small groups of Columbia residents lobby to incorporate. While this has some attraction in terms of local democracy, it has disadvantages in terms of regionalism, given that one of the criticisms of urban sprawl is the fragmentation of the metropolis into multiple jurisdictions, with negative effects on economic efficiency and social equity. If most of the formal government is kept at the county level, this balances some local control with a more regional structure of governance.

The Columbia Association provides a variety of quite local services— recreational facilities, parks, open space, the archives, and covenant enforcement. In the 1990s and early 2000s, however, there were some very bitter controversies. The association was criticized in the press for alleged irregularities in business practices, particularly competitive bids (Morse 1997). People also complained about the cost of services, paid for through the lien, which by 2000 was seventy-three cents per one hundred dollars in assessed valuation. As I explain in chapter 4, the rate in The Woodlands in 2000 was between two-thirds and three-quarters of the Columbia figure, depending on the location in The Woodlands, even though it also paid for waste collection and fire protection. Columbia experienced a very difficult leadership transition after the 1998 retirement of Pat Kennedy, who had been president of the Columbia Association for two and a half decades. Kennedy's first replacement left after less than two years, and a new search collapsed in conflict within the Columbia Council. The ultimately successful result was the promotion of long-time resident Maggie Brown, who had previously worked for Howard County and was working as a vice president of the Columbia Association.

Interfaith.   One aspect of Rouse's interest in the human dimensions of development was spiritual issues and religious groups. This was a multifaceted interest, and Rouse made personal connections with different faith communities. "He would come to different faith institutions, every weekend, and worship with them. You could see him in a synagogue one Saturday; and he came to the Baptist church and he's hooting and hollering along with us, you know; he came to the Catholic church, he goes to mass" (Interview 0123).

Rouse was interested in having such groups share facilities. He had headed the Maryland United World Federalists, so he certainly had an interest in global forms of cooperation. However, part of Rouse's interest in interfaith cooperation was also practical. Congregations had special building needs. They required a lot of space for meetings and classrooms and parking, but only for a few hours a week, and the rest of the time the space lay unused. These needs were expensive for the religious groups, costly for developers, who could generally find more lucrative and efficient uses of land, and awkward for planning purposes, as separate facilities surrounded by separate parking lots tend to spread out development.

During the early planning, Rouse called a meeting of fifteen religious leaders—Protestant, Catholic, and Jewish—and managed to interest the National Council of Churches in some ideas of sharing space. He commissioned a report by the executive secretary of the Department of Church Planning at the Church Federation of Chicago, which showed that such a proliferation of buildings is very expensive. This led to the first interfaith center at Wilde Lake, shared by four Protestant denominations, Catholics, and Jews, who cooperatively raised money to build a complex of worship spaces, meeting rooms, and office facilities. A number of ecumenical congregations were also started. The Archdiocese of Baltimore planned no separate Catholic schools in the new community (Hamilton 1964f; Breckenfeld 1971, 292–94).

This was not totally new. For example, in the earlier planned community of Park Forest a move to promote ecumenical congregations had taken place (Whyte 1956, 369). However, Columbia's was a fairly bold experiment in both the cooperation and the activities of congregations, with a wide range of trial procedures occurring in their organization and in their practice of worship.

At Columbia, the process has not been totally successful. Congregations do share the four centers that have been built. However, over the years a number of groups wanted their own buildings and bought land on the edge of Columbia or in window areas (see Kaboolian and Nelson, n.d.). An important spin-off, however, was the Interfaith Housing task force, which built much of the early subsidized housing in Columbia.

Schools, Colleges, and the Educational Environment. Maryland's county school districts posed a potential difficulty for Columbia in the early years. While Howard County was not poor, schools were not a priority. Columbia had to compete for home sales with counties that spent far more per pupil; in addition, the work group and the planning team had created a development concept focused on education.

However, both the school superintendent and the school board were receptive to new ideas. At the state level, the superintendent of education helped to fund studies about reform and to gain access to Ford Foundation money in order to design two schools in Columbia. The chosen reforms involved open classrooms that included independent work, ungraded classes, and team teaching. Wilde Lake High School, opened in 1971, was the first in the country to use individual-study "learning activities packages" for self-paced learning (Ephross 1988, 87; Karsk 1977, 112). The school board changed the structure of schools, breaking them into years K–5, 6–8, and 9–12. Schools were smaller than is typical in the United States. The first high school was circular in plan, although it was later rebuilt. For its part, from early on in the development, Howard County negotiated to have school sites donated rather than sold by the Rouse Company (Consultants recommend 1967; Odendahl 1969; Avin 1993).

Not all these educational innovations have been maintained. Open schooling, in particular, has been reduced (Ephross 1988, 93–98). However, the school system has been generally regarded as a good one. It has also been kept under close scrutiny. Because Columbia has a high percentage of the county's subsidized housing units, it has had to deal with the perception of being an "inner-city" school district.

While not explicitly related to education, the issue of youth has periodically provoked controversy and debate. For example, in the late 1960s and early 1970s the Columbia Association and Cooperative Ministry created teen centers and a coffee house that attracted a large number of teens, many from outside Columbia, a situation that came to be perceived as a problem. Others complained of boredom among teens and drug problems (Scarupa 1970; Karsk 1977; Wannemacher 1996).

A number of higher-education institutions also established facilities in Columbia, although many for only short periods—the Peabody Conservatory of Music (Baltimore), the Corcoran Art Gallery (D.C.), Antioch College, and Dag Hammarskjold College. The Antioch program was particularly interesting, as it involved students in work-study positions, many of whom became quite active in Columbia's affairs. More long-term has been Howard Community College, opened in 1970 (Breckenfeld 1971, 300–301). Planning in the mid-1960s had envisaged two other unique institutions for research and education. One, the Columbia Center, would conduct research in areas such as employment, family life, health, spiritual issues, altruism, and citizenship. The center would be staffed by research fellows and an annually appointed "resident critic" (CRD 1964d; Hamilton 1964b). The idea shows the idealism and free thinking of Columbia's planning. The second institution, a center for community development, was focused on adult education and life skills (CRD 1964a).

Some of the educational functions of the Columbia Center ended up being carried out at the American City Corporation, founded in the late 1960s. Starting in the 1970s, it hosted the Urban Life Center, where members of the Rouse team conducted classes for new community developers and held conferences on such topics as management and education (The nebulous art 1971). On one level, this shows the extraordinary self-confidence of the Rouse Company. However, it also indicates an astounding openness in a competitive industry that often tries to keep secrets. While the American City Corporation stayed in existence until at least 1987, this educational mission became less important after the early 1970s, and the organization generally conducted planning studies about urban redevelopment.

Mature Planning

When Rouse turned sixty-five, in 1979, he retired, in accordance with Rouse Company policy. Some people saw this as a sign of a well-functioning organization. Others felt that the visionary founder of the company should have been exempted from the rule. Still others thought that he was perhaps ready to leave after all the conflicts over the cost of Columbia. Rouse continued to live in Columbia but put his energy into other things, founding the Enterprise Foundation with his second wife, Patti, in 1982. The administration of Columbia, however, has had some remarkable continuity. The Rouse Company's director of development, Alton Scavo, has worked at the Rouse Company since the 1960s. The current planning director of Howard County, Joseph Rutter, has worked for the county since 1966. The Columbia Association president, Maggie Brown, moved to Columbia in 1970.

The Rouse Company has continued to build out the physical plan, although not without some modifications. The land use was changed several times, with major changes in 1974, the late 1970s, 1992, 1993, and 1995.[29] Because open space and employment areas were increasing, the residential land base was reduced, pushing densities on residential land higher (see table 5). These density adjustments were limited, however, as they aroused controversies in the mid-1970s. Still later, neighboring residents forced a reduction in attached housing in the last village, River Hill. This was part of a general resistance to growth that occurred in the 1980s and 1990s in combination with an increase in low-density development in Howard County. However, the intensity of the town center development has been rapidly increasing, with a renovated library and mid- and high-rise housing (Cadiz 2002).

The Rouse Company still owns a share of all but one of the village centers and has struggled to make these centers work financially as the economics of supermarkets has changed to require larger catchments. After extensive renovations to a number of centers, in 2002 the Rouse Company signed an agreement to create a joint venture with Kimco Realty. In this arrangement, the Rouse Company is the minority partner, with Kimko managing the sites (Columbia Village Centers 2002; Jones 2001). In general, the later villages were not designed with as much attention to detail as is evident in the earlier ones, although the Rouse Company gained experience as it progressed

TABLE 5   Land Use Changes in Columbia

	1965		1974		197–[a]		1992		1993		1995	
	Acres	%	Acres	%	Acres	%	Acres	%	Acres	%	Acres	%
Single-family low-density housing	5,620	36.8	2,560	19.2	1,790	12.7	1,479	10.5	1,479	10.5	1,479	10.4
Single-family medium-density housing	710	4.6	3,328	25.0	2,905	20.7	3,016	21.3	3,015	21.3	3,015	21.1
Apartments	515	3.4	1,256	9.4	1,546	11.0	1,682	11.9	1,695	12.0	1,707	12.0
Employment centers	2,570	16.8	3,094	23.2	2,738	19.5	2,644	18.7	2,629	18.6	2,711	19.0
Open space	2,340	15.3	3,076	23.1	5,068	36.1	5,315	37.6	5,319	37.6	5,360	37.6
Peripheral unplanned acres and other[b]	3,515	23.0										
TOTAL	15,270		13,314		14,047		14,136		14,137		14,272	

SOURCES: Rouse Company land use maps; HRD 1965a, 23.

[a] Exact date on map is unreadable.

[b] This category in 1965 figures only; includes proposed donations.

through the development, so the later villages have the advantage of that experience.

While the profits took a long time to appear, Columbia has met other of its goals: it has become a development with a balance of services, enough jobs for its residents, high-quality open space, and a relatively active public. I examine Columbia's current political, physical, social, and ecological character in more detail in chapters 5 and 6 as I compare the three developments.

Chapter 4

The Woodlands

Houston is renowned as the largest city without zoning in the United States. This has created a very interesting market for real estate, and Houston is the location of a number of large master-planned developments that satisfy some of the demand for an ordered environment. The Woodlands new community entered this market, using landscape as its niche to differentiate it from other Houston developments.[1]

This was not a simple task. The development is designed primarily to protect relatively invisible water systems, allowing aquifer recharge and limiting runoff. It combines this emphasis on hydrology with a striking but somewhat messy aesthetic that uses the original woods to mask and buffer development and to make its approach to protecting the environment more visible. This development strategy was not at all an inevitable one for the pet project of a person who had made his money in oil and gas exploration.

As with the other developments, The Woodlands went through a number of phases:

Phase 1: Early ideas, mid-1960s to 1970: In this period, The Woodlands' developer, George Mitchell, was exploring the possibility of a very large real estate development, involving a significant increase in scale from a few smaller projects that he had done in the region. He assembled the land, worked on two different preliminary plans, and had a preapplication approved for support by HUD under its Title VII new communities program.

Phase 2: Ecological design and the Columbia contingent, 1970 to 1974: HUD's preliminary approval led to bringing landscape architect and environmental planner Ian McHarg into the picture along with William Pereira, who had worked on Irvine. As final HUD approval neared,

TABLE 6 The Woodlands Timeline

Date	General Events	Villages/Facilities Opening
1919	George Mitchell born	
1964	Mitchell Corporation purchases Grogan-Cochran Lumber Company (50,000 acres)	
1965	U.S. Department of Housing and Urban Development created	
1966	Architect Karl Kamrath and land planner Hugh Pickford do first plan for The Woodlands	
1968	Housing and Urban Development Act—creates Title IV new towns	
1969	Cerf Ross completes plan	
1970	Housing and Urban Development Act—creates Title VII new towns	
	Title IV application submitted, February	
	Preapplication approved, June; full application invited	
1971	Meeting with various religious denominations to set up interfaith agreement	
	Tentative HUD agreement, November	
1972	University of Houston Board of Regents accepts offer of campus site	
	Project agreement signed between HUD and The Woodlands Development Corporation	
1974	First resident moves into The Woodlands	Grogan's Mill
	Houston Open golf tournament signs ten-year contract to play in The Woodlands	
	The Woodlands officially opens in October	
1975	Big layoffs from development team	
1978	First supermarket opens	
1979		Circa 1979: Panther Creek
1982	Houston Advanced Research Center announced	Research Forest
1983	The Woodlands formally released from its Title VII new town status	Cochran's Crossing
1984		Indian Springs
1987	Hardy Toll Road opens	
1990		Cynthia Woods Mitchell Pavilion
1992	The Woodlands Community Association transitions to resident control	
1995	Montgomery College opens	Alden Bridge and The Woodlands Mall
1997	The Woodlands sold to Crescent Realty and Morgan Stanley	
2003	The Rouse Company buys 52.5 percent share in The Woodlands from Crescent Realty	

SOURCES: Morgan and King 1987; Kutchin 1998a; TWCSC 2002.

Mitchell started recruiting a large team of people from Columbia, intending the development to combine the expertise of several approaches to new community planning in a way that would potentially build on the strengths of each. However, the opening of the development during the real estate downturn was followed quickly by the resignation and, in some cases dismissal, of many of the Columbia contingent.

Phase 3: Title VII in operation, 1975 to 1983: During the late 1970s and early 1980s the Mitchell team tried to recover from their difficult start and to manage their relationship with HUD. This was not easy.

Phase 4: Community building, 1983 to 1997: The development ended its connection with HUD in 1983 in the early period of the downturn in Texas property prices. However, construction continued and major infrastructure was provided, including the mall in 1994. This was also the period in which residents took more control of service provision.

Phase 5: Post-Mitchell growth since 1997: After George Mitchell sold the development in 1997, its new owners, Crescent Real Estate Equities and the Morgan Stanley Real Estate Fund II, took advantage of good economic times to increase the speed of development, including development in the downtown. In late 2003, the Rouse Company, developer of Columbia, bought a 52.5 percent share in The Woodlands. The long-term effects of this purchase are unclear. (See table 6.)

BACKGROUND TO THE DEVELOPMENT:
GEORGE MITCHELL

In the 1960s George Mitchell, who had been very successful in oil and gas exploration and development, started to think about doing real estate development. He was disturbed by the difficulties of the inner cities, from pollution and traffic to general decay. He was also troubled by the problems of "helter-skelter fragmented development" in suburbs, even in upper-income areas. According to a sympathetic 1987 account of The Woodlands, he came to see that new development could do better. It could be more racially and economically integrated and healthier and more pleasant. If linked governmentally to the urban core, new development areas could funnel taxes back where they were sorely needed. Because of volatility in oil and gas prices, Mitchell was also interested in diversifying his income sources, and real estate seemed to be one option (Mitchell 1998, 204–6; Morgan and King 1987, 7–9).

The planning process for The Woodlands indicates that Mitchell did not have this entire philosophy in place at the start. However, he learned through the process of starting development, and by the late 1960s or early

1970s he had developed his ideas into a package that formed the basis for his long-term commitment to The Woodlands. His approach had many similarities to that of James Rouse, which is not surprising. Mitchell inhabited a world similar to that of Rouse, watching urban events of the 1960s and considering what he could do from the perspective of business. He was a member of a group called the Young Presidents' Organization (YPO), a business group made up of presidents of organizations. Through YPO educational programs he visited both Watts in Los Angeles and Bedford-Stuyvesant in New York during the mid-1960s. The connection with Rouse was also more direct: Mitchell studied at the American City Corporation in Columbia in the early 1970s. However, Rouse's response had been to explore the potential for social science to solve the problems of city building; Mitchell, eventually, looked to the natural sciences and in particular ecology as it was being translated into environmental planning and landscape architecture in the late 1960s and early 1970s. Onto this he grafted many of Columbia's ideas, though indirectly, by hiring many people who had worked on that project (Kutchin 1998b, 10; Mitchell 1998).

Like Rouse's, Mitchell's biography is of some importance to the development he sponsored. He was born in 1919 in Galveston, the youngest son of Greek immigrants—his father's last name was originally Paraskevopoulos. His father had worked as a laborer constructing railroads and later ran a dry cleaning business, first in Houston and then in Galveston. Mitchell worked his way through college. After graduating first in his class at Texas A&M in petroleum engineering, with many classes in geology, Mitchell worked briefly for the American Oil Company, then with the Army Corps of Engineers, and after the war started his own business, which became the Mitchell Energy and Development Corporation. By the 1980s the corporation was on the Fortune 500 list, with key investments in oil and natural gas but also sixty thousand acres held for real estate ventures (Morgan and King 1987, 4–7; Kutchin 1998b; Mitchell 1998, 183). In 2002 Mitchell was the 136th richest person in the United States with assets of $1.6 billion, although by 2003 he had dropped to 139th (Forbes 2002, 2003). Of Mitchell's real estate activities, The Woodlands has been by far the largest. Since the early 1970s Mitchell has also supported a number of sustainability initiatives, many conducted through the Houston Advanced Research Center in The Woodlands.

Many people I interviewed compared Mitchell and Rouse as visionaries; no one was in the equivalent early role at Irvine. When Rouse started Columbia, he had already contributed ideas about urban development to contemporary practices, particularly the early shopping mall and work on urban renewal. He had achieved a national reputation as a speaker on urban issues with numerous invitations to talk to congressional inquiries and major universities in the 1950s and early 1960s, even before Columbia was developed (e.g., Rouse 1955a, 1955b, 1963b; New suburbia 1965). By the early 1960s he had clearly articulated his views on suburban growth and development, authoring a number of papers on the issue. In general, Rouse was a very articulate proponent of his viewpoints, with an obvious commitment to improving the world and spreading development models.

In contrast, when he started The Woodlands, George Mitchell had created only a few small real estate developments. His reputation and significant fortune rested on oil and gas work—he reputedly had a flair for finding oil and a great tolerance for risk. Mitchell was also more low key as a person than Rouse, with aspirations aimed at improving Houston and leaving a legacy there rather than at making a highly visible difference on the national stage. Certainly he had goals about dealing with the environmental crisis, he clearly saw the global implications of his actions, and his entrepreneurship had gained him wide attention. Many of those who worked for him were impressed with his vision and his courage in business. However, he generally kept a lower profile than Rouse.

While Rouse undeniably had charisma and a kind of genius for implementing a vision, it seems to me that at least part of the difference was to do with social background. Rouse had lived and worked close to the center of political power in the Washington-Baltimore area. While he was not extraordinarily rich as a child and had lost both parents by the age of sixteen, he had come from a comfortable social background (Breckenfeld 1971, 202). Mitchell had risen from far humbler beginnings than Rouse. He had come from Galveston and from an immigrant background and had had to struggle more than Rouse to find a place in society. A number of interviewees felt that developing The Woodlands was part of that struggle.

PHASE 1:
EARLY IDEAS, MID-1960s TO 1970

The First Steps: Land Purchase

In the mid-1960s, Mitchell started investing in land to the north and northwest of Houston, along Interstate 45 between Houston and Dallas. The road had been completed in the early 1960s, and the Houston Intercontinental Airport, which was also to the north of Houston, was scheduled for opening in 1968. The traditional growth sector for Houston had been to the south, toward Galveston and the Johnson Space Center, and to the southwest and west, toward the Galleria area. However, with the completion of the interstate, development started to move toward the north of Houston. Mitchell first obtained options to purchase around two thousand acres along I-45, close to Houston along the FM 1960 road, but he let these lapse. Morgan and King argue that Mitchell was moving toward the concept of a very large development, and much of the available land around FM 1960 was already

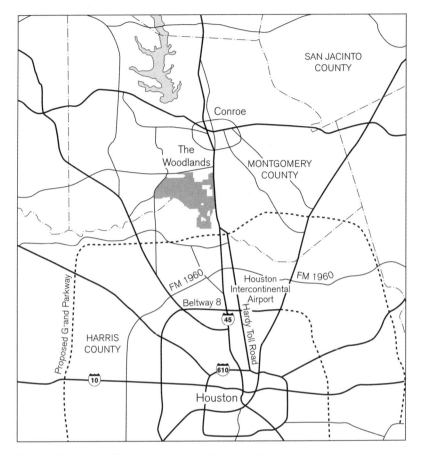

Figure 28. Map of Houston region, with major features.

taken up with a competing residential area, Champions, and a large amount of strip development (Morgan and King 1987, 22–23) (see figure 28).

In 1964, Mitchell purchased the Grogan-Cochran Lumber Company, along with its fifty thousand acres ten miles farther north along I-45 (and over twenty-five miles from the center of the City of Houston). The cost was $6.25 million. With the idea for The Woodlands yet unformed, the potential uses for the land included oil and gas exploration and smaller subdivisions. However, the potential to do a large development was obvious, and eventually twenty-eight hundred acres from this purchase were included in The Woodlands project area (Kutchin 1998b, 10; Morgan and King 1987, 25).

Mitchell started to acquire additional parcels in strategic locations. Land is relatively inexpensive in Texas, and people were used to Mitchell buying land for oil and gas purposes, so he did not use the same elaborate secrecy during the purchase period as Rouse had. Negotiations for the purchase of 1,070 acres of land owned by the Roman Catholic Diocese stretched from April 1966 to March 1970, although negotiations were intensive only after December 1967. Other land deals involved swaps; for example, between February 1968 and October 1970 the Mitchell Corporation negotiated to obtain 4,300 acres of land from the Champion Paper Corporation in exchange for 12,000 acres of timberland in another location (Morgan and King 1987, 25–26).

While a number of transactions were on this scale, many were much smaller, and eventually the development involved between three hundred and five hundred separate transactions, with accounts differing over the exact number (Kutchin 1998b, 11; Lively 1998; Morgan and King 1987, 26). Overall, the land purchase costs for the early stage of the development were $1,688 per acre (Morgan and King 1987, 27). The land was also relatively contiguous—with only 692 acres of outparcels in the initial 20,000-acre site—making it more similar in structure to the Irvine Ranch than to fragmented Columbia. Over the years, The Woodlands Operating Company (earlier, The Woodlands Development Corporation) has continued to buy land to add to the development and close these window areas. Early accounts generally refer to a development area of 17,000 acres; by the late 1990s this was 27,000.

While the land was being bought, George Mitchell was exploring options for the overall design of the new community. The first such plan was prepared by Karl Kamrath and Hugh Pickford in the early part of 1966 and presented in March. Kamrath was a Houston architect who had designed Mitchell's home. The plan covered twenty thousand acres and had a population of fifty thousand, with a low-density housing area and several lakes at the core and multifamily housing and light industry on the edge. A number of commercial and shopping areas were arranged along the boundary between the single-family core and the higher-density edge. The town center was located in the middle of the southern side of the site, quite far from the interstate. It was not unlike a number of other master-planned developments around Houston (Morgan and King 1987, 27, front plate).

Title VII

Working on financial issues, Mitchell started to examine some options for financing the project. He had a great deal of personal wealth, but he also had a great deal of debt. He needed loans or financial partners to do the development. In 1966, Title X was passed, an amendment to the 1965 Housing and Urban Development Act. This provided federal mortgage insurance for developers of new communities, although only for the purchase of raw land and its site improvements. It was not much used, as the private sector already had good access to mortgages, but it did indicate some interest on the part of the federal government (Mields 1973, 24).

This was expanded in the 1968 Housing and Urban Development Act, where Title IV provided federal guarantees for loans to developments as well as making the developments eligible for some federal infrastructure and open space grants. The 1968 act was a compromise. It did not provide significant funds for new communities but gave some limited incentives in exchange for public benefits, such as the provision of affordable housing. After heated debate and the reduction of the overall total of available loan guarantees from $500 million to $250 million, the bill passed (Morgan and King 1987, 16–17; Weiss 1973, 5–6). This bill, like Title X, turned out to offer too few incentives, and few developers applied for the support. The Woodlands was one exception; its initial application was under this program. In addition, in 1969 Nixon came to the presidency, and the administration had a mixed response to new communities.

Congress still had some interest in the idea of new towns, however, and in April 1970 HUD recommended a program to the president involving the construction of ten new towns a year. This was rejected by Nixon, but supporters of the idea introduced House and Senate bills to achieve something of the same program. The bills included a national policy on urban growth and the creation of the Community Development Corporation, which could make direct loans to public and private developers with principal and interest payments deferred for fifteen years (Mields 1973, 26). The bills also provided for direct grants to new community developers for public services. Nixon advocated new communities in his 1970 State of the Union address, but members of his administration, including the new secretary of HUD, George Romney, lobbied to delete the new community program from the 1970 Housing and Urban Development Act. The compromise after machinations in both House and Senate was to put the Community Development Corporation administrative unit inside HUD instead of making it a separate entity. In addition, the federal loans were converted to federal loan *guarantees* (up to $50 million per project, with a total for the program of $500 million). The compromise legislation added fifteen-year interest-free loans of up to $20 million to pay interest on debt for land purchase and development, with a total for the program of $240 million. Developments were also given access to a number of smaller grants for planning and public service, although either Congress or the presidential administration eventually blocked the funding for most of these grant programs (U.S. HUD, NCA 1976, 28–31). Title VII, also known as the Housing and Urban Development Act of 1970, was not signed into law by the president until December 31, 1970 (Mields 1973, 22–23; Morgan and King 1987, 18–20; Weiss 1973, 6).

As Mields summarizes, Congress's goals for Title VII were to encourage good planning, in "relatively self-sufficient communities," for a diverse population, using new technologies, and to channel growth toward both revitalizing older areas and concentrating suburban growth in selected sites (Mields 1973, 2; also Underhill 1976).

Title VII focused on private-sector projects, although public-private partnerships were eligible. However, even private developers had to comply with numerous federal requirements that were being developed while the first round of projects was being processed and approved (see table 7).

For a developer worried about finances, this looked very helpful. Mitchell decided to try the HUD program. He changed architects, and from late 1968 to late 1969 another Houston architect, Cerf Ross, developed a plan for a new town of one hundred thousand on 14,840 acres (Ross 1969, 2, 23).[2] It kept the large loop road around the development but differed from the initial Kamrath and Pickford plan in a number of ways. As the text of the Ross plan explains, this was to be a "city" and not a "super-subdivision." It would be composed of four "communities," each about twenty-five thousand in population, each divided into four neighborhoods, and each providing different household types at a range of costs for people with different incomes. The four communities were arranged as quadrants around the business area, which was in the center of the development, again at some distance from the freeway. A university campus was proposed for the northwestern sector, and an industrial zone was to the north. On-call transit would serve the communities. At the new town level, transit service on dedicated rights-of-way, illustrated by images of monorails, would deal with longer trips between communities (Ross 1969 31, 34). Some form of a transit system remained an option in the 1972 project agreement and later plans (U.S.A. and TWDC 1972, G-19; WMRT 1974b, 40). The Ross plan, however, was an unusual mix of very conceptual bubble diagrams indicating the location of major elements and very detailed site plans and perspective drawings of neighborhood centers and the central business area.

This plan was used as the basis for the preapplication document submitted to HUD under the then Title IV program. The project received preapplication approval on June 17, 1970, but the Mitchell team was told by HUD that the planning would need to be of a higher quality for approval (Morgan and King 1987, 29; McAlister 1970, June 5 memo; Mields 1973, 55). This very early planning had received some nonlocal input, however. James McAlister, director of planning and economics at the Mitchell corporation, corresponded with and visited a number of experts, including Mike Spear, then research director at the Rouse Company (McAlister 1970).

TABLE 7   Federally Assisted New Communities

Name	State	Acres in 1973	Projected Size for HUD Guarantee[a]	Years to Reach Size	Eventual Population[b]	Title VII
Cedar Riverside	Minnesota	336	30,000	20	30,000	Yes
Flower Mound	Texas	6,156	64,000	20	64,000	Yes
Gananda	New York	5,842	50,000	20	82,500	Yes
Harbison	South Carolina	2,000	23,000	20	26,000	Yes
Jonathan	Minnesota	5,856	50,000	20	50,000	Yes, + Title IV
Lysander[c]/Radisson	New York	2,670	18,334	Approx. 10	18,000	
Maumelle	Arkansas	5,319	45,000	20	60,000	Yes
Newfields	Ohio	—	33,500	20	—	Yes
Park Forest South	Illinois	8,291	110,000	15	110,000	Yes
Riverton	New York	2,560	25,600	16	25,600	Yes
Roosevelt Island[c]	New York	—	18,000	18	18,000	
Shenandoah	Georgia	—	70,000	20	—	Yes
Soul City	North Carolina	5,180	44,000	30	44,000	Yes
St. Charles	Maryland	7,900	75,000	20	75,000	Yes
The Woodlands	Texas	16,937	150,000	20	150,000	Yes

SOURCES: Mields 1973, 27–29; U.S. Postal Service 1973; U.S./USSR New Towns Working Group 1981.
NOTE: All figures are approximate because the sources contradict one another.
[a] Data from Mields 1973.
[b] Data from U.S. Postal Service 1973.
[c] Two new communities were not full Title VII new towns, as they received only eligibility for grants rather than grant eligibility and a federal debt guarantee.

PHASE 2:
ECOLOGICAL DESIGN AND THE COLUMBIA CONTINGENT, 1970 TO 1974

Environmental Planning

Mitchell again looked at changing the land planning team for the more expensive process of developing a formal application. Costs to reach the formal commitment stage were estimated to be in the range of $250,000 to $500,000 for a ten-thousand-acre project (equivalent to approximately $870,000 to $1.7 million in 2000 dollars), although costs for the Title VII project Cedar-Riverside were around $1.5 million (Mields 1973, 67–68).[3]

Mitchell looked at several firms but ended up hiring a young Houston architect out of one of the firms to work with him in-house. Robert Hartsfield became the director of planning and design. With Mitchell and James McAlister, now director of economics and real estate, he set about selecting the consultants. Several land planning and marketing firms were asked for proposals during 1970, including Skidmore Owings and Merrill (which had designed Oak Ridge, Tennessee), Victor Gruen and Associates (Valencia and Laguna Niguel, California), McIntire and Quiros (Westlake Village, California), Charles Luckman and Associates, Albert Martin, and William Pereira and Associates. From correspondence in the period, it appears that William Pereira and Associates were front runners, given their experience in Irvine (McAlister 1970). William Pereira came to Houston on other projects, doing an urban design plan for a thirty-two-block area of downtown Houston as well as a forty-story office building that opened in 1974.

Robert Hartsfield came on board in the midst of the selection process. As a University of Pennsylvania graduate, he knew Ian McHarg and suggested that Mitchell look at his work. Mitchell read McHarg's *Design with Nature,* which had been published in 1969, and was very impressed (McHarg 1969; Morgan and King 1987; Middleton 1997; Sutton and McHarg 1975; Hartsfield 1998, 117–19; Kutchin 1998b). Wallace, McHarg, Roberts and Todd (WMRT) were not mentioned in internal status reports on real estate in 1970. Their absence is striking in the case of an August 1970 memo outlining potential teams. McHarg was called on October 13, and by January 1971 had been selected to be part of the team (McAlister 1970, August 11; McAlister 1971, January 22 memo; McHarg 1996, 256). Eventually, the HUD application team included both William Pereira and Associates, employed for master planning and design, and WMRT, for environmental planning. In addition, Gladstone Associates worked on economics and marketing, and Richard P. Browne Associates on development and engineering. Both Gladstone and Browne were consultants who had worked on Columbia. Browne was based in Columbia and also worked with architect-planner Bob Tennenbaum, who had been on the first Columbia planning team. Gladstone was in Washington, D.C. (McAlister 1998, 177; GMA 1971; Browne 1998).

This period, from mid-1970, was somewhat chaotic. The word was out that an oil tycoon wanted to build a new town, and interviewees remember consultants flying in to try to obtain this work (Interview 0502). In addition, those who Mitchell hired each wanted to do a significant part of the project, so there was some jockeying among consultant firms and principals. Together they changed the plan significantly on key dimensions, such as village structure, town center location, circulation, and open space.

In an interview in 2002, George Mitchell indicated that his most important move was to employ McHarg (Mitchell 2002). Although the WMRT work was refined and revised by subsequent consultants, including the firm of land planners from Columbia called Land Design Research (LDR), as well as by various staff members in the Mitchell organization, Mitchell's interview remark seems to be correct. Pereira's role was far less central than it had been on the Irvine Ranch, and he was not commissioned to do major buildings as he had been at both UC Irvine and Newport Center. As was explained in chapter 1, McHarg considered this development to be one of the best examples of his ideas (McHarg 1998).

McHarg, a landscape architect, was interested in working out more systematic ways of analyzing and designing around natural systems. He modified and popularized a system for doing overlays of various natural and human features, eliminating areas of high value from development. However, his approach had a deeper set of principles. In the opening pages of *Design with Nature,* McHarg sketched out his very personal preference for the country over the city. Two images from his early childhood near Glasgow were emblematic. As he described it, in one direction from his childhood home was the industrial city of the 1930s. Although it provided the setting for some "splendid events," such occasions "were interludes in a gray impression of gloom and dreary ugliness" in a city that "was a no-place, despondent, dreary beyond description, grimy, gritty, squalid" (McHarg 1969, 2; McHarg 1996, 14–15). He contrasted that with the other direction, the countryside, which in his childhood was a place of "delight and challenge, meaning and rewards" (McHarg 1969, 2). As he explained:

> We need nature as much in the city as in the countryside. In order to endure we must maintain the bounty of that great cornucopia which is our inheritance. . . . It is not a choice of either the city or the countryside: both are essential, but today it is nature, beleaguered in the country, too scarce in the city which has become precious. . . . Let us then abandon the simplicity of separation and give unity its due. Let us abandon the self-mutilation which has been our way and give expression to the potential harmony of man-nature. The world is abundant, we require only a deference born of understanding to fulfill man's promise. Man is that uniquely conscious creature who can perceive and express. He must become the steward of the biosphere. To do this he must design with nature. (McHarg 1969, 5)

McHarg's perspective also contained an explicit critique of anthropocentric and Western ideas about nature, and particularly economic approaches to the use of land. As he outlined, in these views "neither love nor compassion, health nor beauty, dignity nor freedom, grace nor delight are important unless they can be priced" (McHarg 1969, 25). However, he also rejected the traditional Japanese view of the "harmony of man-nature [which] has been achieved at the expense of the individuality of man" (27–28).

McHarg's solution was to reform the city, including its suburbs, something that he explained was both logical and cosmic in its importance. This approach would move beyond Eastern and Western views to a view informed by ecology.

> Where else can we turn for an accurate model of the world and ourselves but to science? We can accept that scientific knowledge is incomplete and will forever be so, but it is the best we have and it has great merit, which religions lack, of being self correcting. Moreover, if we wish to understand the phenomenal world, then we will reasonably direct our questions to those scientists who are concerned with this realm—the natural scientists. More precisely, when our preoccupation is with the interactions of organisms and environment—and I can think of no better description for our concern—then we must turn to ecologists, for that is their competence.
>
> We will agree that science is not the only mode of perception—that the poet, painter, playwright and author can often reveal in metaphor what science is unable to demonstrate. But if we seek a workman's creed which approximates reality and can be used as a model of the world and ourselves, then science does provide the best evidence. (McHarg 1969, 29)

His approach, demonstrated by the environmental planning in The Woodlands, was not limited to scientific data but also included what is recognizable as a rational planning method, progressing logically from ecological data inventory to interpretation, assessment of landscape tolerance, design synthesis, guidelines, and plans (WMRT 1974b, 6). However, his was not merely a scientific critique; it also had an aesthetic component. For example, McHarg criticized suburbs as "testaments to the American mercantile creed—the hamburger stand, gas station, diner, the ubiquitous billboards, sagging wires, the parking lot, car cemetery and that most complete conjunction of land rapacity and human disillusion, the subdivision" (McHarg 1969, 20). He saw commercial strips as vulgar.

This viewpoint became the intellectual basis for the core vision of The Woodlands. As one of the many professionals who worked on both projects explained to me:

> The big difference between Columbia and the Woodlands reflected the philosophical differences of Jim Rouse versus George Mitchell. Jim Rouse had a ma-

jor, major commitment to social justice. George Mitchell believed in it, but the
intensity of his commitment to it was much less, and he was cautious as to how
well some of those principles would be embraced in Texas, which was a politically conservative environment. He was prepared to do his part. He believed
that the principles of social justice were correct. But he wasn't going to go way
out on a limb in order to prove some points, whereas Jim Rouse was. George
Mitchell's big, big commitment was to environmental principles, and he
adopted this whole Ian McHarg hydrology model. He bought into the whole
thing, and it was the driving force behind land planning in the first village,
and for five years. (Interview 0201)

McHarg's team from WMRT was a large one. In the main ecological plan
for The Woodlands, twenty-three people are credited with planning and scientific roles in addition to those involved in report production and layout
and a separate consultant list. The list included people working in planning
and design as well as analyzing geology, hydrology, soils, plant ecology,
wildlife, and climatology.[4] McHarg did come to The Woodlands for significant periods, but people remember him spending a lot of time with George
Mitchell rather than doing project work. Of course that was part of his role—
a person who promoted a set of ideas: "Ian [McHarg] was an evangelist; the
environment was his religion. . . . He came up with all sorts of ideas; Ian was
always full of ideas, and not all the ideas worked. He needed people to trans-
late them" (Interview 0421). Most of the consulting firms and in-house
project planning groups involved with each of the developments were made
up of similarly large teams, but this case is a particularly striking example of
the problem of assigning authorship to developments. For example, I talk
of the "McHarg-Pereira" plan, but it was obviously the product of the work
of many people. I take up this issue in more detail in chapter 5.

The WMRT team delivered a preliminary report on ecological planning
on March 14, 1971, during a meeting at Columbia, Maryland (Morgan and
King 1987, 33; WMRT 1971, n.p.). A number of key early meetings were held
at Columbia because many of the consultants were located there.

This ecological planning work was submitted as part of the new community proposal (GMA 1971, V2). However, Jonathan Sutton of WMRT continued to work, producing a number of more polished documents in 1973
and 1974 that dealt with site planning, land planning, an ecological inventory, and the final ecological plan. Very few copies of the original planning
study survive; however, the later volumes were widely distributed (also Sutton and McHarg 1975).[5]

The 1971 study, and the later ones, pointed out that The Woodlands area
is relatively flat. Its most prominent feature is its forests, which are dominated
by various species of pines, although also supporting other vegetation. The
area is poorly drained and prone to flooding—one-third of the study area
was within the one-hundred-year floodplains of the three creeks on the site—

creating a set of very real constraints on development (WMRT, n.d., 79). In fact, the WMRT team saw this issue of hydrology, the water system including drainage and aquifer recharge, as the most critical natural system. As they explained: "In The Woodlands then, water became the integrating process which explained the nature of the site. Through the flow of water over the ground, the movement of water in the ground, and the effects of water on soil and vegetation, one can understand the interactions of nature and how to complement them" (WMRT, n.d., 79). As one of the early environmental planners noted:

> One of the things about the piney woods is that there are pines and other trees. The pines are not particularly special, but the rest of the trees, like the big live oaks and magnolias, are really beautiful trees. The problem is, if you change the hydraulic regime even the slightest bit, what happens is virtually all of the broad-leaved evergreens die; you end up with pines. One of the big issues was— One of the reasons we decided to use the natural drainage system apart from infiltration and other stuff is that we didn't want to drop the water table, because we wanted to keep this really diverse vegetation. (Interview 0421)

To the lay public, however, this particular landscape has a scraggly and messy appearance, quite different from the manicured landscapes that planned developments have traditionally had in Houston (see figures 29–34). This made the development approach somewhat more daring than it may at first appear.

Given these constraints, the WMRT team delineated areas where development would have less impact because of soils, slope, drainage, water recharge, erosion, wildlife areas, and opportunities for recreation and open space (WMRT 1974b, 26; also WMRT 1973a, 1973b, 1973c; Hydrological balancing act 1974). This included limits on clearing of building lots, the design of open space, and changes to drainage design. As I explain in chapter 5, landscape has been used very consistently as a basic framework underlying the urban design of The Woodlands, with villages, transportation corridors, and commercial centers having secondary importance. Development would change the hydrology of the system, but it was intended to increase peak flows by only about one-third of the increase in comparable new development (Spirn 1984, 166). While the priority of ecological values is by no means absolute, it is significant when compared with other comparable large developments.

At some stage early in the development, also an idea grew for replicating The Woodlands–type projects with a series of planned developments in a "string of pearls . . . a series of five or six projects, not as big as the Woodlands," around Houston (Mitchell 2000; also Mitchell 1998, 209–10). A 2000 interview with George Mitchell indicated that both he and McHarg were interested, and they even started an additional development, but The

Figure 29. Open drain in residential street. Photographer: Ann Forsyth.

Figure 30. Large drainage channel. Photographer: Ann Forsyth.

Figure 31. Forest buffer near shopping area. Photographer: Ann Forsyth.

Figure 32. Forest playground. Photographer: Ann Forsyth.

Figure 33. Attached housing. While The Woodlands is dominated by detached housing, other options are available. Photographer: Ann Forsyth.

Figure 34. Forest buffer in Research Forest; the area has many reflective glass buildings to literally mirror the forest itself. Photographer: Ann Forsyth.

Woodlands demanded too much attention. WMRT also prepared a feasibility study for a Mitchell property near Aspen in Colorado, but it did not go ahead either (WMRT 1974a).

The Social and Economic Planning Approach

The HUD project agreement of 1972, based on the submission of 1971, used the ecological knowledge but also added a strong land planning and development component. On the basis of marketing consultant Gladstone's experience with Columbia and other developments, the Title VII proposal estimated that 47,375 dwelling units would be built, housing about 150,000 people. The total site area in this version of the plan was 16,939 acres, of which 3,909, or 23 percent, would be open space, including private open spaces such as golf courses; 9,006 acres were saleable, including 6,339 for residential uses and 2,000 for industrial uses (U.S.A. and TWDC 1972, 9–12). Marketing consultant Gladstone proposed a marketable package including recreation areas, preschools, tot lots, an outdoor theater, and a path system (Morgan and King 1987, 37–38).

The development was divided into a range of social groupings: *clusters* of six to twenty-five dwellings on a short street, *sections* of two to eight clusters, *neighborhoods* of two to twenty sections, and *villages* of two to six neighborhoods. Like Columbia, clusters were to be homogeneous in price but mixed in other social characteristics, such as race. All larger areas were to be mixed in all dimensions (U.S.A. and TWDC 1972, G-5). Neighborhoods were organized around an elementary school, and neighborhood centers were to replicate the early idea for Columbia, with the centers containing both recreation spaces and a convenience store. The next level of center, village centers, were to cluster retail, recreation, school uses, and community rooms (U.S.A. and TWDC 1972, G-14; GMA 1971, V2–67, 83). This village center design did not eventuate, in that recreation spaces are separated with the exception of the first village, Grogan's Mill, in which the village center is near the country club and conference center. All village associations meet at the main community association building; the community center spaces in the villages were cut. Even individual churches, and their associated services, were eventually discouraged from locating in the centers because of land prices (Gebert 2000). The overall adherence in the proposal to a Columbia-style village structure is not surprising, given the consultants' experience with Columbia and its reputation as an exemplary new town. This was the period when Columbia's reputation was at its height. While even Columbia has struggled to maintain a few convenience stores in neighborhood centers, it has retained mixed-use village centers. The move away from mixed uses in The Woodlands' village centers has led to their primary use as commercial areas (Morgan and King 1987, 49ff.).

Like many other new towns, the proposed town center was to contain a mix of larger-scale uses: major retail, office, and entertainment areas. The 1972 project agreement indicated approximately two thousand acres of industrial areas. The road network was a loose grid of arterials with a set of loops and culs-de-sac in the interiors of the villages.

The project agreement proposed that 52.5 percent of dwellings were to be rental units in various attached forms, from townhouses to elevator apartments (forty-nine hundred of the latter). However, the project agreement *required* a minimum of only 25 percent of one tenure. This was a much larger percentage of rental units than the other two developments had initially proposed. Only 26 percent of units in The Woodlands were to be single-family detached houses, with other ownership dwellings being attached units. It is interesting that with these high initial expectations, The Woodlands has the lowest percentage of attached and rental units of the three case study developments. In 1990, it had 74 percent detached units and 34 percent renters. By 2000, 79 percent of units were detached, and the proportion of renters had dropped further, to 21 percent, under the minimum level promised in the project agreement (U.S.A. and TWDC 1972, G-7, schedule 8) (see table 12 in appendix B).

Part of the reason that the large number of attached and rental housing units was proposed—large particularly in this suburban area in Texas—was to provide affordability and income mix. The assisted program for low- and moderate-income earners included both homeownership and rental units in a scattered pattern. In the initial proposal, assisted or subsidized units were to constitute 15 percent of all units, although many inexpensive market-rate units would be built in addition, also classified as affordable because of their low cost. The application projected that low- and moderate-income earners would be able to afford about 30 percent of units in The Woodlands because of the inexpensive character of the housing. The market-rate units would, of course, be subject to price escalation, but this problem was not mentioned in the project agreement. In the final agreement no numbers were specified for assisted or subsidized units, although the development was to have 12.8 percent of units affordable to low-income earners and 14.5 percent affordable to moderate-income earners, represented by incomes of $5,300 and $7,155, respectively, for a family of four in 1972. While the ways of achieving such affordability—through subsidies or through inexpensive market units—might seem vague, HUD was serious about the goal of low- and moderate-income housing matching the income profile of the metropolitan area by quartile. If annual goals were not met, the developer was required to set up a revolving fund equal to 10 percent of net earnings, up to $10.5 million, to supply such housing (U.S.A. and TWDC 1972, G-10–11, schedule 12).

Other components gradually came into play. The University of Houston had been interested in a branch campus, and it had been indicated in the 1969 Cerf Ross plan. Negotiations about an offer of land by Mitchell continued from early 1971 to March 7, 1972, when the regents accepted the offer of a donation of four hundred acres for the campus, pending authorization from the Texas State Authorizing Board (Morgan and King 1987, 39–40). The University of Houston campus was a core component of the Title VII program application and part of the marketing plan, in that it would generate demand for housing along with significant retail spending (Morgan and King 1987, 95). As in Columbia, this did not run smoothly. The university never came, and in 1995 The Woodlands ended up with a community college, just as Columbia did, although Mitchell also established the Houston Advanced Research Center in 1982 with input from a consortium of universities (Kutchin 1998a, 25; Tough 1998).[6]

Social planning was less developed than other aspects of project planning, although some staff members were assigned to social and institutional planning, and consultants were employed in public health. Mitchell also conducted a two-day workshop or seminar in October 1971, with a team of experts very similar in character to Columbia's social planning work group (Morgan and King 1987, 40–41). However, compared with the many years of work on ecological issues, the emphasis on social planning was much more minor.

Planning for religious facilities did receive a fair amount of attention. Mitchell was attracted by Rouse's experiment with interfaith. He discussed the issue with his own minister, Reverend Richard Wheatcroft, and in June 1971 had a meeting of leaders from Jewish, Roman Catholic, and Protestant denominations in Houston. The group formed the Religious Institutions Planning group and in February 1972 adopted a statement, "Towards an Interfaith Covenant," which stated support for cooperative planning, ministry, and community service (Morgan and King 1987, 42–43; Franzmeier and Gebert 1979, 5; Wheatcroft 1998). They continued to meet in 1973, forming a group called The Woodlands Religious Community, Inc. (WRC), which later became known as Interfaith (Franzmeier and Gebert 1979, 9).

HUD Approval

Plans for the new town were formally presented to HUD at the end of March 1971, and Mitchell's group submitted the master plan in August (GMA 1971). Tentative approval was given in November 1971, and the project agreement was finally signed in August 1972. Construction started with the ceremonial removal of the first tree in September 1972 (Morgan and King 1987, 44, 49).

This process of becoming a Title VII new town sounds relatively smooth but, in fact, involved a number of judgments about what HUD would approve. A letter dated May 22, 1970, from George Mitchell to HUD secretary

George Romney explained that over one hundred thousand dollars had been spent on planning work and requested a twenty-million-dollar guarantee under the then-active Title IV (McAlister 1970). However, The Woodlands was a big, complex project, and by the time of the mid-1971 presentation to HUD, Title VII was in place, and the development team argued to Mitchell that they should ask for the maximum loan guarantee. James McAlister's brother-in-law was an aid to Senator Lloyd Bentsen and helped to involve Senator John Tower, so they had political support, but Mitchell was still worried. As McAlister explained of the HUD presentation:

> The way that I had it set up was first, to have Jim Veltman get up and go through ecology, then second we went through the social part. . . . This was followed by the development plan with all exhibits. At this point we had never told them how much money we were going to request. . . .
>
> George was nervous all the way on the airplane going up there about the $50 million he wanted. At any rate my economic presentation was the last part. So I went through the economics and was the last speaker. I had to close and state our request. I said, "And, therefore, for the reasons you've just heard, we respectfully request $50 million." Total, total silence for the longest period. . . . Mitchell begins to look around and looks at me like, Oh! Oh! . . . I didn't say one thing. If you know about sales you know that the first person to speak, loses, and I just stood there and thought, "God, I'm going to get fired, my life's over, it's done." Then Nicholson [Nicoson] speaks up and says, "That was a very fine presentation and we will take it under advisement." That's all he said. Then they had some questions as they went through the process and, ultimately, we got the loan guarantee. (McAlister 1998, 179; see almost identical quotes in Kutchin 1998a, 13; McAlister 2000)

Overall, this was quite a coup. Fiscally conservative Senator Tower had testified against the loan guarantees during debates over the 1968 bill and had even offered an amendment to delete Title IV (Morgan and King 1987, 16).

HUD required local approvals from local governments that might be affected by the development—a process called the A-95 clearance—and the entities for The Woodlands were the Houston Galveston Area Council (HGAC) and the Cities of Houston and Conroe. Amazingly the development was kept out of the press until October 1971—Mitchell had briefed the Conroe *Courier* but asked them to keep quiet until the HUD financing was finalized (Morgan and King 1987, 45–46). However, on October 5, 1971, HGAC had a meeting at which the development was announced, bringing it into the open. The Mitchell organization quickly asked the City of Houston to place the new community in its extraterritorial jurisdiction, which it did. It had been planning such a move since at least July 1970 (McAlister 1970, July 10 memo). However, in 1966, the City of Conroe to the north had already declared in its extraterritorial jurisdiction a strip of land along the interstate and would not give this up. In 1974, with the development about to open, this came to a head when citizens in this strip in The Woodlands were given permission to incorporate as the small City of Shenandoah, which included some of the office park area of the new community.[7] However, the majority of the land in The Woodlands did go to the extraterritorial jurisdiction of Houston.

This had a number of benefits. Houston's lack of zoning was useful to The Woodlands, as the development had more flexibility in its overall plan as well as a capacity to modify the plan without having to go through a rezoning. This made it a "a pure subdivision process . . . and that's pretty mechanical stuff—pipe diameters and turning radiuses" (Interview 0201). Unlike the small cities in its immediate vicinity, Houston also had the capacity to process a large number of such applications. Houston was the only city that could annex the land placed in its extraterritorial jurisdiction and would need to give residents of The Woodlands permission if they wanted to incorporate, effectively cutting off the incorporation option to residents of the new development. However, Houston was unlikely to annex the development in its first decades, when it had huge debts and had not yet developed a tax base. Morgan and King describe this as a strategy for the developer to keep "near-absolute control during the development period" (Morgan and King 1987, 46). Finally, it fulfilled Mitchell's regional aims for the development, which he saw as the best of both worlds, providing a suburban environment for those who wanted it and ultimately contributing to the tax base of the center city (Mitchell 1998).

In 1971, as the preliminary HUD agreement was nearing, Mitchell made a number of hires. He had earlier recruited a small number of people who had worked on Columbia to act as consultants to the HUD proposal, but at this stage he hired many more. Not every new hire was from Rouse's team, but Mitchell focused on the Columbia people, many of whom he had met at seminars on new town development at Rouse's American City Corporation in Columbia. One of the professionals working on Columbia described George Mitchell at this time as "recruiting people like baseball players" (Interview 0210).

The Woodlands created attractive packages for many professionals. Len Ivins had been vice president of the Rouse Company and director of development and was hired by Mitchell in late 1971 as senior vice president overseeing real estate. He was later president of The Woodlands Development Corporation, formed in July 1972. Other former Columbia people came to manage utilities, finance, and the proposed community association or as consultants in law and design (Morgan and King 1987, 48). From late 1971, when Ivins was hired and HUD gave tentative agreement to the plan, until the development officially opened in October 1974, this group worked with great intensity. They focused on both completing more detailed planning and getting the development open with the kind of infrastructure that would attract buyers out beyond the edge of suburban Houston.

At about this time the Mitchell corporation went public, having its initial offering in February 1972 (Kutchin 1998b, 34). This provided some access to capital for The Woodlands, but publicly traded companies need to post profits with some regularity, something that is difficult to do in the early stages of new community development. Over the years investors and analysts were also confused by the combination of oil and gas with real estate within one corporation, leading to the eventual splitting apart of the two components in the late 1990s.

In terms of planning, McHarg's ideas needed to be made operational. The general plan was revised in 1973. WMRT remained on the team, but many other consultants were replaced, although a Columbia presence was still strong. Land Design Research, the firm started by former Columbia employees, worked on land use; LWFW, on marketing; Turner, Collie and Braden, on engineering; and still others, on transportation and hydrology (WMRT 1974b, 37). Detailed site planning fell to a range of consultants, although the WMRT team developed prototype designs for areas with different vegetation and soil types (WMRT 1973a). Consultants working on the project at the time remember quite a bit of needed negotiation to bring together McHarg's rather conceptual work with the approach of the engineering firm, which had not previously done this sort of drainage design.[8] It was also necessary to increase the amount of buildable land so that the development was financially viable. In doing this, LDR reworked the land availability analysis over the original WMRT work, simplifying the analysis and adding consideration of views. They also developed prototype housing layouts, to increase development and to make the project economically viable, with the LDR plans being incorporated into the Wallace, McHarg, Roberts and Todd published reports (WMRT 1974b, 37, 55; Interview 0428). Reinforcing the dominance of the economic model, one of the professionals on the real estate side of the Mitchell corporation explained:

> McHarg would have much rather seen much more greenbelt, but that was not consistent with the economic requirement for The Woodlands. That's where we go back to the driving force is economics. . . . You never put into a development anything people will not pay for. . . . If you don't pay attention to solvency and you get too much out on the limb of whatever your objective, be it social, ecological, or whatever, and you push too far in that direction, the whole deal collapses and nothing happens. So you get 65 or 70 percent of what you want. That's better than nothing. (Interview 0507)

Fortunately, given these economic imperatives, the emphasis on water quality in the environmental planning turned out to be less expensive than conventional drainage. The approach included the prohibition of building in recharge areas with a drainage design that emphasized stopping runoff and allowing water to seep into the soil gradually. Early reports priced a conventional system at $18.7 million and a "natural" system at $4.2 million (WMRT 1974b, 3).

The Woodlands lies alongside a small incorporated development, Oak Ridge North, whose homeowners complained vigorously about potential runoff and made sure that eliminating runoff from The Woodlands was a high priority (Morgan and King 1987, 60). However, some aspects of this drainage design were modified over time. The open drains along streets in residential areas were not very popular with residents. A member of the development team recalled: "I believe that was a mistake to the extent that it was unmarketable. Many calls came to my office, two days or three days after rain: 'We've got water in the back yard, my kids play in the mud, we've got mosquitoes. The birds like to play in the water.' Many, many calls" (Interview 0511). After the first couple of villages were built, the design was changed to narrow streets with curb and gutter. However, the more hidden parts of the original water system remain, as do forested areas and open drains in the research and industrial park areas (see figures 29–34).

Overall, the early approach reduced impervious surface and created a landscape of forested drainage swales, buffered natural drainage channels, water retention areas, and partly cleared lots (WMRT 1974b, 54–55). Natural landscape buffers, complete with underbrush, hide commercial buildings and wind through residential areas. In earlier villages, paths are located in forested areas in the interiors of blocks, behind the back yards of houses (see figures 35–37). Covenants limit the clearing possible on residential yards and nonresidential sites.

A number of planting or vegetation styles could have achieved the same hydrological result—theoretically highly geometric layouts could do this—but The Woodlands chose a wild and unkempt aesthetic, with uncut underbrush and forest buffers hiding much of the building. It was, of course, inexpensive in that it did not require special planting—but for the lay public, it was also the only visible sign that this development was different, that it had been designed with nature in mind.

Of the three developments, this creates an aesthetic that is most at odds with the American public's desire for a naturalistic landscape that is cultivated rather than wild (Nassauer 1995). Even wooded Columbia is more rural in feel than The Woodlands, with its unmanicured appearance. For many in the lay public, it is this wooded aesthetic that seems to be the environmental contribution of The Woodlands. While it is only a small part of the hydrological approach, it is the most obvious part and has made The Woodlands distinctive.

Figure 35. Path in center of block in older section of The Woodlands. Photographer: Ann Forsyth.

Figure 36. Pedestrian link from internal path to vehicular
cul-de-sac. Photographer: Ann Forsyth.

Figure 37. Path beside road. Photographer: Ann Forsyth.

One of the marketing professionals explained:

George always had a penchant—and I do think this emanated from George Mitchell—to leave undergrowth, if you will, or understory it's sometimes called, in the medians of divided roadways and in the setbacks and so on. The Woodlands has been religious in maintaining some of those setbacks and divisions as the whole thing matures, and the understory and the pine trees grow back. You do have more sense of vegetation. Anecdotally, The Woodlands has sometimes been said, it always needs a haircut. Places like Kingwood and Cinco Ranch and some of the others are just manicured. The barber calls on them every week. And there are people who like various looks, and there has been some criticism of The Woodlands for looking a little shaggy. On balance, I think it served The Woodlands' interest well, in that you do get this very wooded feel as you drive down the major thoroughfares. (Interview 0418)

Project Management

Project management was continuing at the same time as the basic environmental and land planning, with decisions made about how to build the development and how to market it. This had design and planning implications, as some elements were needed for the Title VII agreement. Others were more important for marketing the project.

Psychologically, The Woodlands was a long way from Houston. Houston was also the site of many partly built subdivisions. In order to entice people to a new community, the developer had to provide a certain amount of infrastructure up front, both to attract people to the development and to assure them of a long-term commitment. However, this involved expensive investments that would take some time to recoup. Mitchell also had some personal preferences for infrastructure: an avid tennis player, he wanted courts built in the early stages of the development.

With these various objectives, the Mitchell Energy and Development Corporation spent a great deal of money at this time, some of which was on controversial items perceived by many as frills. The Woodlands Development Corporation invested a large amount of money in the Commercial, Conference, and Leisure Center—a 335-acre site at Grogan's Mill, including a two-hundred-room inn, golf course, lake, and information center. The high salaries that had been used to attract professionals to the project increased costs now that 365 people were on staff (U.S. HUD, NCA 1976). In addition, the period of the early 1970s was in general a difficult time economically. Housing construction in Houston peaked in 1970–71, and sales a year later (Morgan and King 1987, 76). The 1973 Arab oil embargo hit The Woodlands hard. At that stage a primarily residential area far from Houston, it made people consider the issue of the commute more critically. Rising energy prices did help the oil and gas side of the Mitchell corporation in 1975, alleviating some cash flow problems, but rising mortgage interest rates made home purchases relatively more expensive, depressing sales. Some external factors exacerbated the financial situation, including very heavy rains in the first part of 1973, which slowed construction (U.S. HUD 1984; Kutchin 1998a, 35).

The relationship with HUD was also strained. HUD required a large amount of reporting and paperwork; for example, the project agreement listed 114 "Application Documents," including planning reports, feasibility studies, land title documents, and very extensive correspondence. Many of the "items" consisted of multiple parts, such as series of maps or reports, although some were single letters (U.S.A. and TWDC 1972, Exhibit A).[9] The project agreement had required that Mitchell allow HUD a first lien on the development and that George Mitchell not "sell, transfer or encumber" his shares in Mitchell Energy and Development before 1980 or the year of peak cash flow (whichever came later) without consent of the HUD secretary. At the time this restricted assets worth $45 million. This was removed in 1980 after Mitchell pledged $24.4 million in loans and equity, but the volume of correspondence in the National Archives collection showed that this required much negotiation.[10] Numerous fees were also paid to HUD to manage the program, for example, a $170,000 commitment charge for the $50 million loan guarantee and other annual fees (U.S.A. and TWDC 1972, 1). In early 1973, financing and sales were held up waiting HUD's approval of deed covenants relating to the community association (Morgan and King 1987, 53–54). HUD could also ask for additional low-income housing, and approval from the HUD secretary was needed for such changes as density and housing mix. This had the potential to slow the development and make it hard to respond to market changes.[11] In addition, as interviewees mentioned, the HUD staff were not highly experienced in the financial aspects of new community development, so negotiations over those issues took time.

HUD, of course, was guaranteeing loans and also potentially making grants available, so there were some benefits from these interactions. However, the grant process did not go smoothly. Before 1975 only one federal grant went to The Woodlands, $75,000 for a library from the Department of Health, Education, and Welfare (Morgan and King 1987, 74). By August 1976, $45.5 million of federal basic and supplementary grants had been approved for Title VII new communities, but none appears to have gone to The Woodlands, even though the agreed-upon financial plan for the first year alone included $33.6 million to the development (Booz, Allen, and Hamilton 1976, III-7). Mitchell considered legal action (Morgan and King 1987, 75).

The Title VII program also suffered from problems with its general administration, and these were exacerbated in this period by a reorganization ordered by HUD secretary George Romney and by staff cuts ordered in 1972 (see also Rabinovitz and Smookler 1973).[12] In January 1973 the Nixon administration declared a moratorium on federal grants, and by the middle of the year this affected the new towns, from which money that had been appropriated by Congress in 1972 was even withheld (Morgan and King 1987, 66–67). These changes made relations with HUD chaotic, but an additional level of confrontation seemed evident from my reading of HUD's files on The Woodlands in the National Archives. This conflict was remarked upon by the 1987 monograph on The Woodlands. Morgan and King recount: "By March, 1972 [before the final project agreement], for example, Mitchell's staff had become convinced that HUD viewed them as 'rich, arrogant Texans.' Their equally uninformed view of HUD personnel as incompetent, petty bureaucrats so impeded relations that direct negotiations for approval of the project were turned over to Piper and Marbury, a Baltimore law firm" (the firm of Jack Jones, who had worked on Columbia) (Morgan and King 1987, 73). Resolving these kinds of problems took a great deal of negotiation. In this, The Woodlands team was helped by the Washington contacts of the ex-Columbia group (Ivins 2002).

By the middle of 1974—after people had started to move in but before The Woodlands was officially opened—the Mitchell Energy and Development Corporation had sunk $28 million into development. In 1970 or early 1971, Gladstone and Associates had predicted $30.3 million in investments through 1973 and $140 million over the twenty years projected to build out. Revenues were predicted to be $690 million, giving a return on investment of 23.5 percent from the land development alone. While these were big profits, the developer had significant costs in the early period. According to an early HUD study, basic infrastructure and land costs led to a fixed carrying charge of about $3.5 million per year (U.S. HUD, NCA 1976, 80). A 1973 internal report estimated a net total cash flow from land development of $313 million, although total cash flow would not be positive until 1983 (TWDC 1973, 5, 8). Through 1975, actual disbursements (expenditures) were lower than had been projected in the agreements with HUD, $61.1 versus $71.7 million, and receipts were higher than expected, at $20.2 versus $18.7 million. The Woodlands was the only Title VII new community to have a *better* disbursement-to-receipt ratio than expected, and only the Title VII new community of Jonathan had a *lower* ratio, 2.51, compared with 3.03 in The Woodlands (Booz, Allen, and Hamilton 1976, III-57). In short, debt was high, but that was typical of the early phases of new community development, and the situation was better than had been projected.

People had quite different recollections of this period. One group, including many of those in the Mitchell oil and gas operations as well as some employees of the development arm, saw this period as one of profligacy, with huge expenditures being made for little short-term return. For these people, the "Columbia Mafia" had demonstrated poor management skills and sapped capital from other parts of the Mitchell enterprise (Morgan and King 1987, 76, 79; Kutchin 1998a, 15). Ivins's at times aggressive approach did little to win over this group. Evaluations in the mid-1970s estimated that internal staff were too numerous and the organization was not well structured. The large number of staff, however, was partly due to the internal conflict and the need to separate the two sides of the organization. The tensions between the energy and real estate arms had led to the creation of dual structures in areas such as accounting. The staff was also reduced after opening.

As the development came closer and closer to opening and the key people with a Columbia background spent more and more money, tensions were almost guaranteed. The decision to put in prestige infrastructure such as the conference center, something done with Mitchell's full support, both cost a great deal and made HUD suspicious about The Woodlands' relative level of commitment to low- and moderate-income earners and to racial minorities (U.S. HUD, NCA 1976; ULI 1976). However, a number of interviewees commented that this investment had been essential in marketing terms, in order to avoid The Woodlands being seen as a low-cost government development (Interviews 0418, 0420).

Additional conflicts over personal styles and cultural issues arose as well. The main planning for the development also occurred in the 1970s, at a time of continuing social change. Many planning and development consultants and staff had arrived from the East or West Coast to more conservative Texas. Some people embraced the freedoms of the period. But what might be seen as experimentation for one person was an impropriety of high order for another. The lines were not always clear—fiscally conservative employees could be partygoers. For many this remained part of their private life; however, for others it intersected with their professional relationships. I think this was not a problem of The Woodlands in particular, but rather a characteristic of the time. Regardless, it added considerably to the corporation's tensions in the context of trying to do a large development under intense time and money pressures, worsened by the growing recession. People's differing concepts of legitimate business expenses further added to this resentment. In private development what counts as a valid expense is often a blurry and contentious issue, particularly during periods when companies are prepared to do almost anything for a client in order to create a sale (Kutchin 1998a, 15). As one professional involved in the development at that time put it, "George [Mitchell] was an open-minded guy, but not that open-minded. The culture clash in Houston got really ugly" (Interview 0520).

The Columbia people also came having worked with a person, Jim Rouse, whom they considered to be a genius and the person to have started the most lauded of the new towns of the period. They considered themselves to be, and in some senses were, the world experts on developing new towns. Many had experience not only at Columbia but often in other locations as well. As one said, "We were very cocky at the time because we had come off of some really successful years" (Interview 0428). Others working on The Woodlands, from Texas and elsewhere, didn't have either this camaraderie or this assurance. One of the Columbia professionals remarked to me: "The whole time we were working there, they said the biggest problem that we have with you guys working on this is that you're going to try and transfer Columbia here. . . . So we tried very hard to never say, 'Well, in Columbia we did this'" (Interview 0428).

The people who had worked on Columbia had also lived through Columbia's start-up. Through extraordinary efforts at sales, they had weathered the initial cash flow problems. The economic downtown that came along in the early 1970s, just as The Woodlands was opening, was in this view a piece of bad luck, not to be laid at the door of the project team. Two of the ex-Columbia professionals remarked:

> *A:* They did spend too much money, and they opened the doors right at the recession, which was a problem, and they took the heat for it. . . .
>
> *B:* What was the alternative? Hold back for a couple of years?
>
> *A:* There was no alternative. It had to be done. It was bad timing. (Anonymous interview)

Overall, interviews with many of the people involved in these early years, from both Texas and the Columbia group, paint a similar picture of complex interpersonal and professional dynamics. In the Woodlands I heard the most diverse opinions about who had done what in the early development, particularly whose ideas were most important and who was to blame for problems. This was not merely to do with interpersonal resentment but also reflected the character of the planning. The early planning and design was done in four significant stages: the preapplication, the McHarg-Pereira plan for HUD approval, planning refinement in the early 1970s, and continued planning after the dramatic downsizing of the early 1970s. At each stage, substantial turnover occurred. The extensive use of consultants who reported to only a few people in the corporation made the roles of some much less apparent; and the diverse mix of disciplinary backgrounds involved made the work of others less obvious. Although all three projects in this book involved hundreds of people in significant roles and had something of this confusion, it was particularly striking in The Woodlands.

PHASE 3: TITLE VII IN OPERATION, 1975 TO 1983,
AND PHASE 4: COMMUNITY BUILDING, 1983 TO 1997

The City and Its People

The Woodlands was officially opened in October 1974 with a large amount of infrastructure in place, including a post office, The Woodlands Country Club, three office buildings, the Convention Center, and a number of shopping facilities (Morgan and King 1987, 63–65). On January 16, 1975, HUD gave the development notice of default because it had expended funds on items that were not land purchase and development (e.g., roads and drainage) and because it had not obtained prior HUD approval of transactions between "interested persons." This latter problem involved situations such as the sale of land or reimbursement for staff time between one subsidiary of Mitchell Energy and another (Morgan and King, 1987, 86). While this seems arcane, the larger issues were to do with the relationship between HUD and the development. Was public money being spent in legitimate ways? Was the development being given enough flexibility to compete in the private market? Also in January 1975, HUD imposed a moratorium on Title VII applications (U.S. HUD, NCA 1976, 3).

With opening and the recession, staff were cut back. Accounts of the early part of 1975 vary, but what happened with certainty was an increase in Mitchell's involvement in the day-to-day operations of the development. Some functions, such as social planning, were scaled back with the elimination of the "institutional planning" department responsible for that topic. Len Ivins, who had been a focus for criticism from the oil and gas side, decided to leave early in 1975 along with many of those who had either worked on the planning or been brought in from Columbia. Some resigned, and some were cut or could see cuts coming. Interestingly, Michael Richmond, the CEO of The Woodlands Operating Company in the 1990s and early 2000s, was one of the former Columbia people who stayed (Richmond 1998).[13] The staff, presumably including temporary and construction workers, fell from 365 to 160 (Morgan and King 1987, 92; Booz, Allen, and Hamilton 1976, iii-3, VII-2). Richard Browne, who had been involved with engineering and land development issues on the early Pereira-McHarg plan, was brought back to head community planning and development, and he stayed for two decades.

In a sense, this was an appropriate time for such reductions and changes in staff, because planning had been launched. However, it did undermine social planning and programming. At this stage in Columbia, continuity had been helpful, as a highly skilled and senior team was involved in pushing sales in the newly opened development.

It took several more years to negotiate financial management and reporting that were acceptable to both The Woodlands and HUD. The two, in fact, sponsored a 1976 Urban Land Institute (ULI) panel to examine the development and recommend changes. The nine ULI panelists included Peter Kremer of the new community of Valencia, who became president of The Irvine Company in 1977. The group recommended changes in the organizational structure of The Woodlands Development Corporation (TWDC) but also asked for more flexibility on the part of HUD. While calling it an "exceptional development" and "a grandiose project done in Texas style," the panelists criticized the amount and character of front-end investments (ULI

1976, 19). In their opinion, these investments reflected planning priorities rather than the responsibility to make profits. They pointed out that the cash flow projection of $423 million in the 1972 project agreement was reduced in to $172 million by May 1975, and even this figure was inflated, as HUD used the same data to show a $146 million deficit (ULI 1976, 61). A report of the same year using HUD data indicated that the project agreement projected an annual interest cost on guaranteed debt of $3.625 million but an average annual revenue of $6.25 million. While the revenue for 1975 was $6.731 million and thus within the projected range for the project agreement, this included $15.6 million of sales to companies affiliated with the Mitchell group (Booz, Allen, and Hamilton 1976, III-5). The ULI panel concluded that this demonstrated the uncertainty of such large projects. However, they also concluded that The Woodlands was viable in the short term.

Because of cost problems, not only staffing but also amenities had already been scaled back. The ULI panel reported a May 1975 plan, not yet accepted by HUD, that reduced neighborhood centers from thirty to sixteen, village centers from sixteen to six, paths from fifty-five miles to thirty-two miles, under- and overpasses from twelve to six. Of twelve sorts of amenities and facilities listed in the report, only tot lots were increased, from thirty to thirty-two (ULI 1976, 34). The ULI made recommendations for increasing low-cost housing products and getting approval for FHA and VA home financing, which surprisingly had not been obtained already (16, 50). The major sticking point in FHA funding was getting approval for the residents association and the associated covenants, conditions, and restrictions. It is interesting that Columbia, as a private development, had obtained such permission, but several Title VII new towns such as The Woodlands had difficulties (Burby 1976, 38, 44). The residents association had also been the reason for HUD's earlier rejection of a 340-unit section 235 (low-interest mortgage) project that was turned down in 1974.

In 1975 the economy started to turn. Home sales increased, and the development corporation started to supply more single-family homes. The Woodlands hosted the Houston Open, which had been searching for a site; it signed a contract for a ten-year stint and later extended it. Major events were also attracted to the Swim Center and tennis facilities. The financial difficulties did slow down investment in commercial facilities, and the development did not have a supermarket until 1978. Mitchell Energy did not move its headquarters there until 1980 (Kutchin 1998a, 27; Morgan and King 1987, 102, 106–9, 112).

After a transition period of 1975 to 1977, Edward Lee, who had been vice president of land development in Irvine, was recruited to be president of The Woodlands Development Corporation. He was president from 1977 to his death in 1986 (Morgan and King 1987, 143). Ray Watson, Lee's boss in Irvine, was also asked to lead the project but stayed in California (Watson

2002). From 1977, an annual budget control document (ABCD) provided a mutually acceptable reporting framework. However, correspondence and internal HUD memoranda that I examined at the National Archives, as well as materials examined by Morgan and King at the Mitchell corporation, demonstrate considerable ongoing frustration on the part of HUD, particularly over affirmative action, low- and moderate-income housing, and aspects of financial reporting (see also Morgan and King 1987, 90–91, 143).

The Woodlands Development Corporation (TWDC) earned an operating profit in 1978, partly because it was now receiving grants from the federal government, which totaled $16 million by 1979. The utility districts (elected single-purpose governments set up to provide water and later sewer services in the various villages), county, and other government entities had received $8.8 million more in federal grants for infrastructure, and the utility districts had started to pay back TWDC for infrastructure. By the summer of 1982, Mitchell Energy had reportedly invested $200 million in the project (Morgan and King 1987, 146).

Social Issues.   As was explained earlier, the Title VII designation meant that the development aimed to have a significant amount of affordable housing. In 1978, Mitchell was still being quoted in the local newspaper, the *Woodlands Villager*, as intending to have a cross section of people in The Woodlands that was similar to the Houston area as a whole (Morgan and King 1987, 146). Initial advertising for the development mentioned HUD sponsorship, and early residents were perceived to be people coming from outside Houston, more open to economic and racial integration (Franzmeier and Gebert 1979, 45–46).

It was not until 1979 that Tamarac Pines was opened, the first of the subsidized rental projects in The Woodlands (Morgan and King 1987, 112). As of 1998 almost eleven hundred federally subsidized units existed, making up about 5 percent of the housing stock. As I relate below, most of these were built before the release of the development from its HUD sponsorship in 1983 (Deretchin 1982). However, several staff members explained to me that while The Woodlands staff had continued to apply for subsidies for a number of years, they eventually gave up, as it was made clear to them that they had already received a large share of available money in the region, and no more was to be forthcoming. Since the development was bought in 1997, an increased number of high-end housing units have created an income stream for the partnership. However, in order to increase sales, offerings had to be diversified, which has necessitated increasing supply at the lower-cost end, including a number of attached-housing products. The area still has inexpensive market-rate housing, with new ownership units at $108,000 in 2000 and older housing costing even less (Richmond 2000).

More continuously successful in terms of the social planning was the community-building role of the faith communities—at the beginning, mostly churches. Planning for religious facilities had already started with the creation of the Religious Institutions Planning group in 1972 and the 1973 formation of WRC (known as Interfaith after 1975). In Columbia, Rouse had required that religious groups share "interfaith" facilities rather than have separate buildings, a policy with mixed success. While Mitchell was early on a supporter of a Columbia-style system of shared facilities, he could not get agreement from the WRC. Mitchell, however, still provided support for the group, supplying office space and secretarial help (Franzmeier and Gebert 1979, 25, 32).

Mitchell also thought that Interfaith should supply services such as child care, but the WRC initially disagreed. Interfaith in The Woodlands saw itself as having a different focus, with its role as that of an incubator of congregations and forger of new social ties. Conflicts over the location of buildings and the pricing of land also occurred. The Woodlands Development Corporation charged commercial land prices for groups not willing to conform to a church park or church campus model, clustered with other congregations to share parking and other facilities. A formal letter of understanding in 1974, laying out the roles of The Woodlands Development Corporation and the WRC, did not eliminate all these conflicts. Land pricing remained a contentious issue during a period in which The Woodlands Development Corporation changed its practices a number of times (Franzmeier and Gebert 1979, 29–42).

However, Interfaith had other effects. The first director, arriving early in 1975, was Don Gebert, a Lutheran minister who had worked in a number of situations, including being a community organizer with the Philadelphia Foundation. When he arrived, social planning had been virtually eliminated as a function of the developer, so Interfaith had an opportunity to take an important role. Although Gebert did not work alone, he was very active in helping create venues for community participation. From his initial office in the Information Center he visited all new and current residents. The telephone book for The Woodlands is still sponsored by Interfaith. It started in 1975 as a community directory, complete with children's birthdays. Gebert and volunteers developed the book to make it easier for people to know their neighbors. With Jack O'Sullivan, Gebert also founded the *Grogan's Mill Villager,* the precursor to the *Woodlands Villager,* a multipage weekly initially run by David Slavin (Franzmeier and Gebert 1979, 25–28; Dinges 1997; Morgan and King 1987, 132–33; Gebert 2000).

Village and townwide resident associations were part of the plan for The Woodlands, and Gebert became involved. Like that of Columbia, the townwide Woodlands Community Association was initially dominated by the developer, with a fairly complicated formula for increasing resident participation. This led some residents to resent what they saw as total control by the developer (Morgan and King 1987, 134). Gebert helped to establish the first village resident association at Grogan's Mill, the group that elected the one representative at that time on the nine-member board of directors of the community association (Franzmeier and Gebert 1979, 25–28).

While it had not wanted to provide services, Interfaith nonetheless found itself in the position of sponsoring and providing a number of social services, from self-help groups to child care and services for teens. This was in part a response to the new town blues, or, in Gebert's terminology, the "new town syndrome," which affects most such communities. People had come to the highly planned Woodlands in part to make better lives for themselves, but once there, they discovered that the new environment could have only a limited effect. To this was added the irritation of living on a construction site where many services were still to be built. While the need for social services was apparent, the Mitchell corporation layoffs of late 1974 and early 1975 particularly affected social planning, making the corporation less able to deal with those needs (Franzmeier and Gebert 1979, 42–49). However, TWDC did contribute various spaces and eventually a parcel of land for a head office for Interfaith. By 2002, Interfaith had over 250 employees, primarily doing social service work (Interfaith of The Woodlands 2002).

For the federal government, however, race and affirmative action were central social issues in The Woodlands. In the National Archives are several boxes of correspondence about The Woodlands. Very little deals with the planning and construction of the development in terms of its physical character. The largest groups of materials are on three issues: financial reporting; housing mix; and efforts at marketing to ethnic minorities. One has a sense that the Texans continued to be seen with some suspicion by the HUD central office—a group of cowboys or wildcatters with little sensitivity toward racial issues. This view was apparent in spite of all the Columbia expertise that was in evidence in the period from 1971 to 1975, along with quite significant marketing campaigns targeting African Americans and Latinos in the 1970s. The Woodlands has always been dominated by non-Hispanic whites, at 87 percent in 2000 (see appendix B).

Governance.   Governance in The Woodlands has always been very complex. It is in the extraterritorial jurisdiction of Houston, which has jurisdiction over subdivision control and building regulation. The county provides police and courthouses; roads, drainage, and utility maintenance; public libraries; and a part of subdivision approval mainly relating to engineering issues for the infrastructure that the county will maintain. The Woodlands is in the Conroe Independent School District, although, until a realignment of boundaries in 1992, part was also in the Magnolia Independent School District, making the situation even more complex (Kutchin 1998b, 28). The Town Center Improvement District uses a 1 percent sales tax to provide additional services in the town center area, including added security and maintenance. The Woodlands Road Utility District has taxing powers to pay for roads. Depending on your perspective, it is a "discombobulated mishmash of alphabet organizations" or "a world of partnerships" (Interviews 0422, 0418).

Like Irvine, The Woodlands very early on established municipal utility districts (MUDs) to provide water and sewer services. These could be established on the petition of registered voters in an area.[14] The municipal utility districts were able to issue bonds to reimburse the developer for expenditures on water, sewer, and drainage. Since 1982 the MUDs have cooperated through the Joint Powers Agency, which allows them to share administrative services, staff, and equipment. In The Woodlands, when grants or legal agreements require a municipality to represent The Woodlands, the MUDs, which have elected boards, are that entity. For example, in 1999 the City of Houston signed an agreement not to annex The Woodlands for twelve years; this agreement was signed with the MUDs (MUD 2001; Morgan and King 1987, 55).

The Woodlands Community Service Corporation (CSC), founded in 1992, provides most other typical municipal services to The Woodlands Commercial Owners Association, The Woodlands Community Association (representing the earlier villages and since 1992 under resident control), and The Woodlands Association (in the newer villages and still developer dominated). The CSC was founded in part because The Woodlands was taking longer to develop than had been planned, which disrupted the timetable for turning over control of The Woodlands Community Association to the residents. This timetable was tied to construction of units, though with a deadline for turning over to the residents in 1992 (The Woodlands Association, Inc., 1974, 1993). The compromise, given that The Woodlands would not be completed so soon, was to create a second resident association for the newer villages and a separate business owners association to allow later business development to have covenants tailored more toward commercial needs. The CSC was then initiated as an umbrella group that provides services to the resident associations as well as to the business areas. Services include park and open space maintenance, fire protection, trash and recycling collection, and staffing for residential covenant enforcement. These services are specified in a mutual benefit agreement signed in 1992 and amended in 1998 after the sale of The Woodlands. The CSC communicates through a Web site and a glossy monthly magazine, featuring news from the village associations, community event listings, and a variety of articles dealing with parks, plants, and the logic of covenants.

The community associations can borrow to pay for open space and other infrastructure, just as in Columbia, although in the older association this has been paid off (Interview 0422). Eventually, once development nears completion, the two resident associations will merge.

The Woodlands Community Association had its own financial problems in the early years, when the small population meant that its assessments levied on all properties were also low. In 1976 the ULI panel expressed concern that while the developer in the early stages controlled infrastructure investments, these were paid for over time by the community association.[15] While this followed the Columbia model, the ULI panel wanted the financial situation clarified and maximum tax rates set (ULI 1976, 29). By 1979 vandalism and lack of maintenance threatened the use of many facilities. For a couple of years this was partly overcome by voluntary maintenance activity, at least until the population reached a level where assessments could cover these expenses (Morgan and King 1987, 141).

As the development has matured, most of these problems have been resolved. By 2000, 94 percent of residents surveyed thought that the services provided by the community association were good, very good, or excellent (Creative Consumer Research 2000).[16] Assessments to provide these services were lower than the Columbia rate, which is variable but has a maximum of 75 cents per $100 assessed value, or $750 for a $100,000 house. The Woodlands has the same cap in the older section. In 2000 the rate was 54 cents per $100 assessed value in the newer section of The Woodlands and 48 cents in the older section, compared with 73 cents in Columbia (TWCSC 2002; Columbia Association 2002; The Woodlands Association, Inc. 1974). Of course, some of this difference may be related to how true the underlying assessed values are, as practices differ from state to state.

While this is certainly a private government, many of the CSC's facilities and services are available to the general public, and parks are open and function much as they do in municipalities. Park regulations sound similar to those in cities; for example, people are prohibited from soliciting donations, carrying weapons, having unleashed pets, and removing vegetation. People cannot distribute circulars or post signs, but they can hold a demonstration if it is not too noisy or disorderly (Parks and pathways 2001, 18). However, people seem to use resident association meetings and the *Villager* as the preferred forums for protest and debate.

In the context of this complex web of service providers and regulatory agencies and the claim of Houston to annex the development eventually, incorporation has been periodically raised as an issue. One of the earliest manifestations came in 1981 at a high point of early dissatisfaction with citizen involvement and involved a group from the Village of Panther Creek investigating annexation by Houston (Morgan and King 1987, 135). Resident protest over environmental issues also emerged at about that time through a conflict over a gas station design (Morgan and King 1987, 121). Telephone surveys in 1999 and 2000 found only 1 percent of residents wanting annexation to Houston, with most of the respondents divided between incorporating as a separate city or remaining unincorporated (Creative Consumer

Research 1999, 2000). Incorporation would be advantageous for the Community Service Corporation in some ways. For instance, its municipal equivalent could apply for certain kinds of grants. It could also create and enforce ordinances around issues such as solid waste or fireworks, which are dealt with by the CSC or in the covenants but could be better managed by a formal government. As an employee of the Community Service Corporation explained:

> This year, July the fifth was not a happy day to come to work, if you want to talk to us folks in this neck of the woods. Our deed restrictions say, "Thou shalt not have fireworks." We pronounce it loudly [but] . . . the only enforcement tool we have is to take you to court. . . . Or you'd have a restraining order in your back pocket, which means that I'd have to anticipate which of us guys are going to go off and shoot fireworks. It's not an effective tool. But the angst of the neighborhood is real. They've moved from places where you don't have the kids across the way shooting bottle rockets onto your roof. . . . And it said in the newsletter you can't have fireworks. So the alternative is to fold our tent and not say anything about it, or say it, hoping to raise a level of awareness and common sense and not have fireworks, and then suffer on July fifth when everybody says you're inadequate, you can't do what you said you do, what am I paying for . . . ? (Interview 0503)

While the solution to these kinds of issues in Columbia has been more resident involvement in county politics, The Woodlands residents who I talked to did not seem to think that the county was a viable realm for such political action. While their local county representative was efficient, the minimalist character of the county government in Texas made it more difficult to use the county for such services. However, Mitchell still holds a different position, pointing to the benefits that the City of Houston brings—the port, airport, and major roads—and arguing that residents of The Woodlands should bear the burden of paying for them by agreeing to annexation. In terms of the antisprawl agenda, incorporation is a problem, as it adds to fragmentation and social inequality, given the strong tax base of The Woodlands. Eventually a compromise may be reached to allow some self-government in return for tax sharing. I return to these issues of governance in chapter 7.

Environmental Infrastructure in Practice

As it has matured, the overall development of The Woodlands has shown a continuing commitment to many dimensions of environmental protection, although it also has some weaknesses. The development has largely controlled runoff, is a striking forest area, has a variety of parks, and boasts a path system of over one hundred miles. However, a number of environmental activists have complained that in some areas only a "veneer of woods" or "a forest façade" remains and that the focus on hydrology has detracted from the attention paid to maintaining corridors for wildlife (Interviews 0414, 0429). Some early innovations, funded by demonstration grants, were dropped because of costs. For example, waste water was initially treated using oxygen for recycling, and early experiments were made with a porous asphalt (GMA 1971, 2; Pappas 1998, 249–50, 252; Scarlett 1972).[17]

At an individual level, residents have both promoted and undermined the ecological concept. Individual homeowners have frequently cut back more of the growth than was initially intended, increasing the amount of lawn in their yards. Because of the use of curb and gutter and fewer "natural" yards, the newer areas have a more conventional appearance. However, this may well be because of their newness and because they are in areas where the forest cover was not as thick in the first place. Counter to the ecological focus, The Woodlands did not have recycling service for years, and it was a volunteer group, The Woodlands Recycles (later renamed The Woodlands GREEN), that eventually started the recycling program, which was then taken over by the CSC (The Woodlands GREEN 2003).[18] Curb-side recycling started in 1994.

In terms of automobile dependence, this is a car-based development. The Woodlands Operating Company has been willing to create a local bus service, and a system of commuter buses to central Houston is well used. However, more general bus service is not in place and has reportedly been opposed by residents concerned about opening the borders and being linked to Houston.

George Mitchell has also maintained a more personal interest in ecological issues. He has sponsored conferences on sustainability since the mid-1970s, for example, workshops on costs of growth, with participants including some of the people who wrote the famous Club of Rome report. The Mitchell Center for Sustainable Development, housed in the Research Forest in The Woodlands, still sponsored awards, publications, and conferences during the 1990s (e.g., Meadows 1977; www.harc.edu). It was folded into a more general sustainability initiative at the Houston Advanced Research Center in the new century.

Mature Planning since 1983

In 1983, The Woodlands was released from its Title VII status, although it was not until 1992 that the last of the HUD bonds were retired (Kutchin 1998a, 28). It was reported at the time that all the other Title VII new towns had either gone bankrupt or failed to meet debt service (Thomas 1982). This was not unexpected, as the most profitable developments had not bothered to apply for HUD loan guarantees, given the administrative burden that the relationship created. However, The Woodlands was still bound to affirmative action and low-income housing requirements. The low-income housing requirement was for "15 percent of the total future housing units at The Woodlands to be occupied initially by households within the then current limits of section 8, section 235 or successor programs," programs aimed at both renters and homeowners (Haines 1982, 3). At the time, The Woodlands had actually produced approximately 15 percent of its units as HUD-assisted low- and moderate-income units. As of May 1982, The Woodlands Development Corporation reported 5,712 housing starts, with 993 assisted units, or 17.4 percent—783 in section 8 developments for the elderly, 120 in section 236 rental, and 90 in section 235 low-cost mortgages. The population was 14,233, with 5,915 jobs, although 700 of these were in construction (Deretchin 1982).

Growth was slow in the 1980s. While there had been sixty thousand housing starts in the Houston area in 1983, this had slumped to under fifteen thousand by 1985 and stayed at that level for the rest of the 1980s. Market-rate housing construction increased substantially in the 1990s in The Woodlands, particularly at the high end. However, the subsidized units did not increase; their proportion in 2000 was about one-third of their level in 1982.

The slow start in the area of housing was also reflected in commercial and industrial development, so it took a relatively long time to obtain a full complement of services in the new community. Like Columbia and Irvine, The Woodlands aimed to attract industry. Like the other two developments, it was located near a major airport and had rail service, and an early industry was distribution. A toll road to Houston was completed in 1987, after some lobbying on the part of George Mitchell, making the link quite fast for those who wanted to pay. However, the developer also put a great deal of effort into creating a strong research park and attracting high technology industries. In 1982, George Mitchell sponsored the formation of the Research Forest business park and the Houston Advanced Research Center initially as a collaboration between four universities (Kutchin 1998a, 25–26; Galatas 1998). HARC is, however, only one part of the Research Forest, which holds a diverse group of companies, with an emphasis in high technology industries.

Shopping development also moved slowly. The first supermarket opened in 1978, but negotiations about opening a mall in the early 1980s did not progress because of the downturn in the Houston economy. However, in 1994 a study of The Woodlands found that even before the opening of the mall (which happened late in 1994), the development had 19 percent of Montgomery County's population but 27 percent of its retail sales, 30 percent of its private-sector employment, and 27 percent of its property values (Smith 1994). The Woodlands has always had a strong public sculpture program, but in 1990 the Cynthia Woods Mitchell performance pavilion opened, increasing the capacity for other art events (see figure 38).

Figure 38. Cynthia Woods Mitchell Pavilion. Photographer: Ann Forsyth.

PHASE 5: POST-MITCHELL GROWTH SINCE 1997

The Crescent and Rouse Periods

In 1997, Mitchell sold The Woodlands to Crescent Real Estate Equities and the Morgan Stanley Real Estate Fund II after a competitive auction. The new owners paid $543 million for the development, which gave after-tax proceeds of $460 million (Kutchin 1998a, 38). Most of the existing staff were kept on, and the new owners maintained the overall plan. However, they also started to develop more quickly, partly because they needed cash flow to pay off the debt and partly because they now had more access to capital to do such development. They introduced products that George Mitchell had resisted because they did not fit his vision of a comprehensively planned and open community. These included a large gated area called Carlton Woods, although as noted earlier, the number of smaller and attached units increased. One of the marketing staff from the 1990s explained that Mitchell's resistance had lost The Woodlands some sales earlier in the decade:

> [In the] early 1990s Houston was just coming out of a slump, and I guess things were on the upswing. The primary issue was to get more than our fair share of the piece of the market pie, and the things that I encountered basically— George Mitchell still very much lay in the picture, and his vision was still in force. I would liken his vision and his spin on some things to the restrictor plate

on the NASCAR. It keeps it from going as fast as it really can. And George was, for instance, resistant to a gated community. No matter how you feel about gated communities, there was an appetite in the marketplace, which The Woodlands is now meeting, for a more secure area, due to controlled entrance. So we were missing a bet on that. The development had gotten very dense, and there was some resistance along the way on shoehorning big custom homes onto relatively small lots. (Interview 0418)

The pace of construction increased, ranking fifth nationally among master-planned communities in terms of home sales in 2001 (Lesser 2002). This growth brought some problems, mainly related to traffic issues, but at the same time it made it attractive for the Rouse Company to buy out Crescent Realty in 2003. While at the staff level The Woodlands Operating Company had great continuity until quite recently, the new owners were also perceived as more distant. One resident of The Woodlands explained:

I don't want to stereotype what the relationship was, but you certainly knew how decisions were made and you knew that . . . as a last resort you could appeal to Mitchell's sense of community. And it's hard to do with the [new] developer. Even though we know who the people are who are still here, the developer per se is a nameless, faceless entity that's not part of this community as much as the Mitchells were. (Interview 0429)

However, it has also been in this period that some new initiatives have occurred, notably citizen action to help the few hundred residents of Tamina, a small neighborhood across the interstate from The Woodlands. This community is largely African American. Tamina children go to Woodlands schools, and they are in the service area of Interfaith because they share a zip code with The Woodlands. With unclear title and in an unincorporated area, the Tamina population has also been underserved in municipal services, without sewer, water, or street lighting. Since the late 1990s a nonprofit group, the Friends of Tamina, including a number of people with professional skills in infrastructure and building from The Woodlands, has been working to increase services and help people to maintain their homes. Working with the small City of Oakridge, they have arranged funding to provide a number of these services (Cox 2002).

Overall, The Woodlands is much more a work in progress than the other two developments, opening seven years after Columbia and facing in succession the real estate crash of the 1970s and the slumps in the Houston economy in the 1980s and early 1990s. This is exemplified by the opening of The Woodlands Mall in 1994 two decades after the opening of the development. This opening was much later in the development timetable than the opening of such shopping centers as Fashion Island in Newport Center, in 1967, and the Mall in Columbia, in 1971. The town center is still very much under development but is currently growing rapidly, with expansions planned to the mall (which is already over a million square feet) and the opening of a new 30-story office building as a headquarters for Anadarko Petroleum in 2002 and a 345-room Marriott hotel in 2003. A 400,000-square-foot "main street style" retail area and upgrading of a downtown waterway are other improvements (Town Center Improvement District 2003). The plan for the downtown also includes well over five hundred units of townhouse and midrise housing (Ziegler Cooper 2000). While single-family housing increased in the 1990s, the new owners, seeking to increase sales across all market segments, may in fact be taking the development toward more housing mix, although this was not picked up in the 2000 census.

Like Irvine, The Woodlands came to its overall vision through a series of steps. In this the HUD Title VII application was very important, because it was this process that forced the Mitchell group to search for experienced and high-profile consultants of the kind that could win in the competition for federal support. Mitchell undoubtedly had a sincere interest in improving urban development, but the HUD process definitely applied pressure and made the development team work with social as well as environmental goals.

In terms of providing an alternative to sprawl, The Woodlands has had mixed success, as I explain in the subsequent chapters. I heard a number of complaints about the development becoming expensive and conformist, moving away from both the social goals of HUD and the early environmental aims. However, it has maintained remarkable continuity with its initial vision. Like the other two developments, even civic activists felt that, on balance, the development has made a good ongoing attempt to maintain its initial concept. As one environmental leader explained: "It's been marketed as a place to live, work, and play in harmony with the natural environment, and we have taken that and used that in our whole mission and vision and values. Our first stated value is 'Preserve the natural environment,' and they've kind of put their money where their mouth is" (Interview 0410). While it is unclear what effects the Rouse Company's purchase of a share of The Woodlands will have, in the next chapters I examine the ways in which The Woodlands has created a new kind of environment and how it compares with the other two case studies.

Chapter 5

Organizing the Metropolis

While the preceding chapters have traced the unique paths of each development, many similarities in their social and physical configurations are also obvious. These new communities are organized as balanced developments—with the activities, facilities, and jobs for self-containment—while also functioning as integral parts of a metropolitan area.

After land assembly, the first step in the overall development process was arranging the project areas. The holdings had to be to be broken up into parts that could be designed in detail, built at different times, and managed as independent units. The development teams generally hoped that different parts of the developments would make sense to the residents as distinctive places, although this was not essential for construction and maintenance. In addition, the developments had to be made to fit within their metropolitan regions, which necessitated organizing the new communities with an eye to both internal components and external links. Most obviously this was done physically, but this sense of organizing a metropolitan area went far beyond the physical. For example, resident or homeowner associations were structured to match physically defined villages within the developments, giving a social reality to the organization even when the physical reality of the village was sometimes not so clear. The new community designers often talked about creating areas that were balanced—economically, socially, and in terms of the activities they supported.

The grand scale of these kinds of planning and design activities made the developments large canvases for planning and design experimentation. This was tremendously exciting for those working on the developments. However, while having the potential for innovation, the planning and design teams also arrived with sets of preexisting skills and expectations drawn from their professional backgrounds and knowledge of prototype developments. These backgrounds predisposed them to certain solutions—framing the alternatives that they could imagine.[1]

Irvine's core visions have come from the tradition of the architect-planner and the landscape architect doing urban design. This is not unexpected for a development conceived in the late 1950s. Such a vision was the cutting edge of large developments up to that period, from the much smaller greenbelt towns of the 1930s to Reston, which was envisioned in the 1950s and opened in 1964. A number of other large California developments of the 1950s and 1960s were also designed in this manner by prominent architecture firms such as Victor Gruen and Associates. In this kind of planning, the built structures and lavish plantings were the dominant elements. The existing landscape was perceived as a set of contours, water features, and soil types that provided amenities and constraints for the overall design. This approach was coming under fire by the 1960s, as it was seen as having too narrow a focus, although it has had a resurgence in new urbanism, albeit in a gentler form that has learned something from past decades.

Columbia was quite different. It was very self-consciously created as a humanistic alternative to contemporary physical planning and architecture, melding an advanced social program with an unpretentious suburban aesthetic. Columbia was also much more intentionally designed as a model. Rouse's repeated speeches and the extensive documentation of the work group process were meant to spread the word. Rouse also had a heavy hand—from big ideas such as small-town life to the details of road signage. While the process drew on a number of sources, it was wrapped in the systems thinking of the day, an approach that saw issues as linked in a complex and often adaptive whole and an approach that has something of a resurgence in contemporary debates about sustainability. The coordinator of the social planning work group, Donald Michael, was an expert in systems approaches, and related ideas were used to manage the project.

By the time of intensive planning for The Woodlands, developments such as the Irvine Ranch and Columbia had already demonstrated options for the satellite new town. In addition, Houston had a tradition of master-planned residential developments. Mitchell moved slowly from this local master-planning approach to the satellite new town model, gradually learning the ropes. For the final HUD proposal, the social and architectural ideas that he had seen in the other developments were filtered through an additional layer of ecological thought. In this sense The Woodlands had the potential to be a particularly rich and complex response to contemporary development problems, at the cutting edge of all three dimensions, employing Pereira from Irvine and a whole team from Columbia and adding the ecological approach of the Wallace, McHarg, Roberts, and Todd group. However, some of the conflicts within the Mitchell Energy and Development Corporation, compounded by the property crash of the 1970s, swept away many of the more elaborate aspects of these approaches. The ecological ideas remained for some time, but less integrated with the other dimensions than may have been possible in better times.

This chapter examines the physical layouts of the developments and their social outcomes, focusing on how they were designed to be both self-contained and also parts of their metropolitan regions. It examines their components, laid out in a structure of cells, corridors and centers, and landscape frames, rather than as a carpet of development, a scattering, or a grid. It then describes how they were developed and assesses how social life has intersected with the physical plans. In doing this it traces their many physical and social similarities as well as some significant differences in areas such as family life and economic mix.

OVERALL ORGANIZATION OF NEW TOWNS

Self-Containment and Mixed Use

As was explained in chapter 1, new towns in the United States have taken a variety of forms. What they share is their relatively large size, mixed use, and comprehensive planning. They all occupy a space "in the suburbs but with a little flavor of the city" (Interview 0111).

In the overall design of a new town, at least two big decisions must be made. First is the decision to design a bounded development with a unified identity rather than a series of smaller developments. Second is the internal organization of that entity, a decision with implications both for the new town itself and for the way that it relates to the rest of the metropolis.

None of the three developments is an isolated, completely self-contained new town surrounded by a large greenbelt. Of the three case study developments, Columbia and The Woodlands were the most isolated at the outset, making them seem more self-contained. However, their early development took place in the context of largely rural counties, and they are now increasingly surrounded by urban development. Despite having more jobs than households, they are less rich in jobs than Irvine and have fewer residents working within their boundaries, tying them functionally to the surrounding region. A significant percentage of the housing that has developed at the edges of the new communities is attached, with residents of these peripheral housing areas presumably attracted by the new town amenities. This means that they are now surrounded by fairly intensive development rather than being distinctive, separate new towns. Both Columbia and The Woodlands have bought additional land over the years and are adding areas, also changing the size of the development and therefore the character of their boundaries. The Woodlands is adding extra villages; and Columbia, mainly business development. However, with all this development and change, Columbia and The Woodlands have had years to establish an identity for the new town as a whole, and the encroaching suburban growth has not undermined that yet.

The Irvine Ranch planners took a different approach. The development has its centerpiece in the City of Irvine, but a significant part of its development is not in the city. Suburbanization had literally reached south to the ranch's northern boundaries when its development was started, and short of a dramatic move to keep a belt of land out of development while paying large property taxes on it, it was not possible in the 1960s to design the ranch as a separate and bounded entity. Because the view from the road is important, and the land along the two central freeways has been largely developed, it is also hard to perceive the remaining open space as a boundary, even though it is quite extensive and the developed areas are heavily planted. That the ranch has been divided among several municipalities further confuses the situation. These political and physical features make the identity of "Irvine" much less clear, an ambiguity that has both benefits and problems.

However, even without a greenbelt, a development can be self-contained in the sense of having a comprehensive array of opportunities and services for all residents. This is the case in all three, although it took some decades to achieve. Uses are mixed within each of the developments, within their villages, and within their small neighborhoods and parcels. Frequently classified as an edge city or a suburban downtown, each development has regional-scale business parks, entertainment, and shopping areas, often loosely clustered.

In 1991, journalist Garreau's widely read book *Edge City* described all three developments as being edge cities or emerging edge cities (Garreau 1991, 6–7, 430, 431, 437). Garreau defines an edge city as having at least five million square feet of office space, six hundred thousand square feet of leasable retail space, and more jobs than bedrooms. For Garreau, an edge city also needs to be perceived as one cohesive place with a name, but to have been formerly composed of farms or residential suburbs (Garreau 1991, 6–7). Geographers Hartshorn and Muller (1992, 151) label this kind of environment a *suburban downtown*. They define it as having five million square feet of office space, a one-million-square-foot regional shopping center, fifty thousand or more employees, three or more high-rise office buildings, at least one Fortune 1000 headquarters or regional headquarters, and two or more major chain hotels with four hundred or more rooms in each.[2]

As table 8 demonstrates, the developments do fulfill the edge city criteria and most of those for classification as a suburban downtown in terms of office space, retail space, hotel rooms, job concentration, identity, and newness. However, they are not as chaotic and lacking in design as Garreau suggests such environments are: they were intensely planned in terms of physical design and economic structure, and firms and businesses were very

TABLE 8 Case Study New Communities as Edge Cities

	Location				
Criteria	Irvine Business Complex	Irvine Spectrum	Newport Center	Columbia	The Woodlands
Edge City[a]					
5 mill. sq. ft. office space	48 mill. sq. ft. office, R&D, industrial, and commercial space in 3,500 acres	25 mill. sq. ft. office, R&D, and industrial space in 5,000 acres	600 acres	8.7 mill. sq. ft. office space; 6.2 mill. sq. ft. R&D space	5.4 mill. sq. ft. office space; 3.7 mill. sq. ft. institutional space
600,000 sq. ft. leasable retail space	—	Irvine Spectrum Center: 680,000 sq. ft. and increasing	Fashion Island: 935,000 leasable sq. ft.	Mall in Columbia: 1.3 mill. sq. ft., 450,000 leasable Snowden Square and Columbia Crossing: 500,000 sq. ft. each planned	The Woodlands Mall: 1.1 mill. sq. ft.
More jobs than bedrooms	Yes	Yes	Yes	Depends on boundary	Depends on boundary
Perceived as one place	Yes	Yes	Yes	Yes	Yes
Named	Yes	Yes	Yes	Yes	Yes
Formerly farms or residential suburbs	Yes	Yes	Yes	Yes	Yes

Suburban Downtown[b]

5 mill. sq. ft. office space	48 mill. sq. ft. office, R&D, industrial, and commercial space in 3,500 acres	25 mill. sq. ft. office, R&D, and industrial space in 5,000 acres	600 acres	8.7 mill. sq. ft. office space; 6.2 mill. sq. ft. R&D space	5.4 mill. sq. ft. office space; 3.7 mill. sq. ft. institutional space
1 mill. sq. ft. regional shopping center	Close to South Coast Plaza, north of Irvine Ranch	Irvine Spectrum Center: 680,000 sq. ft.	Fashion Island	Mall in Columbia: 1.3 mill. sq. ft.; 450,000 gross leasable area	The Woodlands Mall: 1.1 mill. sq. ft.
50,000 or more employees	?	55,000 in 2002	15,000 in 1999	66,500 in 1999	26,600 in 2002
3 or more high-rise office buildings[c]	Yes	Yes	Yes	Yes	Yes
Fortune 1000 headquarters or regional headquarters	Home Base	Western Digital	Conexant; Pacific Life Insurance	U.S. Food Service; Magellan Health Service; W. R. Grace	Anadarko Petroleum
2 or more major chain hotels with 400+ rooms each[d]	Hyatt Regency (536); Crown Plaza (335); Embassy Suites (293); and others	No major hotels	Four Seasons (295); North Beach Marriott (570)	Sheraton Columbia (289); Courtyard by Marriott (152)	Marriott (345, plus 7 suites)

SOURCES: GIS Lounge 2004; Rouse Company 1999, 2002; TWOC 2000a, 2002; Irvine Company 1998, 2002d; Destination Irvine 2002.

[a] Data from Garreau 1991, 6–7.

[b] Data from Hartshorn and Muller 1992, 151.

[c] Many are midrise of up to six stories.

[d] I have listed larger chain hotels in each area, and although some do not have the required 400 rooms, they show that the area partly fulfills this criterion for classification as a suburban downtown.

actively courted. However, too often people looking at suburban areas have not distinguished between these new towns and more incrementally developed areas.

Their design as employment centers affects both the internal structure of the developments and their relation to the region. All three developments now use advertising with slogans like "live-work-shop-play-and-learn," but something of this emphasis on multiple uses and comprehensive design was always there. Because of the new communities' large areas, the planning and design teams could lay out these uses in ways that reflect an overall planning vision rather than immediate market forces or the luck and constraints of owning a small parcel in a particular location. In this they had some planning and phasing advantages over the generally smaller developments that new urbanists have created and over the larger regional plans that rely on others to carry out their purposes. The comprehensive planning is certainly noticeable from the overall transportation networks to the details of landscaped areas. However, some mixed-use innovations did not sell well or were ahead of their time. For example, the housing units over the shops in Harper's Choice, one of Columbia's early villages—an arrangement promoted in the current period by new urbanists—were not popular and thus not repeated. In the Irvine Ranch, both county and Irvine Company planners reported county resistance to mixing uses in business areas in the 1960s. Only in the 1990s were significant numbers of housing units placed in commercial areas in any of the developments. Since that time, however, significant numbers of housing units have been placed in town and regional centers and in business parks in each of the new communities, and more such units are planned.

The City in the Region

Held together with vast transportation networks, contemporary metropolitan areas provide tremendous opportunities and diversity. People move to urban areas and stay in them at least partly because they can make better lives for themselves than would be possible elsewhere, although that does not preclude a certain nostalgia for small towns.

In the 1950s and 1960s, as the new communities were being proposed, this metropolitan complexity was not yet completely obvious, but growth was rapid. New kinds of environments were emerging out of the interstate system, the urban renewal programs of the 1950s and 1960s, and suburbanization aided by prefabrication, mass production, and cheap mortgages. City structure was changing as metropolitan areas developed multiple centers and as suburban shops and jobs competed with downtowns (Webber 1964).

These changes provoked some debate about the future of urban or metropolitan areas. Obviously the suburban critique was part of this atmosphere, involving both cultural commentators and academics identifying the problems associated with this tremendous urban expansion. However, the debates about the future of the city often mixed this kind of critique with an excitement about the possibilities unleashed by growth. For example, in 1957 the Connecticut General Life Insurance Company opened its new suburban headquarters in Bloomfield, Connecticut, outside Hartford, in a Skidmore Owings and Merrill office building with Isamu Noguchi landscaping set on a three-hundred-acre site (Rowe 1991, 158–59; Owen 1959, xii). To celebrate the opening, the company held a four-day conference on the theme "The New Highways: Challenge to the Metropolitan Region." A key question was "How can we increase the efficiency and livability of our cities through the national highway program?" (Owen 1959, x, capitalization removed). Fifty-five people wrote papers for the conference or participated as speakers and panelists. They included directors of many federal and state agencies, magazine and newspaper publishers, and representatives of major professional associations. An additional seven hundred guests registered. Opening remarks were by Frazier Wilde, the man who gave his name to the Village of Wilde Lake in Columbia. James Rouse presented prepared remarks, Lewis Mumford attended, and Wilfred Owen, from the Brookings Institution, compiled the sense of the meeting into a 1959 book, *Cities in the Motor Age* (see also Gelfand 1975, 229–30). Also in attendance were architect Victor Gruen, Rouse's former employer Guy Hollyday, and George Romney, later secretary of HUD at the time of The Woodlands' approval as a Title VII new town, but at that time president and chairman of the board of the American Motors Corporation.

In a striking set of introductory images, *Cities in the Motor Age* presented pictures of inner-city slums with "no place to play" and "obsolete streets" and pictures suburban "slums" in the form of strips and "mass produced housing—monotony and conformity." It contrasts these with pleasant pictures of Paris's Champs-Élysées, a Stockholm park, and new suburban malls. As Owen explains in the first pages of chapter one: "After fifty years of the automotive age, we are beginning to wonder if cars and crowded highways are really the best possible way to get around. And despite all the centuries that urban concentrations have grown and prospered, we have begun to doubt that the city can survive the automotive age, or even that it should" (Owen 1959, 3). The answer to these contradictory images and this confused sense of the future was to call for more planning to reclaim the highway program from the engineers and to use it both to renew center cities and to provide a framework for better-designed suburbs. Overall the conference summary presented an optimistic picture of the potential for better planning and design to reshape the metropolitan landscape.

What this case exemplifies is that, in the 1950s and 1960s, people—

including some key players in the later new communities movement—were hopeful that the energy of such activities as the "biggest public-works program in history" could be channeled toward making better urban areas (Owen 1959, 10). Their palette of options now seems dated—early shopping malls and modernist urban renewal projects—but they were sincerely seeking solutions to difficult urban problems. These huge investments seemed open-ended in their possibilities and perhaps instrumental in improving human life, but the narrowness of the engineering-dominated approach of the federal and state road bureaucracies also caused concern.[3]

The early development teams for the case study new towns all prominently displayed the existing and proposed freeway and highway systems in the location maps of their developments and even in more detailed conceptual plans. Development projections were also set in the context of regional growth, showing the economic links of the new communities to the metropolitan region in terms of employment and housing markets. That they were often wrong in their projections, generally overestimating the demand for houses, does not diminish the importance of this regional thinking. These were crucial projections because they provided important information about the financial viability of the developments and about the role they would play within their regions. While the development teams overestimated growth in their regions, it was strong nonetheless and a major factor in the survival of the developments in the early years when expenses were very high. This regional thinking has continued to set these developments apart from more incremental subdivisions.

INTERNAL ORGANIZATION

Complementing this concern with the region was a need to design the internal components of the new town to fit together while also fitting within the larger regional context. Drawing on new and old debates about new town organization, all the developments produced conceptual studies of the arrangements of neighborhoods within villages and the relationship of the neighborhoods and villages to the town.

Internally, there are three ways of reading the physical organization of the case study new towns, although the same elements can be read in multiple ways—it is a matter of emphasis, of what is the figure and what is the ground. One is a pattern of cells within cells; another, a network of corridors and centers; and the third is where natural features such as waterways and forests provide a structure or landscape frame into which other elements are fitted (see figure 39). Of course, the cells in the cellular structure need to be linked together with something that looks like a corridor, but the main focus is on creating bounded units that add together to make up a whole. This structure could also be likened to a mosaic, where the individual tiles

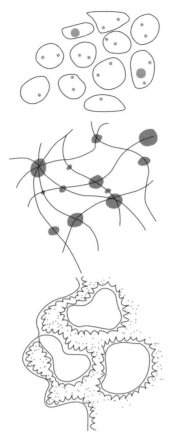

Figure 39. Cell, corridor-and-center, and
landscape-frame arrangements.

are the important elements rather than the grouting between them. In contrast, what makes a system of corridors and centers special is the emphasis placed on circulation and gathering spaces. Having bounded identifiable residential areas is less important, particularly where they are not associated with centers. A corridor-and-center arrangement may be combined with or overlaid on a cellular structure, but it can also lie across a uniform carpet of development. Both arrangements may be modified and fitted within the framework of natural features.

Other arrangements also are possible for organizing a new community—for example, a carpet of development, a random scattering, a uniform grid, large single-purpose areas, linear cities, and developments laid out according to mystical or spiritual principles.[4] Cells, corridors, and centers can also be used to make urban types other than new towns; they can be the elements or framework for a much bigger or smaller area. The elements do not always read on the ground; some of them, like the cells, may make sense in daily life only because they are overlaid with social institutions, such as neighborhood associations. However, in these new communities, they provided a way for the development teams to organize space.

Cellular Structures, the Developer Village Unit, and the Idea of the Balanced Community

As is clear from earlier chapters, planners in all three developments divided the landscape into neighborhoods and villages, a form of cellular structure. From the Abercrombie Plan for London in 1944 to more recent new urbanist proposals, this idea has been a popular way of arranging metropolitan space. What I call the developer village unit drew from a palette of precedents, including Perry's neighborhood unit, Radburn planning, small-town nostalgia, Lynch's districts, and the idea of social balance or social mix.

Reflecting this eclectic ancestry, the village idea has been attractive to professionals from quite different backgrounds with different views on urbanism. For some developers, planners, and designers, village units would create identifiable places in metropolitan areas to promote wayfinding or a sense of belonging. Alternately, they would create microcosms of the functional diversity of the metropolis, developing bounded areas where people could walk to work or school, thus reducing travel and increasing casual social interactions. For others, they could provide for infrastructure in an efficient way through phasing in one neighborhood or village at a time. Finally, village units were designed as areas where people had common ties, which would foster social connectedness and civic engagement.

All these reasons—identity, function, phasing, and community—were important. However, the first three are rather straightforward and practical. It is the fourth reason, the idea that these cells could help create strong community bonds, that has been most slippery and open to critique. Of course *community* is an overused term in design, planning, and urban development, with little agreement about its definition (Hillery 1955). Obviously communities exist that are not based on residence—for example, social networks based on work, family, heritage, and common interests. However, as Raymond Williams has pointed out, it is one of the few terms about social organization that "seems never to be used unfavorably" (Williams 1983, 76). The term *new community* itself obviously plays on this positive association, and marketers of the developments used the term quite freely.

Some proponents of the new communities saw themselves as creating something more than just a convenient, identifiable base for access to the wider metropolis; they were also providing a small-scale setting for important human relationships and institutions tied to a bounded place. People such as James Rouse imagined that new communities would have a significant level of interaction, similar to that obtained in a preindustrial village, with the neighborhood being the dominant geography of both "informal social relationships and . . . the formal organizations to which [residents] would belong" (Willmott 1967, 390).

Similar ideas about balanced community units had been popular in the Mark 1 British new towns of the 1940s. However, studies in the 1950s failed to show that such neighborhood units of five thousand to ten thousand people led to friendships among neighbors (Keller 1968). As Herbert Gans outlined in a 1961 review essay, friendships were formed by socially homogeneous people who share "values with respect to child rearing, leisure-time interests, taste level, general cultural preferences, and temperament, characteristics at least partly due to similar lifecycle stage, income and education" (Gans 1961b, 137). Research from the period found that in suburban and new town areas, the space of the home and the space beyond the neighborhood or "village" were the main geographies of social life (Gans 1961b; Willmott 1967, 390).[5]

Obviously neighbors interact at different levels—from simple recognition, to neighborly chatting, to joint membership of civic associations, to close and intense friendship. All might be called a sense of community. Certainly something of a pioneer effect can manifest in new towns, where many similar people looking for a similar sense of belonging converge on one place at one time and interactions surely occur. People choosing the same new town may also share the kinds of social similarities that Gans pointed to in his 1961 review essay. However, the new town blues, or disappointment in the lack of change after moving to a new community, can also be a problem.

While the developments were talked about and marketed as "new communities," the better-read members of the development teams had seen these analyses and knew that merely putting people in one place would not cause friendships to form. However, they needed to organize the landscape somehow, and the village became a "convenient fiction," with the added benefits of identity, function, and phasing, mentioned above (Ewing 1991, 75). As Hoppenfeld outlined:

> The real community to which individuals belong becomes a function of interest and identification. Sometimes it will correspond with the "physical community" but at other times, for families and individuals at different stages of life, it will cut across service areas resulting in "community patterns" as complex and overlapping as in every living city. Freedom of movement and access to community facility centers via transit and car throughout the city should enhance and foster the sense of real community, based on choice. (Hoppenfeld 1967, 406)

Unfortunately, because marketing departments and some popular versions of the plans so promoted the village as a site of intense neighboring and friendship, any departure from the marketing image seemed like a planning failure (e.g., Burkhart 1981, 151). In addition, residents often did find a sense of community, or at least positive neighboring, at the local level, at least in part because of the pioneer effect and because a range of social activities and organizations was overlaid on and integrated with the physical structure of the new community, including village associations, schools, and shopping areas. One of the residents of the City of Irvine explained in an interview:

> I think the most successful aspect is the neighborhood community sense that exists. The services and the provision of schools, neighborhood shopping centers, parks, give people a sense that they are in a community. It's not like you have to go to some remote place that isn't part of your local area. To me, that's a part of the reason that I like the development [in one of Irvine's villages], because it was very clear as the Irvine Company's planning has evolved that they have really been trying to emphasize the community aspect in that development. The small parks . . . bring out the local people, the neighborhood people, and so it's that neighborhood thing of having an opportunity to meet people, to know people from your own community. That, to me, has been one of the real take-home values, one of the successes of Irvine, that my wife and I both really value. (Interview 0307)

Associated with this idea of community was the issue of balance. A balanced community could mean many things: balance between social groups, economic activities, "man" and nature, and balance as a sense of convenience. As Irvine Company consultants explained in an internal report on the Irvine Ranch in the 1960s:

> The balanced community is one which contains a broad range of mutually supporting activities that tend to foster social and economic heterogeneity in the community population and serve to achieve a measure of economic and functional independence. The balanced community, therefore, contains a reasonably wide variety of land uses, including various types of residential environments and public and commercial facilities. (Kreditor and Kraemer 1968, II-3).

Three decades later, an Irvine Company employee said much the same thing:

> I think the thing that we strive for and we've achieved is a balance in the community. That when people come into it . . . they have, number one, a variety of housing opportunities. They have the opportunity to work within a few miles of their home. They have multiple shopping opportunities, and the best recreation system in terms of parks and things that anyone could find. In addition to that, there are major regional facilities, performing arts centers and things like that. When I worked for [a growing local government area], people would

call and say, "When are the parks coming? When are the libraries coming? When are the schools coming?" The way we're able to develop [at the Irvine Company], the parks and the schools and everything come at the same time or almost at the same time. . . . And so, I think that real balance is what we've been able to achieve in each community as we build it. (Interview 0228)

Although cells or villages could each have a different function and character and be balanced across the entire new town, a more common proposal was for various sorts of balance within each cell or village.

While it was possible to imagine the balanced community as attractive to the wider public, some critics started to see it as reflecting the planners' desire for neatness and a particular sort of order. As Kevin Lynch complained a little later:

Good environments are repeatedly characterized as "balanced." We see the world as a system of polarities—hot and cold, big and little, black and white, dense and sparse, high and low, stimulating and quiet—and expect danger at each end of the spectrum. There must then be an optimum point in between, and this incorporates the idea of equilibrium: equal and opposing forces which kept the world steady, preventing any acceleration into disaster—the yin and yang of Chinese philosophy. The metaphor is so powerful that it can be used without challenge in the sharpest of debates. Who would question that we must have a "balanced population," or a "balanced economy"? Asking what purpose is served by balancing, or worse, advocating imbalance, is greeted with incredulity. (Lynch 1981, 370)

These are opposing views—Lynch questioning balance and the new community planners promoting it. However, even Lynch argued that neighborhoods do have some relevance as social units: "The pleasure of living in an identifiable district which has quiet, safe streets and daily services easily accessible nearby, and within which one can organize politically when the need for control arises, are surely a legitimate feature of good settlement. For certain age groups, moreover, particularly the young child, a place-based social community is quite important" (Lynch 1981, 248–49). For those working on planning and designing the new towns, as opposed to those marketing them, balance, more than "community," remained a core value, a way to articulate their ideas.

Of the three case study new communities, Columbia's plan is the most clearly cellular, repeatedly conceptualized as neighborhoods clustered into villages, with road systems deemphasized and subordinated to village units. However, all three developments have internal village road systems, with many loops and culs-de-sac for vehicles, and pedestrian circulation systems that provide links that are often not obvious to outsiders. This makes the village area a destination rather than a path for all but long-term residents. Overlaid by the village governance structure, which gives an actual social

identity to the physical village, this creates a landscape of insiders and outsiders. Residents from all three developments, even those from the ostensibly more inclusive Columbia, commented on this as an advantage in terms
of excluding unwanted intruders. Residents of The Woodlands and the Irvine
Ranch explained:

> The success of the neighborhoods, I think, creates a real sense of community.
> The basic design philosophy of limited access to residential sections provides
> a sense of security. [It] provides an opportunity for the residents in those areas
> to get to know each other on a much closer scale than in some of the tradi-
> tional subdivisions that we all have referred to as urban sprawl. It's not a grid
> system; it's very much a neighborhood system. And we've been able to incor-
> porate that neighborhood system into our watch programs, which was originally
> called The Woodlands Watch. And that has expanded into an involvement in
> Park Watch, Senior Watch, Apartment Watch, Campus Watch, in addition to
> the original Woodlands Watch, which was tailored to the neighborhoods. (Inter-
> view 0516)

> If you're going to rob somebody's house, you'll have a hell of a time getting
> out. It may only be one way. So it turns out to be a deterrent, just the physical
> layout of it. (Interview 0408)

Overall, the cellular structure had a number of benefits, providing a local
identity and some physical separation for residents while ordering the overall metropolitan landscape in a balanced way. As such, it was quite different
from the scattered subdivisions and the carpet of urban development that
were focuses of critiques of urban sprawl.

Corridors and Centers

As an alternative to the cellular structure of the neighborhood and village
model, others have proposed a corridor-and-center arrangement that focuses on transportation and activity nodes, including shopping, workplaces,
and high-density housing clusters. In many plans the network of corridors
and centers is overlaid on a landscape of neighborhoods and villages, although treated separately in a conceptual sense. This can be seen again in
a variety of plans from Abercrombie's 1944 Plan for London to the Port-
land metropolitan plan of the 1990s. However, at times these corridors and
centers take center stage, becoming the dominant elements, as in many city
beautiful plans of the early twentieth century, which focused on transportation infrastructure, industrial areas, and civic centers and paid scant
attention to housing. Garreau's (1991) edge city idea is essentially a landscape of corridors (freeways) and centers (edge cities) set in a uniform urban field. However, the idea of corridors and centers is also attractive to
those promoting rail-based sustainability, with recent schemes using this

structure devised as walkable nodes along transportation corridors (Newman and Kenworthy 2000).

The three new communities can be read or interpreted in terms of this concept of centers and corridors. In this case each element forms a hierarchy: town center, village center, neighborhood center; interstate, arterial, collector, and residential street. The absence of strip shopping areas in the new communities makes the centers compact and gives an overall character to the corridors that is quite different from generic sprawl. This framework of corridors and centers is overlaid on the mosaic of villages and neighborhoods. While this happens in each development, the way that it happens varies quite a bit.

The structure is perhaps clearest on the Irvine Ranch, where clusters of industrial and commercial development are linked by a freeway system and activity corridors. At a smaller scale, many villages are enclosed in a loose grid of arterials, with village centers generally on the outside edge of the village area so that they are accessible from several villages along the arterial corridors that divide them.[6] The situation is not so neat in The Woodlands, where corridors sometimes pass between villages and sometimes through them.

While Columbia has a more purely cellular structure, this was not the whole story of its initial planning. Originally, the "Columbus" minibus system was to run on a right-of-way that followed a figure-eight path around the development and through the village centers. This was a pattern also seen in British new towns such as Runcorn, designed at the same time as Columbia. Had the Columbia right-of-way been completed, it would have provided a looped central spine clearly connecting centers (see Godschalk 1967, 381). In a 1967 article, urban designer Hoppenfeld portrays this idea of small buses with frequent service as "self-sustaining."

> The choice was made to provide good service to a limited area rather than sporadic service to the entire city. This was a fundamental decision resulting in the coalignment of the high-density dwelling areas and the bus route. This physical plan decision put approximately 35 percent of the population within a 3-minute walk to a bus stop. . . . This choice, coupled with attaining good service to village centers, town center, and selected employment areas, strongly affected the shape of the city. (Hoppenfeld 1967, 406)

While the minibus ran for a few years, it was replaced with a county system, and the right-of-way route was never completed.[7] Without it, the cellular village structure is dominant.

Overall, plans that emphasize a center-and-corridor system deemphasize the residential unit and place more importance on movement corridors and centers of commercial or civic activity that may be linked to a number of residential areas. Rather than local community, it focuses on ties across met-

ropolitan areas, social networks, and associations based on common interests or background or activities, not the accident of residence. It is, in this
sense, a less nostalgic and more forward-looking idea. None of the projects
is a pure center-and-corridor arrangement, but this idea is most obvious on
the Irvine Ranch.[8]

Landscape Frames

People move to the suburbs at least partly to be closer to nature. To some
extent, this has to do with the spatial qualities within the suburban areas
themselves, but it is also related to the closeness of the countryside or of
significant undeveloped parcels of land. The new communities have tried
to enhance these qualities. Planning of the three developments represented
the level of sophistication about ecological issues available in their periods,
with ecology and landscape values becoming more important over time
(Healey and Shaw 1994).

The early 1960s plans for the Irvine Ranch, which came out of an agricultural perspective, essentially ignored ecology but did pay attention to topography. The Irvine Ranch had for a long time been a landscape of industrial-
scale agriculture made possible by increasingly elaborate water infrastructure;
it was not a rural landscape of family farms. Agriculture is an industry; *rural*
refers to a quality of place. A small amount of the early agricultural landscape remains—notably rows of eucalyptus windbreaks in the central valley
area. However, the dominant approach to the new landscape was to build it
from scratch using a lush and formal aesthetic without rural nostalgia. Only
very recently has restored habitat been added to this landscape palette.

Columbia's architect planners of the mid-1960s were working a little later
and did not have such a strong history of agricultural thinking. In contrast,
they started with a mosaic of pieces of farmland and promoted a more rural
image. They preserved buffers along the waterways as well as some forest
areas and did very extensive plantings to create a landscape that was fundamentally recreational—parks, paths, and woods to hike in. An offshoot idea
was to bury the undistinguished architecture in a wooded and naturalistic
setting. That is not to say that the landscape is without habitat values, but it
was not as dominant in the development.

In The Woodlands, McHarg had a team of ecologists, hydrologists, and environmental planners working intensively on natural systems and producing
multiple reports that eventually fed into the master planning of the entire
development, the land planning of neighborhoods, and the site planning of
individual parcels. The site was not an untouched wilderness, as significant
logging had been done, but the planning team looked at the landscape in a
different way, seeing not farms and streams but plant species and soils of dif-

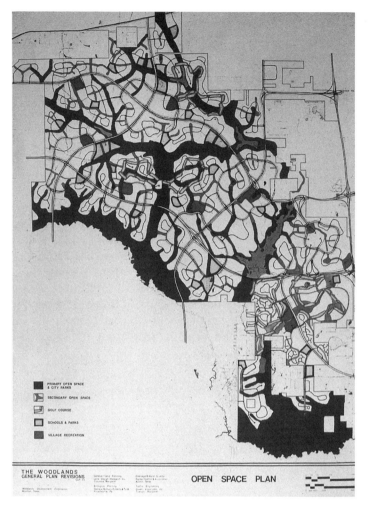

Figure 40. Landscape framework in The Woodlands, early 1970s.
Reprinted with permission from Cy Paumier.

ferent porosities and thus capacities to recharge the aquifer. They certainly
disturbed the environment themselves, inserting houses, industrial buildings,
and several golf courses. However, they did this in a way that was far removed
from the evocation of rural character so prevalent in many generic suburban
areas. The most important element of the ecological planning concept, the
hydrological system, is largely invisible to the general public. The forested aesthetic is also fairly uniform and does not have the variety of the rural land-

scapes that are a more common starting point for suburban planting designs. As a resident in The Woodlands explained: "It's very easy to get lost in this community; that's the thing I hear. And I've done it myself. I'll be on my bike or something, I'll get to an intersection; if I'm not thinking about where I am, I go, 'Wait a minute, where do I need to go?' Every intersection looks the same; there's two roads and trees" (Interview 0410).

Of course, in all three developments, designers and planners became more sophisticated about ecological issues each year and increasingly incorporated these ideas, particularly in The Woodlands and Columbia. On the Irvine Ranch, environmental activists were present from the late 1960s, working to protect various parts of the landscape and significantly reducing the developable land area.

This means that in Columbia and particularly in The Woodlands, open spaces are interwoven with development, reflecting understandings of the 1960s and 1970s and the emphasis on hydrology in The Woodlands (see figure 40). This lowers density. In Irvine, large areas of open land were protected in return for increased density, and so separation between untouched habitat areas and highly designed city is greater here than in the other two developments. This was not in the early plans, of course. It generally reflects a more contemporary understanding of the natural landscape and the emphasis on habitat rather than hydrology, with larger and more contiguous areas protected from development.

DESIGN

Style and Order

To a casual observer, the new towns are unmistakably suburban in appearance, although it is a suburban landscape without overhead wires, large signs, and strip shopping corridors. The common idea of the village, and a hierarchy of corridors and centers, gives a certain uniformity in scale and texture of development. However, the new community developments provided spaces for trying out innovative design concepts at a variety of scales.

This kind of experimentation had different profiles in different professions. For architects, buildings in the new communities stake out an ambiguous ground between the vernacular of builder suburbia and the high style or signature design that fills architecture magazines.[9] For landscape architects, however, the new communities provided the space to develop work that was frequently well respected.

All the developments required architects to design buildings or had extensive design review processes. Certainly many prominent architectural firms worked in these developments. However, their work creating fire stations, shopping centers, visitor centers, office buildings, apartments, and hotels was largely bread-and-butter professional work, working to budget and designed to be appealing to suburban consumers. While competent, interesting, popular, and even innovative, this work was not of the kind to capture national attention among the elites of the architectural profession, even when done by designers such as Frank Gehry or Ricardo Legorreta, who were part of that elite. This has created a continuing tension. Architects had heavily criticized generic suburban sprawl. Architects were also heavily involved in design and design review in these new communities. However, the form of suburban development was not appreciated by high-style professionals in architecture.

It was in the area of landscape architecture that these developments were more easily cutting edge, and it is unsurprising that they have received more attention from that profession. The big moves were made in creating an overall structure for the new town. Landscape architects were lucky because they could clearly help to create this structure both at a broad scale and in its details. In environmental planning, land planning, site planning, and the design of utility easements, streetscapes, parking lots, and parks, the developments received careful attention from some of the top practitioners in the nation (Girling and Helphand 1994; see figures 41–49). In many ways the landscapes are the most memorable aspects of the developments.

In their turn, the various professionals working on all the developments saw themselves creating the kinds of environments that Americans would actually want to live in, rather than the kinds that elite architectural professionals wanted to build. This required strong discipline—if the developments did not sell, the designers would lose future work. The need to appeal to fairly diverse consumers of the landscape was explicitly examined by staff in the three developments (e.g., Finley and Hoppenfeld 1963, 1). Looking back on their past work, two professionals explained in interviews that the new communities had succeeded in terms of popular appeal, which was a key criterion:

> I think [Rouse] had a very good sense of the marketplace, understood what people really wanted. Americans are not urbanists, particularly. They like the idea of going west. They like the idea of having land. . . . I think he sensed all of that and saw it, but he thought that he could do it in a somewhat regulated fashion; with some order. . . . [The Rouse Company planners] saw it as a green country town. That was in their minds. I think that was one of the reasons that they allowed the landscaping and the waterfront to occur. It was critical in their minds that you set the tone for the things that would happen after. The buildings were less important to them, I believe, than the sense of space and place. (Interview 0113)

> I think what I've always enjoyed with the Irvine Company is that the people really are dedicated to creating . . . communities that we think people want. And I think we're always willing to change when we find out that people want some-

thing else. We have elaborate programs of feedback from people. We stay involved in homeowners associations so that we know what are some of the good
things, what are some of the bad things. We like to think that we're constantly
learning on each new community. Unlike some developers where the bottom
line is the only thing they think about, and certainly we do, too—I mean, we're
here to make a profit—but one of the advantages of being a large landowner
is that we're going to stay here, so every community we do ends up putting
value on our next community. And so, it's really important that we keep building quality, that we keep that level. If we start dropping that, then the value of
our next community will decline. And that goes true for office development
and our R&D and our hotels and everything. If we start doing something that
isn't up to what people feel should be the standard that it should be, it'll impact our next products. We can't pick up and leave; we're not building two
hundred homes and then leaving. We live on the quality of what we do. . . .
And I think that attitude really permeates the whole company and has for a
long, long time. And even people in the community that just don't want development, and therefore oppose us, will typically say, "Although I've always
liked the quality of what you do and such, I just don't want you to do it any-
more." (Interview 0228)

Residents and professionals who had not worked on the development
teams had more mixed views about the visual character of the suburban environments in these new towns, dealing with criticisms in a complex way.

I've learned to be a little patient about . . . these snooty reviews from the *New
York Times,* [saying that in Irvine] everything looks alike. Well, what do they
expect in twenty or thirty years? The places that they love in New York City
or even Westwood, Los Angeles, for that matter—these are areas that have
evolved over a hundred years at least. Give us a little time and a little opportunity, and you are beginning to see all kinds of different subcommunities within
the city developing different styles of architecture, different ways of looking
at how you do retain a quality of life within an urban or suburban setting. (Interview 0219)

I think a lot of people are attracted to the idea of Irvine. I was really surprised
when I moved here. I had very strong biases. People told me: "Oh God, you'll
die there. It's so Republican, it's so conservative, it's so new." . . . One of the
things that really struck me in the beginning when I came here . . . [and met]
the local urban design community and planners and so forth—they're really
proud of it. The people who have participated in this development are—I think
in some ways justifiably, in some ways not so—very proud of what they've created here. There's this real pioneer sense of "We carved this out of the land.
Look at what a great job we've done." (Interview 0302)

Overall, the developments did respond to critiques of the organization
and aesthetics of suburban sprawl, becoming more organized and coherent
while maintaining popular appeal. That this was not appreciated by cultural
elites was not a huge problem in marketing terms.

Figure 41. Automotive landscape: Irvine Spectrum Center parking lot, viewed from above. Photographer: Ann Forsyth.

Figure 42. Automotive landscape: Columbia townhouse parking. Photographer: Ann Forsyth.

Figure 43. Automotive landscape: fast food restaurant, The Woodlands. Photographer: Ann Forsyth.

Figure 44. Peopled landscape: Newport Center, on Irvine Ranch. Photographer: Ann Forsyth.

Figure 45. Peopled landscape: Columbia's birthday cake cutting. Photographer: Ann Forsyth.

Figure 46. Peopled landscape: village pool, The Woodlands. Photographer: Ann Forsyth.

Figure 47. Landscape style: formal hedges in Irvine. Photographer: Ann Forsyth.

Figure 48. Landscape style: park landscape in Columbia. Photographer: Ann Forsyth.

Figure 49. Landscape style: drainage area in The Woodlands. Photographer: Ann Forsyth.

Change and Covenants

To build and maintain these designs, the developments imposed a system of architectural controls and common-area maintenance, enforced through covenants, conditions, and restrictions (CC&Rs) and paid for through levies on properties. For many, these restrictions smack of big brother, particularly on the Irvine Ranch, where they seem to be enforced more strictly than in the other developments (McKenzie 1994). In all the case study developments, they are elaborate—for example, requiring approval to change the style of external light fittings or paint colors on houses.

While I am not a fan of such regulations, the CC&Rs have some logic. In a review of all major new communities in the United States, Ewing (1991, 95–96) found several themes in these kinds of elaborate and seemingly rigid documents. In order of prevalence, they were to "hide unsightly elements"; keep views; "keep mature plants"; promote pedestrian activity; "break up masses"; accent entries; encourage visual variety or "simple, clean designs"; "create coherent public spaces"; and avoid abrupt transitions.

Once villages or sections of the developments are completed, enforcement has generally been turned over to voluntary boards of residents who, with the aid of staff at the community associations, enforce the CC&Rs for their neighbors. This enforcement has been more complicated in the case of commercial areas, with only some having independent boards. For example, in Columbia the Architectural Committee for commercial areas is still based at the Rouse Company; in all the developments the developers' significant ownership of commercial areas gives them more continuing power. The restrictions on commercial areas are elaborate in all three developments (e.g., Development Standards Committee 1999). Even in incorporated Irvine, with significant city control over building, the owner associations have more stringent design controls.

However, as is explained in the next chapter, covenants in each of the developments have two components—a set of difficult-to-change legal requirements and a set of guidelines that can be changed more easily. This situation provides more flexibility than may be apparent, and this flexibility has been used to advantage, particularly in Columbia and The Woodlands. It allows a continual reordering or reorganization of the rules that define the built environment, even if this process is cumbersome at times.

The architectural review process also involves engagement in civic life. In both Columbia and The Woodlands, architectural review committee meetings are well-advertised sessions. In Irvine, given that there is also a city process, these are more like the meetings of condominium associations. Everywhere the process is quite decentralized, open to local perceptions. I attended several of these meetings in Columbia and The Woodlands and found quite a lot of diversity in local norms about how strictly to interpret the elaborate guidelines.

The architectural review process obviously creates a forum for political action. Writing about events in the 1970s, Burkhart describes architectural committees in Columbia as the sites of conflicts over class differences, but with outcomes taking different political directions. For example, in one case an architectural committee denied an application for middle-class owners of a townhouse development to place a fence across its border with a low-cost rental apartment complex. However, in another case such a committee tried to deny permission to install play equipment in a subsidized housing development that they thought untidy (Burkhart 1981, 59–61, 115–26).

Obviously CC&Rs constrain choice, but they also give control over the haphazard development characterized as *sprawl*. In the new communities, they have provided predictability for potentially nervous customers in developments where a number of innovative design strategies have been tried. For some of the same reasons, they are used extensively today in new urbanist developments. Generally, in the new towns, they are flexible enough to support different architectural styles (Wood 1985, 199). In this context, a number of designers living in the developments told me stories of being prevented from putting in fences or changing the colors of their own houses; however, they had also managed to do significant renovations.

> I said, "Look . . . let's allow awnings." That was one of our first departures from the CC&Rs, was to allow people to put [up] some canvas awnings. I said, "Why don't we let a whole variety of primary colors—you know, the yellows, reds, blues?" Can you imagine, here's these lay people saying, "Oh, no, we'd better be safe, let's make the awnings [be] tan." They had several shades of tan. (Interview 0301)

> There's a lot of just cookie-cutter regulations, not a lot of room for individual self-expression. On the other hand, I'm not living next door to a bright hot-pink house with a goat in the front yard. (Interview 0430)

While only the more sophisticated residents were likely to know how to push the envelope of design, I was surprised in the architectural committee meetings by how many people requested permission to make changes only after the changes had been made. Most were approved, showing a path to change that did not require sophisticated architectural expertise. The enforcement of these restrictions is in this way generally quite prosaic. A resident of Columbia, reflecting on his own experiences of reviewing plans and also of being reviewed, explained about the CC&Rs:

> They sometimes have been inconvenient. My experience has been, as a member of the [review] board and as a resident with a problem, that people tend to be reasonable. If you can make a reasonable argument for why something

should or should not be done, then you'll be heard, and it will be acted upon favorably. (Interview 0101)

ORDERING DIVERSITY IN THE SOCIAL ENVIRONMENT

The planners, developers, and residents of these new towns assumed that a relationship exists between the physical environment and the kinds of human lives that can be lived in particular places. At a minimum, the physical environment could be made convenient and predictable, giving access to a range of shopping, educational, recreational, cultural, and employment opportunities at the village, city, and regional scale. In Columbia, whether realistic or not, many saw the environment as the setting for increased economic and racial integration and the creation of something akin to small-town life. For each development, this was a reaction to the problem of how to live in a metropolitan area, a problem put quite poignantly by Michael Ignatieff:

> Is there a language of belonging adequate to Los Angeles? Put like that the answer can only seem to be no. Yet we should remember the nineteenth-century city and the richness of its invention of new forms of possibility and belonging. Those great cities—Manchester, New York, Paris—were as strange to those who had to live in them for the first time as ours may seem to us. Yet we look at them now as a time of civic invention—the boulevard, the public park, the museum, the cafe, the trolley car, street lighting, the subway, the railway, the apartment house. Each of these humble institutions created a new possibility for fraternity among strangers in public places. (Ignatieff 1984, 139–40)

As outlined above, the three developments were largely successful in creating a sense of place. This is confirmed by recent survey responses outlined in the next chapter. All the developments have attracted people wanting accessibility and convenience and have increasingly become home to people who also work in the developments. Overall, these exemplary new towns have emphasized an ordered diversity, in both social and physical components, something I heard from a range of people. This is related to the idea of balance but has occurred at a variety of scales, not just at the village level. This issue of ordered diversity forms the focus of the rest of the chapter.

Income and Ethnic Mix, Gender, and Youth

One of the most important dimensions of this idea of ordered diversity within new towns as a whole, and within villages and neighborhoods at a smaller scale, was the idea of social mix, most notably economic and ethnic or racial mix. As was noted previously, all three case study developments had explicit policies to promote some form of economic mix in order to create balanced demographics, promote housing sales, and attract industries and businesses.

In new construction, economic mix is particularly difficult to attain; however, housing units can be made affordable in a number of ways. Land prices can be kept low by a government or a developer subsidy or by increasing the density of the development. Unit prices can be kept low by using less expensive construction methods and self-help or voluntary labor (as in Habitat for Humanity) or by limiting unit size. A government can directly subsidize the overall cost of the housing, either paying for specific units or providing vouchers for people to compete in the private market. Also, as private-market housing ages, it often becomes more affordable than new housing. This lower relative value sometimes comes about because the older housing is smaller than newer housing and has fewer features, such as air-conditioning or fancy appliances, but it may also be more in need of repair.

Obviously all the developments dealt with this differently. The Woodlands had explicit, enforceable legal requirements for affordable housing because of its association with HUD; Columbia had a strong moral commitment because of the vision of James Rouse; and the Irvine Ranch had a more piecemeal approach implemented by both the developer and local government. As I outline in the next chapter, all three were more successful at creating economic mix than generic sprawl is but less successful than many had hoped. Because of this they received mixed reviews. One resident in The Woodlands complained:

> We lived in sections of Panther Creek when we first moved here that was not the higher economic scale, and the school that our little kids went to—they chased my little daughter around at one point in time, calling her Wal-Mart girl because her mommy was not smart enough to know that she was supposed to have fancy clothes. Her mommy's always been a Wal-Mart girl herself. It was hard on my kids to be Wal-Mart kids, but basically their mommy didn't know any better, and I wouldn't have chosen any differently. I thought, "Jeez, is this a real good experience for people in this time, when you're challenged to be global and you're challenged to be accepting, and you're supposed to do good in your life, and you're inside such a kind of weird bubble. . . ." But I think we may be growing out of it. (Interview 0503)

As I explain in more detail in the next chapter, the three new communities had very different initial aims in terms of ethnic mix. Irvine didn't aim for mix but has achieved it with a large population of Asian descent (who may be Asian American, but include recent immigrants as well). Columbia aimed for racial mix and has achieved it; The Woodlands, with an aim similar to Columbia's, did not do so well. However, apart from their homogeneous newness, the developments are more mixed in racial and income dimensions than much of suburbia, and, with age, the homogeneous newness of each development has worn off as well. This does not mean that people are close friends with others who do not share their interests, but in their daily lives people do come across others who are not like themselves.

This was appealing in the market, and not just to liberals. As a Republican Woodlands resident explained:

> I was looking for a place that had land use designations. I was looking for a place that had an education system in place and that had a quality of life that guaranteed I didn't have a Stop and Go next to me. And I wanted a community that would eventually diversify itself so that my children didn't grow up in a strictly white Caucasian environment. And I wanted a place that had a diversity of religion, so that my children didn't grow up in this cloistered environment and they go off to college some day and have the shock of their life. (Interview 0426)

The role of women was an additional area in which society was already changing when the developments were designed and first inhabited. Of the three developments, Columbia made the most explicit early attempts to plan for women through the social planning work group. All three developments talked about being balanced communities with people of different ages, income groups, ethnicities, and life circumstances; however, women were initially imagined as mothers.

While I do not think that it had an enormous or long-term effect, the work of planning these developments was undeniably done primarily by men. In the 1960s, the small number of women involved with early planning generally had short-term or behind-the-scenes roles. Even in socially progressive Columbia, Antonia Chayes was the sole female member of the social planning work group, with her area of expertise described in various documents as either "women" or "family life." Of course, as pictures of the work group show, it was also all white. Even so, its members spent a great deal of time working out how to transform racial relations and the opportunities of African Americans in particular. In contrast, they spent little time considering how the position of women could be transformed dramatically, envisaging only small changes.

Antonia Chayes's draft memorandum for the working group focused on women's education. Her suggestions included a continuing education institute (for training for employment and volunteer duties, as well as for general knowledge), child care and help with family errands and tasks such as shopping and meal preparation, family life education, and a structure for volunteer groups (Chayes 1964). Chayes pointed to the increasing number of women in the workforce and the need for such women to be educated to hold better jobs, but this was not seen as the only path for women.

Of course, women might have been working behind the scenes in planning the new towns. As was discussed in chapter 3, Libby Rouse, married to Jim Rouse for over three decades until their divorce in the 1970s, seems to have had some role in developing the Columbia concept (J. Rouse 1977). However, many wives in that period saw themselves as primarily supporting their husbands, and so I was not able to find the cadre of unrecognized wife-planners that I had imagined might be there. Even James Rouse was not terrifically progressive in his views on women. As late as 1982, he offered the following reflections on changes in women's roles, in response to a query on the state of Christian women, for the magazine *Today's Christian Woman:*

> Women for a long time have been the rock of Christian faith and influence in the family, influencing, leading, guiding their husbands as well as their children. Now as more of them have moved into leadership roles in business, community, politics and church that influence has been extended. . . .
>
> [Women] have tremendous capacities—so much to give—that they must be happier, on the whole, in their new fulfillment, recognition and respect. Women are much more important than men. They are more sensitive, more perceptive, more intricate in their capacity for understanding, and empathizing. I have often said that women are like a Swiss watch—men like a "big Ben." They hold higher values, give themselves more sacrificially; respond with greater warmth. Women excel in the human side of life—in relationships, understanding, service and support—far more important than physical strength, calculation, deal-making, executive management. As they have opportunities to use their gifts in a wider field, it is natural that they would be happier in fulfillment of God's purpose for them. (Rouse 1982)

In the numerous documents produced by the Columbia social planning work group, Herbert Gans seems to have made the most often quoted comments about women. Drawing on his Levittown experience, he pointed to the potential isolation of stay-at-home mothers, particularly those from cultural and racial minorities and from working-class backgrounds. He also articulated class differences in the priorities of women, even among such stay-at-home mothers (e.g., Gans 1964, 5). However, when the work group leader, Donald Michael, produced a lengthy social planning proposal dealing with neighborhood, village, and townwide issues, women were not a prominent group (Michael 1964). The main focus in terms of social innovation was on racial and economic integration and some aspects of education. Adolescents were much mentioned in special sections, but women were subsumed into discussions of family and recreation.

Early marketing for all the developments emphasized family life. For example, a double-page advertisement for Columbia in 1967 featured a white family of two parents, three children, a cat, and a dog, and asked in large text:

> What do you do with a creative wife, a hyperactive Tom Sawyer, an atomic scientist aged 14, a little beauty who simply must have her very own horse, a polygamous housecat, a basset hound—and yourself, if you're a man who thinks living anywhere but in a city is for pioneers?

You move to Columbia, the Next America.
New. Near. Now. (Rouse Company 1967)[10]

This changed during the early 1970s. By the mid-1970s Irvine's market segmentation was responding to changing households. Columbia was also attracting a large number of dual-earner couples: by the 1980 census, 60 percent of married-couple families in Columbia had both husband and wife working, compared with 35 percent in Baltimore City.

At this time women were also taking on more professional roles in planning and urban design, which affected The Woodlands in particular. Specifically, landscape architect Leslie Sauer was an important contributor to some of the early WMRT planning studies in The Woodlands, as was Anne Spirn at the start of her career. More typical was a role in marketing: Judy Neiman at Rouse stands out as creating much-lauded early marketing slide shows for Columbia (incidentally, Neiman was Chayes's sister-in-law) (Neiman 1975).

A parallel situation occurred with people of color. While it is much harder to trace the role of people of color by tracking names, it does not appear that they had prominent roles on the planning and design teams until the 1970s, even though the issue of ethnic relations was one that was discussed on such teams. Even in the 1970s, the people of color on the teams were often foreign-born, such as Narendra Juneja and Mokun Lokhande, originally from South Asia, and members of the WMRT team in The Woodlands. However, in Columbia, many African Americans were prominent in civic organizations and political life; in The Woodlands, a number of HUD staff members were people of color; and there were individuals of color in all three developments working on specific components, such as building designs.

Even today, few women are among the planning and development staff and consultants. For example, a 1976 article on Woodbridge in the City of Irvine showed a picture of thirty-two "planners, architects, engineers, marketing specialists, educators, Irvine commissioners, council and staff" who had worked together on Irvine—including one woman (Hunsinger 1976, 57). Two and a half decades later, an article on architects working on the Irvine Ranch in the area of housing included pictures of twenty-five architects, none of them women; while mostly white, they exhibited much more ethnic diversity than sexual diversity (Conroy 2001).

This situation was not unique to new towns. It was not until the 1970s that a sizable number of women started to move into architecture and physical planning. The first books of feminist critiques of planning and urban design emerged only in the late 1970s and early 1980s (e.g., Hayden 1981; Keller 1981; Wekerle et al. 1980; Stimpson et al. 1980).[11]

In subsequent years, a number of surveys of life have been made in these new communities, although relatively little attention has been paid to sex and gender issues. Unfortunately, while sex was recorded in the North Carolina studies of the early 1970s, it was not used as a major category for analysis. "Women" and "females" do not appear in the indexes of the volumes produced in the studies; few tables, charts, or analyses break out the responses by sex. Those distinctions between men and women were generally reported only in global terms, not by development. For example, men moving to new communities "were more likely to say that the move improved their life quality, but more women reported being completely satisfied with their lives" (Zehner 1977b, 19, 118). Something of the same could be said of African Americans and other people of color: their population numbers were often too small to enable researchers to glean statistically significant findings from one development. However, race has been an important category for discussion in spite of the small sample sizes, and discussion of racial issues has been more central in debates about new communities.

The Columbia Association did conduct an early survey on women's lives, using a stratified random sample of three hundred households based on housing type—apartment, townhouse, and single-family home (Columbia Association 1974, 2). At a time when only 18 percent of adult women in the United States had education beyond high school, 78 percent of the Columbia sample had. In terms of quality of life, people who had lived in Columbia at least two years generally reported feeling settled and having enough friends. However, while 80 percent of women with children ages six to eighteen at home reported that they had no difficulty meeting friends, only 48 percent of women with no children at home reported the same ease of friendships.

In terms of race, more black women than whites reported having as many friends as they wanted (71 versus 52 percent) and being more satisfied in Columbia than their previous location (79 versus 69 percent). However, overall, more black women than whites reported that they did not find their lives to be very satisfying (27 percent versus 9 percent) (Columbia Association 1974, 13).

The three developments have continued to do resident surveys, sponsored by the local government (Irvine) or by resident associations (Columbia, The Woodlands). All have conducted surveys in the period since 1998, and these recent surveys are useful in that they reflect residents' experiences of the more mature or fully developed new communities. In addition, the presence of UC Irvine means that a number of studies have used the ranch as a setting, notably in work on gender, ethnicity, and space by Kristen Day (e.g., Day 1999). Unfortunately, of the large community-wide surveys, Columbia's 1998 survey did not inquire about the sex of the respondent, but focused instead on the household. It also did not ask about race or ethnicity, but focused on household income, tenure, and residential village. Columbia's more recent 2002 survey on governance does break down responses by sex—as well as by race, length of residence, and age—but deals only with a limited number of issues. Irvine's 2000 survey report broke out male and female differences for only a small number of questions, although this was true for ethnic and income differences as well. Only The Woodlands gave a complete set of cross-tabulations by sex and village for every question in its 1996, 1999, and 2000 surveys (Chesapeake Group Inc. 1998; Fairbank, Maslin, Maullin and Associates 2000; Creative Consumer Research 1996, 1999, 2000; Mason-Dixon Polling and Research 2002).[12] However, The Woodlands survey included only residents of houses, not apartments or condominiums. By 2000, 79 percent of the housing units were detached single-family homes, and another 4 percent were attached single-family homes, so this survey eliminated about one-fifth of households. Also, while the survey asked a number of demographic questions, these did not include race,

As I describe in chapter 6, these surveys confirm that developers, government officials, and resident association employees were all correct in claiming to me that residents liked living in these areas, but some gender differences occurred. In Irvine, use of facilities showed little variation in ethnicity or income, although "men are more likely to use an athletic facility, hiking, and biking trails than women are, but women are more likely to use an arts center, community theater, and arboretum" (Fairbank, Maslin, Maullin and Associates 2000, 9). In The Woodlands, in 1999, 47 percent of women but only 35 percent of men ranked the trees, forests, greenbelts, and natural setting as the thing they liked best about living there. However, by 2000 the gap had closed to 47 percent and 44 percent, respectively. In considering threats of annexation by Houston, 38 percent of men were worried but only 31 percent of women were. By 2000 this had dropped to 14 and 12 percent, respectively (Creative Consumer Research 1999, 2000).

Overall, in spite of an early focus on women as mothers, the developments have proved more flexible in their actual use. For example, many of the women in Columbia and Irvine work. In 2000, 71 percent of Columbia women over sixteen were in the labor force, 61 percent of those in Irvine, and 53 percent in The Woodlands compared with 61 percent nationwide, although the proportions in all three new towns had declined since 1990 (see appendix B). Several of the women interviewees mentioned appreciation that their children could walk to school, as this freed their time significantly, particularly in Columbia and Irvine. Findings continue to show that women prefer suburban environments, and the new communities have provided these environments while mitigating some of their disadvantages (Spain 1988).

Single-mother households were between 8 and 10 percent of those in the developments in 1990, a little lower than the state averages but impressive for suburban areas. The job opportunities and housing variety made the areas attractive. Similarly, by 2000, both the City of Irvine and Columbia had virtually the same percentage of single-person households as their respective states—25 percent in Columbia and 23 percent in Irvine—and only The Woodlands remained more family oriented (with 19 percent single-person households compared with 24 percent statewide). These are obviously not exclusively areas for nuclear families, at least partly because the new communities function as employment centers; in the late 1990s, the City of Irvine had about 3.1 jobs per household, Columbia 2.0, and The Woodlands 1.2. However, it is interesting that in Columbia's many planning documents I can find no explicit attention paid to single-person households, except those of older people. In contrast, the more market-driven Irvine Ranch was more responsive to social changes in household types, although not until the 1970s.

Women activists are present in all the new communities. The League of Women Voters has branches in the counties that The Woodlands and Columbia dominate, and several people mentioned its political importance in Howard County. The City of Irvine has had a number of female mayors, and several women have represented Columbia at the county and state levels. Resident associations (Columbia, The Woodlands) and homeowner associations (Irvine) offer opportunities for women to develop leadership skills. For example, a 1975 article on community association newsletters in the Irvine Ranch noted that all but one newsletter was edited by a woman or group of women (Smith 1975). Bloom (2001b, chap. 10) argues that a number of women have been significant political figures in both Columbia and Irvine. In 1973, Charlotte Temple, a visiting developer, found that the women's movement was strong in Columbia, with many women also working outside the home (cited in Bloom 2001b, 214).[13] The current president of the Columbia Association, Maggie Brown, is a long-time female resident. In addition, many activist women moved to the developments, sometimes because of their utopian promise.

Overall, the mixed-use designs and varied housing forms have, interestingly, been flexible enough to unintentionally support the changing roles of women. In spite of the gender stereotypes involved in their early planning and marketing, these developments now rate highly as places for women to live, as exemplified by the *Ladies Home Journal* rating for Irvine. The magazine's selection process involved developing general criteria on the basis of opinions from the readership and then applying those criteria to U.S. cities, which did not involve Columbia or The Woodlands, as they are unincorporated areas in counties (Best Cities 2001, 2002). These environments work because they were planned to be relatively self-contained—people could "live, work, shop, play, and learn," as most still say in their advertising.

An additional sex and gender issue is that of gays and lesbians, and here differences occur among locations and over time. Both the Irvine Ranch and Columbia have a variety of gay, lesbian, and queer organizations, but these are largely absent in The Woodlands. Queer adults in suburban areas often

CHAPTER 5

choose to live fairly quietly and can create social networks that are not necessarily based in their neighborhoods, so the lack of organizations can have many meanings.

However, the issue of younger people is more difficult, and here The Woodlands stands out. The Irvine Ranch is more urban in character, less isolated in its region, and has more varied places to hang out—from parks and beaches to the university and a very wide variety of shopping and entertainment centers. Irvine has hosted a number of gay and lesbian organizations and events at UC Irvine, including the 2001 Orange County gay pride celebration. The Orange County Cultural Pride (OCCP) organization—the county's gay pride group—has its board meetings in the City of Irvine (OCCP, n.d.). Columbia is also accustomed to diversity. By 1999 Columbia had made it into the *Washington Post* for its gay high school prom, sponsored by the local branch of the national organization PFLAG (Parents and Friends of Lesbians and Gays). This is certainly on the cutting edge of acceptance of such diversity in suburban areas. This group also sponsors the Rainbow Youth Alliance of Columbia/Howard County, based at the interfaith center in one of the older villages (Rainbow Youth Alliance, n.d.).

It is not surprising that the most negative events for gays and lesbians emerged from the more conservative Woodlands. Most dramatically, in 1991 ten young men from The Woodlands assaulted and deliberately killed a twenty-seven-year old gay man, Paul Broussard, in Houston. This was the most tragic incident in a long series of gay-bashing events in Houston by young Woodlands residents. The interracial group of young men—seven were seventeen and the oldest twenty-two—received a variety of jail sentences of up to forty-five years (Aston 2001; Baker 2000).[14] John Aston, a professor of education at Southwest Texas State University and a resident of The Woodlands in the late 1990s, interviewed many of those involved and found a number of other elements in the equation, including the perpetrators' use of alcohol and illegal drugs (Aston 2001).

At the time, this incident provoked some, though by no means all, adults to reassess their environment:

> The idea for The Woodlands Teen Center . . . came out of a very tragic event that we'd had here where a couple of our high school kids, recent graduates, went down into Houston into an ostensibly gay area and apparently bashed some guy to death. It was a story that made national news. . . . But it just stunned everybody in this community, and it made people realize two things. One is the level of intolerance with some people, and two, some of the things we're hearing from the kids is The Woodlands is not a good place for kids once they reach a certain age. . . . There was no place to go for the loner couple of kids who like to ride their skateboards. There was no place to go for those kids who maybe didn't fit into the church group or the athletic group.

There was no place to hang out. They were not welcome anywhere. (Interview 0422)

Timing is also an issue: gay and lesbian issues became more mainstream everywhere in the United States in the 1990s, with a number of queer characters appearing on network television in fairly positive roles. Some of the difference between Columbia's prom and the Broussard case reflects simply changes over the decade. However, the distinction still remains. Some interviewees mentioned, unprompted, that gay teens were in a difficult situation in The Woodlands, although the fact that gay teens are a big enough group to warrant comment is in itself evidence of social change in that location.

Youth in general have had some special concerns. For young children, with a smaller home range, the design of each of the developments has enabled them to walk to school and shops in relative safety. However, teens often want access to a wider area. In the Orange County landscape of beaches and entertainment areas, youth at the Irvine Ranch seem to have had fewer problems than they may have had in a more isolated development (Purpura 1999, 29–32). However, youth here, as well as those in the other two developments, have had the most obvious difficulties with the automobile-based design and orderly landscape. The City of Irvine has loosened some land use regulations to allow more youth-oriented entertainment facilities in business and industrial areas, has built a skate park, and has organized a number of task forces on youth. However, in the 1990s the City of Irvine also imposed a curfew on teens and increased police allocated to gangs. Similarly, Columbia early on created centers and coffeehouses for teens, and The Woodlands has a number of recreational facilities but has also struggled with public concerns about the disruptiveness of this age group.

LINKAGES

Organizing the metropolitan landscape is a very complex task. Space that will have social meaning is both created and sold; development is tested against economic models and market acceptance. These developments organized their landscapes to create balance and orderliness in them, and they have largely succeeded in making convenient, distinctive, and well-designed places for people to live. They tried out the cellular, corridor-and-center, and landscape-frame arrangements that are still the basis for proposals for better suburban development and changes in metropolitan design. Aesthetically the designers of the developments pushed the boundaries of suburban style, even if this was not much appreciated by the design elites in architecture.

By overlaying resident associations on the physical structure, developers gave social meaning to physical forms. Thus, even if physical proximity could not create social bonds in the new community villages and neighborhoods, there were social organizations to take on that role. Some groups that have had a difficult time, such as teens, have a difficult time in many other places as well, and it has perhaps been unrealistic to expect them to be enamored with even well-planned suburban environments. Whether the developments created reasonable social environments and also managed to avoid the other problems of urban sprawl is the subject of the next chapter.

Chapter 6

Alternatives to Sprawl?

THE PROBLEM OF SPRAWL

Those planning the developments expended a tremendous amount of effort to create an alternative to sprawl. The book has shown how development teams grappled with how to change development patterns, working to redesign the metropolitan landscape and fashion new kinds of social settings. However, developments could do all this and, as meaningful as the changes might be, still not provide an actual alternative to the perceived problems of sprawling suburban growth. Instead, they might merely repackage the same features into a bundle that would look slightly different but be indistinguishable from other, more incremental and less coordinated development in relation to the issues that have been important in sprawl debates.

This chapter critically assesses the character of these planned developments in terms of a number of key concerns highlighted in debates about suburban growth: density; aesthetics, design, and identity; social equity, diversity, and access; economic efficiency; and environmental issues. It evaluates the developments in these dimensions, showing that they have, in fact, solved many problems identified in the sprawl debates but that in some key areas they have not been able to do so.

Of course, even if they had not solved any of the problems of sprawl, they may still have been quite popular. Postwar sprawl is often portrayed as a problem. In fact, to call it sprawl and not suburban development is generally to imply that something is wrong. However, at least part of the reason that sprawl is so pervasive in the United States is that it has benefits. Certainly federal policies encouraged road building and suburban mortgages and thus pushed people to the suburbs. However, people were also drawn there by the benefits of large amounts of inexpensive private space, easy automobile access, and small government units, giving residents strong local control. The developers of the three new communities knew this, so their capacity to capture or retain many of these benefits of sprawl was a critical aspect of their ability to compete for a large percentage of sales in their regional markets. That they did so while avoiding many of the costs of sprawl is striking. Selling a small, highly designed subdivision to a niche market is one thing, but selling thousands of homes and hundreds of acres of commercial and industrial land decade after decade is much more difficult.

In addition, the development teams working on these new towns differed in their definitions of the problem of sprawl, showing a lack of general agreement about which of its problems needed to be solved. For example, in a 1970–71 Irvine Company draft of the Urban Design Element of its 1970 general plan, sprawl was characterized in physical terms:

> Urban sprawl may be defined as a relatively fine-grain and haphazard distribution of nonresidential uses throughout residential areas, these residential areas themselves being a continuous pattern of low-density housing on standardized lots with uniform setbacks, derived through the application of unimaginative and inadequate zoning and subdivision controls and all acting in response to the presence of the automobile as the universal means of transportation. The effect of sprawl from the point of view of urban design is to create widespread visual monotony and an environment largely devoid of identity and meaning at scales no more intimate than those of the metropolitan region. Because the circulation system must serve this sprawling urban development, it tends to be an inefficient investment of public funds. . . . The auto-oriented and piecemeal development likewise creates notorious conflicts in land uses and, thus, fragile land values which tend to cause people to lose interest in the appearance and maintenance of private property.
>
> The public and quasi-public sectors contribute to the untidy and chaotic appearance of the environment . . . and the lack of adequate and consistent landscaping along streets and roads is a missed opportunity in providing some visual relief and stimulus in the sprawled environment. In addition, public open space tends to be of inferior quality. (Irvine Company 1970–71, 1–2)

Not too surprisingly, descriptions of urban sprawl in Columbia's planning often had a more social focus. As Rouse Company employee Wallace Hamilton explained in an early memo proposing a center for human development in Columbia, the Rouse team rejected the typical urban design approach to counteracting sprawl:

> With the creation of this new community of Columbia, the developers hope to make a response to the present-day dilemma of burgeoning urban growth. On the one hand, too little planning invites sprawl that is depersonalized, inconvenient, and costly. On the other hand, when planning is done, it tends to be focused on the aesthetics of urban design which may or may not coincide with the needs of the people who will be living in the town.

The developers want to make Columbia a place for human growth and the enhancement of human life experience. (Hamilton 1964a)

Or as Columbia was described in materials presented to Howard County citizens and officials:

Columbia is an opportunity for the growth of America to change course away from needless waste of the land, sprawl, disorder, congestion and mounting taxes to a direction of order, beauty, financial stability and sincere concern for the growth of people. (CRD 1964c, n.p.)

In this kind of evaluation, one has to confront a number of issues. The first is characterizing sprawl, not a simple thing, as the quotes above demonstrate. I had originally intended to avoid the term altogether because it is so poorly defined in both public debates and the academic literature and because the term is so often used in a negative manner. However, the term is so pervasive and so much a part of the contexts of these developments that its avoidance was not possible. Instead, as I have explained earlier, I took a very inclusive view of sprawl, seeing it broadly as incremental and uncoordinated suburban development. This includes generic developer subdivisions as well as small, highly planned developments if they are not part of a larger, coordinated development plan.

I have evaluated sprawl, not according to a single dimension, but in terms of over thirty features and effects that form the basic range of characteristics, problems, and benefits attributed to incremental suburban growth. To do this I examined the issues raised in both academic work in urban studies and the popular literature dealing with the problems of suburban growth and the options for sustainability or livability. My examination included checklists of good design and planning and some of the work on sustainability indicators (see appendix A).[1] From these debates I distilled features and effects attributed to suburban growth or sprawl. They are listed in appendix D, organized in relation to three general themes: urban design, environment, and coordination. Features are characteristics of sprawl, and effects are problems or benefits caused by the features. The division into features and effects gets around some conceptual confusion within these critiques between characteristics of sprawl and problems caused by sprawl (Galster et al. 2000). The "dimensions" column of appendix D shows that many features and effects are measurements of, or create problems and benefits in, several dimensions, such as aesthetics, design, social equity, efficiency, and environment, which illustrates the complexity of measuring urban sprawl. One feature or effect can have both positive and negative aspects.

A further difficulty with such evaluations is that both the criticisms of sprawl and the developments' planning responses changed over time. However, one of the reasons for choosing these three developments is that they were planned and built more continuously than most other developments from the 1960s and 1970s. They were created in a period when criticisms of sprawl were not so different from those of today, and they generally used planning, design, and development approaches that are either still on the cutting edge or else have become fairly standard in the field. While the maturing of the developments has been very important in terms of such issues as the ultimate jobs-housing balance and the extent of open space, the trajectories have been relatively constant, making evaluation more reliable.

I also compare key aspects of the developments with some projects considered to be exemplary in the smart growth and new urbanist movement (see table 9). The first is Duany Plater-Zyberk's Kentlands development (Southworth 1997; Lee and Ahn 2003). This is the most complete nonresort new urbanist development to date and will buildout at about five thousand people on 356 acres. The second is the Stapleton Airport reuse proposal, featured in Calthorpe and Fulton's *The Regional City* (2001). At 4,700 acres and around thirty thousand people, it is one of the largest and densest of the new urbanist project proposals to date and has the added benefit of being an infill rather than a greenfield site, with significant employment. For comparison, Celebration, Florida, had a population of about thirty-five hundred in 2001 and will buildout at twelve thousand to fifteen thousand people in an area of 4,900 acres and a 4,700-acre greenbelt (Celebration Corporation 2001). This is very low density. Other well-known smart growth standards, such as Maryland's priority funding area criteria, are also used in this evaluation (Maryland Office of Planning 1997).

However, some proponents of new urbanism argue that basing judgments of the movement on its partly implemented products rather than on its stated aims "result[s] in a preoccupation with new urbanist projects as end states, elevating mishaps at the expense of undermining the legitimacy of its stated principles" (Talen 2000, 321). While new urbanist built subdivisions or projects are very visible parts of the movement, the movement has also done significant work on long-term regional planning and on changing local development regulations. These last—regional plans and local regulations—potentially have an enormous impact but will take years to implement. However, at a project level, new urbanists themselves criticize other developments, such as modernist public housing developments, on the basis of their practice rather than their stated aims. Further, the developments that I selected for comparison are those that the new urbanists praise or promote, and I avoided projects that have received more mixed reviews within the movement. For example, developments such as Seaside (an expensive resort) and Celebration (very low density) are too easy to criticize from the criteria that I developed.

The new urbanist developments are smaller than the new communities

TABLE 9   Basic Data on Case Study Developments Compared with Two New Urbanist Projects

General Features	Irvine, CA (census City of Irvine only)	Columbia, MD (census CDP)[a]	The Woodlands, TX (census CDP)[b]	Kentlands, MD[c]	Stapleton Airport Reuse, CO
Developer	The Irvine Company (TIC)—majority-owned by James Irvine Foundation until 1977; consortium included Donald Bren until 1983; owned since 1983 by Bren	James Rouse Company affiliates, with early backing from Connecticut General Insurance (CIGNA)	George Mitchell of Mitchell Energy and Development; sold in late 1990s to Crescent Operating, Inc., and Morgan Stanley	Joseph Alfandre	Stapleton Development Corporation and Forest City
Metro area/state	Orange County, CA	Baltimore, MD (and Washington, D.C.)	Houston, TX	Washington, D.C.	Denver, CO
Proposed population in early plans	Over 400,000 (1970 TIC and 1973 City of Irvine plans)	110,000	150,000 (1972 HUD Project Agreement)	5,000	28,800–38,400 (calculated from 12,000 units)
Population (2000 census)	143,072 in city; more nearby; totaling 200,000	88,254 (2000 census); 88,370 (Rouse Company 1999)	55,649	5,000 (estimate)	None
Households	51,119 (2000 census)	34,199	19,881 (2000 census)	1,600 units (estimate)	None
Approximate total size (acres)	Originally 93,000; 29,376 in City of Irvine; 29,758 in census	14,272 (Rouse Company, n.d.); 17,705 in 2000 CDP	Originally 17,000; by 2000, 27,000; 15,284 in 2000 CDP	356	4,700

(continued)

TABLE 9 (continued)

	Irvine, CA (census City of Irvine only)	Columbia, MD (census CDP)[a]	The Woodlands, TX (census CDP)[b]	Kentlands, MD[c]	Stapleton Airport Reuse, CO
General Features					
Starting date	1959: UCI campus study 1964: southern sector plan 1970: overall plan	1962: first land bought 1965: plan approved 1967: first projects completed	1964: first land bought 1971: HUD approves Pereira-McHarg plan 1974: first buildings occupied	1989, with planned buildout in 1997	Mid-2000s
Density					
Units	53,711 (2000 census)	35,281 (2000 census); 32,629 (Rouse Co. 1999)	21,014 (2000 census)	1,600 (estimate)	12,000 (proposal only)
City-level population density (persons/acre, circa 2000)	4.8 for census area	6.2 using Rouse Co. definition; 5.0 for CDP	3.6 for CDP	—	6.13–7.66 calculated from units at buildout[d]
City-level dwelling density (units/ acre)	1.8 for census area	2.3 using Rouse Co. definition, 2.0 for CDP	1.4 for CDP	Too small to include all the functions	2.6 (at buildout)
Village population density (persons/acre)	Appendix E shows 11 villages: 5.2 to 16.0 persons/acre; average 11.5	—	Appendix E shows 5 villages: 3.3 to 6.2; average 4.6	11.5 to 15.3, calculated from 4.8 units/acre	—
Village dwelling density (units/ acre)	Appendix E shows 11 villages: 2.1 to 6.7; average 4.6	—	Appendix E shows 8 villages: 1.3 to 2.7; average 1.8	4.8	—

Detached housing (1990/2000 census)	39%/40%	39%/42%	74%/79%	Not enough constructed at 1990 census	—
Jobs	168,000	66,500	24,700	921	—
Jobs/acre	5.7	4.7	0.9	2.6	—
Environment					
Parks and open space	Over half of ranch, about 50,000 acres	38% public open space (about 5,360 acres)	16% for villages and town center at buildout (see appendix E)	About 28%, 100 acres, public open space	23% open space
Employment					
Edge city	1.5 full and 1 emerging	1	1 emerging	Gaithersburg area	Not applicable
Employment[e]	168,000[f]/TIC claims another 40,000 on ranch	66,500[g]	24,700[h]	400,000 sq. ft. of retail	Up to 10 million sq. ft. of offices

SOURCES: Three new communities: City of Irvine 2000, 2002; Irvine Company 1970c, 2001a, 2002d; Rouse Company 1999, 2002, n.d.; TWOC 2000a, 2001; U.S.A. and TWDC 1972; U.S. Census 1990. Kentlands: Southworth 1997. Stapleton: Calthorpe and Fulton 2001.

[a] The Columbia CDP does not exactly correspond with the Columbia new town zoning area. The CDP includes significant outparcels within the general outline of Columbia and does not include some commercial and industrial areas and the Village of Dorsey's Search.

[b] The Woodlands CDP excludes land in Harris County, not yet developed, and some land in Montgomery County, notably in the new Village of College Park. For density calculations, I use census definitions of area and people, as the excluded areas are general.

[c] Kentlands not constructed for 1990 census. As it is only part of a tract, 2000 census data would have to be compiled from blocks. For this reason, socio-economic data have not been compiled for the two new urbanist developments.

[d] Population densities sometimes calculated from units, assuming household of 2.4 to 3.0 persons per household.

[e] City and developer figures used for employment because of suppression of data from economic census at this level.

[f] From City of Irvine 2002.

[g] From Rouse Company 1999.

[h] From TWOC 2000a.

that I studied, but that is actually a factor in their favor in key dimensions such as density. It is much easier to increase average densities or maintain an innovative housing mix in five-hundred-acre developments than on twenty-thousand-acre ones. However, because of scale differences, where this issue is relevant I take the new community *village*, rather than the whole development, as the most appropriate comparison. I have also compared the projected *final* figures for the new urbanist developments with both incomplete and completed components of the case study developments, in all cases giving the new urbanist developments the benefit of the doubt. Projected final figures are almost always better than those either for not-yet-completed developments (because more development will occur) or for finished developments as built (because compromises are made). New urbanist projects, like the case study new communities, are also competing for sales in the contemporary suburban market. This makes them a more realistic comparison than prewar suburbs, which were developed in a far different economic and technological context.

However, for those developing the new communities, this comparison with the best face of new urbanism seems to give too many concessions in this evaluation to the quite small and relatively uncomplicated new urbanist developments. That the new communities fare well in this comparison shows their significant achievement, given the added complexity of these very large, very long-term projects. Appendix D, appendix B, which summarizes socioeconomic data, and table 9 show the new community developments mitigating many of the costs and keeping most of the benefits of sprawl. In the following section, I examine in more detail how this occurs, linking the material in the appendices and table 9 to the case histories. Because various measures of density are so often used as indicators of sprawl, the chapter starts with a discussion of this issue. While it is only one feature of sprawl, it is probably the most studied feature. The rest of the chapter is divided into sections relating to the dimensions highlighted in appendix D: aesthetics, design, and identity; social equity, diversity, and access; efficiency and costs; environmental issues; and benefits.

DENSITY

Density is the most frequently used measure of sprawl or its absence and is believed to have implications for energy use, accessibility, walkability, and land conservation (e.g., Malpezzi and Guo 2001). The Irvine Ranch and Columbia clearly meet smart growth criteria for density, and while this saves land it has not had much effect on transportation choices.

Density is a measure of a number of elements per unit area. It is hard to measure because of the many different standards for what to include in the base land area calculation, even for residential or housing density. Should it include just the lot, internal roads, local streets, neighborhood level facilities, or the entire land area of the city? While residential density is important, employment density also has implications for urban form, although it is not often used as a measure because obtaining figures on employment in small areas is difficult.[2] Given these limits, I developed six residential and employment density measures, although not all were available for each development. The first four densities involve both population and dwelling units per acre, with the two measures giving slightly different results because of different household sizes. The first five densities can all be considered to be gross density calculations—that is, measuring land area beyond the house lot or development site.

- City-level population density: the total area of the development (or for Irvine, the City of Irvine) divided by the total population. This is a gross density, including open space, roads, easements, commercial areas, institutions, industrial areas, and currently unbuilt areas.
- City-level dwelling density: the total area of the city or development divided by the number of housing units.
- Village population density: the total area of a residential village divided by the population. This is a different kind of gross density calculation, including housing, open space, neighborhood commercial and institutional uses, local roads, easements, and so on, but not such uses as regional open space, specialized industrial areas, and major shopping malls.
- Village dwelling density: the total area of the village divided by the number of housing units.
- City-level jobs density: the total number of jobs divided by the area.
- Proportion of detached single-family housing: This is a measure of perceived density, as attached housing is often perceived as denser than detached houses.

As table 9 indicates, the three new communities have fairly low overall city-level population and dwelling unit densities, ranging from 3.6 to 6.2 persons per acre and from 1.4 to 2.3 units per acre. However, the new urbanist Stapleton Airport reuse proposal, at 2.6 units per acre, is only a little higher than Columbia's 2.3. The City of Irvine's very significant agriculture and open space lower its densities. These uses take up 54 percent of the zoned area of the City of Irvine *and its sphere of influence* (and some areas, for example, the freeways, are not zoned). A more accurate perspective of the character of the Irvine Ranch's built-up areas is provided by the village densities, calculated for eleven largely completed villages with a total population of over 121,000 people (see appendix E). In these villages, densities range from 5.2 to 16.0 persons per acre and average about 11.5. In addition, these figures are lowered by just one older hillside development, Turtle Rock. Its exclusion takes the average to 12.9 persons per acre and well within the range for new urbanist developments. The signature Irvine Company village of the 1970s, Woodbridge, has a gross population density of 14.6 persons per acre, compared with 11.5 to 15.3 persons per acre for the village-level density in the new urbanist Kentlands, and Woodbridge, with a population of 26,000, maintains this density for a far larger population (see appendix E).

Interestingly, none has the 8 to 13 persons per acre across a metropolitan area that Newman and Kenworthy (2000, 100) suggest is needed for viable transit. With comparable city-level densities of 3.6 to 6.2 persons per acre, the new communities are below this threshold. However, so is the much smaller new urbanist Stapleton Airport, unless it achieves household sizes of well over 3.0 persons per unit, which seems unlikely when even in the family-oriented Woodlands the average household size in 2000 was only 2.8.

The City of Irvine and Columbia are also above the density thresholds for designation as priority funding areas (PFAs) under the State of Maryland's smart growth regulations. Under these regulations, the state will place infrastructure only in areas that fulfill certain requirements. Specifically, they have to be planned for 2.0 units per net residential acre (excluding public recreation, habitat, wetlands, and public open space) in areas with existing sewer or water. For greenfield or peripheral sites, this is raised to 3.5 units per net acre excluding those same public uses. The City of Irvine has only 1.8 units per acre across the entire city; however, only 8,205 acres are zoned residential (in the city *and* its sphere of influence). The actual residential density is at least 6.5 units per acre. In addition, presumably more construction will occur on this residentially zoned land, further increasing densities. The signature Woodbridge Village has a gross village-level density of 5.2 dwelling units per acre. Excluding only its 340 acres of public parks and public open space easements but counting all the other uses above, the density is 6.4 units per acre, much higher than the Maryland threshold. Ten of the eleven villages for which the Irvine Company has compiled data meet the Maryland standard. Similarly, Columbia has about 5,360 acres of public open space, which makes its first-cut Maryland smart growth density about 3.7 units per acre, even including industrial and commercial areas, major roads, and institutional uses. In residential density terms, among others, two of these new communities are exemplars of current practices of smart growth. They also have a significant number of jobs per acre (see table 9).

The Woodlands is the only development of the three to have densities, on the face of it, too low for the Maryland standard. It has much more single-family detached housing than the other two areas. In 1990, 74 percent of its housing was detached compared with only 39 percent in the other two developments (Columbia CDP and the City of Irvine). By 2000 the figures were 79 percent in The Woodlands, 42 percent in Columbia, and 40 percent in Irvine. Interestingly, the original 1972 project agreement proposal was for 74 percent *attached* housing in The Woodlands, and early projections of over 47,000 units led to a gross citywide density of 2.8 units per acre (U.S.A. and TWDC 1972, 95; Underhill 1976, I-29). In contrast, in early plans Columbia proposed 53 percent attached houses but by 1990 had increased its attached housing to 61 percent (HRD 1965a, 24). The Irvine Company mapped only general densities, and it calculated demand by income levels for housing in its 1970 central sector plan and associated documents. However, in its 1964 southern sector plan, only part of which is in the City of Irvine, 81 percent of units were to be at densities of 6.5 or fewer dwellings per acre, generally associated with detached housing. The other 19 percent were to be at fairly high densities possible only with attached housing (Irvine Company 1970a, 1970c; William L. Pereira and Associates 1964b, 6). Again, it has increased its attached housing substantially over the years.

It is interesting that if the developments had been compared at the time of their planning, The Woodlands would have seemed the most compact in terms of housing type, but this is not at all how the developments have turned out. It shows the effects of responding to market demands as well as the flexibility of the urban structures put in place that were capable of dealing with a number of densities, sometimes increasing and sometimes decreasing and sometimes a mix of the two. This is evident on the Irvine Ranch, where some of the low-density housing of the 1964 plan became habitat protection areas, and other parts became the sites of more intense development.

In The Woodlands, gross densities are also reduced by a layout that emphasizes natural drainage, with open areas woven into the fabric of the development. This exemplifies the tension in planning for environmental protection, in that designs that emphasize on-site water treatment are often very low-density, leading to high energy use in transportation. It is also less fully built out than the other developments. However, a third reason that its density is found too low for the Maryland regulations has to do with the way densities are calculated. While the original project agreement was for 23 percent open space, this included such private spaces as golf courses. If built today in Maryland, the general design could be similar, but the designation of public and private and public space could likely be manipulated to fit the density criteria.

AESTHETICS, DESIGN, AND IDENTITY

The case study developments made aesthetic and urban design innovations that were important in their period. While apparently liked by residents, these aesthetic innovations are not easily measured and are not of the kind valued in high-style design debates. The three developments have all been criticized on aesthetic grounds as being full of houses that are similar (Irvine) or architecturally undistinguished (Columbia, The Woodlands). Garage doors are prominent in the dwellings built before the 1990s. They have used the loop and cul-de-sac road layouts that limit options for vehicular movement. All developments are large, and arterials are lined with long planted buffers that are perhaps less interesting to walk along than quaint main streets.

However, they have taken care with landscaping, creating identities for subdistricts, placing utilities underground, strictly regulating signage, building landscaped paths for pedestrians and cyclists, and banning strip shopping areas. Columbia and especially The Woodlands have invested in public art. All three have paid great attention to the details of design, mixing uses in a way that fosters a sense of place that goes beyond the merely residential. They have created clearly defined edges of villages, just as new urbanists propose should be done (although I do wonder if clearly defined edges are really so much better than developments where the fabric is more continuous).

All the developments use an elaborate set of architectural and land use covenants to make the environment more predictable and certain. These covenants restrict the potential for altering or retrofitting these suburban landscapes and, as was discussed in chapter 5, the ideas that they encoded were generally not of a character valued in high-style design debates. However, covenants are enforced with different levels of vigilance, even within one development, and can be changed over time. For example, while the basic legal restrictions have remained in place, design guidelines in both Columbia and The Woodlands have been changed over the years to allow more variations without needing approval, for example, more types of home businesses. As was outlined in chapter 3, Columbia has been the least aggressive in enforcing covenants but is starting a rolling program of inspections because of maintenance problems with some units, particularly those owned by absentee landlords. Not all the covenants are self-perpetuating, meaning that for parts of the developments they will expire at some point. Others can be altered through voting. Certainly some of the controls may be too rigid, but they did help sell certain design innovations, such as attached housing and mixed-income villages to an unsure market, and current residents also have opportunities to review and change them.

As was discussed in chapter 5, the developments were designed using a structure of villages—or, in the terms of the Charter of the New Urbanism, "neighborhoods and districts"—as a way of breaking the large developments into smaller identifiable units. Each development drew on slightly different sources, and each has slightly different arrangements of housing, schools, parks, institutions, and commercial space.

Have these strategies of mixed-use villages with well-thought-out circulation patterns, aesthetic controls, and designed open space made these new communities better places? The North Carolina study in the early 1970s found that people appreciated neighborhood pools, culs-de-sac, underground utilities, and good maintenance, and residents of attached units also appreciated neighborhood services such as stores and gas stations (Burby and Weiss 1976, 203–4). However, the study found little difference in satisfaction between residents of planned and residents of conventional communities, because the major contributors to satisfaction were housing tenure and the characteristics of the dwelling units, factors that were rather similar between planned and less-planned developments (Burby and Weiss 1976, 209). The high-design quality, "meticulous landscaping," and recreational amenities in Irvine's apartment complexes, generally developed and managed by the Irvine Company, did result in a statistically significant difference in satisfaction in that community (Burby and Weiss 1976, 213–14). The Irvine Ranch and Columbia also rated highly in terms of quality-of-life questions in that same survey, with 21 percent of Irvine Ranch residents and 15 percent of those in Columbia mentioning the community plan as one reason for the high ratings (Burby and Weiss 1976, 368).[3]

Several recent surveys of the three new communities update these findings. A telephone survey of Columbia residents was conducted for the Columbia Association in 1998, using a random sample of one thousand residents, stratified so that each village was equally represented. It found that residents stated they had moved to Columbia because of its location relative to employment (29 percent), housing opportunities (17 percent), family reasons (15 percent), and quality of life (11 percent). For Columbia residents, 79 percent were "happy with their decision to continue to live in Columbia." This is similar to the figure obtained in the University of North Carolina study of the early 1970s, which found that 82 percent of interviewees rated Columbia as an excellent or good place to live. Given differences in wording, however, it seems lower than the 1978 Columbia Association survey of two hundred randomly selected residents, which found 95 percent "very" or "somewhat" satisfied with living in Columbia (Burby and Weiss 1976, 365; Columbia Association 1978b, 14; Columbia Association 1978a). In the 1998 survey, respondents' top reasons for staying in Columbia included "nice place to live/good community" (28 percent), employment (16 percent), family (15 percent), schools (9 percent), location (6 percent), housing opportunities (4 percent), and racial diversity (4 percent) (Chesapeake Group Inc. 1998; see also L. Parker 1997; Rouse Company, Research and Site Strategy 1982, 1984, 1991).

The 2000 City of Irvine satisfaction survey relied on a sample of four hundred residents (Fairbank et al. 2000). With a margin of error of plus or minus 4.9 percent, this telephone survey found that 95 percent of Irvine's residents ranked the quality of life as excellent (64 percent) or good (31 percent). This was basically the same figure obtained in the 1970s, at which time 95 percent of ranch residents rated the community as an excellent or good place to live (Burby and Weiss 1976, 365). The main reasons for moving to the City of Irvine were schools (30 percent) and safe neighborhoods (25 percent). The top priorities for government spending were park maintenance (75 percent) and "preserving a well planned community with a proper mix of homes, businesses, and open space" (74 percent).

The Woodlands Community Service Corporation surveyed residents of houses, not apartments, in February 1999 (575 respondents) and October 2000 (634 respondents). In these phone interviews in both years, residents named four aspects they liked most about The Woodlands: its trees and natural setting (41 percent in 1999, 46 percent in 2000), self-containment with everything nearby (18 percent, 22 percent), friendliness and good neighbors (17 percent, 16 percent), and hike and bike trails (16 percent, 15 percent). Suggestions for changes to improve the development reflect the increased pace of construction under the new owners, with two issues topping both years: slower growth (11 percent, 15 percent) and improving and reducing traffic (10 percent, 24 percent) (Creative Consumer Research 1999, 2000).

Overall, it seems that these urban design strategies have made the planned environments pleasant ones with high quality of life, whether or not they represent a significant alternative to sprawl. Inasmuch as the current generation of planning proposals shares the characteristics of these case study communities, it seems that newer developments will be pleasant and functional for the residents who choose to live in them.

SOCIAL EQUITY, DIVERSITY, AND ACCESS

All three new communities are focused on the middle class, although with ethnic mix. Through what seem to be unusual efforts, they have also managed to have small but significant proportions of government-backed or -sponsored affordable housing. However, in new communities, affordable market-rate units are difficult to create until the housing stock ages.

Obviously, the three developments have managed to mix housing types in a sophisticated and cutting-edge way for their regions, and Columbia and the Irvine Ranch have very significant proportions of attached housing. The proportions of such housing increased over the years until the 1990s, when they stabilized at around three-fifths of the housing stock in those two developments (see appendices B and E). The Irvine Ranch mixed housing types to preserve open space, attract businesses by improving affordability of housing for workers, and increase housing sales in general. Housing professionals from Columbia inspected Irvine's innovations in attached housing and took them back to Columbia in the 1960s and early 1970s (Interview 0210).

The Irvine Company also pioneered market segmentation in the 1970s in villages such as Woodbridge, with housing for different household types.

The other two developments had loftier social goals but were more concerned with providing housing for nuclear families. However, as was explained in chapter 5, by the 1990s Columbia and the City of Irvine both had high proportions of working women and of single-person households. In contrast, The Woodlands initially aimed for a very high proportion of attached and rental housing but is now dominated by detached houses and nuclear families, although this is in line with the outer areas of Houston (see table 12 in appendix B).

Columbia aimed at mixing economic and racial groups, though it was always more successful at the latter than the former and was known in its region as a place where interracial couples could find housing. It did include a number of federally subsidized developments in its early period, but as federal funding dried up in the early 1970s a high level of production of subsidized housing was not sustained. The Woodlands was required to have income mix because of its federal funding. By the late 1970s when activists sued the City of Irvine and the Irvine Company to create more affordable housing, they too came up against this reduction in federal funding for construction (Settlement Agreement 1977; Banzhaf 1980).

By the late 1990s all the developments had around 5 to 6 percent of their stock as subsidized housing or housing in local programs for affordable units, lower than the initial aims for Columbia and The Woodlands. It is particularly striking that after all the early verbal commitments to housing mix, Columbia does not do much better than the other locations. Even in the early days, however, much of the low-income or affordable housing was created through programs for moderate-rate housing, not public housing. Would more have been created if the federal government had kept funding construction of low- and moderate-income housing? Certainly, but that would also have been the case in the other developments.

However, the developments are often not given credit even for this level of "affordable" units, because the high quality of design renders low-cost units invisible, particularly in the City of Irvine and The Woodlands (see table 9 and appendix D). The City of Irvine's units are also the result of innovative local programs, such as linkage schemes in which developers of a large number of units have to provide a certain percentage that are affordable. This makes these units harder to track than federally supported projects and also more awkward to access, as there are separate waiting lists for each development (Schiesl 1991).

In the absence of unified developers either to promote such housing or to be sued to provide it, greenfield smart growth strategies such as mixing housing types are unlikely to do much better in solving the affordability issue. After trying relatively hard, having a relatively large number of attached units, and being able to give some concessions on price because of their size, these developments still don't do particularly well on affordability, especially with their new housing stock. In 2000 in the City of Irvine, 45 percent of renters and 31 percent of owners paid more than 30 percent of their income for housing. While this was roughly the same as the situation in Orange County and, as I explain below, may be related to the student population, it was also not significantly better than its region. The comparable figures for Columbia were 33 percent of renters and 19 percent of owners, and for The Woodlands 38 percent of renters and 18 percent of owners, again in line with the county (except for renters in The Woodlands). In the 2000 City of Irvine Citizen Satisfaction Survey, 56 percent of the population saw a lack of affordable housing as a serious problem in terms of overall concern, ahead of traffic congestion (42 percent) and behind only the ultimately defeated plan to build an international airport on the El Toro Marine Corps base (66 percent). This indicates some of the limits of the private-sector provision of truly affordable housing, particularly in desirable places.

Partly as a result of the lack of inexpensive housing, few poor people live in these developments; they ranged from 3 to 6 percent in 1990. Interestingly, in 1990 Columbia's poverty rate was half that of the other two in spite of its goals of economic integration and the much more substantial debate in Columbia about the perceived problems of low-income populations. By 2000, the City of Irvine still had the highest poverty rate, at 9 percent, compared with Columbia at 5 percent and The Woodlands at 4 percent.

In cultural and racial terms, by 2000 the City of Irvine had a significant resident population of the census category of Asian, and Columbia had a significant population of blacks or African Americans (the figures included people of all citizenships), and they contained 57 and 64 percent non-Hispanic whites, respectively. The variety of housing types provides an underlying structure for this mix, as did all three developments' marketing strategies that stressed forms of diversity. Columbia, of course, deliberately targeted African Americans, and the City of Irvine seems to have just been part of wider changes in California. As mentioned in chapter 3, work by Kato has found that the three developments are much less racially segregated than their metropolitan areas, and this is particularly significant in Columbia, where general racial/ethnic diversity is also high (Kato 2002).

However, in 2000, per capita and household income for whites was significantly higher than for other ethnic groups in all three developments, and poverty rates were lower for whites, as is shown in appendix B, although certainly affluent members of these other ethnic groups live in the new towns, indicating income diversity. Further, a close reading shows some anomalies among the developments. While 16 percent of the census-defined "Asian alone" population was below the poverty rate in Irvine, 85 percent of the poor were eighteen or over, indicating very few families with children are poor, and the median household income for the group was over sixty-seven thousand dollars, indicating a significant affluent segment. In contrast, 11 percent of the single-race black or African American population in Irvine was poor, but only 63 percent of these were over eighteen, and the median household income for the group was under fifty-three thousand dollars. This unusual pattern may indicate that some of the circumstances of poverty among Asians—Asian Americans and Asian noncitizens—involved low student incomes or a very poor immigrant population. Half of UC Irvine's student body is in this ethnic group, and in 2000, college students made up about one-fifth of Irvine's population. Although college students are a real and important part of the population, which is my reason for not distinguishing their role in the City of Irvine more generally, their low incomes are generally not a permanent situation.

In 2000, Irvine's population included 17 percent noncitizens; and the county, 19 percent. No other case study new town or county had more than 7 percent noncitizens, which was perhaps part of the reason for the Pledge of Allegiance at the start of public meetings in Orange County. Interestingly, 31 percent of those in poverty in the City of Irvine were noncitizens compared with 17 percent in Columbia and 9 percent in The Woodlands. Whether these are students, new immigrants, or others is an important question for issues of social equity (see appendix B).

As was explained in chapters 3 and 4, Columbia and The Woodlands have also experimented with religious institutions. Both of these new towns took a different approach, but in both cases the experiment used the term *interfaith*. All three developments have provided spaces for performances and other cultural events—from Halloween parties in an Irvine Ranch shopping center and gay pride at UC Irvine to symphony and rock concerts in the pavilions in Columbia and The Woodlands. These cultural events and institutions have all involved a great deal of effort and have made sense only because of the large size of the developments. Even the best-designed subdivisions on their own will not inevitably lead to such efforts and innovations.

Government is fairly open. The Irvine Ranch became part of several municipalities—the largest portion is in the City of Irvine, but significant parts are in Newport Beach and several other locations—giving formal political representation to residents (at least those who are U.S. citizens). Columbia and The Woodlands are not incorporated but at the town scale have resident, not homeowner, community associations. Community associations seem to have been a path to political office for many women and, in Columbia, African Americans (Bloom 2001b). Resident associations also allow representation for noncitizens. While critics have certainly pointed to the strong influence of the development companies on local politics, particularly in Irvine, undoubtedly forums exist for participation of residents in government.

However, as has also been explained, even these developments, which have been conceived of as integrated wholes, are starting to have some gated or fenced sections—proposals that were resisted in the earlier decades by the earlier new community planners and developers because gating undermines comprehensiveness, complicates circulation patterns, and has implications for social life. Irvine Company planners indicated that they are trying to keep pedestrian paths open through these areas, as they had done with walled edges of ungated villages before, and this attempt was confirmed in my interviews with both residents and city staff members.[4] In this sense the gated areas operate quite differently for those in cars and on foot. In Columbia the area called gated by some residents is small, with a low unlocked iron fence around condominiums in the town center. In The Woodlands, under the new owners, the gated area is quite large and surrounds a golf course but is fairly far from the town center, meaning that the main circulation patterns are less affected than might have been the case had it been in a more central location.

The development companies' marketing departments, however, have made significant inroads regarding gated communities. This is particularly obvious along the coastal areas of the Irvine Ranch, where very high-priced housing is made even more exclusive with walls. While, this is not exactly new, as such developments have occurred in the coastal areas of the Irvine Ranch since at least the 1970s, these trends obviously represent challenges (Hunsinger 1976, 63–64). However, the cul-de-sac layouts of the road networks *within* the villages of all three developments have always been difficult for outsiders to navigate, even without walls—a lack of openness to strangers often noted as an advantage by residents.[5]

Overall, these suburban areas have a certain amount of income and ethnic diversity and are certainly not totally homogeneous enclaves. They provide for a variety of cultural activities. However, they are also facing challenges, given market trends toward exclusivity.

EFFICIENCY AND COST

While on open land beyond the metropolitan edge, these were not isolated developments but were deliberately integrated with existing and planned infrastructure, supporting both jobs and housing. However, potential economic benefits from location and coordination were obviously counterbalanced by additional costs due to such characteristics as added amenity levels.

As was explained in chapter 1, all three communities were in or beside the three metropolitan areas in the nation that grew fastest in sheer numbers in the 1960s. All three communities took advantage of the existing and planned public infrastructure in these fast-growing areas: freeways, train lines, and airports in or near their developments. The Woodlands was located north of the new Houston Intercontinental Airport; the John Wayne Airport is on land originally part of the Irvine Ranch; and Columbia is west of the Baltimore/

Washington International Airport. However, each one has taken at least four decades to reach buildout. The Irvine Ranch will take twice that long, increasing development costs.

Issues of costs were a key topic in the developments. The 1970s brought a number of well argued criticisms of the inefficiency of urban sprawl, most notably the Real Estate Research Corporation's *Costs of Sprawl* report (1974), sponsored by HUD, the EPA, and the Council on Environmental Quality. This controversial study found significant infrastructure savings in higher-density development. Although it was attacked on methodological grounds, other studies came up with similar findings of small but still measurable savings from more compact and planned development (Frank 1989; Hughes et al. 1991; Windsor 1979). Most other studies in the United States have found small savings from compact development and coordinated infrastructure provision—on the order of up to 10 percent.[6] However, in new community developments, the advantages of coordination are counterbalanced by the added costs of preservicing and the large holding costs of having to purchase extensive tracts of land that must be paid for decades before being developed.[7]

These developments were devised before this debate reached its peak but reflected some awareness of concerns about the inefficiency of sprawl. In fact the Howard County Planning Commission projected significant savings in Columbia, up to $2,453 per dwelling unit for infrastructure, services, and land costs (Underhill 1976, I-15). Two other studies confirmed this, including an unpublished 1974 study prepared for HUD by Richard Anderson, former general manager of Columbia, using actual Columbia data, and another by George Anderson of the New Communities Administration, using data from Title VII new communities, including The Woodlands. Both found per capita costs for land development and infrastructure to be even lower in these developments than the *Costs of Sprawl* study had projected for "planned mix developments," the second most efficient pattern after "high density planned" (cited in Underhill 1976, I-24–I-30, I-34; Real Estate Research Corporation 1974). While these studies suffered some limitations relating to incomplete data, they showed how in the early 1970s it seemed that the actual experience of new community development confirmed costs savings with planning and coordination (Short 1973).

Given the lengthy development time frames, as explained earlier, the developments all faced tremendous problems with start-up funding for infrastructure, exacerbated by downturns in real estate and the need to have at least some of the basic structure of the community in place at the start. All of the developments produced initial projections of sales that were too high, which must certainly have affected their cash flows, because they were paying interest on loans for the early infrastructure but receiving payment for it from sales at a much lower rate than their early projections. The Irvine

Company solved the funding problem by using agricultural production as an income stream and focusing on high-end housing first (which was overdetermined by the location of the UC Irvine campus close to Newport Beach). Columbia used backing from Connecticut General Life Insurance Company for the majority of its initial funding and was virtually owned by that company at one stage. The Woodlands used federal loan guarantees, revenues from George Mitchell's gas and oil ventures, lines of credit from banks, and some logging income from the forests it was holding for development. As it was coming on line during the property crash of the early 1970s, The Woodlands had particularly severe problems with cash flow. This is perhaps the biggest problem for market approaches to greenfield smart growth: the sale of some of the design innovations depends on having infrastructure in place at the very start of sales, but this requires large amounts of capital. While the compact designs and coordinated development phasing may have saved some money in terms of infrastructure, these savings many not have made up for the costs of accelerating the provision of major items and of increasing quality, let alone the cost of holding very large parcels of land.

ENVIRONMENTAL ISSUES

All three developments were ahead of their time in terms of open space provision. In Columbia and The Woodlands in particular, accessible open space, distributed throughout the developments, tends to spread out development. This provides space for pleasant paths but lowers densities. In such low-density environments people drive a lot for utilitarian reasons. However, open space is undeniably salable and has helped these developments survive in the market place. It has also had benefits for habitat and water quality.

All the physical plans emphasize open space and landscape character—working with the existing agricultural, rural, or timber industry landscapes of the developments. All mix local parks with regional recreation and environmental protection areas. The Irvine Ranch, in particular, has very lush and distinctively formal plantings, even in its parking lots and roadsides, and balances these with very separate habitat areas; The Woodlands really does live up to its name; and Columbia has protected the surroundings of its many rivers and streams.

Habitat protection has become more important in each development over time, just as it has become more important for society as a whole. Although not in the initial plan, the Irvine Ranch has done better at habitat protection than the other developments. In late 2001 Donald Bren announced that he would donate additional land for a permanent preserve of forty-four thousand acres of habitat, or nearly half of the ranch. An additional six thousand acres of the ranch will end up as other forms of open space. While the Irvine Company has had many conflicts over wetlands and other habitat issues, it has certainly adapted to environmentalism, from its early installation of double piping for water recycling to its later habitat protection (Jasny 1997; Irvine Company 2000a, 2000b). At a smaller scale, appendix E shows that open space makes up about 29 percent of the land in the eleven villages for which such data are available, and most of this is public open space. This is largely in addition to habitat protection areas, few of which lie within villages.

The Woodlands has emphasized water systems, natural drainage, and protection of the aquifer, and its early planning involved very extensive ecological studies (e.g., WMRT 1971, 1974b). Since the early 1970s George Mitchell has funded conferences, awards, and research on sustainable development and, for a while, a center for sustainable development. Following a planning process in 2000, over the next three years the Houston Advanced Research Center as a whole was reorganized to concentrate on sustainability across all its programs. Columbia, though without such an explicit environmental program, seems to have taken up some of the ideas that were obviously coming into currency.[8] In particular, it protected its rivers and streams, and the overall new town is 38 percent open space.

The developments have not been as successful in promoting alternatives to the private car, even though all of them examined the issue. Columbia had an early minibus system, which it had initially promised would run at five-minute intervals. However, the minibus never gained sufficient ridership (Minibus to separate road system 1966, 3; Sunderland 1970). All three of the developments had, at some stage, proposals for monorails, but these were never implemented. By the 1990s Columbia had municipal buses; the Irvine Ranch, buses and an Amtrak line; and The Woodlands, a well-used commuter shuttle to Houston. Columbia had a very high carpool rate in 1980, at 25 percent. However, 1990 census data in appendices B and D indicate that by 1990 the three developments had from 78 to 82 percent of people driving to work alone, 10 percent higher than the state average in California and Maryland and 2 percent higher than that of Texas. By 2000 this had not changed significantly, with all three developments having 80 or 81 percent of commuters driving alone.

Overall, commute patterns have been remarkably persistent, although with some drop in the use of cars. At the time of the new communities studies in the early 1970s, 93 percent of residents of Columbia drove or carpooled to work compared with a figure of 92 percent in 1990, and 90 percent in 2000. The figures for the City of Irvine were 96 percent in the 1970s, 91 percent in 1990, and 87 percent in 2000 (Burby and Weiss 1976, 336). In 1969, when early residents of Columbia's detached and townhouse units were interviewed about transportation issues, 66 percent of households owned two or more cars, and none was car free. These figures were roughly in line with national figures for households at similar income levels, although the proportion of households with two or more cars in Columbia was lower than in less-planned developments, with a difference of up to 20 percent between Columbia and the least-planned developments (Lansing et al. 1970, 138, 140, 141). By 2000, 6 percent of households in Columbia did not have a car, compared with 4 percent in the City of Irvine and The Woodlands (see appendix B). While 17 percent of Columbia households and 18 percent in the City of Irvine and The Woodlands had three or more cars at the time of 2000 census, this figure was lower than those in their counties, which were at 22, 21, and 19 percent, respectively, a considerable difference in the case of Columbia.

The slight improvement in the figures may reflect the increase in the number of jobs in each new community—by the late 1990s ranging from 1.2 per household in The Woodlands to 3.1 per household in the City of Irvine.[9] According to the census, fairly high proportions of workers live and work in all three developments, though this fell in Columbia in the 1990s. In the decade from 1990 to 2000, the percentage of workers living and working in the City of Irvine rose from 37 to 39 percent; for Columbia it dropped from 27 to 26 percent; and for The Woodlands it increased from 5 to 31 percent (see appendix B). In 2000, the average commute time for residents of the City of Irvine was 23 minutes (compared with 27 in its county), 30 minutes in Columbia, and 33 in The Woodlands (both equivalent to their counties). Many of the jobs in these developments are taken by people outside them, who, if without cars, must cope with buses in Columbia and some limited train service in the City of Irvine (Cadiz 2002).

The analysis of nonwork trips, a major area of transportation, is hampered by a lack of place-level data. However, Burby and Weiss (1976, 340–42) described how, in the early 1970s, respondents in the Irvine Ranch and Columbia reported slightly *more* vehicle miles traveled per family per year compared with people in their less-planned counterparts. They surmised that the convenient layout of new communities might actually promote more social, recreational, and shopping trips. Of the ten developments in the 1969 study by Lansing et al., Columbia's families drove the third most overall, at 21,700 miles per year (Lansing et al. 1970, 143).

It is interesting that while Columbia and The Woodlands explicitly planned for transit, it is the Irvine Ranch, with its central location, large university, and strong jobs spine, that is most likely to have the most sophisticated system in the next decades. The ranch is part of a large urban county bus system. Light rail options are under investigation by the county. The City of Irvine is also conducting a pilot program with shared electric vehicles available for rail commuters using the Amtrak line between San Diego and Los Angeles. Vehicles are used in the day by workers in Irvine going from train to job and in the mornings and evenings by residents going from home to the train (ZEV NET 2002).

The developments do allow for pedestrian and nonmotorized modes of transportation. The development teams treated pedestrian and bicycle paths with care, seeing them as often separate from the road network, at first considering the home-to-school route and recreational uses and, later, nonmotorized trips to work and services (although in Columbia the recreational focus is still strong, and paths could be more continuous).[10] By 1990 walkers made up 7 percent of commuters in the jobs-rich City of Irvine, although by 2000 they had dropped to 5 percent.

Frequently these developments are criticized for their walkability after an analysis of their vehicular road networks, which contain a large number of loops and culs-de-sac—a structure that is difficult for walking. Given the separate design of pedestrian and vehicular networks, this at least partly misrepresents the pedestrian experience of these communities in which the path system is more continuous and connected, particularly in the Irvine Company developments and The Woodlands. Of course, road design is not the only thing to influence transportation choices. A study comparing the transportation modes in some areas of the Irvine Ranch with very curvilinear street patterns and more gridded areas in Orange County found that people took more automobile trips and walked less in the curvilinear areas; however, those who conducted the study argued that this difference was explained by income: people who are more affluent drive more (McNally and Kukarni 1997).

For their path systems, Columbia and The Woodlands have very helpful pedestrian maps created by their resident associations, and the City of Irvine has created an excellent bike map. However, in many parts of the Irvine Ranch, parking spaces are difficult for outsiders to find, particularly on main roads, where bike lanes take up the edge of the road. This does limit outsiders' access to parking and walking, although it provides space for cyclists on these busy roads. If one thinks about the more attractive parts of many major cities, parking restrictions in walkable and cycle-friendly areas are fairly common. Obviously having a path network doesn't necessarily lead to walking and biking, but it is still important to recognize the differences among the pedestrian, biking, and motorized vehicular networks.

Overall, these cases seem to show that densities that conform to smart growth and new urbanist practices, pedestrian paths, and even mixed-use layouts are not enough in themselves to significantly shift inhabitants away from car use. As the developments keep expanding their employment areas and more people need to commute to those suburbs, this issue will become even more complex. The large proportions of attached-dwelling units in the City of Irvine and Columbia, rather than density per se, and the early interest in climate-sensitive house siting in The Woodlands may have some benefits in terms of energy use in housing, but this has not been the case in the transportation realm.

MAINTAINING THE BENEFITS OF SPRAWL

Finally, as can be seen in appendix D, incremental and uncoordinated suburban development, or sprawl, does have benefits in terms of affordability to the owner, private open space, and other aspects of choice. These new communities have had to compete with more generic development for sales, meaning they have had to provide similar benefits, particularly in the private realm, although sometimes private space has been traded for public space. Furthermore, within this larger landscape, the new communities have provided the additional choice of planned development, including such things as land use and architectural covenants, which, though perceived as one of the major drawbacks of such developments, in fact supply a market demand for order.

HOW THEY DID BETTER AND HOW THEY DID NOT

These new communities are often seen by those proposing smart growth and the new urbanism as rather dated in their urban designs—with low densities, culs-de-sac, and automobile-based shopping. This is certainly true for some parts of these developments, although it glosses over variations within them, their detailed design, and change over time, with all of them having newer sections with a new urbanist flavor.

All three case study developments involved planners, designers, and developers who thought long and hard about what it was to live in the new extensive metropolitan areas where the developments are located. However, while these developments are special places—they are large, with continuous ownership—they are not unique. It is possible for both business and government to replicate at least some of their characteristics and techniques. The question, however, is which parts should be replicated, and which instead show the limits to current thinking about better urban development?

The new community planning and design techniques that are particularly interesting in this assessment are those that are widely used and promoted in smart growth. The techniques include breaking the developments into "villages," creating jobs-housing balance, building pedestrian and biking paths, creating distinctive identities through landscape design, and mixing housing unit types. Judged against the criteria developed by proponents of smart growth and new urbanism, the developments fare very well on such issues as density, pedestrian paths and access, income and ethnic mix, neighborhood identity and layout, and open space (also Ewing 1991). The new communities have balanced connections to the wider metropolis with self-containment and a sense of place at the local level. They have achieved a range of positive outcomes from fine-grained racial mix to strong visual identity and are still close to the cutting edge. One of the members of the development team and a great supporter of new communities explained:

> Even as terrible as the Columbias and the Irvines and the Restons and The Woodlands, quote, all are—we're not perfect—some of the alternatives are just atrocious. You would have thought the state of the art would have progressed to a point that whoever's doing the next one, in 2001, would have had this all worked out . . . all of the imperfections and impurities would have been washed. . . . It hasn't happened. (Interview 0208)

Residents also expressed appreciation for the comprehensive design. This comment from a person of color in one of the developments is fairly typical:

> I like the open space concept [and yet] the feeling of having people live relatively close to you. You're in the suburbs but not an acre apart. I like the proximity of the neighbors, and I like the open space and the ready availability of recreational facilities and the fact that you can also both live and work here. (Interview 0101)

Overall, they really do what most proponents of smart growth and new urbanism think should be done in urban development and, in this, have distinguished themselves from generic sprawl over a period of decades. Where they have weaknesses, so do the current proposals for a new generation of best practices, because in large part the new practices mirror this older generation of responses to urban sprawl. Here, the case study communities clearly have not been uniformly successful across all dimensions of development. They have done better at such tasks as developing systems for incorporating natural processes into suburban development and creating a new suburban aesthetic than they have at providing housing for very-low-income population and real alternatives to the car. They show how providing transportation options does not necessarily lead to people using those options as an alternative to the automobile. They demonstrate that urban designs emphasizing open space, recreation, habitat, and water quality are not always consistent with those emphasizing energy conservation.

Overall, it seems that many of the techniques shared by new communities and smart growth proponents are not enough on their own to reorganize their metropolitan landscapes to be smarter, fairer, or more sustainable. This is true even though they were implemented in almost ideal circumstances by very sympathetic developers with innovative professional teams, long time horizons, deep pockets, and large areas at their disposal. That these developers created environments that generally do well when compared with current ideas about good urban development shows what it is possible to do in the United States. That these communities have blemishes despite their almost ideal situation is extremely challenging for urban planners and urban designers.

In particular, the case study communities cause one to wonder about the basic idea behind smart growth and new urbanism. This idea is a hopeful one: that people in the United States can continue to use resources freely, and with some small changes this can turn out all right. However, many of those who support smart growth criticize new towns such as the case study developments, although the findings of this study indicate that in smart growth and even new urbanist terms there is very little to criticize about these developments. People there certainly drive a lot, their covenants slow change, and they could be more economically integrated, but it is not at all obvious that many high-profile smart growth and new urbanist proposals will do better, particularly those in suburban areas. The new communities certainly fulfill the general aims for development outlined in the preamble to the Charter of the New Urbanism:

> Neighborhoods should be diverse in use and population; communities should be designed for the pedestrian and transit as well as the car; cities and towns should be shaped by physically defined and universally accessible public spaces and community institutions; urban places should be framed by architecture and landscape design that celebrate local history, climate, ecology, and building practice. (Leccese and McCormick 2000, vi)

This means that the high hopes in many current smart growth proposals that small design modifications can lead to large benefits are almost certainly misplaced, and more dramatic changes are needed (Beatley 2000).

In addition, although they have made money, the new communities have not always been models for nearby development, showing the limits to a voluntary transfer of ideas from exemplary developments. Other places in Orange County may have copied Irvine's formal look but not the mixture of uses. Columbia is seen as the inner city of Howard County, with a racial mix that the rest of the county does not share. The shaggy look of The Woodlands has not been replicated; other master-planned new communities in Houston are more manicured.

However, the weaknesses and limits of these developments do not mean that sprawl is better. Rather, they show that in the United States it is difficult to beat a market that is dominated by products that externalize the costs of growth. By this I mean that consumers looking for housing, particularly suburban housing, will frequently be attracted to lower-cost products. Such products lack services, skimp on public amenities and spaces, are at densities too low to ever support alternatives to the car and thus build in long-term congestion problems and private transportation costs, and use (temporarily) undeveloped land to substitute for permanent open space. The new communities were certainly responses by private-sector developers who saw problems with typical sprawl patterns of development and imagined some marketing advantages in providing more comprehensively planned alternatives. However, competition with less planned areas put real constraints on the level of services, the density, and the design features that even the best-intentioned developers could provide before becoming uncompetitive in the market-place. In responding to a complicated cluster of phenomena such as urban sprawl, it is difficult to solve every problem and particularly difficult to solve them and remain profitable.

Even limited successes are important, however. In terms of recent moves toward smart growth, it so often seems that the United States needs to learn from Europe, Canada, Australasia, or some of its own unique locations, such as Oregon. Critics of alternatives to growth point to the move in many parts of Europe and Asia toward lower-density "American" models of urbaniza-tion, arguing that it is a global trend. These three case study developments provide important lessons from within the U.S. planning tradition involving deep suburban areas, which are not normally associated with the cutting edge of planning practice. The case study developments certainly didn't change the whole culture, but they shifted preferences a little. Some people bought into the whole new community package, some came for the good schools and convenience, but the developments wooed a market, and they did this at a very large scale within their regions. They show that it is possible to make changes in the market, but they also show two major problems. First, the changes might not be enough to achieve real progress in areas such as hous-ing affordability and energy use reduction; and second, influencing others to adopt even the level of change that has occurred is difficult to do.

Chapter 7

New Town Planning
and the Paradoxes
of Private Innovation

Why do the stories of these new communities matter today? This book started out with a number of questions about Irvine, Columbia, and The Woodlands. How well did these planned communities avoid the problems of sprawl? What can they tell us about current attempts to create more sustainable or livable places? Are the techniques that they used still viable alternatives to sprawl, or are they now part of the problem? Can private-sector planning achieve important public purposes?

These new communities did manage to compete in the market against incremental, unplanned suburban growth, which externalizes the costs of sprawl. They also conform to contemporary ideas about better development that is an alternative to sprawl and have done this at an extraordinary scale and scope, representing some of the largest continuously planned developments in the United States. Creating architecturally reviewed villages, in mixed-use towns, with orderly movement systems and designed open space, these private-sector developments have provided a planned and coherent alternative to both the high-style individually designed house and the incremental subdivision. By showing that it is possible to sell such products at a large scale, they give hope to those proposing current innovations in a similar vein. However, for those who think even more dramatic changes are needed in urban patterns, they also serve as useful warnings of the difficulty in making such changes.

Earlier chapters have explored how the developments organized the social and physical landscape and provided an alternative to sprawl. This chapter examines their specific lessons for current attempts to create more comprehensive and well-planned urban development, focusing on the roles of the public and private sectors.

It presents this examination in three parts. First, it explores how these private entities interacted with government. Government is often seen as having a strong role in urban development, both at a local level and through state and federal policies in individual sectors such as housing and transportation. The logic of these new towns demanded comprehensiveness and coordination among levels of government and among policy areas focused on the specific locations of the new towns. The developers were thrust into a coordinating role, obtaining legitimacy for this role through property ownership rather than democratic elections. The problems that these powerful development corporations had in managing this coordination provide important lessons about its general difficulty. This has implications for the capacity of any group to do the kind of urban development that deals with multiple dimensions over a long time frame. Even governments will likely have difficulties, given their fragmentation and periodic turnover due to elections.

In the second part of the conclusion, I turn to the key question of the possibility of innovation in suburban development. A key concept is the "paradox of private innovation," or the tension between the largest window of opportunity for innovation that occurs early in such developments and the timing of profits decades later. This creates strains within development companies, often putting planners and designers at odds with the real estate and marketing arms.

Finally, I examine the issue of comprehensive development and the public interest. Compared with generic, incremental growth, comprehensive development is difficult to achieve in the United States. This raises a key issue of whether the private sector can achieve something that conforms with public interest, and if so how.

These three issues of public-private interactions, innovation, and comprehensiveness and the public interest raise one last question about the *power* of private developers. It would be possible at this stage to spend much of the conclusion tracing the role of these large development corporations as part of a growth machine or growth coalition, a group from government and the private sector coalesced around a commonsense understanding that growth brings benefits (Logan and Molotch 1987, 32). For example, part of the reason that the Irvine Company supported the incorporation of the City of Irvine was that over time the county had become less supportive. However, while such analyses of pro-growth groups are an important background to urban development, they say little about why particular design and planning strategies were chosen. Why did development teams take on unusual development strategies for the period, including attached housing, racial and household mix, open drains, bans on strip developments, and distinctive planting palettes? As I pointed out in chapter 1, it is here that other kinds of analyses are important, ones that examine the internal workings of development companies and the larger political context, and ones that examine the role of ideas in shaping options.

Large new community developers are certainly powerful and profit seeking, attempting to affect local politics enough to achieve power and profits, and it is possible to achieve those aims while building developments using a variety of planning and urban styles. However, if we observe suburban development in the United States, it is apparent that most developers choose to do smaller, less comprehensive developments, with fewer design innovations—the kind that can turn a more predictable profit far more quickly than a new town can. In fact, parts of the development companies of the three case study communities made the argument for doing more conventional, less expensive, and more clearly marketable developments, and this internal conflict is an important part of the stories of these developments.

Holding on to their plans was certainly an expression of corporate power—showing they had the resources and relationships to achieve their purposes over decades. But their plans were also attractive to many residents and represented some of the best thinking among urbanists at the time of their design. Some residents later wanted changes to peel back growth—for reasons of quality of life and homeowners' investments—and this was done very clearly in Irvine. However, the comprehensive concept that attracted many residents and business people could be comprehensive in reality only if most of the developments' parts were built; thus, others in addition to the company personnel had an interest in sticking to the plans. Obviously the impetus for and the opposition to urban developments can be explained in terms of the political and economic interests of various actors. The companies used their power to shape perceptions of what was possible in urban development. However, these visions of the future were complex and innovative, and such innovation was not inevitable given the aim of profitability (Gottdiener et al. 1999).

PRIVATE PLANNING AND GOVERNMENT

In the United States, urban development, particularly residential development, is most often seen as the domain of private developers working in the context of local government or large-scale federal programs, such as urban renewal or the Federal Housing Administration. This book shows a more complex development process, involving many parts of government and a number of groups within the private development arena, including development company leadership, staff, and consultants.

The case study sites are very large and complicated projects that have intersected geographically with many jurisdictions and programmatically with numerous policy and regulatory areas (Forsyth 2002b; Watson 1973, 1975).[1] Obviously they interacted with local governments for zoning, schools, and infrastructure. Government interest and interaction was not merely local—these developments were big enough to be on the state and even federal radar screen. They dealt with federal government at several levels, from specific changes in FHA, taxation, and endangered species regulations to the more general federal programs of military expenditures, affordable housing programs, environmental regulations, and interstate construction. In a sense they also dealt with weaknesses or gaps in federal policies, in areas from education to urban agriculture. While The Woodlands was the only Title VII new community of the three, members of all three development teams participated in government-sponsored seminars and exchanges on the topic of new communities.

These intersections were not easy to manage, given the fragmented character of government. Government agencies are typically organized by specialty, such as transportation, energy, environment, or housing. Agencies at the same level of government and in the same geographical area do interact with one another, although often these interactions are limited. Governments also interact across levels, typically within one "sector" or "vertically linked chain of federal, state, area wide, and local agencies addressing a common functional specialization through interdependent tasks and procedures" (Christensen 1999, 66). While these government interactions may be cooperative, they can also be obstructive. Christensen (1999, 33–39) outlines a range of collaboration from autonomy (no collaboration) though information exchange, joint learning, review and comment, joint planning, joint funding, joint action, joint venture, and merger. She also describes a range of obstruction techniques between government agencies from autonomy (no obstruction) to contradictory information and theory, negative comments, competitive and isolative planning, prohibitory legislation and judicial action, and counterprograms and -funding (Christensen 1999, 39–43).

The potential for difficult relations was very clear to developers, not only in terms of government staffs, but also in view of the multiple constituencies that these disparate agencies and departments relate to. A member of one of the development teams complained:

> The criticism I have for public agencies generally is they tend to look at things in a fragmented view. . . . They tend to have a more narrow focus because someone will be in traffic or someone will be in zoning or someone will be in urban design, and that's their focus. And that's what it should be. But the problem is, sometimes they don't have the perspective of how what they're asking for will be implemented. . . . So often you're dealing with a fragmented process where you have a series of agencies, and you're having to deal with each one of them, and there's nobody on the other side trying to bring them together. That's a major problem, especially for large, comprehensive projects. Everybody will agree in abstract that comprehensive planning is the right thing to do . . . but in many ways it's the hardest thing to do, because by its very definition a large project creates concerns. It impacts more people. . . . You'll, by na-

ture, have more opposition. So in some cases it's better to have a very small subdivision and do ten of those and link them together and stay below the radar screen than to come in with one large project. So what people on both sides, private and public, agree is the best, many times the rules and regulations and the policies and the way people operate work exactly opposite that. It doesn't foster comprehensive planning. (Interview 0110)

In response and in order to get their developments finished, developers took over a significant number of roles traditionally undertaken by government. This was unavoidable because of their large scale, which necessitated that they cross jurisdictions, and because of their comprehensive planning, which necessitated crossing sectors. They were providing not only housing but also schools, retail, and open space, employment, cultural facilities, habitat protection, and elaborate recreational programs. There was no government agency set up to do this coordination, and, with their huge holding costs, the developers had a great deal of incentive to take on the role in order to get their developments done with the various pieces in place at much the same time or according to some conception of phasing.

The coordination role was reminiscent of special purpose governments, such as urban renewal authorities. Many new towns built in other countries are actually developed by such special public development corporations, but in the United States this role is generally taken by the private sector.[2] For the developer this quasi-governmental role was most obvious in the initial and ongoing physical master planning of the development. However, it continued as the developers administered private development controls, took large infrastructure loans, set up neighborhood associations and other bodies to administer common and recreational areas, built public spaces, and attracted employers and retailers to the new communities. The developers also initiated the formation of local and specialized governments, as the Irvine Company did in establishing the Irvine Ranch Water District in 1961 and The Woodlands did in creating its many municipal utility districts.

The ownership of very large tracts of land gave the developers some legitimacy in dealing with governments and initiating planning and development activity, but it often forced a strained relationship between the private and public actors. As a government representative from the City of Irvine explained: "In Irvine, it's like living in a society where you can't get a divorce. We're married to the Irvine Company. They're the only landowner, we're the government entity. And we have to figure out how to develop a plan that everybody can live with" (Interview 0329). The developers also saw this clearly; unable to exit easily they were forced to negotiate: "We can't afford to fall on the sword, so to speak, to fight for an issue with the Howard County planning department the way another developer would, because we're going to be in there again tomorrow. So there's a relationship" (Interview 0116).

It is worthwhile here to distinguish between speculators or even master builders—bent on making profits from land value increases or from basic building—and community builders. The latter have a long-term vision and rely on planning to sell their developments (Eichler and Kaplan 1967; Ewing 1991). Of course, not all community builders have wonderful plans. However, private-sector urban development is not generally done in such a comprehensive manner but is the product of many companies doing relatively small projects over short time frames that end up often with fragmented and uncoordinated results.

Of course, another view is that this relationship between government and the private developers was still too cozy, and even well-intentioned governments are often co-opted by the development teams, which in this coordination role set the development agenda, frame potential alternatives, and control others' options. I heard many such stories about the Irvine Company. It had negotiated agreements that froze development regulations in the Irvine Spectrum area in return for infrastructure provision and had used a form of transfer of development rights to protect open space in some areas while increasing density in others (e.g., Pincetl 1999; Gaventa 1980; Forester 1989).[3] Critics saw this as using private power to manipulate public processes.

While many large corporations face similar tasks of managing multiple interactions among agencies and making different sectors and levels of government aware of conflicts among policies—for instance, large manufacturers—the unique character of land development injects some added complexities. These involve its fixed location, cultural impact, and cyclical nature (Fainstein 1994, 219). As explained earlier, much more than typical developers who manage smaller projects in different locations either simultaneously or sequentially, new community developers are tied to a specific place for decades with a set of clear expectations of continued master planning from both residents and governments. While private developers want coordination, there are no incentives on the part of government to produce such coordination, except perhaps on the part of the very weak planning agencies.

The Woodlands was in a special situation because of its early federal support. This imposed significant reporting requirements and regulations. However, it also gave the development access to some federal grants in competition with actual city governments. Later, when it was no longer a Title VII community, the company staff used the experience to continue grant writing. That they were able to gain a number of these grants, particularly in the transportation area, caused some local resentment. One interviewee remarked, "One of the things that The Woodlands Operating Company has done really well is OPM, other people's money" (Interview 0518).

As very visible projects, the case study developments faced some additional political challenges in terms of local opposition, often channeled through government. They were all started in the 1960s and early 1970s, before there was significant nationwide citizen opposition to development, although the developers all spent time monitoring and managing local opposition, even in the early years.[4] All three created an early track record of fairly responsible development. While subsequent development in all three projects was opposed by neighboring residents or municipalities, the opposition was muted by this track record. However, because these were very large and identifiable projects, the companies did receive added attention and criticism from both inside and outside the developments, being held accountable for the high standards they had proclaimed and having to fight to maintain their development program.

Even if the local population has moved to the area because they were attracted to its plan, they will not predictably support that plan in the future. Across the nation, residents of some developments have blocked future stages of projects. When this has happened in the middle of the decades-long new community building process, it has had enormous financial implications for developers who required major loans for infrastructure (Godschalk 1973, 198). As a professional working on the Columbia project explained:

> It is immensely complicated. . . . The interrelationship of customers, new residents, old residents, governments that constantly change, et cetera, creates a very complicated matrix of issues. One of the issues we're going to face . . . [is] we've saved the best land till last, [but] since it is last, everybody that's here is going to think that it should stay green forever, or it certainly shouldn't be urban. The planners in the county will think urban makes all the sense in the world, creates a sense of vitality. All the people who are here will say traffic, environmental issues, smoke, noise, "them," whoever "they" are. . . . (Interview 0116)

The developers, then, want to negotiate a highly predicable future that they can plan investments around (Marris 1996). This has to be agreed upon by all major players with a long time frame, including the public sector and the electorate as well as private groups such as banks and builders. The initial new town zoning for Columbia and Irvine's 1988 memorandum of understanding transferring development rights for open space both perform this function, creating a high level of certainty and allowing investments in comprehensive planning. In contrast with the goals and needs of the developers, residents and governments can come to see development differently over time, questioning the planning of an earlier era. For some this can be a self-interested desire to stop development, but for others it reflects a more general transformation of understanding about the importance of various facets of development. The negotiations over habitat protection and coastal development on the Irvine Ranch are both examples of this kind of transformation.

Overall, it is difficult to get multiple public and private players to share something of the same vision, and it is difficult to maintain circumstances enough to build out over a long period. As one of the development team members explained:

> When it gets down to it, big projects draw lots of attention, and lots of attention draws political fire. Political fire, chest pounding—know what I mean? It's just a hell of a lot easier chopping and dicing up the agricultural land in the rural jurisdictions. It's cheaper, less time-consuming, better to market. You can reach more people in the pyramid because the housing's less expensive, because the land's less expensive out there. And there are fewer neighbors to argue about it. I'm being very candid. (Interview 0208)

In an interesting twist, through housing and land sales, the developers of these new communities created the public that would eventually vote for the governments who would administer and approve many of their proposals for future stages of the development. The design of the new towns—physically, socially, and governmentally—grappled with this issue. Early plans for the developments explored both the importance of communication and new methods to achieve it, including interactive television (e.g., Withey 1964). The developers built a range of physical public spaces throughout the developments.

However, in general, I think it would be hard to argue that physical design in itself has had a lot to do with how people in these new communities have eventually become involved with civic and political activities. I am not of the opinion that much democratic argument occurs on the street or in public parks among strangers, although the neighborhood may be a base for organizing around local issues (Lynch 1981; Forsyth 2000).[5] Instead, political and civic activity often happens in the private and, in Lofland's terms, parochial, social realms. These are generally spatially located in private homes, clubs, and work places, in local streets, and in programmed and more highly regulated spaces such as community centers, libraries, religious facilities, sports facilities, and coffee shops (Lofland 1998).[6]

Usefully, all three developments provided just the kinds of programming that results in such significant interactions—in resident associations, governments, and elsewhere. While Columbia provided more civic facilities in the village centers, the Irvine Ranch had more formal government. In all three, the structure of villages with their associated village committees, which are in charge of covenant enforcement, varying amounts of open space maintenance, and other local issues, has provided an easy forum for participation for those who want to be involved in governance. That is, the social structure created through the community associations gave the village structure a reality that it would not have had if it were merely a physical entity and provided a forum for resident and even business involvement in governance.

Some commentators have been struck by the high level of participation evident in the new communities once built, even though their initial development was not particularly participatory (e.g., Bloom 2001b; Baggett 1975). However, many of the civic activities and protest campaigns of the three new communities reminded me of life in college towns, which tend to have similarly highly educated populations. Whether extraordinary in terms of activism or merely reflecting such socioeconomic variables, this relatively active citizen involvement affected later development plans. As an employee from of one of the development companies complained: "Our big challenge for the community is . . . that they can accept that more growth isn't necessarily going to harm their quality of life. That it can be accommodated. That it's been planned for. And I think that's a constant battle for us, because it's the public opinion which drives the political guys" (Interview 0401).

Overall, while private, these cases show that new community developers have been deeply affected by government and in turn have shaped governments: working to coordinate government activities enough to build their new towns, creating new publics to participate in governance, and dealing with the protests of these publics in later stages of development. While these large developments have some unique ways of intersecting with governments, they are also only extreme versions of what is typically a complex set of interactions between private and public sectors in urban development. This combination of typicality and uniqueness makes such developments important, as they can clarify what can often seem to be a messy and diffuse set of government effects on urban form, particularly the effects of higher levels of government, where the interactions are often indirect. This kind of complexity can be missed by analyses that focus on individual policies (such as the interstate highway program), on sectors (such as housing), or on small developments, which raise a narrower range of issues. New community development is difficult both because of its initial costs and also because of the complexity of these governmental relations.

INNOVATION AND THE PRIVATE SECTOR

Obviously, reorganizing a metropolitan area is a difficult thing. There are tremendous problems of vision, technique, coordination, financing, and marketing. It is easier to do small, incremental projects that externalize the costs of amenities and public spaces and provide the maximum internal space. Sprawl is, in fact, very good at providing private household space for people who use private motorized transportation and want small government that provides services tailored to people much like themselves. It is good at deferring payment for amenities and providing for short-term needs, though often it also creates longer-term problems. The private developers of the three case study communities tried to break that pattern, and they did it in a complex way: for example, by providing more housing choices and more public spaces, but also by creating more regulations and controls. It was not a simple task, and many innovative ideas were dropped because of costs.

Could the development teams have done more to push the boundaries of suburban design? Certainly the development companies could have made additional innovations and the designers and planners could have perhaps pushed harder for them. They could have used mechanisms being developed in the 1960s, such as land trusts, to protect affordability of at least some housing;[7] increased densities significantly in key locations to make transit and walking more viable as means of transportation; focused more on passive solar design and other energy efficiency strategies emerging during the 1970s; provided more options for design spontaneity and diversity; and incorporated more or better-designed civic spaces in village and town centers. The planners of each of the developments investigated at least some of these strategies but implemented them partially at most. Examples of early attempts at such strategies in the 1970s were certainly available for their investigation, though in developments of a smaller scale (Corbett and Corbett 2000).

However, in very large developments, a crucial paradox makes additional innovations, beyond those already outlined in earlier chapters, very hard to do. The early period of a development is both the easiest time and an almost impossible time to push the limits of design and planning. It is the easiest time because the company has on board the initial highly innovative design and planning team, and few or no residents are in place, so few or no resident expectations can be violated. In a later period, the development staffs in place are generally more skilled at careful implementation than at broad innovation, and the residents who have moved in are concerned about their own values, which probably don't involve changes to the plan, except possibly to reduce development. To change the plan too much at later stages is to undermine a set of shared expectations. The early period, however, is also the time when innovations are most difficult to make, because money is tightest then and the need to make sales is at its greatest (Watson 1971, 19). For a very large development, as opposed to a subdivision of a few hundred acres, early sales are particularly important, as failure up front can make the whole development appear unsuccessful and suppress sales for a long time, leading to bankruptcy.

This does not mean that the very large developments are irrelevant to a discussion of urban innovation; rather, their size is essential for true innovation to break the prevailing pattern of suburban development. However, the stories of these new communities show how difficult it is to develop and sell a very large amount of a new style of development, particularly without special government financial support. It is risky and expensive. In this sense large innovative developments provide a better test case about the broad market for urban development than much smaller innovative subdivisions can.

The case study developers certainly did innovate early on, with attached housing, racial and household mix, and open drains, setting in place innovations that became part of what was commonplace for the new residents. However, all the developers balanced risky innovations with known market acceptance of more generic products; they could innovate but only as far as they could sell, so they tried some innovations and not others. Could they have pushed the boundaries of innovation more? The Irvine Company is the organization that could have done this most easily; development was well underway by the time of the early 1970s property crash, which deeply affected the other two developments. It was criticized at the time. A number of early publications by Irvine Company staff are in the form of defenses of its position on issues such as racial and economic mix (Dienstfrey 1971), which, along with natural environmental issues, were the focus of Irvine's critics. They were also the focal areas of innovations by those who were working on the other two developments. Those working on the Irvine Ranch focused more on innovations in physical design and environmental perception. Over the years the Irvine Company has also given concessions in open space and made some innovations in that area, but those actions have been responses to both increasing public concerns about habitat and a more conservative desire by existing residents to limit new development. For the other developments, the early financial picture was more challenging. They might have been able to innovate in different dimensions but not dramatically more in quantity.

Would a government new towns program have been different? Probably, but in the United States, with many competing interests, such a program would likely have been far less coherent than the new towns programs in Europe and Asia. In those locations either governments are stronger or a greater social consensus exists about public intervention (Strong 1971; Van Der Wal 1997; Phillips and Yeh 1987). Certainly the federal government supports urban development in the United States and has even shaped these new towns extensively, but, as was explained earlier, it has done this in the kind of piecemeal manner that is characteristic of American ambivalence toward urban policy (Forsyth 2002b).[8]

The U.S. public new town program that was launched and provided loan guarantees for The Woodlands struggled for support. However, if its launch had been a little more successful, it may have been a true disaster, starting many more projects than could be finished, given the likely inconsistent government support and administrative staffing, which occurred at a small scale even with Title VII. Only a very different kind of program might have succeeded (Peiser and Chaing 1999). In the end, the private new communities I studied look rather like public ones elsewhere in physical terms, but they have a more middle-class population, given their need to make money through sales.

Finally, one can ask whether it was worth trying out innovation in new town development when existing cities were so in need of investment. While the Irvine Company did not choose its location but responded to both market demands and government pressures to develop, developers Rouse and Mitchell did choose suburban locations. Rouse hoped that the new communities could create models for center-city development, and certainly he became involved in center-city revitalization in subsequent decades. Mitchell envisaged The Woodlands as part of the City of Houston, contributing taxes. Given the wide preference in the United States for suburban living, these developments showed alternative designs for such environments. If we look back after some decades, it is possible to criticize their decision to build on the urban edge. However, metropolitan areas are many times larger than they were at the time that these three developments were conceived. Today, there is far more potential for redeveloping already urbanized areas, and redevelopment is occurring within the new communities as well, particularly in the industrial and commercial areas of Irvine.

COMPREHENSIVENESS AND GOOD URBAN FORM

New community development is not easy for private-sector developers, particularly publicly traded companies that need to show a profit. However, long-term projects are not unusual in business. In fact, it seems no surprise that these big, long-running developments were carried out or funded by those involved with agriculture, insurance, and oil and gas exploration, as all of these businesses require "patient money" and a commitment to planning.

The companies that took on these developments were, then, skilled in considering the long term. However, in new town developments there are some added problems to do with vision and government. Important in new towns, an overall comprehensive vision needs to be articulated clearly, in spite of all the disagreements over development priorities and over who has done the most important work. This vision must then be maintained among people who have quite different personalities and work styles and who work in different kinds of organizational structures, more suited to the long haul. The private sector alone is not the only entity involved in this transition of vision, because in the long run the public governments will maintain the plan as phases are completed. None of the developers of these new communities intended to leave entirely—all the developers continue to own apartments, shops, offices, and industrial areas—and the construction is taking decades. However, eventually all the developers have to create an exit strategy for most of their properties. So the private sector needs the public sector, not only for approvals and infrastructure funding, but also to perpetuate the comprehensive vision.

In this perpetuation, the public sector is not merely taking over a typical city general plan. Such plans reflect the ideas of the professional planners, vocal citizens, and elected representatives about the best achievable future. Many people expect these general plans to be renegotiated periodically. In contrast, the private new community plans were literally bought into by residents, who were purchasing a set of hopes and expectations about the future with highly elaborated visions of physical layout, recreation, and neighborhood governance. Not all residents of a county or municipality might live in the planned development, but in the later years of development a significant portion did in each case.

This raises the issues of how the public sector can tell if the private-sector vision is a good one, worth taking over, and how it can add its own concerns. I have framed this analysis in terms of responses to criticisms of urban sprawl. However, at a deeper level the master plans that these new communities developed were based on ideas about creating the best kinds of environment for human life, in the context of having to sell those ideas quite literally. The new communities of the 1960s and 1970s were a kind of development and were from a period in the history of urban development when quite fundamental questions were being asked about how to organize the metropolis for the public good. It was a period when the private sector was centrally engaged in those conversations. Of course, it is obvious that great disagreement has always occurred about the character of such "good urban forms"—for lack of a better shorthand. Even among the case study development teams, people disagreed about what makes the good life and how to build an environment to support that. At times they had ideas that were internally inconsistent and differentially attainable, which was particularly obvious in tradeoffs between such values as privacy and community, locality and region. However, this set of ideas was part of the background of their thinking as the companies worked to coordinate government and make innovations.

The relationship between private interests and the common good or public interest can be conceptualized in several ways. While the public interest is often associated with government, a potential role for the private sector exists in all of the models. They include the following:

· *The public interest is determined by aggregating private interests through what are seen as fairly neutral systems, such as voting, the market, and cost-benefit calculations.* In this context, private-sector developers hold interests that can be added into the mix. They can also have a role creating a market or even governmental mechanisms for the expression of others' interests. This aggregation leaves the ultimate decision about the good, and the balancing of short- and long-term perspectives, to the individual or household, although even the "neutral" systems for aggregation have biases. The numerous referenda in the Irvine Ranch that increased open space and ultimately defeated the reuse of the El Toro

Marine Corps base as an airport are examples of such aggregated interests.

- *The public good is conceptualized as a unified common good that exists outside individual interests and can be represented by professions, governments, elites, or activists.* This conceptualization of the public interest potentially has a place for private-sector developers or the professionals they employ to define or perceive the common good. In this case the common good is something that informed and sophisticated people can perceive. It is often thought that governments are uniquely situated to work for the public interest and that corporations serve private interests. However, professionals in fields such as urban planning also often see themselves as well situated to determine the public interest.[9]
- *The public interest is operationalized as a set of core values or goals that can be agreed upon through deliberation.* The private sector, in this model, can be part, even a key part, of a deliberative group convening the various players. This model sees multiple interests, but instead of aggregating them, it proposes a model of debate (Meyerson and Banfield 1955; Reich 1988; Howe 1992; Forsyth 1999).

All these ways of determining the public interest can fit with a market system, although obviously the market is most central in the first theory, where it can be the mechanism for determining the good. However, while the private development companies certainly built to the market, they and their professional staff and consultants also had a wider vision that was not merely an aggregation of the preferences of consumers.

In the new communities, professional and development elites obviously thought that they could determine what was better urban development, relating to the second view. Columbia's Finley and Hoppenfeld explained in language that, while not mentioning the public interest, could have appeared in a public document:

> We look upon physical planning as the manifestation of social and aesthetic objectives. As a minimum the physical plan provides for the efficient (economical) day-to-day working of all aspects of the community, i.e., the elimination of frictions caused by distance, by incompatible activities, sounds, odors, and the establishment of proper functional relationships. At its best, the physical environment will enhance and augment the total life of the community. It will not only respond to known stated requirements but, by its quality, create new opportunities for personal and group interaction with nature, the urban environment, and society. Finally, it should provide for the widest range of personal interests and for aesthetic satisfaction and excitement of all kinds. (Finley and Hoppenfeld 1963, 1)

However, as in Irvine's negotiations over the fate of the coastal and habitat areas, a process of deliberation or intensive negotiation over goals and values also occurred from time to time. In these kinds of cases the public sector was not the sole voice claiming a wider public purpose, and, in fact, because of government's fragmentation even when government agencies claimed to work in the public interest, other agencies and groups made counterclaims.

Was this a benign and useful role of having the private sector help define the public interest? People disagree, depending on whether they like the overall vision of a particular development. These were certainly rich, politically connected developers, and they used their economic and political power to further their development aims. They also tried to shape public ideas by selling particular visions. This visionary aspect can be seen as merely a way of molding the development agenda. However, even if a comprehensive vision was chosen just for business reasons, it was still a challenging path, again because of the difficulties of sticking to comprehensiveness over a long period.

Whether or not this was in the public interest, there certainly was a comprehensive vision, and one of the issues raised by these kinds of discussions about planning and design is who was responsible for the vision. This is slightly more than simply a question of interest to planning historians and members of the development teams. These were vastly complex undertakings with shared responsibilities between public and private entities, and the ways that those responsibilities were shared and disciplinary or professional barriers were overcome matter for contemporary attempts of do better suburban development.

The situation in each development was complex. For example, while it may be easy shorthand to talk about Rouse's Columbia, or even a Rouse-Finley-Hoppenfeld Columbia, it is obviously only a shorthand. The legal work that created the new town zoning, the programming work in managing the complex design and development tasks, the development and maintenance of the Columbia economic model, and the sales work to integrate the residents racially were at least as important early on. Many people remarked about the primacy of economic analyses or models in these private developments, and while such analyses did allow some discretion in the area of the design, they also provided a set of fairly firm limits. In Columbia, the role of Howard County was also not trivial, as a great deal of cooperation was necessary. Those working on the new town over a number of years were also important. For those interested in the power of the private sector, however, the development is more accurately the Rouse Company's Columbia, with all that that implies about an underlying quest for financial returns. Similar analyses can be made for the other developments, showing their complexity (and also showing the reason for so much disagreement about who had had the key role in each development).

Overall, these were contested visions. Certainly the marketing and economics departments of the development companies had strong roles in shaping the concept. The owners or presidents of the development companies also had personal preferences, from tennis courts to racial mix. The companies may well have disliked having a comprehensive governmental planning agency that had a different view of the public interest and disagreed with their private plans. However, the planners, designers, and other professionals working for the development companies were interested in a broader conception of good design and planning, making these new communities more closely in tune with public planning ideas than is frequently the case. Thus, where they seem to have failed as development ideas, so will many other publicly promoted development strategies conceived as representing the public interest.

THE NEW COMMUNITIES IN RETROSPECT

The three case study developments matter today because many of their planning techniques can be used in smaller developments, making their stories relevant beyond the new town movement. The developments provide some important lessons about whether it is worth using specific planning techniques that can be implemented at a smaller scale, that is, if they really do make a difference when put in place across a large area. However, beyond the issue of techniques to ameliorate sprawl, these developments matter because they also raise questions about how far the private sector can go in achieving real alternatives to urban sprawl and highlight where new forms of government intervention are needed.

Constraints on better development come from both the private and public sides of urban development. Together they create a set of hurdles for innovative ideas, particularly as they are implemented over a long period through different business, economic, and electoral cycles. Private developers need to make money in order to make business, and most need to make money within a short time frame, meaning they have to build a product that will sell in the market. Even when private developers are focused on the longer term, the complexity of dealing with sometimes dozens of government agencies working in an uncoordinated way with different agendas can make innovative development difficult. It is easy enough to propose better plans. It is much harder to implement them over time and space.

The stories of these developments are, then, a reminder of how difficult it is to actually construct large, coordinated, comprehensively planned developments in the United States. This is a warning about the difficulties of thinking that the private sector can provide a solution on its own, even with good intentions, great skill, and plentiful resources. It is a caution that public purposes often require public interventions to create the regulatory frameworks or financial incentives both to create better developments and to make it more difficult to create bad ones. When similar alternative development patterns are built in smaller private-sector projects, in a necessarily more piecemeal manner, government has a role in coordinating this work. However, the track record of governments in this area is not exemplary, as there has been little commitment to coordination. The very structure of government makes it difficult to be more comprehensive, and the lack of consensus about government intervention in the property market makes it difficult for the United States to follow models from other countries. For those who think that smart growth, new urbanism, and these new towns do not go far enough in creating real alternatives to existing development patterns, these warnings are even more salient.

Of course, for some it does not matter that incremental uncoordinated growth continues to be the easy option for developers, because it represents the choices of many individuals in the market, people who chose it because it has benefits (Gordon and Richardson 1997). That such development has many benefits is certainly clear. However, the reason the private developers of these three new communities tried to create an alternative to sprawl was that that pattern of development has had long-term costs that are evident even to the private sector.

These three developments are, then, a reminder that the current generation of smart growth and new urbanist proposals is not the first to grapple with the issue of extensive urban growth. This analysis also highlights some of the problems likely to be faced as governments promote smart growth or sustainable development in the balkanized U.S. governmental system. Like new towns, these innovative forms of development provide mixed-use, phased, serviced environments that preserve open space and place people near jobs. They also, like new towns, have a regional vision and are seen as a solution to problems of metropolitan growth. However, the story that these case studies tell in terms of smart growth is of the difficulty of doing comprehensive planning. How will fragmented and uncoordinated governments cooperate to promote these difficult kinds of development? The complexity of new community development is a warning about the difficulty of change, particularly in situations with less coordinated, persevering, wealthy, or influential proponents.

Ahwahnee Principles, Charter of the New Urbanism, and EPA Smart Growth Principles

AHWAHNEE PRINCIPLES

By Peter Calthorpe, Michael Corbett, Andres Duany, Elizabeth Plater-Zyberk, Stefanos Polyzoides, and Elizabeth Moule (1991). Used by permission of the Local Government Commission.

Preamble

Existing patterns of urban and suburban development seriously impair our quality of life. The symptoms are: more congestion and air pollution resulting from our increased dependence on automobiles, the loss of precious open space, the need for costly improvements to roads and public services, the inequitable distribution of economic resources, and the loss of a sense of community. By drawing upon the best from the past and the present, we can plan communities that will more successfully serve the needs of those who live and work within them. Such planning should adhere to certain fundamental principles.

Community Principles

1. All planning should be in the form of complete and integrated communities containing housing, shops, work places, schools, parks and civic facilities essential to the daily life of the residents.
2. Community size should be designed so that housing, jobs, daily needs and other activities are within easy walking distance of each other.

3. As many activities as possible should be located within easy walking distance of transit stops.

4. A community should contain a diversity of housing types to enable citizens from a wide range of economic levels and age groups to live within its boundaries.

5. Businesses within the community should provide a range of job types for the community's residents.

6. The location and character of the community should be consistent with a larger transit network.

7. The community should have a center focus that combines commercial, civic, cultural and recreational uses.

8. The community should contain an ample supply of specialized open space in the form of squares, greens and parks whose frequent use is encouraged through placement and design.

9. Public spaces should be designed to encourage the attention and presence of people at all hours of the day and night.

10. Each community or cluster of communities should have a well-defined edge, such as agricultural greenbelts or wildlife corridors, permanently protected from development.

11. Streets, pedestrian paths and bike paths should contribute to a system of fully-connected and interesting routes to all destinations. Their design should encourage pedestrian and bicycle use by being small and spatially defined by buildings, trees and lighting; and by discouraging high speed traffic.

12. Wherever possible, the natural terrain, drainage and vegetation of the community should be preserved with superior examples contained within parks or greenbelts.

13. The community design should help conserve resources and minimize waste.

14. Communities should provide for the efficient use of water through the use of natural drainage, drought tolerant landscaping and recycling.

15. The street orientation, the placement of buildings and the use of shading should contribute to the energy efficiency of the community.

Regional Principles

1. The regional land-use planning structure should be integrated within a larger transportation network built around transit rather than freeways.

2. Regions should be bounded by and provide a continuous system of greenbelt/wildlife corridors to be determined by natural conditions.

3. Regional institutions and services (government, stadiums, museums, etc.) should be located in the urban core.

4. Materials and methods of construction should be specific to the region,

exhibiting a continuity of history and culture and compatibility with the climate to encourage the development of local character and community identity.

Implementation Principles

1. The general plan should be updated to incorporate the above principles.
2. Rather than allowing developer-initiated, piecemeal development, local governments should take charge of the planning process. General plans should designate where new growth, infill or redevelopment will be allowed to occur.
3. Prior to any development, a specific plan should be prepared based on these planning principles.
4. Plans should be developed through an open process and participants in the process should be provided visual models of all planning proposals.

CHARTER OF THE NEW URBANISM

Used by permission of the Congress for the New Urbanism.

The Congress for the New Urbanism views disinvestment in central cities, the spread of placeless sprawl, increasing separation by race and income, environmental deterioration, loss of agricultural lands and wilderness, and the erosion of society's built heritage as one interrelated community-building challenge.

We stand for the restoration of existing urban centers and towns within coherent metropolitan regions, the reconfiguration of sprawling suburbs into communities of real neighborhoods and diverse districts, the conservation of natural environments, and the preservation of our built legacy.

We recognize that physical solutions by themselves will not solve social and economic problems, but neither can economic vitality, community stability, and environmental health be sustained without a coherent and supportive physical framework.

We advocate the reconstruction of the public policy and development practices to support the following principles: neighborhoods should be diverse in use and population; communities should be designed for the pedestrian and transit as well as the car; cities and towns should be shaped by physically defined and universally accessible public spaces and community institutions; urban places should be framed by architecture and landscape design that celebrate local history, climate, ecology, and building practice.

We represent a broad-based citizenry, composed of public and private sector leaders, community activists, and multidisciplinary professionals. We are committed to reestablishing the relationship between the art of building and the making of community, through citizen-based participatory planning and design.

We dedicate ourselves to reclaiming our homes, blocks, streets, parks, neighborhoods, districts, towns, cities, regions, and environment.

We assert the following principles to guide public policy, development practice, urban planning, and design:

The Region: Metropolis, City, and Town

1. Metropolitan regions are finite places with geographic boundaries derived from topography, watersheds, coastlines, farmlands, regional parks, and river basins. The metropolis is made of multiple centers that are cities, towns, and villages, each within its own identifiable center and edges.

2. The metropolitan region is a fundamental economic unit of the contemporary world. Governmental cooperation, public policy, physical planning, and economic strategies must reflect this new reality.

3. The metropolis has a necessary and fragile relationship to its agrarian hinterland and natural landscapes. The relationship is environmental, economic, and cultural. Farmland and nature are as important to the metropolis as the garden is to the house.

4. Development patterns should not blur or eradicate the edges of the metropolis. Infill development within existing urban areas conserves environmental resources, economic investment, and social fabric, while reclaiming marginal and abandoned areas. Metropolitan regions should develop strategies to encourage such infill development over peripheral expansion.

5. Where appropriate, new development contiguous to urban boundaries should be organized as neighborhoods and districts, and be integrated with the existing urban pattern. Noncontiguous development should be organized as towns and villages with their own urban edges, and planned for a jobs/housing balance, not as bedroom suburbs.

6. The development and redevelopment of towns and cities should respect historical patterns, precedents, and boundaries.

7. Cities and towns should bring into proximity a broad spectrum of public and private uses to support a regional economy that benefits people of all incomes. Affordable housing should be distributed throughout the region to match job opportunities and to avoid concentrations of poverty.

8. The physical organization of the region should be supported by a framework of transportation alternatives. Transit, pedestrian, and bicycle systems should maximize access and mobility throughout the region while reducing dependence upon the automobile.

9. Revenues and resources can be shared more cooperatively among the municipalities and centers within regions to avoid destructive competition for tax base and to promote rational coordination of transportation, recreation, public services, housing, and community institutions.

The Neighborhood, the District, and the Corridor

1. The neighborhood, the district, and the corridor are the essential elements of development and redevelopment in the metropolis. They form identifiable areas that encourage citizens to take responsibility for their maintenance and evolution.
2. Neighborhoods should be compact, pedestrian-friendly, and mixed-use. Districts generally emphasize a special single use, and should follow the principles of neighborhood design when possible. Corridors are regional connectors of neighborhoods and districts; they range from boulevards and rail lines to rivers and parkways.
3. Many activities of daily living should occur within walking distance, allowing independence to those who do not drive, especially the elderly and the young. Interconnected networks of streets should be designed to encourage walking, reduce the number and length of automobile trips, and conserve energy.
4. Within neighborhoods, a broad range of housing types and price levels can bring people of diverse ages, races, and incomes into daily interaction, strengthening the personal and civic bonds essential to an authentic community.
5. Transit corridors, when properly planned and coordinated, can help organize metropolitan structure and revitalize urban centers. In contrast, highway corridors should not displace investment from existing centers.
6. Appropriate building densities and land uses should be within walking distance of transit stops, permitting public transit to become a viable alternative to the automobile.
7. Concentrations of civic, institutional, and commercial activity should be embedded in neighborhoods and districts, not isolated in remote, single-use complexes. Schools should be sized and located to enable children to walk or bicycle to them.
8. The economic health and harmonious evolution of neighborhoods, districts, and corridors can be improved through graphic urban design codes that serve as predictable guides for change.
9. A range of parks, from tot-lots and village greens to ballfields and community gardens, should be distributed within neighborhoods. Conservation areas and open lands should be used to define and connect different neighborhoods and districts.

The Block, the Street, and the Building

1. A primary task of all urban architecture and landscape design is the physical definition of streets and public spaces as places of shared use.
2. Individual architectural projects should be seamlessly linked to their surroundings. This issue transcends style.
3. The revitalization of urban places depends on safety and security. The design of streets and buildings should reinforce safe environments, but not at the expense of accessibility and openness.
4. In the contemporary metropolis, development must adequately accommodate automobiles. It should do so in ways that respect the pedestrian and the form of public space.
5. Streets and squares should be safe, comfortable, and interesting to the pedestrian. Properly configured, they encourage walking and enable neighbors to know each other and protect their communities.
6. Architecture and landscape design should grow from local climate, topography, history, and building practice.
7. Civic buildings and public gathering places require important sites to reinforce community identity and the culture of democracy. They deserve distinctive form, because their role is different from that of other buildings and places that constitute the fabric of the city.
8. All buildings should provide their inhabitants with a clear sense of location, weather and time. Natural methods of heating and cooling can be more resource-efficient than mechanical systems.
9. Preservation and renewal of historic buildings, districts, and landscapes affirm the continuity and evolution of urban society.

EPA SMART GROWTH PRINCIPLES

U.S. Environmental Protection Agency (2001).

1. Mix land uses
2. Take advantage of compact building design
3. Create a range of housing opportunities and choices
4. Create walkable neighborhoods
5. Foster distinctive, attractive communities with a strong sense of place
6. Preserve open space, farmland, natural beauty, and critical environmental areas
7. Strengthen and direct development towards existing communities
8. Provide a variety of transportation choices
9. Make development decisions predictable, fair, and cost effective
10. Encourage community and stakeholder collaboration in development decisions

Census Data for Irvine, Columbia, and The Woodlands, 1980–2000

TABLE 10 Irvine

| | 1980 | 1990 | | 2000 | | |
	Irvine City	Irvine City	California	Irvine City	Orange County	California
Population						
Total	62,134	110,330	29,760,021	143,072	2,846,289	33,871,648
% under 18 years	28	24	26	23	27	27
% 65 years and over	1	6	11	7	10	11
% high school graduates (persons over 25)	95	95	76	95	80	77
% non–U.S. citizens	—	—	—	17	19	16
Households						
Total number of households	21,337	40,257	827,066	51,199	935,287	11,502,870
% family households	75	69	69	67	71	69
% married-couple families	63	56	53	54	56	51
% nonfamily households	25	31	31	33	29	31
% householders living alone	17	20	23	23	21	23
Average household size	2.77	2.74	2.79	2.66	3.00	2.87
Race and Hispanic Origin[a]						
% White	88	78	69	64	68	63
% Black	1	2	7	2	2	7
% American Indian, Eskimo, or Aleut	0	0	1	1	1	2
% Asian or Pacific Islander	8	18	10	32	15	13
% other race (balance, 1980)	3	2	13	5	17	19

Total % of races	100	100	100	104	103	104
% Hispanic origin (of any race)	6	6	26	7	31	32
% non-Hispanic white	84	74	57	57	51	47

Housing

% 1-unit detached	52	39	55	40	51	56
% 1-unit attached	27	28	7	24	13	8
% 2 to 4 units	7	6	9	8	9	8
% 5 to 9 units	6	12	6	9	6	6
% 10 or more units	5	12	17	18	18	17
% mobile home, trailer, or other	3	3	6	2	3	5
% owner occupied	73	62	56	60	52	57
% renter occupied	27	38	44	40	48	43
Median value of owner occupied ($)	137,800	294,700	195,500	316,800	270,000	211,500
Median rent ($)	454	913	561	1,272	923	747
% persons spending more than 30% of income for owner costs	—	—	—	31	32	31
% persons spending more than 30% of income for renter costs	—	—	—	45	42	42

Income^b

Median household income ($)	31,300	56,307	35,798	72,057	58,820	47,493
White	31,550	58,572	37,724	76,648	62,037	51,279
Black	29,135	36,723	26,079	52,443	49,972	34,956
Asian	30,458	51,100 ^c	39,769	67,246	58,501	55,366
American Indian	18,889	47,452	27,818	69,125	50,833	36,547
Hispanic/Latino	27,925		28,209	62,616	44,676	36,532

(continued)

TABLE 10 (continued)

| | 1980 | 1990 | | 2000 | | |
	Irvine City	Irvine City	California	Irvine City	Orange County	California
Income[b]						
Per capita income ($)	12,169	25,332	16,409	32,196	25,826	22,711
% persons below poverty level	4	6	13	9	10	14
% persons 65 years and over below poverty level	7	3	8	6	6	8
Labor Force (LF)						
% persons 16 years and over in LF	75	75	67	69	66	62
% males 16 years and over in LF	86	83	76	77	74	70
% females 16 years and over in LF	64	67	58	61	57	56
Commuting (workers 16 years and over)						
% who drove alone	80	82	72	79	77	72
% in carpools	12	9	15	8	13	15
% using public transportation	1	1	5	1	3	5
% using other means	3	2	2	2	2	2
% who walked or worked at home	3	7	7	10	6	7
% who worked in place of residence[d]	26	37	17	39	23	36
Mean travel time to work (minutes)	23.4	23.2	24.6	22.8	27.2	27.7

Vehicles Available

% with none	—	—	2	9	4	6	10
% with three or more			21	20	18	21	19

SOURCES: U.S. Census 1980, 1990, and 2000.

[a] Per the race definitions in the census, race figures for 2000 are numbers alone and in combination with other races.

[b] Income by race is for one race alone; in 1990, income figures for races include Hispanic/Latino population, and Hispanic/Latino incomes include all races.

[c] Income available for populations of 1,000 or more.

[d] *Place* is a census term that refers to the city- or census-designated place.

TABLE 11   Columbia

| | 1980 | 1990 | | | 2000 | | |
	Columbia CDP	Columbia CDP	Maryland	Columbia CDP	Howard County	Maryland
Population						
Total	52,518	75,883	4,781,468	88,254	247,842	5,296,486
% under 18 years	35	27	24	26	28	26
% 65 years and over	3	5	11	7	8	11
% high school graduates (persons over 25)	94	95	78	94	93	84
% non–U.S. citizens	—	—	—	7	5	5
Households						
Total households	17,965	28,591	1,748,991	34,199	90,043	1,980,859
% family households (families)	77	70	71	68	73	69
% married-couple families	65	58	54	53	61	50
% nonfamily households	23	30	29	32	27	31
% householders living alone	18	22	23	25	21	25
Average household size	2.92	2.65	2.73	2.58	2.71	2.67
Race and Hispanic Origin						
% White	77	76	71	67	76	64
% Black[a]	19	18	25	23	16	29
% American Indian, Eskimo, or Aleut[a]	0	0	0	1	1	1
% Asian or Pacific Islander	3	5	3	8	8	5
% other race[a]	1	1	1	2	2	3
Total % of races	100	100	100	101	103	102

% Hispanic origin (of any race)	2	3	3	4	3	4
% non-Hispanic white	76	74	70	64	73	62
Housing						
% 1-unit detached	46	39	49	42	54	51
% 1-unit attached	26	27	21	27	21	21
% 2 to 4 units	1	1	5	2	2	5
% 5 to 9 units	10	8	6	9	6	6
% 10 or more units	13	24	16	21	15	15
% mobile home, trailer, or other	0	0	2	0	2	2
% owner occupied	65	66	65	66	65	68
% renter occupied	35	34	35	34	35	32
Median value of owner occupied ($)	84,300	150,500	116,500	180,500	206,300	146,000
Median rent ($)	302	652	473	922	879	689
% persons spending more than 30% of income for owner costs	—	—	—	19	22	23
% persons spending more than 30% of income for renter costs	—	—	—	33	33	35
Income[b]						
Median household income ($)	29,858	55,419	39,386	71,524	74,167	52,868
White	30,013	57,294	41,964	77,709	78,976	57,831
Black	29,176	46,580	30,746	54,663	57,476	41,652
Asian	23,563	58,875	45,446	68,293	67,450	59,589
American Indian	c	c	35,249	52,375	65,156	52,372
Hispanic/Latino	27,727	49,219	37,300	68,802	62,821	48,257
Per capita income ($)	10,557	23,538	17,730	32,833	32,402	25,614
% persons below poverty level	3	3	8	5	4	9
% persons 65 years and over below poverty level	8	11	11	11	7	9

(continued)

TABLE 11 *(continued)*

	1980	1990		2000		
	Columbia CDP	Columbia CDP	Maryland	Columbia CDP	Howard County	Maryland
Labor Force (LF)						
% persons 16 years and over in LF	83	83	71	77	76	68
% males 16 years and over in LF	92	90	79	84	83	73
% females 16 years and over in LF	75	77	63	71	69	63
Commuting						
% who drove alone	65	80	70	81	82	74
% in carpools	25	12	15	10	9	12
% using public transportation	6	3	8	3	3	7
% using other means	1	1	1	1	1	1
% who walked or worked at home	4	4	6	6	6	6
% who worked in area/place of residence[d]	25	27	19	26	18	21
Mean travel time to work (minutes)	29.2	28.1	27.0	30.2	30.2	31.2
Vehicles Available						
% with none	—	4	12	6	4	11
% with three or more	—	18	18	17	22	18

SOURCES: U.S. Census 1980, 1990, and 2000.

[a] Per the race definitions in the census, race figures for 2000 are numbers alone and in combination with other races.

[b] Income by race is for one race alone; in 1990, income figures for races include Hispanic/Latino population, and Hispanic/Latino incomes include all races.

[c] Income available for populations of 1,000 or more.

[d] *Place* is a census term that refers to the city- or census-designated place.

TABLE 12 The Woodlands

	1990			2000			
	The Woodlands CDP	Texas		The Woodlands CDP	Montgomery County	Texas	
Population							
Total	29,205	16,986,510		55,649	293,768	20,851,820	
% under 18 years	32	28		32	30	28	
% 65 years and over	7	10		8	9	10	
% high school graduates (persons over 25)	93	72		96	82	76	
% non–U.S. citizens	—	—		5	6	10	
Households							
Total households	10,497	6,070,937		19,881	103,296	7,393,354	
% family households (families)	77	72		78	78	71	
% married-couple families	68	57		69	64	54	
% nonfamily households	23	28		22	22	29	
% householders living alone	20	24		19	18	24	
Average household size	2.78	2.8		2.80	2.83	2.82	
Race and Hispanic Origin							
% White	94	75		92	90	71	
% Black[a]	2	12		2	4	12	
% American Indian, Eskimo, or Aleut[a]	0	0		1	1	1	
% Asian or Pacific Islander[a]	2	2		3	1	3	
% other race[a]	2	11		2	6	13	
Total % of races	100	100		100	102	100	

(continued)

TABLE 12 (*continued*)

	1990		2000		
	The Woodlands CDP	Texas	The Woodlands CDP	Montgomery County	Texas
Race and Hispanic Origin					
% Hispanic origin (of any race)	6	26	7	13	32
% non-Hispanic white	90	61	87	81	52
Housing					
% 1-unit detached	74	63	79	65	63
% 1-unit attached	3	3	4	2	3
% 2 to 4 units	1	6	1	2	5
% 5 to 9 units	3	5	2	2	4
% 10 or more units	18	15	13	8	14
% mobile home, trailer, or other	1	8	1	20	9
% owner occupied	66	61	79	58	64
% renter occupied	34	39	21	42	36
Median value owner occupied ($)	101,800	59,600	168,300	114,800	82,500
Median rent ($)	430	328	760	617	574
% persons spending more than 30% of income for owner costs	—	—	18	17	19
% persons spending more than 30% of income for renter costs	—	—	38	32	34

Median household income ($)	50,929	27,016	85,253	50,864	39,927
White	51,433	29,728	86,611	52,588	42,941
Black	c	17,853	34,750	24,455	29,305
Asian	c	30,792	89,073	75,673	50,049
American Indian		23,340	80,981	43,026	34,926
Hispanic/Latino	41,382	19,233	65,357	37,004	29,873
Per capita income ($)	21,414	12,904	37,724	24,544	19,617
% persons below poverty level	6	18	4	9	15
% persons 65 years and over below poverty level	19	18	11	10	13
Labor Force (LF)					
% persons 16 years and over in LF	69	66	67	66	64
% males 16 years and over in LF	86	76	83	78	71
% females 16 years and over in LF	55	56	53	55	56
Commuting					
% who drove alone	78	76	80	80	78
% in carpools	12	15	10	13	15
% using public transportation	4	2	3	1	2
% using other means	1	1	1	1	1
% who walked or worked at home	4	5	6	4	5
% who worked in place of residence[d]	5	49	31	13	44
Mean travel time to work (minutes)	30.5	22.2	32.5	32.9	25.4

(continued)

TABLE 12 (continued)

	1990		2000		
	The Woodlands CDP	Texas	The Woodlands CDP	Montgomery County	Texas
Vehicles Available					
% with none	6	8	4	5	7
% with three or more	17	16	18	19	16

SOURCES: U.S. Census 1980, 1990, and 2000.

NOTE: In 1980 The Woodlands was not yet a CDP.

[a] Per the race definitions in the census, race figures for 2000 are numbers alone and in combination with other races.

[b] Income by race is for one race alone; in 1990, income figures for races include Hispanic/Latino population, and Hispanic/Latino incomes include all races.

[c] Income available for populations of 1,000 or more.

[d] *Place* is a census term that refers to the city- or census-designated place.

Study Methods

Study methods are described briefly in chapter 1. These include site selection, data sources, reflections on the interview process, and a longer reflection on the issue of audience. This appendix provides additional detail, explaining the multiple methods used:

- the case study approach, including details about site visits and observations
- work with original documents
- interviews
- analyses of existing census and social survey data
- mapping

I also discuss a number of research directions that I did not take.

While much research on urban growth, particularly the issue of sprawl, focuses on a metropolitan level of analysis and a limited number of indicators, this book evaluates significant submetropolitan case study communities on a number of characteristics. This multimethod approach was deliberate. Sprawl is a multifaceted phenomenon and has been described, criticized, and evaluated according to very different disciplinary approaches. By using multiple methods, I hoped to present a more complete picture of urban growth.

THE CASE STUDY APPROACH

Case studies are useful when topics are broad, context matters, and multiple sources of evidence are useful (Yin 1993, xi). Yin distinguishes between a number of methods in social sciences: case studies, experiments, surveys, archival analyses, and histories, with case studies focused on contemporary events and capable of answering questions about how and why certain phenomena occur (1984, 17). Obviously this study employs most of these methods, except experiments. I call the three new communities the case study communities because they are the cases that I am examining, even though technically I am using a number of other methods in combination.

In terms of practicalities, I started the main site visits for this research in November 1999 and completed the last visits in 2002. I broke the research roughly into weeklong trips—four each to Columbia and The Woodlands, and six to Irvine. I also took short side trips to New York and Philadelphia, where some early professionals and activists now live, and I interviewed others in Cambridge, Massachusetts, where I lived at the time. This travel totaled a little under four months, although each trip took several more weeks to set up and process upon my return, so that the actual site visit time was efficiently used.

On each weeklong trip, I interviewed ten people, attended one or two public meetings, took about a hundred photographs, and spent a day in a library or archive or at someone's office looking at documents. I spent a weekend day walking on paths, hanging out at the shopping and entertainment centers, or driving to see other new communities or town centers in the region. In each place, I spent much of my first trip driving and walking—getting a feel for the land, finding my way around. I am a committed pedestrian, but these are all automobile-based environments, and so a car was an important part of my research kit. On each subsequent visit, I was less confused by the layout and more comfortable that I knew good places to hang out.

As I outline in my acknowledgments, I received tours from a staff member of the Howard County planning department and several tours of The Woodlands. These were very helpful, as I began to see some of the parts of the developments as a resident would.

ORIGINAL DOCUMENTS

I gained access to a number of original documents: plans, internal and public reports, image collections, correspondence, and local magazines and newspapers, including ones started by the development companies, for example, *Columbia Today* and *New Worlds of Irvine*. Some historians had looked at sections of these documents before I did. Morgan and King (1987) examined public government records, some public reports and evaluations, and back issues of *The Woodlands Villager* and had access to corporate records from Mitchell Energy. Bloom (2001) had done intensive work on local newspapers and some planning documents in Columbia and Irvine, tracing the social history of those developments. Kane's (1996) dissertation also provided a very detailed and very helpful review of every step in the planning of Irvine. I did not do as much work with local newspapers as Morgan and King (1987) or Bloom (2001), and given my questions, I had a different emphasis from Kane's—but I am very grateful that they had gone before me.

I generally had access to the same materials as these historians had used, except for the internal files of The Woodlands Operating Company, which was under new ownership and less open to research (though see below). However, given my focus, I searched for specific planning documents and found them in firms, personal collections, and archives. As I write in the acknowledgements, many people and organizations helped me to find these documents.

Companies were not a particularly rich source, as they had thrown out many documents over the years, although the Irvine Company generously gave access to their extensive slide collection, and the Rouse Company shared large and hard-to-find land use maps. In the cases of Irvine and Columbia, however, many original documents had found their way to collections at the University of California Irvine, the private Columbia Archives (now affiliated with the Columbia Association), and the Howard County Historical Society. For The Woodlands, a number of Title VII–related files were in the National Archives. I also obtained a list of early documents still kept by TWOC, and while I did not gain access to the company's files, I managed to find many documents in other locations, such as personal files and the files of firms that had consulted on The Woodlands. My reliance on personal files highlights a related problem: as those people who were involved in work in the 1960s and 1970s age and downsize their houses, many important documents from this period may well be lost.

INTERVIEWS

The interviews are explained in some detail in the introductory chapter, as is the issue of audience. Overall, my experience was similar to that of the late Joseph Kutchin, the editor of an oral history collection about the rise of the Mitchell Energy and Development Corporation. He explained that he found "conflicting opinions about who did what with what to whom, and 'it was my idea,' 'no it was my idea,' or 'I caused it to happen.' But what I did get was pretty much across the board a dedication to the project and to the concept" (Kutchin 2000).

Interviewees were initially identified by reading articles, reports, and books as well as corporate and new community Web sites. Early in my work, I also contacted the developers and the community association or city government for each development, so that they knew they were being studied. These early investigations identified some core people involved with the early development, some involved in the current period, as well as those who had made the newspapers though their activism and protests about various aspects of the development. Some of these informants in turn led me to others, including those with similar and different opinions. I aimed to talk with people for whom the developments had absorbed much of their time over many years and those who had worked for shorter periods or with less central roles. I interviewed people who had been involved with early, middle, and recent periods of the developments; defenders and critics; those currently employed, elected, or active and those who had moved on to other things, including retirement. Some people had been involved with the developments for decades, some had come early and left soon after, and others knew them only in their fairly mature state. They covered a range of roles, and many had multiple roles. I used this strategy to avoid the bias of interviewing only people centrally involved in the developments. The interviewees helped me to frame the histories of the developments and to humanize statistics.

Although it was not a reason for choosing The Woodlands and Columbia, a great deal of staff movement had occurred between the two areas, which allowed me to interview people in Texas who had had key roles in Columbia and vice versa. A smaller amount of movement occurred between Irvine and the other two developments. It also turned out that concentrations of people who had worked in the projects lived near each site, in New York, Philadelphia, Massachusetts, and Northern California (the last of which I did not make it to). I corresponded with and phoned a few people who had ended up in more dispersed locations.

I brought a certain identity to these interviews. I am an Australian citizen and a U.S. permanent resident, and at the time I was working at Harvard. This created some baggage: after almost fifteen years in the United States, I sometimes still need to have issues of U.S. popular culture explained to me. A number of people in Texas and Maryland were worried about being criticized by a northeasterner. A few others thought that their position could be vindicated by a Harvard study. Overall, however, I think my position as a planner and urban designer interested in important experiments in city building was the dominant identity that others perceived.

I transcribed some interviews myself and then found funding to have the rest transcribed by the wonderful Elissa Malcohn. I used the qualitative software N4/NUDIST to organize my transcripts. I also did rather more mundane kinds of analysis, reading all the transcripts several times, using NUDIST to search for key words. I read all the documents at least once, but many several times.

CENSUS, SOCIOECONOMIC DATA, AND SURVEYS

Many people studying the Irvine Ranch focus on the City of Irvine. While that is only the central two-thirds of the development, I have also followed this practice in the assessments using census data, although for other parts of the analysis I have examined the larger ranch area. This has some logic, because the approximate city area was conceptualized as a coherent unit, with other parts of the development seen as extensions of other municipalities. Columbia has very significant outparcel areas within its boundaries, which, while not part of the plan, are nevertheless part of the urban fabric and the census designated place. While Irvine also has outparcels, they are relatively fewer, and the Irvine Company worked harder with their owners to coordinate the planning. This is not quite as big an issue in The Woodlands, although The Woodlands census designated place incorporates some of the very small neighboring cities.

The census data involve some other limits. I had originally intended to trace the development of each area at tract level from 1960. Two problems intervened. First, the census geographies of each development changed dramatically in the 1960s and 1970s. Tracts were not only split but also reorganized. The boundaries of the census designated places and of the City of Irvine also changed dramatically. These changes reflected the growth of the developments, but this made comparative work extremely difficult. Second, the developments really did not have significant populations until after 1970. The City of Irvine was not established until 1971, so the 1980 census was the first one in which it appeared. Columbia's first sales were in 1967. The Woodlands did not open until 1974. Given these issues, I have traced all three developments from the 1980 census, except for The Woodlands, which became a census designated place in 1990.

In addition to the census, I used other socioeconomic data when available, including federal consolidated funds reports and data from the Bureau of Labor Statistics. Along with local opinion survey results, they provide a frame into which the more qualitative research can be fitted.

MAPPING

I had initially intended mapping to be an important part of the work and, with the helpful labor of Robert Gilmore, compiled figure ground and street pattern diagrams of all three developments over time, using USGS maps and recent aerial photos. In addition, I traced some key sites in more detail. While this took some time, it did not reveal much analytically. The one finding is that, early in their development, all these new communities looked like classic leapfrog sprawl, even though they were tightly phased.

RESEARCH DIRECTIONS NOT TAKEN

There were obviously some research directions that I did not take. I could have gained extra insights had I been able to live longer in each location, as

Lynne Burkhart (1981) did in her participant-observation study of Columbia. While long-term participant observation in one location would have allowed more depth, it would have precluded comparison, particularly given my other academic responsibilities. Many people had commented on the developments after brief visits or by using already collected data. My compromise was to spend about four to six weeks in each place over a two-year period and to pack each visit with activities. For quite a long period my university breaks were focused on these trips. In long-term participant observation, much of the time is spent in the kind of data-collection setup and processing that I completed at a distance, so the approach I took was very efficient.

I would have also liked to interview a random sample of hundreds of residents in each development, to replicate the NSF-funded University of North Carolina studies of the 1970s. However, such expensive data collection did not seem fundable when I started my research, and the presence of recent random-sample surveys of residents in each location made it less pressing. When I started work on these developments, they had been largely overlooked as relevant examples of solutions to contemporary planning concerns, and I would have been hard pressed to make them seem like a high priority for funders of large-scale surveys. Since the 1970s studies, the developments have also grown and become quite differentiated among villages; thus, larger samples would be needed than had been used in the 1970s, and these would need to be stratified by village. This would all add to costs. My hope is that, with this book completed, funders may see some interest in such a survey, particularly one that compares these new communities with other planned and more incremental developments using different urban design strategies.

Criticisms and Benefits of Suburban Growth with Evaluation of Case Study New Communities

TABLE 13

Criticisms/Benefits of Suburban Growth Features and Effects	Dimensions	General Comments	Irvine, CA[a]	Columbia, MD[b]	The Woodlands, TX[b]
URBAN DESIGN					
Features of Growth					
1 Lack of definition/identity of neighborhoods, both centers and edges	Aesthetics, identity	Identity is an aim	Has clearly named villages, differentiated architecturally and with landscape themes; population varies from about 2,000 to 26,000	Composed of villages; uses landscape areas between villages to define boundaries, though not very clearly	Uses extensive greenbelt and parkway areas to define villages; has been done more clearly than in Columbia
2 Widespread commercial strip development	Aesthetics, identity	Strips have basically been eliminated	Very proud of having no strips	Has some window areas with strips	Most shopping centers buried in forest
3 Road patterns that limit options for movement	Social equity, diversity, access Efficiency, costs	Limitation true of new communities: all have many culs-de-sac; in some cases, pedestrian paths are more gridlike	Good overall way-finding, with loose arterial grid into which villages are inserted; residential streets in cul-de-sac and loop structures; pedestrian system generally more gridlike	Confusing, limited set of primary roads; pedestrian system recreationally focused, although attention paid to school routes	Modified grid as in Irvine, although not all primary roads built; good and improving major pedestrian paths, although not all streets have sidewalks (perhaps to limit impervious surfaces)

4	Spatially segregated land uses developed at a coarse grain	Density Social equity, diversity, access Efficiency, costs	All have some kind of land use and housing mix within overall development and within villages	Offices and shops mixed in many village shopping centers; research parks and mall areas gradually being retrofitted with more uses, including residential	Village centers contain shops and civic, recreation, and educational facilities; some supermarkets have struggled, but commendable mix of public and private space provided	Each village has commercial village center; developing town center will mix residential, entertainment, retail, and office space
5	Low density	Density Social equity, diversity, access Efficiency, costs	Columbia and Irvine have more attached and apartment housing than comparable developments in their regions	Pioneered attached upper-income housing; tradeoff was linked open space; in 2000, only 40% 1-unit detached	Significant apartment and town-house development near neighborhood centers, but overall low density; in 2000, only 42% 1-unit detached	More detached housing units than the other developments; in 2000, 79% 1-unit detached

Effects of Growth

6	Aesthetic issues—monotony	Aesthetics, identity	Developers haven't been daring about mixing housing styles	Clusters of similar housing units and village design themes criticized as monotonous	More variety in housing than Irvine, even with comparable percentage of detached houses	Like Columbia

(continued)

TABLE 13 *(continued)*

Criticisms/Benefits of Suburban Growth	General Comments	Irvine, CA[a]	Columbia, MD[b]	The Woodlands, TX[b]
Features and Effects	Dimensions			
URBAN DESIGN				
Effects of Growth				
7 Reliance on filtering for low-income housing[c]	Social equity, diversity, access			
	Each made some attempt at low-cost housing: 5–6% of units delivered through affordable-housing programs; subsidized housing is of high design standard	City of Irvine has 6% units in government affordable-housing programs: 3,233 total units (only 717 federally subsidized); new housing started at $144,000 in 2000	Around 5% (1,800 units) subsidized, 1,498 federally; much subsidized housing clustered near village centers, making it more visible; new housing started at $108,000 in 2000	Low-income housing a criterion for HUD Title VII; over 1,000 federally subsidized units in 1998; new housing started at $108,000 in 2000
8 Social, economic, civic, cultural (arts) isolation/ inequality within region	Social equity, diversity, access			
	Each worked hard to attract such facilities/ opportunities; good school systems	Has UC Irvine, with many cultural facilities and Irvine Spectrum entertainment complex	Has music pavilion and African American history museum	Has music pavilion and extensive public art program

9	Lack of locations for public or community activities and interaction	Social equity, diversity, access	Has been an interest for all; while imperfect, all have some strengths; some facilities require resident association membership	Municipalities provide typical civic centers, open spaces; Irvine Company provides shopping areas, builds some parks; also funds events (e.g., Halloween costume competitions)	A strength: village centers have shops mixed with community facilities; have had to be redesigned, but basic concept is good; interfaith centers rather than separate facilities for each congregation	Schools used for community activities; resident association provides extensive park system with innovative recreational facilities for people of all ages
10	Disinvestment in historic commercial areas	Social equity, diversity, access Efficiency, costs	Historic commercial areas nearby have not declined	Nearby Newport Beach and Laguna Beach have boomed	Ellicott City (nearby county seat) has redeveloped	No real signs of change in seat, Conroe
11	Lack of useable, designed, accessible open space	Social equity, diversity, access Environmental issues	Extensive path/recreation/open space systems designed for variety of uses; see also item 9	Of 11 villages studied by Irvine Company, park/open space varied from 17–50% of land area	Columbia Association maintains wide array of indoor and outdoor recreation facilities	Over 100 miles of trails and walkways; very comprehensive park system
12	Isolation of those without cars	Social equity, diversity, access Efficiency, costs	Has been a difficult issue	Has Amtrak, county bus system, well-developed biking community	Planned bus system failed, although there is county service	Sole transit is well-used commuter bus to Houston

(continued)

TABLE 13 (*continued*)

Criticisms/Benefits of Suburban Growth	Dimensions	General Comments	Irvine, CA[a]	Columbia, MD[b]	The Woodlands, TX[b]
Features and Effects					

URBAN DESIGN

Effects of Growth

13 Automobile dependence due to density and overall urban structure	Social equity, diversity, access Efficiency, costs Environmental issues	All were automobile based; located/developed because of existing/proposed interstates In 1990, 78–82% of commuters drove alone; by 2000, 78–81%; see also item 12	Potential for transit/nonmotorized transportation because of high job density In 1990, 82% of commuters drove alone (compared with 72% in CA), and 9% drove in carpools; by 2000, 79% drove alone	Path system circuitous, designed for recreation and schoolchildren In 1990, 80% of commuters drove alone (compared with 70% in MD), and 12% drove in carpools; by 2000, 81% drove alone	Like Irvine, has fairly good path system along major roads In 1990, 78% of commuters drove alone (compared with 76% in TX), and 12% drove in carpools; in 2000, 78% still drove alone
14 Long commute times for journey to work and other trips	Efficiency, costs Environmental issues	All have attempted jobs-housing balance; see employment figures in table 9 and item 13 above	Jobs-housing ratio in late 1990s: 3.1:1 In 1990, 37% of residents worked in City of Irvine (compared with 17% in CA); by 2000, 39%	Jobs-housing ratio in late 1990s: 2.0:1 In 1990, 27% of residents worked in CDP (compared with 19% in MD); by 2000, 26%	Jobs-housing ratio in late 1990s: 1.2:1 In 1990, 5% of residents worked in CDP (compared with 49% in TX); by 2000, 31%

				Typical municipal	Columbia Association	Resident association
15	Lower levels of neighboring, civic involvement, etc.	Social equity, diversity, access	Unclear if new towns do better than elsewhere	Typical municipal boards, committees, councils	Columbia Association has active village and town-wide boards	Resident association has many boards but is in earlier stage of development
16	Large amounts of private space, both indoor and outdoor		All trade some private space for common areas yet have much private space	See general comment to left	See general comment to left	See general comment to left
17	High levels of individual mobility (transportation)		New communities unlikely to be worse than generic sprawl; may give some extra options (e.g., bike paths)	See general comment to left	See general comment to left	See general comment to left
18	Good fit with cultural perceptions: home, success, etc.		Each uses "home-town" imagery in marketing	See general comment to left	See general comment to left	See general comment to left

ENVIRONMENT

Features of Growth

				Typical municipal	Columbia Association	Resident association
19	Unlimited outward extension	Density Efficiency, costs	Developments re-shape expansion but do not stop growth; see item 5	Much attached housing and relatively compact suburban form	Much attached housing and relatively compact suburban form	The lowest density
20	Lack of consideration of natural habitat	Environmental issues	Increasing issue	Approximately 44,000 acres in habitat protection, not part of initial plan	Focus on parks more than habitat; early protection of river and stream areas	Extensive ecological surveys before planning; focus mostly on hydrology

(continued)

TABLE 13 (continued)

Features and Effects	Criticisms/Benefits of Suburban Growth	Dimensions	General Comments	Irvine, CA[a]	Columbia, MD[b]	The Woodlands, TX[b]
ENVIRONMENT						
Effects of Growth						
21	Loss of agricultural land, open space, vegetation, habitat	Environmental issues	Open space lost, but each development protected it more than typical subdivisions did	Protected large areas of coastal sage scrub; see item 20	Protected rural atmosphere	Maintained forest; research park and shopping areas hidden by wide forest buffers. Declining value?
22	High energy use/ waste production	Efficiency, costs Environmental issues	Developments may have few advantages; see exceptions listed to right	High percentage of attached houses and people who work in place of residence may have some benefits	Like Irvine	Early concern for microclimate in house siting
23	Water quality problems: erosion, runoff	Environmental issues	All paid some attention	Source of some conflict with EPA	Protected streams, which has had benefits	Clear strength— aimed for zero runoff
24	High water consumption	Efficiency, costs Environmental issues	Similar to generic development	Innovative water recycling program	Information unavailable	Information unavailable

25	Air quality problems from automobile use	Environmental issues	Work trips mostly by car; would be useful to examine nonwork trips; see item 13	See general comment to left	See general comment to left	See general comment to left
26	Spaciousness and closeness to nature		All use design to create this sense	Formal, modernist plantings; habitat protection areas	Rural and forested character	Wooded aesthetic complete with understory

COORDINATION

Features of Growth

27	Leapfrog development	Efficiency, costs	All were phased; only The Woodlands seems to have been phased very sequentially; superficial fragmentation masks underlying logic	Irvine Company forced into developing on multiple fronts because it earlier had sold central valley land to landowners who wanted to develop	Very discontinuous landholding with many outparcels; development was and is a patchwork	Seems to avoid appearance of leapfrog
28	Land uses not coordinated with (existing) infrastructure	Efficiency, costs	Coordination highly valued, although as fast-growing developments, all have had some lagging infrastructure	See general comment to left	See general comment to left	See general comment to left

(continued)

TABLE 13 (*continued*)

Criticisms/Benefits of Suburban Growth	Dimensions	General Comments	Irvine, CA[a]	Columbia, MD[b]	The Woodlands, TX[b]
Features and Effects					
COORDINATION					
Features of Growth					
29 Fragmented land use control	Social equity, diversity, access Efficiency, costs	Strong companies worked around fragmentation issue	County and seven local governments have control—often new areas approved by county, then annexed	County has approval authority	Subdivision approval only required, by City of Houston; coordinated with other government agencies
Effects of Growth					
30 Expensive or delayed infrastructure	Social equity, diversity, access Efficiency, costs	Inefficiency and delays avoided, but infrastructure still expensive because of high amenity levels and early provision	See general comment to left	See general comment to left	More isolated development, so delays greater issue

31	Variation in local fiscal capacity (affecting education, public services)	Social equity, diversity, access Efficiency, costs	Complex issue; in each new community, residents expect high service levels, but large employment areas also supply tax dollars	Because Irvine is incorporated, it hasn't avoided problem of variations in local fiscal capacity at regional level	County benefits from taxes; added parks and recreation paid for through separate fee, part of early agreement with county to limit costs of development	In extraterritorial jurisdiction of Houston, as George Mitchell wanted it to contribute taxes to city
32	Slow emergency-service response times	Social equity, diversity, access	Developments all dense enough for this criticism to be less relevant	See general comment to left	See general comment to left	See general comment to left
33	Less expensive housing due to lower land costs		All competing successfully with unplanned sprawl; see item 7	See general comment to left	See general comment to left	See general comment to left
34	Choice among municipalities providing different bundles of services		New communities add to choice, as they do not make up whole housing market in their regions	Large, but areas within development have different service bundles; falls in multiple municipalities	Urban center for Howard County, providing an option previously unavailable	This and other master-planned communities in Houston region (which does not have zoning) provide planned alternative

SOURCES: Bloom 2001a, 173; City of Irvine 2000, 2002; Irvine Company 2000a, 2000b, 2002a; Rouse Company 1999; TWOC 2000a, 2000b, 2001; U.S. Census 1990, 2000; U.S. HUD 1998.

[a] Census data for Irvine are for the City of Irvine only.

[b] Data for Columbia and The Woodlands are from the CDP. (See notes to table 9 for explanation of relationship between these new communities and their census-designated places.)

[c] Sources for entries in this row are Bloom 2001; Irvine Company 2000; Rouse Company 1999; and U.S. HUD 1998.

Densities of Typical Residential Villages in Irvine and The Woodlands

TABLE 14

Village Name	Total Dwellings	Population	Residential Acres	Parks and Open Space	Public Open Space Only	Roads	Total Acres in Village	Persons per Acre	Persons per Residential Acre	Dwellings per Acre	Dwellings per Residential Acre	Dwellings per Acre Excluding Open Space	% Open Space
Irvine													
East Bluff	1,988	5,785	200	253	253	101	632	9.2	28.9	3.1	9.9	5.2	40
Spyglass Hill	2,933	8,605	498	257	253	206	1,018	8.5	17.3	2.9	5.9	3.9	25
Northpark	2,600	5,000	188	80	65	94	392	12.8	26.6	6.6	13.8	8.3	20
Northwood	9,439	22,055	874	239	192	479	1,747	12.6	25.2	5.4	10.8	6.3	14
Oak Creek	3,104	7,800	162	159	152	108	488	16.0	48.1	6.4	19.2	9.4	33
Westpark	7,983	19,521	560	308	275	240	1,226	15.9	34.9	6.5	14.3	8.7	25
Woodbridge	9,292	26,036	844	422	340	316	1,786	14.6	30.8	5.2	11.0	6.8	24
Rancho San Joaquin	1,735	3,962	118	178	169	46	377	10.5	33.6	4.6	14.7	8.7	47
University Park	2,739	7,362	246	147	79	170	630	11.7	29.9	4.3	11.1	5.7	23
Turtle Rock	3,850	9,625	637	866	828	227	1,868	5.2	15.1	2.1	6.0	3.8	46
University Town Center	2,409	5,297	141	140	140	43	358	14.8	37.6	6.7	17.1	11.1	39
FOR ALL VILLAGES	48,072	121,048	4,468	3,049	2,746	2,030	10,522	11.5	27.1	4.6	10.8	6.4	29
The Woodlands[a]													
Grogan's Mill	6,125	13,300	1,546	752	—	983	4,032	3.3	8.6	1.5	4.0	1.9	19
Panther Creek	5,585	12,830	1,125	4	—	743	2,070	6.2	11.4	2.7	5.0	2.7	0
Cochran's Crossing	5,425	15,610	1,657	335	—	964	3,361	4.6	9.4	1.6	3.3	1.8	10
Alden Bridge	9,091	20,230	1,579	658	—	902	3,575	5.6	12.8	2.5	5.8	3.1	18
Sterling Ridge	5,668	—	1,558	246	—	1,035	3,635	—	—	1.6	3.6	1.7	7

(continued)

TABLE 14 (continued)

Village Name	Total Dwellings	Population	Residential Acres	Parks and Open Space	Public Open Space Only	Roads	Total Acres in Village	Persons per Acre	Persons per Residential Acre	Dwellings per Acre	Dwellings per Residential Acre	Dwellings per Acre Excluding Open Space	% Open Space
The Woodlands[a]													
Indian Springs	2,357	6,700	864	566	—	378	1,879	3.6	7.8	1.3	2.7	1.8	30
Village 7	5,639	—	1,318	1,144	—	513	3,990	—	—	1.4	4.3	2.0	29
Town Center	2,153	—	—	14	—	273	835	—	—	2.6	—	2.6	2
Total for 5 close to buildout	28,583	68,670	6,770	2,315	—	3,970	14,916	4.6	10.1	1.9	4.2	2.3	16
TOTAL	42,043		9,646	3,719	—	5,790	23,376	—	—	1.8	4.4	2.1	16

SOURCES: Irvine Company 2001a; TWOC 2000a, 2001.

[a] Figures for The Woodlands are at buildout except figures for villages, which are 2004 estimates for population. These are similar to current figures except for Sterling Ridge, still under construction at the time of writing. The development also includes the Research Forest.

NOTES

CHAPTER 1. THE NEW COMMUNITY EXPERIMENT

1. Weiss (1973, 6–8) cites an increase from 53 proposed new communities in 1968 to 151 in 1972, although only 28 of these had a population of five thousand or more as of the beginning of 1972. Ewing (1991) counted 58 new communities that were established after 1960 and large enough to be studied in the late 1980s. More have since opened.

2. This discussion of private planning relates to more general histories of suburbia such as Fishman 1987, Hayden 2003, and Jackson 1985.

3. For histories of the ranch, see chapter 2 and Bloom 2001b, Cleland 1962, Cameron 1979, Griffin 1974, and Hellis 1992.

4. The 1970 general plan prepared by the company proposed 430,000 people on fifty-three thousand acres, but because of its focus on the central part of the ranch, it omitted the coastal development between Laguna Beach and Newport Beach that had been part of the 1964 southern sector plan (Irvine Company 1970c).

5. In the first draft of the book, I used the term *Irvine* to indicate the entire ranch, but because this was very confusing for residents of the city, I adopted the approach of specifying each geography.

6. These diagrams are now located in the marketing department of the Irvine Company.

7. The top development in 2000 for home sales was Summerlin, near Las Vegas, a Rouse Company–owned new town started in the 1990s; Columbia's residential areas are almost completely built out (Lesser 2002).

8. A policy of desegregation was in place since May 1956, but actual implementation was slow (Ephross 1988).

9. For histories of Columbia, see chapter 3 and Hoppenfeld 1971, Breckenfeld 1971, Tennenbaum 1996a, and Bloom 2001b.

10. Several other new towns were close runners-up in terms of becoming case studies, but they were rejected for this study because either their final populations will be well under one hundred thousand or they were biased toward either jobs or housing, undermining the potential for comprehensiveness. Others had departed significantly from their initial plans, generally because of major financial problems. Developments considered included Clear Lake City, First Colony, and Las Colinas in Texas; Peachtree City, Georgia; Reston, Virginia; and Valencia and Westlake Village in California.

11. Finley later transferred to city planning.

12. There were a number of additional links. For example, Watson and Rouse had been part of a small group of developers who worked on the Ford Foundation–funded community development project starting in 1964 (Eichler and Kaplan 1967, x–xi, xiii).

13. Garreau's (1991, 6–7) criteria for an edge city include five million square feet of office space, six hundred thousand square feet of leasable retail space, more jobs than bedrooms, and a settlement that is perceived as one place with a name but as recently as thirty years ago was composed of farms or residential suburbs. Geographers Hartshorn and Muller (1992, 151) have tougher criteria for what they call a suburban downtown, with five million square feet of office space, a one-million-square-foot regional shopping center, fifty thousand or more employees, three or more high-rise office buildings, at least one Fortune 1000 headquarters or regional headquarters, and two or more major chain hotels with four hundred or more rooms in each. See also chapter 5.

14. This cost does not include the cost of interest on borrowing to build the tunnel, but my rough estimate of the value of the Irvine Ranch does not either.

15. After resigning, Nixon then moved back to San Clemente, Orange County, until relocating to New York in 1980 (Nixon Foundation 2001).

16. My thanks to Glen Worthington, from the City of Irvine, for pointing this out. This process has meant that TIC has had to deal with local government reviews but has benefited in terms of land values from the prestige of city, rather than county, addresses.

17. The Rouse Company is no longer in the mortgage business, and Rouse is no longer living.

18. Rouse and Mitchell seemed to have tolerated considerable conflict within their companies and, in different ways, expected things to turn out for the best.

19. Thanks to Scott Bollens and Glen Worthington for clarifying this for me.

20. Detached houses generally use more energy than attached ones.

21. Thanks to Guy Stuart and Glen Worthington for their stimulating comments on this quote from Rouse.

22. From the late 1920s until the late 1950s, CIAM was a central forum for modernists.

23. Two additional communities—Roosevelt Island and Lysander, both in New York State—received determination of grant eligibility rather than a federal debt guarantee.

24. Work by Lansing et al. (1970) was one of the earliest studies to distinguish between different levels of planning.

25. The fourth form of power that is customarily discussed—that of military power

or state violence—is not much used in such new community development, at least in the United States (Mann 1986).

26. Allison and Zelikow (1999) have come up with typology focusing on three types of analysis in a review of theories of political decision making.

27. The work on innovative milieus comes from planning history; the work on framing and attention shaping, from planning theory. The two have not been explicitly linked but obviously could be.

28. For comparison, Popenoe's study of social life in Sweden's Vallingby and in Levittown, Pennsylvania, was based on secondary sources, "weeks" of observations, fifty interviews with households (119 people), forty interviews with other informants, and fifteen additional interviews in Sweden about general housing and urban policy issues (Popenoe 1977, 19–20).

29. For The Woodlands, eighteen relevant interviews were found in Kutchin 1998a. For Columbia, seven relevant interviews were found in Olsen 2000. There was one relevant oral history for the Irvine Ranch (Hellis 1992).

30. Because of involvement in multiple projects, of the thirty-five people who read the draft, thirteen knew about the Irvine Ranch; thirteen, about The Woodlands; and fifteen, about Columbia.

31. More specifically, I asked people for a history of their involvement in the new communities, their assessments of their successes and problems, how they would change the developments, where the developments were headed, why people lived there, the impacts of government, the likely effects of changing technologies, and some questions about their concepts of the good city.

32. Thanks to research assistant Robert Gilmore for his cheerful work on the mapping part of this project.

CHAPTER 2. THE IRVINE RANCH

1. Histories or case studies of Irvine include a comparative social history by Bloom (2001b); a planning and development history by Schiesl (1991); a very comprehensive architectural history dissertation by Kane (1996); a comparative planning dissertation by Nishimaki (2001); an extended essay on the architecture of the development by Rocca (1996); the account of a former public relations director at the Irvine Company from 1973 to 1985 by Brower (1994); an urban land institute publication by Griffin (1974); and a work focused on the agricultural period by Cleland (1962). A popular picture-book history is also available (Liebeck and Malone 1990). The Irvine Company and its employees also produced a number of histories (Cameron 1976, 1979; Irvine Company 1965). UC Irvine and its staff produced some accounts of the ranch's development (e.g., UC Irvine 1970; Moffitt 1967). It is of course mentioned in a number of other books and articles, including Eichler and Kaplan's (1967) study of community builders, Campbell's (1976) more journalistic account of new towns, a study of growth politics by Pincetl (1999), and a history of UC Irvine (McCulloch 1996).

2. Bren did not actually own 100 percent of the company until 1996, when he bought out the last shareholder (Irvine Company 2002d).

3. A number of legal decisions up to the level of the U.S. Supreme Court (*United States v. Flint* [1878]) and opinions by the U.S. attorney general in the 1920s val-

idated the ownership of the parcels that had been established in 1851 (Cleland 1962, 128–31).

4. Joan Irvine also went by her married names (Burt and Smith) at times, which various sources show, but to avoid potential confusion I've used her maiden name throughout.

5. The foundation, still owning a majority share of the company, elected Loyall McLaren as president, separating the roles of foundation and company president (Brower 1994, 11–13).

6. McFadden had been fishing with James Irvine II at the time of his death in 1947, a circumstance that prompted accusations of foul play from Joan Irvine.

7. The dissertation by Kane (1996) provides an excellent and very detailed history of the planning of the ranch. My emphasis has been on those issues relevant to the debates about urban sprawl.

8. Five of the UC Irvine quadrangles were for academic areas, such as engineering, and one was for shared facilities, such as central administration and the library.

9. While I cite the plan as being by William Pereira Associates, the 1964 southern sector plan was really an Irvine Company interpretation of the WPA work.

10. Pereira was still present at meetings at which a larger development was discussed, although he was working with the university by then (Minutes of the meeting . . . 1968).

11. A close reading of the 1964 and 1970 plans shows over thirty-two thousand acres were in the central sector and another thirty-four thousand acres were in the southern sector. The central sector and part of the southern sector would be in the City of Irvine (fifty-three thousand acres); the rest of the southern sector would be split between Newport Beach and Laguna Beach.

12. For example, an internal Irvine Company memo to Vice President Ray Watson and the chief of planning Richard (Dick) Reese on January 5, 1967, discussed options for and the detailed process of incorporation. They estimated this process would take nine to ten months (Haworth 1967, 7). At that time the key issue was finding "enough qualified signers within the new city boundaries" to sign the notice of intention; they needed twenty-five to fifty signatures (Haworth 1967, 1–3). The process involved providing notice of intention, approval by the Orange County Local Agency Formation Commission (LAFCO), circulation and filing of a petition with the County Board of Supervisors, a hearing by the board, and then elections. In the actual petition to incorporate, 25 percent of owners needed to sign (Haworth 1967, 5). The rule was that qualified signers needed to own land within the boundaries of the city. However, because of the Irvine Company's policy to lease land rather than sell it, there were only twelve business landowners (counting the Irvine Company, and the Irvine Industrial Complex) and eleven governmental landowners in the area (Haworth 1967, 8–9). The Irvine Company needed a legal opinion about lessees signing. The company continued to examine the incorporation issue through a number of studies (e.g., Bollens 1969).

13. The quote in this section's heading is from Irvine Company materials (Irvine Company 1970b, 20).

14. The lack of a downtown is a frequently mentioned issue with Irvine. If the civic

center had remained close to the university and mixed in with shops, as was initially proposed in the 1960 and 1964 plans, there may have been something of this feel, but only in that one area.

15. Lynch was the author of a number of books over a twenty-year period. After his early work on the *Image of the City,* he went on to change his ideas about the important issues in development, focusing on a more general theory and a number of performance dimensions: vitality or the support of biological functions of humans, sense related to legibility and culture, fit for human activities, access, control by users, and the "meta-criteria" of efficiency and justice (Lynch 1981, 118).

16. Along with Jacobs's *Death and Life of Great American Cities* (1961) and Cullen's *Townscape* (1961), Lynch's *Image of the City* (1960) helped reorient the field of urban design away from architecture toward perception and experience.

17. Elsewhere, TIC lists its planning principles for a village as distinctive character and identity, distinguished edges and entries, village centers, pedestrian orientation, distinctive neighborhoods, and organized neighborhoods (Irvine Company 2002b).

18. By 1983 Ray Watson was on the Irvine Company board, though in his capacity as chairman of the board of Walt Disney Productions (Irvine Company 1983).

19. Also important, but harder for the general public to grasp, is "the exclusion of homeowners' implicit rental income from taxable income" (Carliner 1998, 301).

20. Table 3 presents summary figures for Orange County and the City of Irvine from 1987 and 1996, both in 1996 dollars—using the earliest and latest years from a helpful summary provided by the U.S. Census and compiled by Oregon State University. Because the other two developments are not incorporated, it was not possible to get similar figures about federal funds. Of course, the City of Irvine is only part of the overall ranch, so even these figures are approximate.

21. Markusen explains its effects: "Military budgets have run at about five to seven percent of American GNP over the entire postwar period. Particularly in the 1950s this investment was heavily shifted toward areas of the country that had not up to and even during World War II been prominent" (Markusen 1989, 10–11).

22. Several new communities have been built for defense purposes, including Los Alamos in New Mexico, Oak Ridge in Tennessee (Hales 1997), and Clear Lake City, a suburban area near NASA's Johnson Space Center in Houston.

23. This acreage did not include UC Irvine, the freeways, or the El Toro air station.

24. The 1997 Economic Census estimated 127,605 jobs in the City of Irvine in 1997, but at the place level the data for a number of industries are not released, so the actual number would have been higher.

25. The 1990 category is Asian and Pacific Islanders; in 2000, Asian alone or in combination.

26. My thanks to Frank Hotchkiss for comments on this issue.

CHAPTER 3. COLUMBIA

1. Histories and assessments of Columbia are numerous and include a journalistic account by Breckenfeld (1971), an evaluation in terms of garden city prin-

ciples (Christensen 1986), a comparative social history (Bloom 2001b), and memoirs or analyses of those involved in its early planning (Tennenbaum 1996a; Ivins 1976). Unpublished studies include a paper by Schuman and Sclar (n.d.) assessing the new town from an architectural and planning perspective, and a study on the interfaith experiment in process by Kaboolian and Nelson (n.d.).

2. Its president was Leo Molinaro (Rouse Company 1970, 36).

3. A number of works have examined Rouse's biography, including a master's thesis by Olsen (2000), an assessment by Gillette (1999), and an account in Breckenfeld (1971). Olsen and historian Bloom are currently working on biographies of Rouse.

4. While she does not appear to have been involved in the formal planning, Libby Rouse is mentioned as hosting a number of social events and going on trips to visit new towns. As of 2002 she was writing her memoirs.

5. The interest rate was 8 percent.

6. My thanks to Len Ivins for this comment.

7. See other accounts of the work group in CRD 1963b, Michael 1996, and Breckenfeld 1971, 251–52.

8. This history was never completed, although Breckenfeld's *Columbia and the New Cities* (1971) drew extensively on this material (see also Hamilton 1964l).

9. The group met six times (CRD 1964a; CRD 1964e, 2).

10. The issue of social mix in many new towns outside the United States is different—that of mixing middle-income people into predominantly low-cost and social housing developments (e.g., Peel 1995).

11. Only three of the village centers are linear designs—Dorsey's Search, Oakland Mills, and River Hill. The others all have more complex layouts.

12. The Columbia Association has not always been in this town center site, but moved to its current headquarters in 1992 (Kennedy 1998, 6).

13. Some original diagrams are still available at the Columbia Archives.

14. McHarg was also associated with the Space Cadets group, brought together by Len Duhl of the NIMH, having one of the articles published in their collection, *The Urban Condition* (Duhl 1963; McHarg 1963). Thanks to Jim Wannemaker and Uri Avin, who both mentioned Wallace-McHarg's *Plan for the Valleys* to me.

15. McHarg invited Sears to speak at Penn in 1959 (McHarg 1996, 167).

16. Zoning categories are not consistently defined across jurisdictions but are often specified in terms of numbers and letters. Residential zoning might be R1 for the lowest density and R2 for slightly denser areas, and so forth. M1, M2, and M3 generally indicate different intensities of manufacturing uses.

17. The county also engaged in its own planning, producing *Howard County 1985* (Howard County Planning Commission 1967).

18. Rouse managed to avoid direct liability for the $50 million loan (Rouse Company 1970; Breckenfeld 1971, 308).

19. One problem was that the Columbia team was responsible only for residential sales at first, with other parts of the Rouse Company involved in other development types.

20. Columbia's homebuilding had some notable effects—Ryland Homes built its first homes in Columbia and went on to build nationwide (Ditch 1996).

21. Thanks to Len Ivins for this insight.

22. Geis's study on bird populations found a decline in field and woods birds and a rise in urban birds during the first few years of Columbia's development (Geis 1974).

23. On social planning, governance, and community facilities, see Appletree 1978, Ben-Zadok 1980, Ford 1975, and Roch 1982.

24. Their wider study involved ten communities that represented different levels of planning and different locations in the urban fabric, including Reston and Radburn. All residents in their study lived in single-family homes—detached or attached (townhouses). All were the household "head or wife of the head," with the exact person randomly determined; 97 percent were homeowners rather than renters; 93 percent were married (Lansing et al. 1970, iv, 20, 24). The study found not much of a preference for modern architecture, not surprising given that people with that preference could have chosen other developments.

25. This work was partly the result of sophisticated residential land sales (under Malcolm Sherman) and sophisticated marketing (under Scott Ditch) (Ditch 1996; Sherman 1996).

26. For such studies of the importance of social ties, such as kinship and common interests, see Young and Willmott 1957, and Keller 1968.

27. Up to 1950 the ethics code of the National Association of Real Estate Boards prohibited brokers from introducing races into an area if their presence would decrease property values (Gelfand 1975). Other procedures were biased toward new construction over renovation and toward homeownership over rental housing (Gelfand 1975, 217, 220; Nivola 1999, 22).

28. There are, however, a large number of civic groups in Columbia. One particularly interesting group was the Columbia Forum, which in 1992 prepared "An Agenda for Columbia," a citizen-initiated vision document.

29. The source for these dates is land use maps kept by the Rouse Company. In regard to the major changes in the late 1970s, the date on the map is not legible but appears to be 1978.

CHAPTER 4. THE WOODLANDS

1. Histories of The Woodlands include a planning history by Morgan and King (1987), a collection of oral histories edited by Kutchin (1998a), and a popular history edited by Malone (1985). Some accounts of its architecture and landscape architecture also include histories of its development (e.g., Ingersoll 1994; and McHarg 1998, chapter 19). Claus 1994 is an unpublished critique.

2. According to James McAlister (2000), who was the Mitchell Corporation's director of real estate at the time, Cerf Ross actually told Mitchell about the HUD program.

3. A figure of $250,000 in 1970 dollars is $866,000 in 2000 dollars. As of 1973, fifteen new towns had been approved by HUD (two of these for reduced support), and twenty more were completing applications (Mields 1973, 80).

4. For the planning and design elements of the project, a number of people were mentioned, and participants had different memories of who had the largest roles,

but reports of the period mention such key WMRT staff as Narendra Juneja, Colin Franklin, and Leslie Sauer. Also on the project were Mokun Lokhande, Anne Spirn, Jonathan Sutton, and James Veltman, who later joined The Woodlands' staff (WMRT 1974b, n.p.). Mihran Nalbandian was an important figure in the area of hydrology. Of course, the reason I can list these names is that WMRT left an unusually long paper trail. With others, Sauer and Franklin eventually formed the distinguished landscape architecture firm Andropogon. Spirn became a faculty member at Harvard, the University of Pennsylvania, and later MIT. McHarg also credits Carol Franklin and Rolf Sauer with important roles in the project (McHarg 1996, 259).

5. The office of Wallace Roberts and Todd in Philadelphia could not locate a copy of the early study. The copy that I saw came from the collection of James McAlister Sr., who had worked on land assembly and economic feasibility in the early part of the project. In contrast, the volumes from 1973 and 1974 are in numerous libraries and collections.

6. In August 1974, the university purchased the former South Texas Junior College in downtown Houston, which had come up for sale, essentially replacing The Woodlands site. While the formal decision not to go ahead with The Woodlands was not made until 1977, by which time there were considerable concerns about the costs of higher education in Texas, this disrupted The Woodlands' trajectory (Morgan and King 1987, 96–97).

7. However, The Woodlands Development Corporation tried to negotiate a settlement wherein The Woodlands' land in Shenandoah would be deannexed and placed in Houston's extraterritorial jurisdiction in return for a number of services such as water, sewer, fire, and police. In 1975 such a compromise was reached (Morgan and King 1987, 94).

8. Espy, Houston and Associates developed a computer model to design retention ponds; Turner, Collie and Braden did overall engineering of the natural drainage system (Hydrological balancing act 1974, 394).

9. Unfortunately, these documents were not filed with the project agreements in the National Archives.

10. There were numerous papers, including a number in Box 18, NN3–207, 99–002.

11. These issues were discussed internally in the Mitchell Corporation (McAlister 1971, September 2 memo).

12. Romney was secretary of HUD from 1968 to 1972.

13. Richmond had been with Coopers Lybrand while working on the Columbia project (Richmond 1998, 270).

14. Obviously, there were few registered voters to create such petitions in an entirely new development, and so a series of townhouses was built and eleven were sold, mostly to employees of the corporation, who moved in starting January 31, 1974; in March they approved a $20.75 million bond issue (Morgan and King 1987, 59, 61).

15. For 1977, such infrastructure was projected to have a cash flow deficit of $766,000, given the small assessable base (ULI 1976, 57).

16. The Woodlands Community Service Corporation surveyed residents of houses

by phone in February 1999 (575 respondents) and October 2000 (634 respondents) (Creative Consumer Research 1999, 2000). This survey is described further in chapter 6, but included residents of houses only.

17. Former Woodlands engineer Plato Pappas also mentioned these environmental innovations in his 2001 interview with me.

18. Lynne Aldrich also recounted a similar history of recycling in a 2002 interview.

CHAPTER 5. ORGANIZING THE METROPOLIS

1. This issue of framing is dealt with in more depth in my own earlier work on suburban development "perspectives" (Forsyth 1999), as well as analyses of "frames" by Schon and Rein (1994) and planning doctrines by Faludi and van der Valk (1994).

2. These concepts of edge cities and suburban downtowns are more useful in this study than the related idea of the "boomburb" or fast-growing suburban city, because the boomburb is an incorporated city of over one hundred thousand in population (Lang and Simmons 2001). This privileges accidents of incorporation and political boundaries, while the suburban downtown idea focuses on the function of a place regardless of its political geography.

3. These bureaucracies failed to coordinate with other federal programs, including urban renewal, created in the 1949 and 1954 federal housing acts. They even ignored the 1960 directive by President Eisenhower that the focus of road building should be on nonurban areas and that the "amelioration of the rush-hour traffic mess was not to be considered a function of the Interstate System" (see also Gelfand 1975, 230). However, the car certainly demanded attention; by 1955 two-thirds of households had an automobile, and transit was in deep decline (Gelfand 1975, 231).

4. Lynch (1981) focuses on designed urban forms, but more incremental and generic urban forms are also important.

5. This led many British new towns of the 1960s to reject the neighborhood unit, instead building more densely and emphasizing access to the town center. However, by the 1970s there was a return to neighborhood units, now smaller at around four thousand to five thousand people and focused on an elementary school catchment, as well as a return to the idea of social balance or social mix (Thorns 1976, 86). However, in an evaluation of the idea of community, Thorns proposed that these changes reflected the ideas of planners rather than the preferences of future residents (Thorns 1976, 86).

6. In some older villages, such as East Bluffs, the center is toward the geographic middle of the village; in the very large village of Woodbridge, the center is in the middle, which can also be interpreted as being on the edge of two major halves.

7. Not everyone involved with Columbia's planning thought the bus system would be used much. Among the skeptics was James Rouse (Hamilton 1964c, 4). However, the issue was studied intensively (e.g., Voorhees and Associates 1964).

8. Variation on this linear organization occurs in villages that are strung along a

transportation corridor like a set of beads. This can be seen in the Swedish new town of Vallingby and its neighbors Blackeberg, Grimsta, Racksta, Hasselby Gard, and Hasselby Strand (Godschalk 1967, 376–83).

9. The exception involves the later buildings on the UC Irvine campus, where a series of high-profile architects, including Frank Gehry, Venturi Rauch and Scott Brown, and James Stirling, worked on signature buildings in the 1990s.

10. The advertisement also contained six photos of this family in place in Columbia, with a few column inches in a small font explaining the new city's benefits. The Rouse Company denied me permission to reprint this image.

11. Of course, a number of individual papers on feminism and the suburbs were published in the 1970s, but these were few in number. Some of the early 1980s works on women explicitly dealt with suburban areas (e.g., Popenoe 1980; Fava 1980). Subsequent scholarship has also examined women in new towns (e.g., Hintz 1989).

12. Irvine's survey was based on a random sample of 400 residents over eighteen years of age. These were residents of the City of Irvine, the core two-thirds of the Irvine Ranch. Columbia's survey was a stratified random survey of "slightly more than one thousand" residents of Columbia, with the sample drawn from an equal distribution of households among Columbia's villages. The Woodlands telephone surveys included interviews in February 1999 (575 respondents) and October 2000 (634 respondents) (Chesapeake Group Inc. 1998; Fairbank, Maslin, Maullin and Associates 2000; Creative Consumer Research 1999, 2000).

13. The document was not available at the source Bloom cited, the Columbia Archives, at the time that I visited it.

14. According to Baker (2000), five were white, one African American, and four Hispanic.

CHAPTER 6. ALTERNATIVES TO SPRAWL?

1. Burchell et al. 1998 and Ewing 1996 provide particularly useful reviews of problems and benefits. See also Arendt 1999; Beatley 2000; Calthorpe et al. 1991; Calthorpe 1993; Calthorpe and Fulton 2001; Duany et al. 2000; Esseks et al. 1999; Galster et al. 2000; Leccese and McCormick 2000; Newman and Kenworthy 2000; Southworth 1997; and Southworth and Owens 1993. Some work has been done to quantify effects. For instance, studies have been done on what densities are necessary to support public transportation and to lower infrastructure costs. However, many of the critiques of sprawl involve qualitative assessments.

2. Employment figures are frequently available only for cities and counties.

3. As previously noted, The Woodlands was not constructed at the time of the University of North Carolina study; interviews for that study were conducted in 1973.

4. The gating in Irvine has some fiscal advantages for the city, as roads and parks inside the gates are classed as private and not maintained by the city.

5. It is not possible to compare these findings to the two comparison new urbanist developments. In 2000, Kentlands was part of a tract, and only limited variables are available below the tract level. Stapleton was a proposal.

6. Burchell et al. (1999, 3) estimate that cost savings through compact develop-

ment would save only about 10 percent of infrastructure costs overall. Similarly, Peiser's analysis of costs of planned versus less-planned development, using the case of a seventy-five-hundred-acre site in Houston, found land development, social, and transportation cost savings of only 1 to 3 percent in planned versus unplanned development at the same density, considering within-site transportation and omitting analysis of "interior streets and utility costs for residential subdivisions" (Peiser 1984, 424).

7. Holding costs include the cost of the land or of the loan to buy the land; the costs of owning the land, such as property taxes; and the lost income from alternative investments.

8. Thanks to Uri Avin and Jim Wannemacher for this insight.

9. The 1997 Economic Census estimated 127,605 jobs in the City of Irvine in 1997, but at the place level, the data for a number of industries are not released, meaning the actual number would have been higher. This makes the 2002 figure of 168,000 plausible (City of Irvine 2002).

10. Lansing et al., in their 1969 interviews of 216 residents of Columbia, found that 65 percent of Columbia's residents went hiking or walking five or more times in the previous year—the surprise is that 35 percent did not do even this much walking (Lansing et al. 1970, 88). In addition, 21 percent went bicycling with the same frequency.

CHAPTER 7. NEW TOWN PLANNING
AND THE PARADOXES OF PRIVATE INNOVATION

1. A range of national policies and policy areas that have been in place for some decades has promoted growth, particularly support for transportation (especially highways) and incentives for private homeownership. However, a wider range of policies can also be seen as having promoted suburban growth: environmental regulations; siting of federal buildings and post offices; regulatory review mechanisms such as the National Endowment Policy Act; utility pricing; a relative lack of support for agriculture; and water and sewer regulations (General Accounting Office 1999; Nivola 1999). In addition, military policies that channeled contracts and activities to the Sun Belt, transferring a high level of economic activity and thus housing growth to areas such as Orange County (Irvine) and federal support for new communities (The Woodlands), directly affected these new communities. Works dealing with this issue include Burchell et al. 1998; Burchell et al. 1999; Checkoway 1980; Fishman 1999; Glickman 1980; Hanchett 1994; Markusen 1989; Nivola 1999; Popper 1988; Katz 2000; and Bloom 2001a.

2. There are many legal similarities between local governments and private corporations, in terms of functions such as borrowing, and this has been made extremely clear in new community development (Monkkonen 1988, xii; Frug 1999).

3. Thanks to Scott Bollens for articulating this view.

4. For example, the Rouse Company polled Howard County residents periodically (Sidney Hollander Associates 1965, 1970b).

5. Elsewhere I have defined "as public those spaces that strangers are expected to enter frequently, for at most a minimal fee, with a relatively low level of regula-

tion consistent with access for others, and that can give access to sociability, or political and economic opportunities, or public education (broadly defined)" (Forsyth 2000, 127).

6. Even very public debates occur in private spaces, as when someone composes a letter to the editor in the kitchen. That is not to say that the kind of casual interactions and broad sociability possible in truly public spaces—open to strangers at minimal cost and with few regulations—is unnecessary, but rather to argue that it is only one physical setting for only some forms of communication.

7. Community land trusts were developed in the 1960s by the founders of the Institute for Community Economics (ICE). In this model, the nonprofit land trust owns land under a home and leases it to a low-income resident. The resident owns his or her home, but limits are placed on the sale—it must be sold to another eligible buyer, and restrictions are imposed on the profit that can be taken from the sale (Institute for Community Economics 2003).

8. Irvine did have a highly public planning process in the 1970s, but with the exception of those living in some of the window areas, it was residents who had bought into the plan who participated in this process.

9. In my previous book, *Constructing Suburbs*, this was perhaps the dominant approach to defining the public interest, although people vehemently disagreed about the substance of the common good (Forsyth 1999).

REFERENCES

Agid, Ken. 1972. Consumer segmentation by life style characteristics—interim inter-office memorandum, The Irvine Company, November 9. Collection of Gerald Brock.

Alexander, Christopher. [1966] 1972. The city is not a tree. In *Human identity and the urban environment,* ed. Gwen Bell and Jacqueline Tyrwhitt. Harmondsworth: Pelican.

Allison, G., and P. Zelikow. 1999. *Essence of decision.* New York: Longman.

Alonso, William. [1970] 1977. The mirage of new towns. In *New towns and the sub-urban dream,* ed. Irving Allen. Port Washington, NY: Kennikat Press.

Altshuler, Alan, and David Luberoff. 2003. *Mega-projects: The changing politics of urban public investment.* Washington, DC: Brookings Institution Press.

Anderson, J. W. 1964. A brand new city for Maryland. *Harper's,* November, 99–106.

Apgar, Mahlon. 1971a. *Managing community development: The systems approach in Colum-bia, Maryland.* New York: McKinsey and Company.

———. 1971b. New business for new towns? *Harvard Business Review* 49 (1): 90–109.

Appletree, Roy. 1978. The political economy of a new town community association: Columbia, Maryland. PhD dissertation, Public Administration, University of Southern California.

Architectural Committee, The. 1970. *Columbia Today,* February/March, 8–15.

Arendt, Randall. 1999. *Growing greener.* Washington, DC: Island Press.

Ashley, Thomas. 1969. An approach to planning the central sector of the Irvine Ranch. Internal Irvine Company memorandum to planning department staff, May 1. UC Irvine, University Archives.

Aston, John. 2001. Ten years later. *Out Smart,* July. Retrieved from www.outsmart magazine.com/issue/io7–01/broussard.html.

Avin, Uri. 1993. Chewing the cud with a PUD: Lessons from Howard County and Columbia New Town. In *Proceedings of the institute on planning, zoning, and eminent domain,* ed. Carol Hogren. Philadelphia: Matthew Bender.

Baggett, Nancy. 1975. Columbia: Did the planning pay off? *Columbia Flier,* June, 14, 16–18. Columbia Archives.

Baker, Michael. 2000. Community divided by convicted killer's parole. *Texas Triangle.* Retrieved from www.txtriangle.com/archive/906/topstories.htm.

Banerjee, Tridib, and William Baer. 1984. *Beyond the neighborhood unit: Residential environments and public policy.* New York: Plenum Press.

Banzhaf, M. 1980. Letter to Carlyle Hall, Center for Law in the Public Interest, re *Orange County Fair Housing Council vs. The City of Irvine.* OC Super Ct #225824, July 11. UC Irvine, Orange County Collection.

Barton-Aschman Associates. 1971. Orange County, Santa Ana, and Irvine: Making the development of Irvine a countywide success. Prepared for the City of Santa Ana. UC Irvine, Orange County Collection.

Beatley, Timothy. 2000. *Green urbanism: Learning from European cities.* Washington, DC: Island Press.

Ben-Zadok, Efraim. 1980. Economic and racial integration in a new town. PhD dissertation, Philosophy, New York University.

Berger, Bennett. 1960. *Working class suburb.* Berkeley: University of California Press.

Best Cities. 2001. *Ladies' Home Journal.* Retrieved from www.lhj.com/lhj/category.jhtml ?categoryid=/templatedata/lhj/category/data/BestCities2001.xml.

———. 2002. *Ladies' Home Journal.* Retrieved from www.lhj.com/lhj/category.jhtml ?categoryid=/templatedata/lhj/category/data/BestCities2002.xml.

Blake, Peter. 1964. *God's own junkyard.* New York: Holt, Rinehart and Winston.

Bloom, Nicholas. 2001a. The federal Icarus: The public rejection of 1970s national suburban planning. *Journal of Urban History* 28 (1): 55–71.

———. 2001b. *Suburban alchemy: 1960s new towns and the transformation of the American dream.* Columbus: Ohio State University Press.

Bollens, John. 1969. Irvine central areas governmental study. Prepared for the Irvine Company, August. UC Irvine, Orange County Collection.

Booz, Allen, and Hamilton. 1976. Appendix: An assessment of the causes of current problems. In *New communities: Problems and potentials,* ed. US New Communities Administration. Washington, DC: US Department of Housing and Urban Development.

Brand, Joanna. 1991. Laguna Greenbelt archives. *Journal of Orange County Studies* 5/6: 42–48.

Breckenfeld, Gurney. 1971. *Columbia and the new cities.* New York: Washburn.

Brooks, Richard. 1971. Columbia, Maryland, a suburban middle income biracial community. In *New community development,* ed. S. Weiss, E. Kaiser, and R. Burby. New Towns Research Seminar series. Chapel Hill: Center for Urban and Regional Studies.

Brower, Martin. 1994. *The Irvine Ranch: A time for people.* Newport Beach: Orange County Report.

Browne, Richard. 1998. Interview by Joseph Kutchin, September 1996. In *How Mitchell Energy and Development Corp. got its start and how it grew: An oral history and narrative overview,* ed. Joseph Kutchin. Parkland, FL: Universal Publishers.

Burby, Raymond. 1976. *Recreation and leisure in new communities.* Cambridge, MA: Ballinger.

Burby, Raymond, and Shirley Weiss. 1976. *New communities USA.* Lexington, MA: Lexington Books.

Burchell, Robert, David Listokin, and Catherine Galley. 1999. Smart growth: More than a ghost of urban policy past, less than a bold new horizon. In *Legacy of the 1949 Housing Act: Past, present, and future of federal housing and urban policy,* ed. Fannie Mae Foundation. Washington, DC: Fannie Mae Foundation.

Burchell, Robert, N. Shad, D. Listokin, H. Phillips, A Downs, S. Seskin, et al. 1998. *The costs of sprawl revisited.* Transit Cooperative Research Program Report 39. Transportation Research Board, National Research Council. Washington, DC: National Academy Press.

Burkhart, Lynne. 1981. *Old values in a new town: The politics of race and class in Columbia, Maryland.* New York: Praeger.

Businessman in the news: The profits in building well. 1969. *Fortune* 80 (1): 40.

Cadiz, Laura. 2002. Suburban Columbia seeks an urban core. *Baltimore Sun,* May 26, 1B.

Calthorpe, Peter. 1993. *The next American metropolis.* New York: Princeton Architectural Press.

Calthorpe, Peter, and William Fulton. 2001. *The regional city: New urbanism and the end of sprawl.* Washington, DC: Island Press.

Calthorpe, Peter, Michael Corbett, Andres Duany, Elizabeth Plater-Zyberk, Stefanos Polyzoides, and Elizabeth Moule. 1991. Ahwahnee principles. Retrieved from www .lgc.org/ahwahnee/principles.htm. Sacramento: Local Government Commission.

Cameron, Donald. 1976. Innovations in design and planning methods of new communities: The Irvine experiment. In *Innovations for future cities,* ed. Gideon Golanyi. New York: Praeger.

———. 1979 (edited 1980). An overview of the Irvine Company general plan for the City of Irvine Staff. Duplicated. UC Irvine, Orange County Collection.

Campbell, Carlos. 1976. *New towns: Another way to live.* Reston: Reston Publishing Company.

Carliner, M. 1998. Development of federal homeownership "policy." *Housing Policy Debate* 9 (2): 299–321.

Celebration Corporation. 2001. *Celebration, Florida.* Retrieved from www.celebrationfl .com/press_room/faq07.html.

Cervero, Robert. 1995. Planned communities, self containment and commuting: A cross-national perspective. *Urban Studies* 32 (7): 1135–61.

Charles Luckman Associates. 1959. *University of California site selection study: A report on the search for new campus sites, Southern California metropolitan center section, south cross section.* March. Los Angeles: Charles Luckman Associates.

Chayes, Antonia. 1964. Draft memorandum for Columbia session of January 24–25. Collection of Herbert Gans.

Checkoway, Barry. 1980. Large builders, federal housing programmes, and postwar suburbanization. *International Journal of Urban and Regional Research* 4 (1): 21–45.

Chesapeake Group Inc. 1998. Survey of Columbia households: Executive summary. Prepared for the Columbia Association, November. Baltimore: The Chesapeake Group Inc. Columbia Association, Columbia Archives.

Christensen, Carol. 1986. *The American garden city and the new towns movement.* Ann Arbor: UMI Research Press.

Christensen, Karen. 1999. *Cities and complexity: Making intergovernmental decisions.* Thousand Oaks, CA: Sage.

City of Irvine. 1980. *City of Irvine general plan.* Irvine: City of Irvine.

———. 1999. *General plan comprehensive update.* Irvine: City of Irvine.

———. 2000. *City of Irvine annual traffic management report 1999–2000.* Retrieved from www.ci.irvine.ca.us/departments/public_works/TrffcMgmtRep.pdf.

———. 2002. *City of Irvine, demographics.* Retrieved from www.cityofirvine.org/about/demographics.asp.

———. 2003. The Orange County Great Park plan for the sale and development of the El Toro Marine Corps Air Station. Fact sheet. Retrieved from www.cityofirvine.org/pdfs/great_park_01–28–03/fact_sheets/great_park_fact_sheet.pdf.

Clapp, James. 1971. *New towns and urban policy: Planning metropolitan growth.* New York: Dunellen.

Clark, Michael. 1971. Boy, 3, is symbol of Columbia. *Baltimore Sun,* March 1.

Clark, S. D. 1966. *The suburban society.* Toronto: University of Toronto Press.

Claus, Russell. 1994. *The Woodlands, Texas: A retrospective critique of the principles and implementation of an ecologically planned development.* MCP thesis, MIT, Cambridge, MA.

Cleland, Robert. 1962. *The Irvine Ranch.* San Marino, CA: Huntington Library.

Columbia Association. 1974. A study of women's needs in Columbia. Duplicated. Columbia Archives.

———. 1978a. The Columbia survey background and methodology. July 21, Duplicated. Columbia Archives.

———. 1978b. 1978 Columbia survey preliminary results. July, Duplicated. Columbia Archives.

———. 2002. Web site. www.columbiaassociation.com/.

———. 2003. *Annual report 2003.* Columbia: Columbia Association.

Columbia Association Governance Structure Committee. 2002. Final report. Columbia: Columbia Association. www.columbiaassociation.com/governance_committee_html.

Columbia Commission. 1971. Impact of new town zoning on Howard County, Maryland. Report for the County Executive and County Council, Howard County, Maryland. Collection of Len Ivins.

Columbia Forum. 1992. An agenda for Columbia. Columbia Archives, open shelves.

"Columbia has already changed the county": An interview with the commissioners. 1966. *Columbia* [a newsletter published by Community Research and Development], spring, 15–16.

Columbia Village Centers. 2002. Retrieved from www.columbiavillagecenters.com/.

Congress for the New Urbanism. 1998. Charter of the New Urbanism. www.cnu.org/cnu_reports/Charter.pdf.

Conroy, Claire. 2001. Masters of the suburbs. *Residential Architect Online.* January. www.residentialarchitect.com/.

Consultants recommend new school programs. 1967. *Columbia,* winter, 12–13.

Corbett, Judy, and Michael Corbett. 2000. *Designing sustainable communities: Learning from village homes.* Washington, DC: Island Press.

Cotton/Beland/Associates and others. 1999. Millennium plan phase II: MCAS El Toro Plan. A Report for the City of Irvine.

Cox, Tom. 2002. Interview by Ann Forsyth, The Woodlands.

CRD (Community Research and Development). 1962. *Proposed new city.* September. Columbia Archives, loose file.

————. 1963a. Howard County project staff. Duplicated. Collection of Herbert Gans.

————. 1963b. Program planning consultants. List of work group participants. Duplicated. Collection of Herbert Gans.

————. 1964a. A center for human development in Howard County new town: Some preliminary considerations. Working Paper. August 26. Columbia Archives, RCI, RG1, Folder 21.

————. 1964b. *Columbia: A new town for Howard County.* 16-page newspaper-style publication. November 12. Copy with Ann Forsyth.

————. 1964c. Columbia: A presentation to the officials and citizens of Howard County, Maryland. November 11. Columbia Archives, loose file.

————. 1964d. Columbia Center. Columbia Archives, RCI, RG1, Folder 21.

————. 1964e. The why and how of social planning for the new community. Revised May. Howard County Project. Columbia Archives, RCI, RG1, Folder 21.

Creative Consumer Research. 1996. *Statistical tables, 1996 residents study.* Prepared for the Woodlands Community Service Corporation. Stafford, TX: Creative Consumer Research.

————. 1999. *Statistical tables, 1999 residents study.* Prepared for the Woodlands Community Service Corporation. Stafford, TX: Creative Consumer Research.

————. 2000. *Statistical tables, 2000 residents study.* Prepared for the Woodlands Community Service Corporation. Stafford, TX: Creative Consumer Research.

Cullen, Gordon. 1961. *Townscape.* London: Architectural Press.

Dannenbrink, Robert. 1976. Developing community identity. *Practicing Planner* (December): 27–30.

————. 2002. Letter to Ann Forsyth commenting on draft manuscript of the book, May 10.

Davis, M. 1990. *City of quartz.* London: Vintage.

Day, Kristen. 1999. Introducing gender to the critique of privatized public space. *Journal of Urban Design* 4 (2): 155–78.

Deretchin, Joel. 1982. Letter to Warren Lindquist, NCDC. National Archives, The Woodlands, Box 4.

Destination Irvine. 2002. Web site. www.destinationirvine.com/siteinfo/realestate/overview.htm.

Development Standards Committee. 1999. The Woodlands commercial planning and design standards. Adopted March 31. Available from The Woodlands Operating Company.

Dienstfrey, Ted. 1971. Moral issues in new town development. In *New community development,* ed. S. Weiss, E. Kaiser, and R. Burby. New Towns Research Seminar series. Chapel Hill: Center for Urban and Regional Studies.

Dinges, Gary. 1997. Day 1. In *The Villager celebrates twenty years,* ed. Darilyn Gayle. The Woodlands: The Villager.

Ditch, Scott. 1996. The selling of Columbia. In *Creating a new city,* ed. Robert Tennenbaum. Columbia, MD: Partners in Community Building and Perry Publishing.

Duany, Andres, Elizabeth Plater-Zyberk, and Jeff Speck. 2000. *Suburban nation.* New York: North Point Press.

Duhl, Leonard. 1963. Introduction. In *The urban condition,* ed. Leonard Duhl. New York: Basic Books.

————. 1999. Community as a commons. Notes from presentation at ISSS Meeting, Asilomar. Retrieved from http://isss.org/1999meet/ing99/701091.htm.

Eichler, E., and M. Kaplan. 1967. *The community builders.* Berkeley: University of California Press.

Eichler, Edward. [1969] 1977. Why new communities? In *New towns and the suburban dream,* ed. Irving Allen. Port Washington, NY: Kennikat Press.

Ephross, Peter. 1988. Pragmatic idealism and the perfect match: Open education in the new town of Columbia, MD. Columbia Archives, front shelves.

Epstein, Gady. 2000. Two cities emerge in Rouse's Columbia. *Baltimore Sun,* December 1, 1A.

Esseks, J. Dixon, Harvey E. Schmidt, and Kimberly L. Sullivan. 1999. *Fiscal costs and public safety risks of low-density residential development on farmland: Findings from three diverse locations on the urban fringe of the Chicago metro area.* Rev. version. Retrieved from http://farm.fic.niu.edu/cae/wp/98–1/wp98–1.html.

ETERPA (El Toro Reuse Planning Authority). 1998. Millennium plan: MCAS El Toro reuse plan. A report prepared by Cotton/Beland/Associates and others.

Evans, Hugh, and Lloyd Rodwin. 1979. The new towns program and why it failed. *Public Interest* 56: 90–107.

Ewing, Reid. 1991. *Developing successful new communities.* Washington, DC: Urban Land Institute.

————. 1996. *Best development practices.* Chicago: Planners Press.

Fainstein, Susan. 1994. *The city builders.* Oxford: Blackwell.

Fairbank, Maslin, Maullin and Associates. 2000. *Irvine citizen satisfaction survey.* Prepared for the City of Irvine. Retrieved from www.ci.irvine.ca.us/irvinecitizensurvey.pdf.

Faludi, Andreas, and A. J. van der Valk. 1994. *Rule and order: Dutch planning doctrine in the twentieth century.* Dordrecht: Kluwer Academic Publishers.

Fava, Sylvia. [1973] 1977. The pop sociology of suburbs and new towns. In *New towns and the suburban dream,* ed. Irving Allen. Port Washington, NY: Kennikat Press.

————. 1980. Women's place in the new suburbia. In *New space for women,* ed. Gerda Wekerle, Rebecca Peterson, and David Morley. Boulder, CO: Westview Press.

Finley, William. 1996. The general planning and development process. In *Creating a new city,* ed. Robert Tennenbaum. Columbia, MD: Partners in Community Building and Perry Publishing.

————. 2001. Email comments to Ann Forsyth on work in progress. December 6.

Finley, William, and Morton Hoppenfeld. 1963. Physical planning process: Urban design. Confidential memorandum to James Rouse, October 7. Columbia Archives, RCI, RG1, Folder 1.

Fishman, Robert. 1987. *Bourgeois utopias.* New York: Basic Books.

————. 1999. The American metropolis at century's end: Past and future influences. In *Legacy of the 1949 Housing Act: Past, present, and future of federal housing and urban policy,* ed. Fannie Mae Foundation. Washington, DC: Fannie Mae Foundation.

Flagg, Michael. 1990. Key figures in the dispute. *Los Angeles Times,* June 26, A20.

Forbes. 2002. World's richest people lists. Retrieved from www.forbes.com/2002/02/28/billionaires.html.

————. 2003. World's richest people lists. Retrieved from www.forbes.com/2003/02/26/billionaireland.html.

Ford, James. 1975. *Social planning and new towns: The case of Columbia, Maryland*. PhD dissertation, University of Michigan.

Forester, John. 1989. *Planning in the face of power*. Berkeley: University of California Press.

Forma. 1998. Newport Coast master coastal development permit, 6th amendment. Submitted by Irvine Community Development Company to Orange County. UC Irvine, Government Publications.

Forsyth, Ann. 1999. *Constructing suburbs*. Amsterdam: Gordon and Breach; New York: Routledge.

————. 2000. Analyzing public space at a metropolitan scale: Notes on the potential for using GIS. *Urban Geography* 21 (2): 121–47.

————. 2002a. Planning lessons from three US new towns of the 1960s and 1970s: Irvine, Columbia, and The Woodlands. *Journal of the American Planning Association* 68 (4): 387–415.

————. 2002b. Who built Irvine? Private planning and the federal government. *Urban Studies* 39 (13): 2507–30.

Frampton, Kenneth. 1985. *Modern architecture: A critical history*. Rev. ed. London: Thames and Hudson.

Frank, James. 1989. *The costs of alternative development patterns: A review of the literature*. Washington, DC: Urban Land Institute.

Franzmeier, Alvin, and Don Gebert. 1979. *The Woodlands experience: An unfinished history of the interfaith movement in a new town in Texas*. The Woodlands, TX: The Woodlands Religious Community (PO Box 7186, TX 77380).

Friedan, Betty. 1963. *The feminine mystique*. New York: Norton.

Frug, Gerald. 1999. *City making*. Princeton: Princeton University Press.

Galatas, Roger. 1998. Interview by Joseph Kutchin, August 1995. In *How Mitchell Energy and Development Corp. got its start and how it grew: An oral history and narrative overview*, ed. Joseph Kutchin. Parkland, FL: Universal Publishers.

Galster, George, Royce Hanson, Hal Wolman, Stephen Coleman, and Jason Freihage. 2000. Wrestling sprawl to the ground: Defining and measuring an elusive concept. Paper presented to Fannie Mae Conference on Fair Growth: Connecting Sprawl, Smart Growth, and Social Equity. November 1, Atlanta.

Gans, Herbert. 1961a. The balanced community: Homogeneity and heterogeneity in residential areas. *Journal of the American Institute of Planners* 27 (3): 176–84.

————. 1961b. Planning and social life: Friendship and neighbor relations in suburban communities. *Journal of the American Institute of Planners* 27 (2): 134–40.

————. 1962. *The urban villagers*. New York: Free Press.

————. 1963. Effects of the move from city to suburb. In *The urban condition*, ed. Leonard Duhl. New York: Basic Books.

————. 1964. The everyday life and problems of the average Columbia resident. Final copy, February 1, based on presentation on January 25. Collection of Herbert Gans.

————. 1967. *The Levittowners: Ways of life and politics in a new suburban community*. New York: Vintage.

————. 1968. *People and plans*. New York: Basic Books.

————. 2001. Interview by Ann Forsyth, New York.

Garreau, Joel. 1991. *Edge city*. New York: Doubleday.

Gass, Marion. 1976. Potential effects of industrial zoning and phased development on low and moderate income housing in the City of Irvine. Master's thesis, California State University at Fullerton.

Gaventa, John. 1980. *Power and powerlessness.* Urbana: University of Illinois Press.

Gebert, Donald. 2000. Interview by Ann Forsyth, The Woodlands.

Geis, A. D. 1974. Effects of urbanization and type of urban development on bird populations. In *Wildlife in an urbanizing environment,* ed. J. H. Noyes and D. R. Progulske. Amherst: Cooperative Extension Service, University of Massachusetts.

Gelfand, Mark. 1975. *A nation of cities: The federal government and urban America, 1933–1965.* New York: Oxford University Press.

General Accounting Office of the United States. 1999. *Extent of federal influence on "urban sprawl" is unclear.* Resources, Community, and Economic Development Division. Report 99–87. Washington, DC: General Accounting Office.

Gillette, Howard. 1999. Assessing James Rouse's role in American city planning. *Journal of the American Planning Association* 65 (2): 150–67.

Girling, C., and Kenneth Helphand. 1994. *Yard, street, park: The design of suburban open space.* New York: John Wiley.

GIS Lounge. 2004. Fortune 1000 companies by state. http://gislounge.com/freisin/blfortunetbl2.shtml.

Glickman, Norman, ed. 1980. *The urban impacts of federal policies.* Baltimore: Johns Hopkins University Press.

GMA (George Mitchell and Associates). 1971. *Title VII application: A new community in metropolitan Houston.* 3 vols. Application to Office of New Community Development. August 10; third revision of environmental statement, November 27. Collection of James McAlister Sr.

Godschalk, David. 1967. Comparative new community design. *Journal of the American Institute of Planners* (November): 371–87.

———. 1973. New communities or company towns: An analysis of resident participation in new towns. In *New towns symposium, Los Angeles 1972,* ed. Harvey Perloff and Neil Sandberg. New York: Praeger.

Goldberger, Paul. 1988. Orange County: Tomorrowland wall to wall. *New York Times,* December 11, 32, 36.

Gordon, Peter, and Harry Richardson. 1997. Are compact cities a desirable planning goal? *Journal of the American Planning Association* 63 (1): 95–106.

Gordon, Richard, Katherine Gordon, and Max Gunther. 1960. *The split level trap.* New York: Bernard Geis and Random House.

Gottdiener, Mark, Claudia Collins, and David Dickens. 1999. *Las Vegas: The social production of an all-American city.* Malden, MA: Blackwell.

Griffin, Nathaniel. 1974. *Irvine: The genesis of a new community.* Washington, DC: Urban Land Institute.

Hadden, Jeffrey, and Josef Barton. [1973] 1977. An image that will not die: Thoughts on the history of anti-urban ideology. In *New towns and the suburban dream,* ed. Irving Allen. Port Washington, NY: Kennikat Press.

Haines, [illegible]. 1982. The Woodlands—Termination documents, press release. Memo, June 14. National Archives, The Woodlands, Box 4.

Hales, Peter. 1997. *Atomic spaces: Living on the Manhattan project.* Urbana: University of Illinois Press.

Hall, Peter. 1988. *Cities of tomorrow.* Oxford: Blackwell.

Hamilton, Wallace. 1964a. A center for human development: Draft. October 1. Columbia Archives, RCI, RG1, Folder 20.

———. 1964b. Columbia center: A proposal for a new institution for the enhancement of human development in a planned urban environment. November. Columbia Archives, RCI, RG1, Folder 21.

———. 1964c. Interim memorandum, communications and transportation, HRD History, to James Rouse and five others. August 10. Columbia Archives, RCI, RG1, Folder 3.

———. 1964d. Interim memorandum, financial projections, to James Rouse and five others. November 30. Columbia Archives, RCI, RG1, Folder 3.

———. 1964e. Interim memorandum, government 1, HRD history, to James Rouse and five others. July 28. Columbia Archives, RCI, RG1, Folder 3.

———. 1964f. Interim memorandum, religion, HRD history, to James Rouse and five others. July 20. Columbia Archives, RCI, RG1, Folder 3.

———. 1964g. Interim memorandum, schools, HRD history, to James Rouse and two others. June 15. Columbia Archives, RCI, RG1, Folder 3.

———. 1964h. Interim memorandum, social structure, HRD history, to James Rouse and two others. July 1. Columbia Archives, RCI, RG1, Folder 3.

———. 1964i. Interim memorandum, the evolution of the physical plan, to James Rouse and five others. September 17. Columbia Archives, RCI, RG1, Folder 3.

———. 1964j. Interim memorandum, the presentation of the plan, HRD history, to James Rouse and five others. August 10. Columbia Archives, RCI, RG1, Folder 3.

———. 1964k. Interim memorandum, zoning, HRD history, to James Rouse and five others. September 21. Columbia Archives, RCI, RG1, Folder 3.

———. 1964l. Memorandum, HRD history progress report, to William Finley. June 22. Columbia Archives, RCI, RG1, Folder 3.

Hanchett, Thomas. 1994. Federal incentives and the growth of local planning, 1941–48. *Journal of the American Planning Association* 60 (2): 197–208.

Hanson, Royce. 1971. *New towns: Laboratories for democracy.* New York: Twentieth Century Fund.

Harris, Richard. 1999. The making of American suburbs, 1900–1950s: A reconstruction. In *Changing Suburbs,* ed. Richard Harris and Peter Larkham. New York: Routledge.

Harris, Tom. 1996. Fitting Columbia into Howard County: The planners' view. In *Creating a new city,* ed. Robert Tennenbaum. Columbia, MD: Partners in Community Building and Perry Publishing.

———. 2000. Interview by Ann Forsyth, Columbia.

Hartsfield, Robert. 1998. Interview by Joseph Kutchin, August 1995. In *How Mitchell Energy and Development Corp. got its start and how it grew: An oral history and narrative overview,* ed. Joseph Kutchin. Parkland, FL: Universal Publishers.

Hartshorn, Truman, and Peter Muller. 1992. The suburban downtown and urban economic development today. In *Sources of metropolitan growth,* ed. Mary McLean. New Brunswick: Rutgers University Press.

Harvey, David. 1973. *Social justice and the city.* Baltimore: Johns Hopkins University Press.

Haworth, Ed. 1967. Incorporation of the new City of Irvine. Irvine Company memo to vice president Ray Watson and chief of planning Richard (Dick) Reese. January 5. UC Irvine Archives, Box 153, Folder 747–10.

Hayden, Dolores. 1981. *The grand domestic revolution.* Cambridge, MA: MIT Press.

———. 2003. *Building suburbia.* New York: Pantheon.

Healey, Patsy. 1996. The communicative turn in planning theory and its implications for spatial strategy formation. *Environment and Planning* B 23: 217–34.

Healey, Patsy, and Tim Shaw. 1994. Changing meanings of "environment" in the British planning system. *Transactions of the Institute of British Geographers* 19 (4): 425–38.

Hellis, William. 1992. Interview, 1970. In Recollections of early Orange County and the Irvine Ranch. Fullerton: Orange County Pioneer Council and California State University Oral History Program.

Hilderbrandt, Donald. 2001. Interview by Ann Forsyth, Columbia.

Hillery, George. 1955. Definitions of community: Areas of agreement. *Rural Sociology* 20: 111–23.

Hintz, Marilyn. 1989. Women's place in the vision, planning and development of the new towns in England. PhD dissertation, University of Wisconsin–Milwaukee.

Hise, Greg. 1997. *Magnetic Los Angeles: Planning the twentieth-century metropolis.* Baltimore: Johns Hopkins University Press.

Hoppenfeld, Morton. 1961. The role of design in city planning. *Journal of the American Institute of Planners* 27 (2): 98–103.

———. 1963a. Memorandum, general objectives for community development (preliminary), to work group. November 4. Columbia Archives, RCI, RG1, folder on correspondence of the incoming work group, 1963–64.

———. 1963b. Memorandum, working procedures for program planning, to members of work group. November 4. Columbia Archives, RCI, RG1, folder on correspondence of the incoming work group, 1963–64.

———. 1967. A sketch of the planning-building process for Columbia, Maryland. *Journal of the American Institute of Planners* (November): 398–409.

———. 1971. The Columbia process: The potential for new towns. *Architects Yearbook* 13: 34–47.

Howard, Ebenezer. 1898. *Tomorrow: A peaceful path to real reform.* London: S. Sonnenschein.

Howard County and Columbia. 1971. Report filed in precis of documents from the Columbia papers. Columbia Archives, open shelves.

Howard County Planning Commission. 1967. *Howard County 1985.* Ellicott City: Howard County Planning Commission.

Howe, Elizabeth. 1992. Professional roles and the public interest in planning. *Journal of Planning Literature* 6 (3): 230–48.

HRD (Howard Research and Development Corporation). [Ca.] 1965a. The general plan and development program for the new town of Columbia, Maryland. Collection of Len Ivins.

———. 1965b. Petition: To Board of County Commissioners of Howard County. Case 412, June 3. Howard County Historical Society, Holway Box 5.

———. 1972. *Columbia's progress measured against its goals is impressive.* Columbia: HRD. Columbia Archives, RCI, RG13, Folder 51.

Hughes Trueman Ludlow and Dwyer Leslie. 1991. *Public sector cost savings of urban consolidation*. Final Report. Prepared for the NSW Department of Planning, Sydney Water Board and [Australian] Department of Industry, Technology and Commerce. Sydney: Department of Planning.

Hunsinger, Jan. 1976. What Woodbridge is. *New Worlds of Irvine* 7, 1: 53–65.

Hydrological balancing act on a Texas new town site. 1974. *Landscape Architecture*, October, 394–95.

Ignatieff, Michael. 1984. *The needs of strangers*. New York: Viking.

Ingersoll, Richard. 1994. Utopia, Limited. *Cite* 31, winter/spring. Retrieved from www .rice.edu/~lda/sprawl_Net/Features/INGEutopia1.html.

Institute for Community Economics. 2003. Web site. www.iceclt.org/.

Interfaith of The Woodlands. 2002. Employment opportunities. Retrieved from www.woodlandsinterfaith.org/employment_opportunities.htm.

Irvine Company, The. 1965. *The Irvine Ranch: Highlights of the history of the Irvine Ranch*. N.p.: The Irvine Company.

———. 1970a. Housing element data for central Irvine general plan. November. UC Irvine, Orange County Collection.

———. 1970b. *Irvine: A city for all tomorrow*. Brochure. UC Irvine, Orange County Collection.

———. 1970c. Irvine general plan. The Irvine Company.

———. 1970–71. General plan program urban design element: Urban design goals and objectives. Collection of parts dated 1970–71. UC Irvine, Orange County Collection.

———. 1972a. *General plan program urban design element: Urban design concepts and policies*. Collection of Robert Dannenbrink.

———. 1972b. University town center: A preliminary statement of development objectives. UC Irvine, Orange County Collection.

———. 1975. Irvine sign manual. Newport Beach: Irvine Company. UC Irvine, Orange County Collection.

———. 1983. Press release: Irvine board approves merger with Newco. October 17. Businesswire/Lexis Nexis.

———. 1987. The Irvine coast proposed land use amendment, executive summary. Based on Orange County's coastal program submittal for the Irvine coast. March. Newport Beach: Irvine Company. UC Irvine, Government Publications.

———. 1998. Irvine Spectrum and Irvine Spectrum Center. Internal report. Copy with Ann Forsyth.

———. 2000a. Guide to the great outdoors: Irvine. *Planning Ahead*, July. Retrieved from www.irvineco.com/aboutus/pa_info/pa_index.asp.

———. 2000b. Irvine's housing: Balanced best. *Planning Ahead*, May. Retrieved from www.irvineco.com/aboutus/pa_info/pa_index.asp.

———. 2001a. Comparative community study, Irvine Ranch. Newport Beach: The Irvine Company.

———. 2001b. More than half of 93,000-acre Irvine Ranch will be permanently preserved for open space and recreation. Press release, November 28. Retrieved from http://irvineco.com/aboutus/News.asp?type=news&archive=2001&release=388 &category=17&cid=.

———. 2002a. Irvine Ranch land reserve. Retrieved from www.irvineco.com/good planning/land_reserve/landreserve15.asp.

———. 2002b. It takes a village. http://irvineco.com/goodplanning/master
    _planning/master_planning_article.asp?id=18.

———. 2002c. Planning principles. Retrieved from http://turtleridgeupdate.com/
    aboutus/pa_info/communities/turtle_ridge/planning/planning.asp.

———. 2002d. Web site. http://irvineco.com.

———. N.d. Irvine Ranch: A chronological history. Collection of Ray Watson.

Irvine Company and Nature Conservancy. 1992. The Irvine Company open space
    reserve stewardship plan. UC Irvine, Government Publications.

Irvine Smith, J. 1971. Speech given by Mrs. Joan Irvine Smith before the Associated
    Students of the University of California, Irvine, December 7. UC Irvine Archives,
    Box 158, Folder 747–50–0.

Ivins, Leonard. 1976. Toward a national urban policy: The American new town ex-
    perience. Duplicated. Collection of Leonard Ivins.

———. 2001. Interview by Ann Forsyth, Houston.

———. 2002. Written comments to Ann Forsyth on work in progress, July 29.

Jackson, Douglas, and Melani Smith. 1999. The role of congregational life in devel-
    oping a sense of place and sense of community in the post-suburban city. Master
    of Urban and Regional Planning, professional report, University of California,
    Irvine.

Jackson, Kenneth. 1985. *Crabgrass frontier.* New York: Oxford University Press.

Jacobs, Jane. 1961. *The death and life of great American cities.* New York: Random House.

Jasny, M. 1997. *Leap of faith: Southern California's experiment in natural community con-
    servation planning.* Los Angeles: Natural Resources Defense Council.

Jencks, Christopher. 1964. Educational programs for a new community. April 1. Draft.
    Collection of Herbert Gans.

Jones, John Martin. 2000. Interview by Ann Forsyth, Columbia.

Jones, Sabrina. 2001. It breaks a village to lose a grocery. *Washington Post,* June 11, E1,
    E15.

Kaboolian, Linda, and Barbara Nelson. N.d. Unpublished notes on the Columbia
    interfaith centers.

Kaiser, Edward. 1976. *Residential mobility in new communities.* Cambridge, MA: Ballinger.

Kane, Diane. 1996. *Westlake and Irvine, California: Paradigms for the 21st century?* PhD
    dissertation, University of California, Santa Barbara.

Karsk, Roger. 1977. *Teenagers in the next America.* Columbia, MD: New Community
    Press.

Kato, Yuki. 2002. *Defining and designing balanced communities: Diversity, residential seg-
    regation & American new towns.* Unpublished final master's paper, University of Cali-
    fornia, Irvine.

Katz, Bruce. 2000. The federal role in curbing sprawl. *Annals of the American Acad-
    emy of Political and Social Science* 572: 66–77.

Keats, John. 1957. *The crack in the picture window.* Boston: Houghton Mifflin.

Keller, Suzanne. 1968. *The urban neighborhood: A sociological perspective.* New York:
    Random House.

———. 1981. Women and children in a planned community. In *Building for women,*
    ed. Suzanne Keller. Lexington, MA: Lexington Books.

Kelly, Stephen. 1999. *Designing for the physical and social senses of Irvine's parks.* Master of
    Urban and Regional Planning, professional report, University of California, Irvine.

Kennedy, Davis. 1974. Columbia developer changes plans for refinancing. *Sunday Sun* (Baltimore), October 20, K7.

Kennedy, Padraic. 1981. Remarks by Padraic Kennedy, president, Columbia Association, at the Judge William Hastie luncheon award/symposium. Collection of Padraic Kennedy.

———. 1998. "Seven": Seven stages in the Columbia Association's history. Draft paper. July. Collection of Padraic Kennedy.

Kittamaqundi Community. 2002. Web site. www.kittamaqundi.org/.

Kling, R., S. Olin, and M. Poster, eds. 1991. *Postsuburban California*. Berkeley: University of California Press.

Knepper, Cathy. 2001. *Greenbelt, Maryland: A living legacy of the New Deal*. Baltimore: Johns Hopkins University Press.

Kotkin, Joel. 1999. A place to please the techies. *New York Times*, January 24, B4.

Kreditor, Alan. 2000. Interview by Ann Forsyth, Los Angeles.

Kreditor, Alan, and Kenneth Kraemer. 1968. *Final report: Southern sector general plan*. May. Draft for TIC. UC Irvine, Orange County Collection.

Kutchin, Joseph, ed. 1998a. *How Mitchell Energy and Development Corp. got its start and how it grew: An oral history and narrative overview*. Parkland, FL: Universal Publishers.

———. 1998b. When you're convinced you're right, go for it. In *How Mitchell Energy and Development Corp. got its start and how it grew: An oral history and narrative overview*, ed. Joseph Kutchin. Parkland, FL: Universal Publishers.

———. 2000. Interview by Ann Forsyth, The Woodlands.

Lamb, Karl. 1974. *As Orange goes: Twelve California families and the future of American politics*. New York: Norton.

Landscape design in progress for village and town centers. 1966. *Columbia* [a newsletter published by Community Research and Development], spring, 4.

Lang, Robert, and Patrick Simmons. 2001. "Boomburbs": The emergence of large, fast-growing suburban cities in the United States. Fannie Mae Foundation, Census Note 06, June.

Lansing, John, Robert Marans, and Robert Zehner. 1970. *Planned residential environments*. Ann Arbor: Survey Research Center, University of Michigan.

Leccese, Michael, and Kathleen McCormick. 2000. *Charter of the new urbanism*. New York: McGraw Hill.

Lee, Chang-Moo, and Kun-Hyuck Ahn. 2003. Is Kentlands better than Radburn? *Journal of the American Planning Association* 69 (1): 50–71.

Lesser, Charles. 2002. Top selling master planned communities. Retrieved from http://biz.yahoo.com/bw/020205/52774_1.html.

Levinson, David. 2003. The next America revisited. *Journal of Planning Education and Research* 22 (4): 329–44.

Liebeck, Judy, and Myrtle Malone. 1990. *Irvine: A history of innovation and growth*. Houston: Pioneer Publications.

Lively, Charles. 1998. Interview by Joseph Kutchin, February 1996. In *How Mitchell Energy and Development Corp. got its start and how it grew: An oral history and narrative overview*, ed. Joseph Kutchin. Parkland, FL: Universal Publishers.

Lofland, Lyn. 1998. *The public realm*. New York: Aldine de Gruyter.

Logan, John, and Harvey Molotch. 1987. *Urban fortunes*. Berkeley: University of California Press.

Lynch, Kevin. 1960. *The image of the city.* Cambridge, MA: MIT Press.

———. 1981. *Good city form.* Cambridge, MA: MIT Press.

Macey, Gregg. 1999. Public spheres in planned communities. Master of Urban and Regional Planning, professional report, University of California, Irvine.

Malecki, Edward. 1982. Federal R. and D. spending in the United States of America: Some impacts on metropolitan economics. *Regional Studies* 16 (1): 19–35.

Malone, Myrtle, ed. 1985. *The Woodlands: New town in the forest.* The Woodlands, TX: Pioneer Publications.

Malpezzi, Stephen, and Wen-Kai Guo. 2001. Measuring "sprawl": Alternative measures of urban form in U.S. metropolitan areas. Center for Urban Land Economics Research, University of Wisconsin–Madison.

Mann, Michael. 1986. *The sources of social power.* Vol. 1. New York: Cambridge University Press.

Mann, Peter. 1958. The socially balanced neighborhood unit. *Town Planning Review* (July): 91–98.

Markusen, Ann. 1989. *Regional planning and policy: An essay on the American exception.* Working Paper Number 9. Piscataway, NJ: Center for Urban Policy Research.

Marris, Peter. 1987. *Meaning and action.* Rev. ed. London: Routledge.

———. 1996. *The politics of uncertainty.* London: Routledge.

Marshall Kaplan Gans and Kahn. 1976. The fiscal and economic analysis of general plan options. City of Irvine, California, November 15. UC Irvine, Orange County Collection.

Martinez, Gebe. 1990. Laguna Laurel Q&A. *Los Angeles Times,* Orange County edition, October 21, 3.

Maryland Commission on Interracial Problems and Relations. 1955. *An American city in transition.* Baltimore: Baltimore Commission on Human Relations.

Maryland Office of Planning. 1997. Designating Maryland's growth models and guidelines: Smart growth, designating priority funding areas. Retrieved from www.mdp .state.md.us/INFO/download/pfa.pdf.

Maryland's "new town" may make it big. 1968. *Business Week,* March 9, 132–36.

Mason, W. R. 1971. Letter to County of Orange, Local Agency Formation Commission, January 5. UC Irvine, Orange County Collection.

Mason-Dixon Opinion Research. 1991. Columbia resident knowledge and attitudes on local governance. Survey Report, conducted for The Columbia Forum, November. Columbia Archives, loose collection.

Mason-Dixon Polling and Research. 2002. *Columbia strategic issues community survey.* Available from www.columbiaassociation.com/survey.htm.

———. 2003. Community-wide survey of strategic issues. Survey commissioned by the Columbia Association.

Master builder with a new concept. 1966. *Business Week,* August 20. Unpaginated reprint.

McAlister, Jim, ed. 1970. The Woodland history reading file. Memoranda and correspondence from 1970. Collection of James McAlister.

———, ed. 1971. The Woodland history reading file. Memoranda and correspondence from 1971. Collection of James McAlister.

———, ed. 1972. The Woodland history reading file. Memoranda and correspondence from 1972. Collection of James McAlister.

————. 1998. Interview by Joseph Kutchin, October 1995. In *How Mitchell Energy and Development Corp. got its start and how it grew: An oral history and narrative overview,* ed. Joseph Kutchin. Parkland, FL: Universal Publishers.

————. 2000. Interview by Ann Forsyth, The Woodlands.

McCulloch, Samuel. 1996. *Instant university: The history of the University of California, Irvine, 1957–1993.* Irvine: University of California, Irvine.

McGirr, Lisa. 2001. *Suburban warriors: The origins of the New American Right.* Princeton: Princeton University Press.

McGuire, Chester. 1975. Operational problems of new communities. *Journal of Sociology and Social Welfare* 3 (2): 136–40.

McHarg, Ian. 1963. Man and environment. In *The urban condition,* ed. Leonard Duhl. New York: Basic Books.

————. 1969. *Design with nature.* Garden City, NY: Natural History Press.

————. 1996. *A quest for life.* New York: John Wiley.

————. 1998. *To heal the earth: Selected writings of Ian L. McHarg.* Edited by Ian L. McHarg and Frederick R. Steiner. Washington, DC: Island Press.

McKenzie, Evan. 1994. *Privatopia: Homeowner associations and the rise of residential private government.* New Haven: Yale University Press.

McNally, Michael, and Anup Kulkarni. 1997. Assessment of influence of land use-transportation system on travel behavior. *Transportation Research Record* 1607: 105–15.

Meadows, Dennis, ed. 1977. *Alternatives to growth: A search for sustainable futures.* Cambridge, MA: Ballinger.

Memorandum of understanding implementing initiative resolution 88–1. 1988. Between the City of Irvine and the Irvine Company. Collection of the City of Irvine.

Meyerson, Martin, and Edward Banfield. 1955. *Politics, planning and the public interest: The case of public housing in Chicago.* New York: Free Press.

Michael, Donald. 1964. Recommendations for the social planning of Columbia: Physical facilities and social organization. Abstracted and extended from the deliberations of the CRD Social Planning Work Group. Draft, July. Columbia Archives, RCI, RG1, Folder 15.

————. 1996. The planning workgroup. In *Creating a new city,* ed. Robert Tennenbaum. Columbia, MD: Partners in Community Building and Perry Publishing.

Middleton, Scott. 1997. The Woodlands: Designed with nature. *Urban Land* 55 (6): 26–30.

Mields, Hugh. 1973. *Federally assisted new communities.* Washington, DC: Urban Land Institute.

Miles, Matthew, and Michael Huberman. 1994. Qualitative data analysis: An expanded sourcebook. 2nd ed. Thousand Oaks, CA: Sage.

Minibus to separate road system. 1966. *Columbia* [a newsletter published by Community Research and Development], spring, 3.

Minutes of the meeting on the incorporation of the university of community. 1968. Meeting, October 3, minutes dated October 16. UC Irvine, University Archives.

Mitchell, George. 1998. Interview by Joseph Kutchin, August 1995. In *How Mitchell Energy and Development Corp. got its start and how it grew: An oral history and narrative overview,* ed. Joseph Kutchin. Parkland, FL: Universal Publishers.

————. 2000. Interview with Ann Forsyth, The Woodlands.

———. 2002. Interview with Ann Forsyth, The Woodlands.

Moffit, Leonard. 1967. Community and urbanization: Orange County California. Manuscript. UC Irvine, Orange County Collection.

Monkkonen, Eric. 1988. *America become urban: The development of U.S. cities and towns, 1780–1980.* Berkeley: University of California Press.

Moore, Lawrence. 1976. A forum for planning. *New Worlds of Irvine,* June/July, 115–20.

Morgan, George, and John King. 1987. *The Woodlands.* College Station: Texas A&M University Press.

Morse, Dan. 1997. In Columbia, questions about ethics, favoritism. *Baltimore Sun,* April 27, 1, 10.

Moxley, Robert. 1996. Land acquisition: The realtor's perspective. In *Creating a new city,* ed. Robert Tennenbaum. Columbia, MD: Partners in Community Building and Perry Publishing.

MUD (The Woodlands and Montgomery County Municipal Utility Districts). 2001. *Reference manual for the directors.* The Woodlands: MUD.

Mumford, Lewis. 1957. Preface. In *Toward new towns for America,* by Clarence Stein. New York: Reinhold.

Nasar, Jack, and David Julian. 1995. The psychological sense of community in the neighborhood. *Journal of the American Planning Association* 61 (2): 178–84.

Nassauer, Joan. 1995. Messy ecosystems, orderly frames. *Landscape Journal* 14 (2): 161–70.

Nebulous art of new community management, The. 1971. *Columbia Today,* March, 8–10.

Neely, Tim. 2000. Interview by Ann Forsyth, Santa Ana.

Neiman, Judy. 1975. Columbia, Maryland—a better kind of city. HRD Exhibit Slide Show. Script. Columbia Archives, RGIIN, Series 13, 1; Folder 1.

Newman, Peter, and Jeff Kenworthy. 2000. *Sustainable cities.* Washington, DC: Island Press.

New suburbia, The. 1965. Transcript of panel session with FitzGerald Bemiss, Beverly Briley, Neil Connor, Frank Gregg, Matthew Rockwell, James Rouse, Hideo Sasaki, and Robert E., Simon. In *Beauty for America,* Proceedings of the White House Conference on Natural Beauty, chap. 15. Washington, DC: GPO. Columbia Archives.

Nishimaki, H. 2001. *The making of garden cities: Case studies of Milton Keynes, Irvine and Tskuba.* PhD dissertation, University of California, Berkeley.

Nivola, Pietro. 1999. *Laws of the landscape: How policies shape cities in Europe and America.* Washington, DC: Brookings Institution Press.

Nixon Foundation. 2001. Biography of president Richard Nixon. Retrieved from www.nixonfoundation.org/Research_Center/Nixons/RichardNixon.shtml#Top OfPage.

OCCP (Orange County Cultural Pride). N.d. Web site. http://ocgaypride.com/.

Odendahl, Anne. 1969. The schools go modern. *Columbia Today,* August/September, 19–21.

Olsen, Josh. 2000. *Understanding urban place formation through biography.* Master's thesis, School of Geographical Sciences, University of Bristol.

Orange County Planning Department. 1970a. Staff recommendations on the land use, circulation and housing elements of the central section Irvine Ranch general plan and the proposed City of Irvine general plan. For submission to the Orange County Planning Commission, December 17. UC Irvine, Orange County Collection.

———. 1970b. Staff report on the proposed City of Irvine general plan. For submission to the Orange County Planning Commission, November 12. UC Irvine, Orange County Collection.

Orange County Transportation Authority. 2002. Centerline project Web page. http://centerline.octa.net/.

Oregon State University Libraries. 2002. GovStats Web site: Consolidated federal funds report. http://govinfo.library.orst.edu/.

Owen, Wilfred. 1959. *Cities in the motor age.* New York: Viking Press.

PADCO. Ca. 1966. Preliminary planning model study. Prepared for the Rouse Company. Washington, DC: PADCO. Collection of Len Ivins.

Pappas, Plato. 1998. Interview by Joseph Kutchin, August 1995. In *How Mitchell Energy and Development Corp. got its start and how it grew: An oral history and narrative overview,* ed. Joseph Kutchin. Parkland, FL: Universal Publishers.

Parker, Andrew. 1997. A stealth urban policy in the US? Federal spending in five large metropolitan regions, 1984–1993. *Urban Studies* 34 (11): 1831–50.

Parker, Larry. 1997. 30 years and counting. *Columbia Flier* 13 (26): 1, 26–28, 30.

Parks and pathways in The Woodlands. 2001. *The Woodlands Community Magazine,* July, 18.

Parman, John. 1990. Utopia revised. *Architecture* (January): 66.

Pasco, Jean, Scott Martelle, and Dan Weikel. 2002. In jolt to Orange County, navy to sell El Toro land. *Los Angeles Times,* March 7.

Peattie, Lisa. 1987. *Planning: Rethinking Ciudad Guayana.* Ann Arbor: University of Michigan Press.

Peel, Mark. 1995. The rise and fall of social mix in an Australian new town. *Journal of Urban History* 22 (1): 108–40.

Peiser, Richard. 1984. Does it pay to plan suburban growth? *Journal of the American Planning Association* (autumn): 419–33.

Peiser, Richard, and Alain Chaing. 1999. Is it possible to build financially successful new towns? The Milton Keynes experience. *Urban Studies* 36 (10): 1679–704.

Perloff, Harvey, and Neil Sandberg, eds. 1973. *New towns symposium, Los Angeles 1972.* New York: Praeger.

Perry, Clarence. 1929. The neighborhood unit. In *Neighborhood and community planning* (comprising three monographs). New York: Regional Plan of New York and its Environs.

———. 1939. *Housing for the machine age.* New York: Russell Sage Foundation.

Phillips, David, and Anthony Yeh, eds. 1987. *New towns in East and South-east Asia.* New York: Oxford University Press.

Pincetl, Stephanie. 1999. The politics of influence: Democracy and the growth machine in Orange County, U.S. In *The urban growth machine,* ed. Andrew Jonas and David Wilson. Albany: SUNY Press.

Plan approved for Village of Wilde Lake. 1966. *Columbia* [a newsletter published by Community Research and Development], spring, 1–3.

Planning Center. 1996. *MCAS Tustin specific plan/reuse plan.* Prepared for City of Tustin. UC Irvine, Government Publications.

Popenoe, David. 1977. *The suburban environment: Sweden and the United States.* Chicago: University of Chicago Press.

———. 1980. Women in the suburban environment: A U.S.-Sweden comparison. In *New space for women,* ed. Gerda Wekerle, Rebecca Peterson, and David Morley. Boulder, CO: Westview Press.

Popper, Frank. 1988. Understanding American land use regulation since 1970. *Journal of the American Planning Association* 54 (3): 291–301.

Purpura, James. 1999. *Look who's hanging out: Assessing recreational opportunities for Irvine teens.* Master of Urban and Regional Planning, professional report, University of California, Irvine.

Rabinovitz, Francine, and Helene Smookler. 1973. Rhetoric versus performance: The national politics and administration of the U.S. new communities development legislation. In *New towns symposium, Los Angeles 1972,* ed. Harvey Perloff and Neil Sandberg. New York: Praeger.

Radburn: A planned community. 2002. Retrieved from www.radburn.org/geninfo/radburn-intro.html.

Rainbow Youth Alliance. N.d. Web site. Retrieved from www.geocities.com/WestHollywood/7162/.

Randall, Gregory. 2000. *America's original GI town: Park Forest, Illinois.* Baltimore: Johns Hopkins University Press.

Real Estate Research Corporation. 1974. *The costs of sprawl: Environmental and economic costs of alternative residential development patterns at the urban fringe, detailed costs analysis.* Washington, DC: United States Government Printing Office.

Reich, Robert. 1988. Policy making in a democracy. In *The power of public ideas,* ed. Robert Reich. Cambridge, MA: Ballinger.

Richmond, Michael. 1998. Interview by Joseph Kutchin, 1995. In *How Mitchell Energy and Development Corp. got its start and how it grew: An oral history and narrative overview,* ed. Joseph Kutchin. Parkland, FL: Universal Publishers.

———. 2000. Interview by Joe Kutchin, The Woodlands. Transcript.

Riesman, David. 1950. *The lonely crowd.* New Haven: Yale University Press.

Rocca, A. 1996. Irvine, plan and architecture of the campus and Irvine Ranch of Orange County: The city which does not imitate the city. *Lotus* 98: 7–102.

Roch, D'Ann. 1982. *The role of community facilities in promoting community ties in planned communities.* PhD dissertation, Pennsylvania State University.

Rogers, Millard. 2001. *John Nolen and Mariemont.* Baltimore: Johns Hopkins University Press.

Ross, Cerf. 1969. Woodland Village: University of Houston North Campus. A report for Mitchell Gas and Oil Corporation, November 30. Collection of James McAlister Sr.

Rouse, James. 1955a. Statement on Housing Amendments of 1955. *Hearings before a Subcommittee of the Committee on Banking and Currency, United States Senate, Eighty-fourth Congress.* Washington, DC: United States Government Printing Office.

———. 1955b. Statement on housing amendments of 1955, HR 5827. *Hearings before the Committee on Banking and Currency, House of Representatives, Eighty-fourth Congress.* Washington, DC: United States Government Printing Office.

————. 1959. Talk at conference on family happiness and security. Insurance Company of North America. Columbia Archives, MCII, James Rouse Papers, Folder 1A.

————. 1963a. It can happen here: A paper on metropolitan growth. Presented at the Conference in the Metropolitan Future, Berkeley. Columbia Archives.

————. 1963b. The regional shopping center: Its role in the community it serves. Speech at the Seventh Urban Design Conference, Harvard Graduate School of Design, April 26. (Attached to July 15 memo distributing the speech to all Rouse Company officers.) Columbia Archives.

————. 1964. Letter to Dr. Herbert Gans. November 10. Collection of Herbert Gans.

————. 1966a. In *Hearings before Subcommittee Number 5, of the Committee on the Judiciary, House of Representatives, Eighty-ninth Congress, on miscellaneous proposals regarding the civil rights of persons within the jurisdiction of the United States.* Washington, DC: United States Government Printing Office.

————. 1966b. Statement of James B. Rouse, president, the Rouse Company. Before the Executive Reorganization Subcommittee, Senate Committee on Government Operations, December 7. Columbia Archives, MCII, James Rouse Papers, Folder 4A.

————. 1969. Letter to the editor, July 5, *The Times* (Ellicott City). Columbia Archives, RCI, RG2, Folder 3.

————. 1970. Memorandum: To everyone in the Columbia and Baltimore offices. Subject line: Lenten Lunches. Columbia Archives RCI, RG2, Folder 2.

————. 1977. The values of wildlife as an integral part of the urban community. Remarks by James Rouse at a seminar on Wildlife in Urban Areas, Howard Community College, Columbia, MD, June 18. Columbia Archives, MCII, James Rouse Papers, Folder 21.

————. 1982. Letter to Ron Wilson, senior editor, *Today's Christian Woman.* Columbia Archives, MCII, James Rouse Collection, Folder 29.

Rouse, Libby. 1977. The spiritual dream behind Columbia and the vision still hopefully ahead for it. A paper prepared for the Kittamaqundi Community, Columbia, MD. Columbia Archives, James Rouse Papers, MCIII, Folder 20.

Rouse, Patty. 2001. Remarks at the Enterprise Foundation network conference. Retrieved from www.enterprisefoundation.org/resources/Trainingconf/conferences/networkConference/2001highlights/patty.asp.

Rouse Company. 1966. *Columbia: A new city.* Baltimore: Rouse Company.

————. 1967. The story of Columbia, Maryland. Bound set of advertising images. Columbia, MD: Rouse Company. Columbia Archives.

————. 1970. Annual report for the year ended May 31, 1970. Columbia, MD: Rouse Company.

————. 1971. Rouse Company profile. Special issue, June 1. Columbia Archives.

————. 1999. 1999 community profile. Retrieved from www.columbia-md.com/col community.html.

————. 2002. Web site. www.therousecompany.com/.

————. N.d. Rouse Company history. Retrieved from www.therousecompany.com/whoweare/history/index.html.

Rouse Company, Research and Site Strategy. 1982. Consumer research, Columbia residents, Columbia, Maryland. March. Columbia Archives, RCI, RG17, Folder 14b.

————. 1984. Consumer research, Columbia residents, Columbia, Maryland. August. Columbia Archives, RCI, RG17, Folder 14c.

————. 1991. Columbia resident survey. January. Columbia Archives, Howard Research and Development Corporation. Columbia Archives, RG17, Folder 14d.

Rowe, Peter. 1991. *Making a middle landscape.* Cambridge, MA: MIT Press.

Ryder, Sharon. 1976. A Rousing place. *Progressive Architecture* 76 (2): 58–63.

Sandberg, Neil. 1978. *Stairwell 7: Family life in the welfare state.* Beverly Hills, CA: Sage.

Sarkissian, Wendy. 1976. The idea of social mix in historical perspective. *Urban Studies* 13: 231–46.

Saunders, Peter. 1986. Social theory and the urban question. 2nd ed. New York: Holmes and Meier.

Scarlett, Harold. 1972. "New town" will use porous streets. *Houston Post,* February 24. Collection of City of Houston Planning and Development Department.

Scarupa, Harriet. 1970. Youth in Columbia. *Columbia Today,* July, 8–23.

Schaaf, Dick. 1977. Irvine Center. *New Worlds of Irvine* 8 (1): 58–64.

Schiesl, Martin. 1991. Designing the model community: The Irvine Company and suburban development, 1950–88. In *Postsuburban California,* ed. R. Kling, S. Olin, and M. Poster. Berkeley: University of California Press.

Schon, Donald, and Martin Rein. 1994. *Frame reflection: Toward the resolution of intractable policy controversies.* New York: Basic Books.

Schuman, Tony, and Elliott Sclar. N.d. The enterprise of American city building: The exceptional case of Columbia, Maryland. Manuscript available from the authors.

Scott, Allen. 1993. *Technopolis: High-technology industry and regional development in Southern California.* Berkeley: University of California Press.

Scott Brown, Denise. 1967. Team 10, Perspecta 10 and the present state of architectural theory. *Journal of the American Institute of Planners* (January): 42–50.

Sears, David. 1947. Importance of ecology in training engineers. *Science* 106 (2740): 1–3.

Sennett, Richard. 1970. *The uses of disorder.* New York: Knopf.

Settlement Agreement. 1977. Settlement agreement among all the parties to *Orange County fair housing et al. v. City of Irvine et al.* Orange County Super. Ct. No. 225824. UC Irvine, Orange County Collection.

Sherman, Malcolm. 1996. Early home building. In *Creating a new city,* ed. Robert Tennenbaum. Columbia, MD: Partners in Community Building and Perry Publishing.

————. 2000. Interview by Ann Forsyth, Baltimore.

Short, James. 1973. *Total new town building costs and comparison with an alternative development.* PhD dissertation, University of California, Los Angeles.

Sidney Hollander Associates. 1965. Attitude of Howard County residents to the Columbia plan. Prepared for Community Research and Development Inc., February 27. Columbia Archives, RCI, RG17, Folder 11.

————. 1970a. The Columbia housing market: Recent buyers. Prepared for the Rouse Company, June. Columbia Archives, RCI, RG17, Folder 13f.

————. 1970b. Howard County looks at Columbia. Prepared for the Rouse Company, October. Columbia Archives, RCI, RG17, Folder 14.

Sills, David. 2002. Letter to Ann Forsyth, commenting on draft manuscript, July 25.

Silver, Chris. 1985. Neighborhood planning in historical perspective. *Journal of the American Planning Association* 51 (2): 161–74.

Simon, Norton. 1970. Letter and accompanying materials to the regents of the University of California, October 9. UC Irvine, Orange County Collection.

Smith, Barton. 1994. The role of The Woodlands in the economic development of Montgomery County. Collection of Ann Forsyth.

Smith, Beverly. 1975. The community association press corps: Have they got news for you. *New Worlds* [of Irvine] 6 (5): 61–66.

Smookler, Helene. 1975. Administration hara-kiri: Implementation of the urban growth and new community development act. *Annals of the American Academy of Political and Social Science* 422: 129–40.

———. 1976. *Economic integration in new communities.* Cambridge, MA: Ballinger.

Southworth, Michael. 1997. Walkable communities? An evaluation of neotraditional communities on the urban edge. *Journal of the American Planning Association* 63 (1): 28–44.

Southworth, Michael, and Peter Owens. 1993. The evolving metropolis: Studies of community, neighborhood, and street form at the urban edge. *Journal of the American Planning Association* 59 (3): 271–87.

Spain, Daphne. 1988. An examination of residential preferences in the suburban era. *Sociological Focus* 21: 1–8.

Spear, Michael. 1971. Economic modeling for new town evaluation. In *New community development,* ed. S. Weiss, E. Kaiser, and R. Burby. New Towns Research Seminar series. Chapel Hill: Center for Urban and Regional Studies.

Spirn, Ann. 1984. *The granite garden.* New York: Basic Books.

Stein, Clarence. [1950] 1957. *Toward new towns for America.* New York: Reinhold.

Steiner, Fritz. 1981. *The politics of new town planning.* Athens: Ohio University Press.

Stimpson, Catharine, Elsa Dixler, Martha J. Nelson, and Kathryn B. Yatrakis, eds. 1980. *Women and the American city.* Chicago: University of Chicago Press.

Strong, Ann Louise. 1971. *Planned urban environments.* Baltimore: Johns Hopkins University Press.

Sunderland, Lowell. 1970. Can mass transit really work? *Columbia Today,* September, 8–14.

———. 1971. How Columbia manages its amenities while gearing for public control. *Columbia Today,* March, 11–15.

Sutton, Jonathan, and Ian McHarg. 1975. Ecological plumbing for the Texas coastal plain. *Landscape Architecture* 65 (1): 78–89.

Talen, Emily. 2000. New urbanism and the culture of criticism. *Urban Geography* 21 (4): 318–41.

Taylor, Brian. 2000. When finance leads planning: Urban planning, highway planning, and metropolitan freeways in California. *Journal of Planning Education and Research* 20 (2): 196–214.

Tennenbaum, Robert, ed. 1996a. *Creating a new city,* ed. Robert Tennenbaum. Columbia, MD: Partners in Community Building and Perry Publishing.

———. 1996b. Physical planning and design. In *Creating a new city,* ed. Robert Tennenbaum. Columbia, MD: Partners in Community Building and Perry Publishing.

————. 2000. Interview by Ann Forsyth, Columbia.

————. 2002. Letter to Ann Forsyth, commenting on draft manuscript, May 23.

The Woodlands Association, Inc. 1974. Covenants, restrictions, easements, charges and liens of The Woodlands. Available from the association.

————. 1993. Covenants, restrictions, easements, charges and liens of The Woodlands. Available from the association.

The Woodlands GREEN. 2003. Web site www.thewoodlandsgreen.org/twg-History.htm.

Thomas, Kate. 1982. Woodlands to be cut loose from federal loan program. *Houston Post,* August 4.

Thorns, David. 1976. *The quest for community: Social aspects of residential growth.* New York: John Wiley.

Timmins, Terry. 1993. Structural speculation as a dynamic of urban growth: A case study of the Irvine Company. PhD dissertation, Fielding Institute, Santa Barbara.

Toner, Bill. 1970. Interview package: New city analysis. For the Orange County Planning Commission. UC Irvine, Orange County Collection.

Tough, Coulson. 1998. Interview by Joseph Kutchin, August 1995. In *How Mitchell Energy and Development Corp. got its start and how it grew: An oral history and narrative overview,* ed. Joseph Kutchin. Parkland, FL: Universal Publishers.

Town Center Improvement District. 2003. Web site. www.town-center.com/.

TWCSC (The Woodlands Community Service Corporation). 2002. Web site. Retrieved from www.wcscwoodlands.com/index-ns.html.

TWDC (The Woodlands Development Corporation). 1973. Board report as of March 20. National Archives, Maryland, The Woodlands, Box 3.

TWOC (The Woodlands Operating Company). 2000a. *The Woodlands.* Marketing brochure. TWOC, The Woodlands, TX.

————. 2000b. The Woodlands, Texas, demographics. January 1. (Photocopied sheet in marketing and information packet.) TWOC, The Woodlands, TX.

————. 2001. Internal figures on village densities. Collection of Ann Forsyth.

————. 2002. Community facts. Retrieved from http://thewoodlands.com/business/comm_facts.html#.

Tyrwhitt, Jacqueline. 1950. Surveys for planning. In *Town and Country Planning Textbook,* ed. Association for Planning and Regional Reconstruction. London: Architectural Press.

ULI (Urban Land Institute). 1976. The Woodlands: An evaluation of development strategies for the New Communities Administration of the US Department of Housing and Urban Development. ULI panel service report, January 12–16. Washington, DC: Urban Land Institute. National Archives, The Woodlands, Box 4.

Underhill, Jack. 1976. Appendix D: Achievements and Potentials. In *New communities: Problems and potentials.* U.S. New Communities Administration. Washington, DC: HUD.

University of California, Irvine, Office of Physical Planning and Construction. 1970. Progress report, Development of the University Community, Irvine Campus, September 1. UC Irvine Archives, Box 158, Folder 747–50–1.

U.S.A. and TWDC (The Woodlands Development Corporation). 1972. Project agreement. August 23. National Archives, The Woodlands, Box 27.

U.S. Census. 1980. U.S. Census of population and housing, STF 1 and STF3. Washington, DC: U.S. Dept. of Commerce, Bureau of the Census.

————. 1990. American fact finder. Census of population and housing. Retrieved from http://factfinder.census.gov/servlet/BasicFactsServlet.

————. 2000. American fact finder. Census of population and housing. Retrieved from http://factfinder.census.gov/servlet/BasicFactsServlet.

U.S. EPA (Environmental Protection Agency). 2001. What is smart growth? Smart Growth Fact Sheet RPA 231-F-01-001A, April. Retrieved from www.epa.gov/dced/pdf/whtissg4v2.pdf.

U.S. HUD (Department of Housing and Urban Development). 1984. *An evaluation of the federal new communities program.* Washington, DC: HUD.

————. 1998. A picture of subsidized households. Retrieved from www.huduser.org/datasets/assthsg/statedata98/index.html.

U.S. HUD (Department of Housing and Urban Development), NCA (New Communities Administration). 1976. *New communities: Problems and potentials.* Washington, DC: HUD.

U.S. Postal Service, Economic Analysis Division. 1973. *New towns and the US Postal Service: Some guidelines for postal officials and new town developers.* Washington, DC: U.S. Postal Service.

U.S./USSR New Towns Working Group. 1981. *Planning new towns: National reports of the US and USSR.* Washington, DC: HUD, Office of International Affairs.

Van der Wal, Coen. 1997. *In praise of common sense.* Rotterdam: 010 Publishers.

Van Zandt, Victor. 1999. *The role of public elementary schools in increasing sense of community in Irvine, California.* Master of Urban and Regional Planning, professional report, University of California, Irvine.

Village Center, The. 1966. *Columbia* [a newsletter published by Community Research and Development], spring, 3.

Von Eckhardt, Wolf. 1971. A fresh scene in the clean dream. *Saturday Review,* May 15, 21–23.

Voorhees, Alan, and Associates. 1964. Feasibility of transit services for Columbia, March 23. Columbia Archives, RCI, RG1, Folder 19a.

Wallace, Amy. 1999. *Don't fence me in: Communities, conflicts, and rights.* Master of Urban and Regional Planning, professional report, University of California, Irvine.

Wallace-McHarg Associates. 1964. *Plan for the valleys.* Towson, MD: Green Spring and Worthington Valley Planning Council.

Wannemacher, James. 1996. Early buildings: People and projects. In *Creating a new city,* ed. Robert Tennenbaum. Columbia, MD: Partners in Community Building and Perry Publishing.

Ward, Stephen. 2002. *Planning the twentieth-century city.* Chichester: John Wiley.

Watson, Raymond. 1971. Phasing growth—a process of a plan. Presentation to the American Institute of Architects New Communities Conference, Washington, DC, November 3–6. UC Irvine, Orange County Collection.

————. 1973. The changing role of the private developer. An address to the 7th Pan American Congress, American Institute of Real Estate Appraisers, San Francisco, September 25. UC Irvine, Orange County Collection.

————. 1975. How one developer lives with government controls. An address before the Southwest Regional Conference, American Institute of Real Estate Appraisers, Anaheim, April 17. UC Irvine, Orange County Collection.

————. 1999. Interview by Ann Forsyth, Newport Beach.

———. 2002. Email letter to Ann Forsyth, commenting on draft of book manuscript, May 21.

Webber, Melvin. 1964. The urban place and the nonplace urban realm. In *Explorations into urban structure*, ed. Melvin Webber. Philadelphia: University of Pennsylvania Press.

Weiss, Mark. 1987. *The rise of the community builders.* New York: Columbia University Press.

Weiss, Shirley. 1973. *New town development in the United States: Experiment in private entrepreneurship.* Chapel Hill: Center for Urban and Regional Studies, University of North Carolina.

Weiss, Shirley, and Ray Burby. 1976. Preface. In *Residential mobility in new communities,* by Edward Kaiser. Cambridge, MA: Ballinger.

Wekerle, Gerda, Rebecca Peterson, and David Morley, eds. 1980. *New space for women.* Boulder, CO: Westview Press.

Wheatcroft, Richard. 1998. Interview by Joseph Kutchin, August 1996. In *How Mitchell Energy and Development Corp. got its start and how it grew: An oral history and narrative overview,* ed. Joseph Kutchin. Parkland, FL: Universal Publishers.

Whyte, William H. 1956. *The organization man.* New York: Simon and Schuster.

———. 1958. *The exploding metropolis.* Garden City, NY: Doubleday.

Wilbur Smith and Associates. 1961. *The Irvine Ranch traffic planning study.* Prepared for the Irvine Company. San Francisco: Wilbur Smith and Associates.

William L. Pereira and Associates. 1959. *A preliminary report for a university-community development in Orange County.* October. UC Irvine, University Archives.

———. 1960. *Second phase report for a university-community development in Orange County.* Prepared for the Irvine Company. May. UC Irvine, University Archives.

———. 1963. *Long range development plan, University of California, Irvine.* William L. Pereira and Associates.

———. 1964a. A guide to the master plan for the southern sector of the Irvine Ranch as presented to the Orange County Planning Commission on January 15, 1964. UC Irvine, University Archives, 535–1.

———. 1964b. *Master plan submittal.* UC Irvine, University Archives, 535–1.

———. 1970. *Long range development plan, University of California, Irvine.* William L. Pereira and Associates.

Williams, Carroll. 1969. Impact. *Columbia Today,* August/September, 5–7.

Williams, Raymond. 1983. *Keywords: A vocabulary of culture and society.* London: Fontana Paperbacks.

Willmott, Peter. 1967. Social research and new communities. *Journal of the American Institute of Planners* (November): 387–98.

Wilsey and Ham. [1973] 1974. *General plan for the City of Irvine.* Irvine, CA: City of Irvine.

Windsor, Duane. 1979. A critique of the costs of sprawl. *Journal of the American Planning Association* 45 (3): 279–92.

Withey, Stephen. 1964. Communications systems and sense of community. Work group paper. Columbia Archives RC1, RG1, Folder 19.

WMRT (Wallace, McHarg, Roberts and Todd). 1971. *Ecological planning study for the new community.* Philadelphia: Wallace, McHarg, Roberts and Todd.

————. 1973a. *Woodlands new community: Guidelines for site planning.* Philadelphia: Wallace, McHarg, Roberts and Todd.

————. 1973b. *Woodlands new community: Phase one, land planning and design principles.* Philadelphia: Wallace, McHarg, Roberts and Todd.

————. 1973c. *Woodlands new community: Phase one, progress report on land planning and design principles.* Philadelphia: Wallace, McHarg, Roberts and Todd.

————. 1974a. *Owl Creek: A feasibility study for future development.* Prepared for Mitchell Energy. Philadelphia: Wallace, McHarg, Roberts and Todd. Collection of Wallace, McHarg, Roberts and Todd.

————. 1974b. *Woodlands new community: An ecological plan.* Prepared for The Woodlands Development Corporation. Philadelphia: Wallace, McHarg, Roberts and Todd.

————. 1977. *Urban design implementation plan: City of Irvine horizon year policies.* Prepared for the City of Irvine and The Irvine Company. Harvard University, Loeb Library.

————. N.d. *Woodlands new community: An ecological inventory.* Prepared for The Woodlands Development Corporation. Philadelphia: Wallace, McHarg, Roberts and Todd.

Wood, Peter. 1985. Throwing MUD at Taft. *Cite,* summer, 6.

Yankee discipline. 1969/1970. *Columbia Today,* December/January, 14–18.

Yin, Robert. 1984. *Case study research.* Beverly Hills: Sage.

————. 1993. *Applications of case study research.* Newbury Park, CA: Sage.

Young, Michael, and Peter Willmott. 1957. *Family and kinship in East London.* London: Routledge and Kegan Paul.

Zehner, Robert. 1977a. *Access, travel, and transportation in new communities.* Cambridge, MA: Ballinger.

————. 1977b. *Indicators of the quality of life in new communities.* Cambridge, MA: Ballinger.

ZEV NET. 2002. Zero emission vehicle • network enabled transport (ZEV • NET) provides consumers an alternative. ZEV • NET Web site. www.zevnet.org/.

Ziegler Cooper. 2000. Town center urban residential. Report for The Woodlands Operating Company.

INDEX

Page numbers in italics indicate figures and tables.

Text: 10/12 Baskerville
Display: Baskerville
Cartographer: Bill Nelson
Compositor: Integrated Composition Systems
Printer and Binder: Thomson-Shore, Inc.